DATE DUE

DEMCO 38-296

Wayne Jones
Editor

E-Serials: Publishers, Libraries, Users, and Standards

E-Serials: Publishers, Libraries, Users, and Standards has been co-published simultaneously as *The Serials Librarian*, Volume 33, Numbers 1/2 and 3/4 1998.

Pre-publication
REVIEWS,
COMMENTARIES,
EVALUATIONS . . .

"Can a print monograph still offer valuable information, analysis or commentary about the fast moving Internet world? With respect to Haworth Press's *E-Serials: Publishers, Libraries, Users, and Standards*, edited by Wayne Jones, the answer is a decisive "Yes!" Thoughtful contributions from a wide range of perspectives offer advice . . . and analysis . . . which will stand the test of time. Libraries and publishers will find this book helpful in developing strategies, policies and procedures. Of particular interest are discussions of actual and possible roles and responsibilities of various players in the serials life cycle."

Nancy Brodie
National Library of Canada
Ottawa, Ontario

More pre-publication
REVIEWS, COMMENTARIES, EVALUATIONS . . .

"***E**-Serials: Publishers, Libraries, Users, and Standards*, edited by Wayne Jones, is a diverse collection of thought-provoking articles on the impact of electronic serials on library staff, publishers and vendors and is essential reading for serials librarians and other library managers, educators and staff interested in the changes that electronic journals and the Internet have brought to our work lives. Publishers and vendors interested in the impact of the Internet on the creation, distribution and bibliographic control of electronic serials would also benefit from a reading, especially to see what other publishers and vendors are doing. Reading and reflecting on a variety of problems, changes and innovations created as a result of the impact of the electronic world should result in even more and better services in the electronic world.

Initiatives underway in publishing are described, many new products and services in development are described, and new and more collaborative work flows are outlined. Specific topics include the role of a university press in electronic journal publishing; online journal pricing; new complexities in work flows for collection development and acquisitions of electronic journals; the difficulties of following print-based cataloging rules for the cataloging of electronic serials; metadata and its conversion for use in OPACs; preservation of scholarly electronic resources; the future of uniform resource identifiers; and preferred methods of citing electronic journal literature. For anyone wishing to participate in effectively moving his/her library, journal publishing, or vendor services from the print-based to electronic world, this volume illustrates many practical issues and solutions for improving services to libraries and patrons."

Kristin Lindlan, AM
Head of Serials Cataloging Section
Serials Division
University of Washington Libraries
Seattle

E-Serials: Publishers, Libraries, Users, and Standards

E-Serials: Publishers, Libraries, Users, and Standards has been co-published simultaneously as *The Serials Librarian,* Volume 33, Numbers 1/2 and 3/4 1998.

The North American Serials Interest Group (NASIG) Series

The Serials Information Chain, edited by Leigh Chatterton and Mary Elizabeth Clack

Serials Information from Publisher to User, edited by Leigh A. Chatterton and Mary Elizabeth Clack

The Serials Partnership, edited by Patricia Ohl Rice and Joyce L. Ogburn

The Future of Serials, edited by Patricia Ohl Rice and Jane A. Robillard

A Changing World, edited by Suzanne McMahon, Miriam Palm, and Pamela Dunn

If We Build It, edited by Suzanne McMahon, Miriam Palm, and Pamela Dunn

New Scholarship: New Serials, edited by Gail McMillan and Marilyn Norstedt

A Kaleidoscope of Choices, edited by Beth Holley and May Ann Sheble

Serials to the Tenth Power, edited by Mary Ann Sheble and Beth Holley

Pioneering New Serials Frontiers, edited by Christine Christiansen and Cecilia Leathem

These books were published simultaneously as special thematic issues of *The Serials Librarian* and are available bound separately. Visit Haworth's website at http://www.haworth.com to search our online catalog for complete tables of contents and ordering information for these and other publications. Or call 1-800-HAWORTH (outside US/Canada: 607-722-5857), Fax: 1-800-895-0582 (outside US/Canada: 607-771-0012), or e-mail getinfo@haworth.com

E-Serials: Publishers, Libraries, Users, and Standards has been co-published simultaneously as *The Serials Librarian,* Volume 33, Numbers 1/2 and 3/4 1998.

The development, preparation, and publication of this work has been undertaken with great care. However, the publisher, employees, editors, and agents of The Haworth Press and all imprints of The Haworth Press, Inc., including The Haworth Medical Press and The Pharmaceutical Products Press, are not responsible for any errors contained herein or for consequences that may ensue from use of materials or information contained in this work. Opinions expressed by the author(s) are not necessarily those of The Haworth Press, Inc.

Cover design by Thomas J. Mayshock Jr.

Library of Congress Cataloging-in-Publication Data

E-serials : publishers, libraries, users, and standards / Wayne Jones, editor.
    p. cm.
    Co-published simultaneously as The Serials librarian, Vol. 33, No. 1/2 and 3/4 1998.
    Includes bibliographical references and index.
    ISBN 0-7890-0514-X
    1. Libraries–Special collections–Electronic journals. 2. Libraries–United States–Special collections–Electronic journals. I. Jones, Wayne, 1959- .
Z692.E43E7 1998
025.2′832–dc21   98-5627
                                                            CIP

E-Serials:
Publishers, Libraries, Users, and Standards

Wayne Jones
Editor

E-Serials: Publishers, Libraries, Users, and Standards has been co-published simultaneously as *The Serials Librarian,* Volume 33, Numbers 1/2 and 3/4 1998.

The Haworth Press, Inc.
New York • London

INDEXING & ABSTRACTING

Contributions to this publication are selectively indexed or abstracted in print, electronic, online, or CD-ROM version(s) of the reference tools and information services listed below. This list is current as of the copyright date of this publication. See the end of this section for additional notes.

- *Academic Abstracts/CD-ROM,* EBSCO Publishing Editorial Department, P.O. Box 590, Ipswich, MA 01938-0590

- *Academic Search: database of 2,000 selected academic serials, updated monthly,* EBSCO Publishing, 83 Pine Street, Peabody, MA 01960

- *Cambridge Scientific Abstracts,* 7200 Wisconsin Avenue, #601, Bethesda, MD 20814

- *Chemical Abstracts,* Chemical Abstracts Service Library, 2540 Olgentangy Road, P.O. Box 3012, Columbus, OH 43210

- *CINAHL (Cumulative Index to Nursing & Allied Health Literature), in print, also on CD-ROM from CD PLUS, EBSCO, and Silver-Platter, and online from CDP Online (fomerly BRS), Data-Star, and PaperChase. (Support materials include Subject Heading List, Database Search Guide, and instructional video.)* CINAHL Information Systems, P.O. Box 871/1509 Wilson Terrace, Glendale, CA 91209-0871

- *CNPIEC Reference Guide: Chinese National Directory of Foreign Periodicals,* P.O. Box 88, Beijing, People's Republic of China

- *Current Awareness Abstracts,* Association for Information Management, Information House, 20-24 Old Street, London, EC1V 9AP, England

(continued)

- *Current Contents: Clinical Medicine/Life Sciences (CC: CM/LS) Weekly Table of Contents Service), and* Social Science Citation Index. *Articles also searchable through* Social SciSearch, *ISI's online database and in ISI's* Research Alert *current awareness service,* Institute for Scientific Information, 3501 Market Street, Philadelphia, PA 19104-3302

- *Hein's Legal Periodical Checklist: Index to Periodical Articles Pertaining to Law,* William S. Hein & Co., Inc., 1285 Main Street, Buffalo, NY 14209

- *IBZ International Bibliography of Periodical Literature,* Zeller Verlag GmbH & Co., P.O.B. 1949, d-49009 Osnabruck, Germany

- *Index to Periodical Articles Related to Law,* University of Texas, 727 East 26th Street, Austin, TX 78705

- *Information Reports & Bibliographies,* Science Associates International, Inc., 6 Hastings Road, Marlboro, NJ 07746-1313

- *Information Science Abstracts,* Plenum Publishing Company, 233 Spring Street, New York, NY 10013-1578

- *Informed Librarian, The,* Infosources Publishing, 140 Norma Road, Teaneck, NJ 07666

- *INTERNET ACCESS (& additional networks) Bulletin Board for Libraries ("BUBL") coverage of information resources on INTERNET, JANET, and other networks.*
    - <URL:http://bubl.ac.uk/>
    - The new locations will be found under <URL:http://bubl.ac.uk/link/>.
    - Any existing BUBL users who have problems finding information on the new service should contact the BUBL help line by sending e-mail to <bubl@bubl.ac.uk>.
    The Andersonian Library, Curran Building, 101 St. James Road, Glasgow G4 0NS, Scotland

- *Journal of Academic Librarianship: Guide to Professional Literature, The,* Grad School of Library & Information Science, Simmons College, 300 The Fenway, Boston, MA 02115-5898

(continued)

- *Konyvtari Figyelo-Library Review*, National Szechenyi Library, Centre for Library and Information Science, H-1827 Budapest, Hungary

- *Library & Information Science Abstracts (LISA)*, Bowker-Saur Limited, Maypole House, Maypole Road, East Grinstead, West Sussex, RH19 1HH, England

- *Library and Information Science Annual (LISCA)*, Libraries Unlimited, P.O. Box 6633, Englewood, CO 80155-6633. Further information is available at www.lu.com/arba

- *Library Digest,* Highsmith Press, W5527 Highway 106, P.O. Box 800, Fort Atkinson, WI 53538-0800

- *Library Hi Tech News,* Pierian Press, P.O. Box 1808, Ann Arbor, MI 48106

- *Library Literature,* The H. W. Wilson Company, 950 University Avenue, Bronx, NY 10452

- *MasterFILE: updated database,* EBSCO Publishing, 83 Pine Street, Peabody, MA 01960

- *Newsletter of Library and Information Services,* China Sci-Tech Book Review, Library of Academia Sinica, 8 Kexueyuan Nanlu, Zhongguancun, Beijing 100080, People's Republic of China

- *PASCAL, c/o Institute de L' Information Scientifique et Technique,* Cross-disciplinary electronic database covering the fields of science, technology & medicine. Also available on CD-ROM, and can generate customized retrospective searches. For more information: INIST, Customer Desk, 2, allee du Parc de Brabois, F-54514 Vandoeuvre Cedex, France, http//wwwinist.fr

- *Periodica Islamica,* Berita Publishing, 22 Jalan Liku, 59100 Kuala Lumpur, Malaysia

- *Referativnyi Zhurnal (Abstracts Journal of the All-Russian Institute of Scientific and Technical Information),* 20 Usievich Street, Moscow 125219, Russia

- *Sociological Abstracts (SA),* Sociological Abstracts, Inc., P.O. Box 22206, San Diego, CA 92192-0206

(continued)

SPECIAL BIBLIOGRAPHIC NOTES

related to special journal issues (separates)
and indexing/abstracting

☐ indexing/abstracting services in this list will also cover material in any "separate" that is co-published simultaneously with Haworth's special thematic journal issue or DocuSerial. Indexing/abstracting usually covers material at the article/chapter level.

☐ monographic co-editions are intended for either non-subscribers or libraries which intend to purchase a second copy for their circulating collections.

☐ monographic co-editions are reported to all jobbers/wholesalers/approval plans. The source journal is listed as the "series" to assist the prevention of duplicate purchasing in the same manner utilized for books-in-series.

☐ to facilitate user/access services all indexing/abstracting services are encouraged to utilize the co-indexing entry note indicated at the bottom of the first page of each article/chapter/contribution.

☐ this is intended to assist a library user of any reference tool (whether print, electronic, online, or CD-ROM) to locate the monographic version if the library has purchased this version but not a subscription to the source journal.

☐ individual articles/chapters in any Haworth publication are also available through the Haworth Document Delivery Service (HDDS).

E-Serials:
Publishers, Libraries, Users, and Standards

CONTENTS

ABOUT THE EDITOR

Wayne Jones is Head of the Serials Cataloging Section at the Massachusetts Institute of Technology, where he manages all aspects of serials cataloging as well as supervises MIT's CONSER operations. Mr. Jones was formerly Leader of the Serials Team at the National Library of Canada, where he supervised serials cataloging, ISSN Canada, and CONSER operations. He has contributed several articles and reviews to professional journals and edited the book *Serials Canada: Aspects of Serials Work in Canadian Libraries* (The Haworth Press, Inc., 1995). He is also the Associate Editor of *The Serials Librarian*.

Preface

As I write this on a Sunday morning, I am listening to Bruce Springsteen on CD and hoping that I will be able to see at least one football game later in the day–nice, familiar luxuries.

The serials world before the arrival of e-serials was a relatively calm and luxurious one, too. E-serials have turned a lot of things around and upside-down. Some people predict even more profound shifts as e-serials become common and entrenched: the "demise of the scholarly journal," for example, was to have happened by now, or will happen by the end of this century, or by the middle of the next century.

There is, of course, some irony in the fact that a publication about e-serials is being issued as a special volume of *The* (printed) *Serials Librarian*, as well as in (printed) book form. Such a practice might seem quaintly retro fifty years from now, but in 1998 I am happy to have edited this collection of articles which attempts to present a fairly comprehensive view of some of the most important aspects of e-serials. Not everything is (or could be) included, for sure, but I feel confident that readers will find something of value in the writings of authors whose experiences with e-serials can be instructive for us all.

I'd like to thank these authors for agreeing to put their thoughts to, yes, paper, and for enduring with good humor the gentle proddings of an editor. Jim Cole, the editor of *The Serials Librarian*, also deserves my gratitude for his unfailing patience and for his encouragement of this volume. And, finally, I would also like to thank MIT for allowing me the communications resources to facilitate both the technical and the human aspects of my editing.

[Haworth co-indexing entry note]: "Preface." Jones, Wayne. Co-published simultaneously in *The Serials Librarian* (The Haworth Press, Inc.) Vol. 33, No. 1/2, 1998, pp. xv-xvi; and: *E-Serials: Publishers, Libraries, Users, and Standards* (ed: Wayne Jones) The Haworth Press, Inc., 1998, pp. xv-xvi. Single or multiple copies of this article are available for a fee from The Haworth Document Delivery Service [1-800-342-9678, 9:00 a.m. - 5:00 p.m. (EST). E-mail address: getinfo@haworth.com].

xv

And a final note also on nomenclature: e-serials. That is the title of this volume, but I don't think the naming has really "settled" yet on what to call these serials. What name unambiguously establishes the fact that they are available electronically via a computer or a computer network, that they may or may not be published in some other (physical) medium, but that they are not CD-ROMs or diskettes? I posted the question to the discussion group ARL-EJOUR-NAL, and informally polled the contributors to this volume, and got a good variety of suggestions: ejournals, e-journals, electronic journals, eserials, e-serials, electronic serials, e-zines, Internet-based electronic journals, Internet-based serials, networked electronic journals, networked electronic resources, on-line journals, or just plain Web sites. Jeff Pache said they should be called "n-e-serials" (for "networked electronic serials"), but that people would end up calling them "n-e-thing" they wanted to. That same freedom has been permitted in this volume.

Wayne Jones
Somerville, MA

PUBLISHING

D-Lib Magazine:
Publishing as the Honest Broker

Amy Friedlander, PhD

Illustrations by Catherine Rey

SUMMARY. This paper describes the organization of material in *D-Lib Magazine* <http://www.dlib.org>, an online reference collection of pointers to sites containing resources in networked information and digital libraries, and a monthly, which addresses developments in advanced research and implementation projects in digital libraries and related topics. The importance of persistent, location-independent identifiers (or names) is discussed primarily from the perspectives of information organization and the associated issues in cataloging resources in the MARC environment. *[Article copies available for a fee from The Haworth Document Delivery Service: 1-800-342-9678. E-mail address: getinfo@haworth.com]*

Amy Friedlander is Editor of *D-Lib Magazine* (email: afriedl@cnri.reston.va.us).

Catherine Rey is Web Designer, Corporation for National Research Initiatives, 1895 Preston White Drive, Suite 100, Reston, VA 20191-5434, USA.

[Haworth co-indexing entry note]: "*D-Lib Magazine:* Publishing as the Honest Broker." Friedlander, Amy. Co-published simultaneously in *The Serials Librarian* (The Haworth Press, Inc.) Vol. 33, No. 1/2, 1998, pp. 1-20; and: *E-Serials: Publishers, Libraries, Users, and Standards* (ed: Wayne Jones) The Haworth Press, Inc., 1998, pp. 1-20. Single or multiple copies of this article are available for a fee from The Haworth Document Delivery Service [1-800-342-9678, 9:00 a.m. - 5:00 p.m. (EST). E-mail address: getinfo@haworth.com].

KEYWORDS. Digital libraries, electronic publishing, persistent identifiers, Digital Libraries Initiative, editorial practices

D-Lib Magazine <http://www.dlib.org> is a project of the Corporation for National Research Initiatives (CNRI) in Reston, Virginia, with sponsorship from the US Defense Advanced Research Projects Agency (DARPA) in support of the Digital Libraries Initiative (DLI).[1] We are available free-of-charge to anyone who finds us on the Web and maintain a "subscriber" list only to offer priority announcement of each monthly issue. Each issue consists of an editorial, several stories about current research contributed by members of the research community, and two columns: one called the "Technology Spotlight," in which we provide a pointer to interesting sites featuring new technologies or new applications, and a second called "Clips and Pointers," in which we identify interesting new or updated resources on the Web, announce meetings, and run short news items and abstracts of important, forthcoming reports. There are many topics that we could discuss in this story but have chosen to describe our basic policies and then focus on the core issue of how we manage and structure the information since it is a topic with implications not only for publishing and libraries but also for the underlying communications architecture.

When we released our first issue in July 1995, our goal was to support the DLI by offering investigators an opportunity to exchange early and speculative results in a setting that was more structured than a listserv but less formal than a peer-reviewed journal. We also knew that substantial research pursuing related or convergent goals was undertaken outside of the six university-based partnerships that constitute the DLI. The Brittle Books program at the National Endowment for the Humanities is a case in point. Moreover, there were numerous research programs in universities and corporate labs that were yielding or were likely to yield results of interest to the DLI projects. So *D-Lib Magazine* undertook to stimulate synergies across the nascent communities of researchers and observers (among whom we count ourselves) by courting stories from as broad a population as would respond to e-mail messages and telephone calls.

We have been remarkably lucky. Because of our association with the DLI, we have had access to an important segment of the research community and to the major funding agencies: the National Science Foundation (NSF), DARPA, and NASA, who provided additional introductions and contacts for stories. Timing was also with us. There had been enough work to create a backlog of material that could be molded into stories. Yet the field of digital libraries is growing so rapidly that we find ourselves in an expanding environment rather than a competitive market. As a result, we have found that we have become less reliant on the DLI projects for material and for readers. Although estimates of the size of our readership are inexact at best, we know that we have a broad readership at home and overseas. Moreover, in the last year, we have run relatively few stories from the DLI projects. We see this as progress, that we are resisting the tendency to become parochial and are moving toward our fundamental goal of building community.

So much for the big picture. On a daily basis, *D-Lib* borrows heavily from models set by earlier media: print, broadcasting, and film. Some of these precedents concern the legal framework within which we operate, and discussion of them is outside the scope of this story. With respect to content, we follow traditions of print publishing in our insistence on scheduled monthly releases on or near the 15th (rather than casual and asynchronous updates) and in our acquisitions and editing policies. We *invite* stories from important researchers and projects, which we develop on an individual basis, and we encourage would-be authors to "pitch" ideas by e-mail and abstracts rather than by throwing a 5,000-word item over the virtual transom.

Editing, of course, has been seen as an eternal war between the author and editor, where "writers write primarily to advance themselves, and editors edit to satisfy readers."[2] We beg to differ. At least in the world of research, good stories will attract both readers and writers, and the role of the editor is to help the writer tell the story he or she wishes to tell. Then, the passion and excitement will come through and sweep the reader along. Thus, we pursue an "author-centric" policy, inviting our writers to experiment with the capabilities of the digital medium within a very few limits: English is our language of publication (although parallel versions in other languages have been run). Copyediting is consistent with *The Chi-*

cago Manual of Style (with healthy assistance from the *Editorial Eye*). And we always add minimal visual cues (such as a bar at the head of the story) and navigational tools so that the story will not lose the reader. Since we are not juried, senior researchers have, in some cases, been willing to provide us "thought" pieces and essays that would not be appropriate for professional journals. We have also observed that writers are informally re-creating aspects of peer review, circulating stories among their colleagues for input on content before sending the material to us for formal editing and HTML mark-up. Finally, we are very much aware of issues that arise from the library side of the house. This means questions of long-term archiving and preservation as well as of resource discovery and identification.

In the digital environment, identification of resources–a concept fundamental to notions of cataloging in the print world–is closely allied with the question of naming. One of the major issues in the digital information infrastructure is the question of persistent, location-independent names or identifiers for digital items. Looked at solely as a question of names, the issues concern syntax, organization, and semantics–that is, should the sequence of bits that comprise the name also contain meaning? Or should the bit string be meaningless? And if meaningless, meaningless to whom or to what? To a traditional librarian, the distinction between semantic and non-semantic naming is similar to the difference between a classification number, which assigns an alphanumeric code to a work that captures its content, and a simple inventory control or acquisitions number that merely identifies the sequence in which an institution acquired an item. CNRI has developed the concept of a handle, which is a unique, location-independent string that identifies an Internet resource. There are other approaches to persistent naming, but the important point is to choose a system that is interoperable, enabling users with one to find the others.[3]

The issues surrounding naming, thorny though they are, beg a second question: to what do these identifiers point? That is, what entity does the "name" identify? And how, then, is that entity described so that it can be found, traditionally the concern of catalogers? Not surprisingly, there is disagreement. The architecture set forth by Robert Kahn and Robert Wilensky and subsequently developed by CNRI builds up digital libraries from the core concept of a "digital object," that is, "a way of structuring information in digital form."[4]

> However, the information in the digital library is far from simple. A single work may have many parts, a complex internal structure, and one or more arbitrary relationships to other works. To represent the complexity of information in the digital library, several digital objects may be grouped together. This is called a set of digital objects. All digital objects have the same basic form, but the structure of a set of digital objects depends upon the information it represents.[5]

However, others—researchers at IBM, for example—describe an expanded notion of a "document," where "document means any package of information that can be conveyed digitally, e.g., a film together with associated administrative information, pre-recorded music, a set of web pages, etc."[6]

D-Lib presently observes a compromise position that we hope will accommodate change while not forcing our readers to translate between useful and familiar concepts and new and alien ones now meaningful primarily to the technical community. We recognize three entities or sets of digital objects:

- the *site*, which is equivalent to the magazine in the same way that the serial means, for example, *The New Yorker* as the totality of all issues or *60 Minutes* means the television show, which airs at a given time, but is an abstraction above any weekly edition;
- the *issue*, which appears each month and maps respectively to weekly issues of *The New Yorker* or weekly editions of *60 Minutes*; and
- the *components*, which break down into stories, columns, and various elements such as the contents page, access terms and conditions page, etc., which are more or less standard from issue to issue but may change slightly.

This much is familiar. The question is how do these entities map onto the organization of material as files and directories? Or alternatively, what is the object to which we give a name and, presently, a location? The most inclusive and complex object is the magazine or the site: *D-Lib Magazine*, which presently has the URL: <www.dlib.org> (Figure 1). There exists a server at CNRI that contains the directories and files that constitute the magazine. Conceptually, these are subdivided into two principal sections: the issues which change monthly, and a small reference collection of pointers identifying materials on the Web of interest to researchers in digital libraries and networked information; these change asynchronously and infrequently, at most once or twice year. This top-level directory, which corresponds to the site or to the abstraction roughly equivalent to the "serial" looks like this (see Figures 1a, 1b, 1c).

Note that the directory (Figure 1c) contains the graphics (*.gif) as well as the text files (*.html) that collectively make up the display that the user sees (Figure 1a, 1b) as well as the sub-directories containing the monthly issues. Each of these elements is an object,

FIGURE 1a. Home page of *D-Lib Magazine* (as displayed to the reader) [portion]

FIGURE 1b. Source file for Home Page [portion]

```
Source of: file:///D|/DLIB/www.dlib.org.html - Netscape

<HTML>
<HEAD>
<TITLE>D-Lib Magazine</TITLE>
</HEAD>
<BODY background = "lgray_bg.gif" width = 700 height = 16>
<img src = "dlib_mag.gif">
<p>
<h4>Welcome to <B>D-Lib Magazine</B>, a single site with
monthly stories, commentary, and briefings and a collection
of resources for digital library research.
Visit <a href = "dlib/july97/07contents.html">D-Lib Magazine
This Month</a> for new material; visit
<a href = "#ready">D-Lib Ready Reference</a> for
pointers to projects and collections concerning
digital library research.</h4>
<IMG SRC = "d-line1.gif">
<p>
<A NAME = "month"></a>
<TABLE><TR VALIGN=TOP><TD>
<a href = "dlib/july97/07contents.html"><img src =
"dingb.gif" border = 0></a>
</TD><TD>
<FONT SIZE = +2><b>D-Lib Magazine This Month</b>:
<a href = "dlib/july97/07contents.html">July/August
1997</a></FONT>
</TD></TR>
<TR VALIGN=TOP>
<TD>
<BR>
<A HREF= "http://www.dlib.org/Architext/AT-dlib2query.html">
Search</a> the contents of the monthly magazine and reference
pages; or<p>Browse <a href = "back.html">back issues</a> of
<b>D-Lib Magazine</b>.<BR>or <b>D-Lib Magazine's</b> stories,
editorials, and briefings by <a href = "title-index.html">
title</a>or <a href = "author-index.html">author</a>.
</TD></TR></TABLE>
<IMG SRC = "d-line1.gif">
</BODY>
</HTML>
```

FIGURE 1c. Directory/file structure [portion]

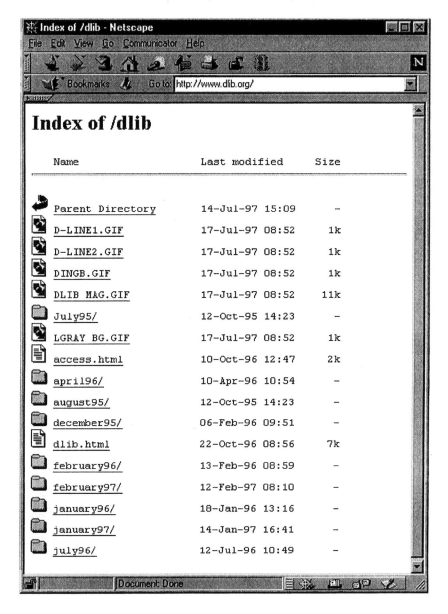

but note that we have opted to identify the item, in this case the home page for *D-Lib Magazine*, in terms of the display–that is, in terms of *what the user sees*. This means that it maps relatively intuitively into the familiar world of cataloging and print publishing and thus facilitates use within existing technologies.

At the next level down, monthly issues of the magazine occupy their own directories (Figure 2c). To the user, each monthly issue contains familiar components: there is a contents page listing individual columns and stories as well as the stories and columns themselves. But again, the similarity to print is in the display and not in the actual assembly, so that the contents page for the June 1997 issue of *D-Lib Magazine* is, like the home page, a composite of images and text, and some of the text (i.e., pointers) invoke sub-routines so that not all sequences of characters are the same. Consider the display as it appears (Figure 2a) and the text (or source) as it is, in fact, written (Figure 2b).

When users point to the June 1997 issue of *D-Lib Magazine*, they typically expect to see the contents page: <http://www.dlib.org/dlib/june97/06contents.html>. But in fact, the cataloging equivalent to the issue is the directory <http://www.dlib.org/dlib/june97> and constituent sub-directories and files together with the files that are identified as part of the "Technology Spotlight," <www.dlib.org/dlib/*.*>. For historical reasons, the "Technology Spotlight" has been maintained separately. Although readers see the column as part of the magazine, the "Spotlight" is a separate set of objects comprising three files, each of which is typically updated monthly. Because pointers to sites identified on a monthly basis are moved to an archive, which is part of this object, we do not maintain historical copies of each month's "Technology Spotlight." The name of the current site is identified on the contents page for the month in which it is featured, so that future users might reconstruct the magazine in its entirety, if they so desired. In this sense, then, archival and magazine functions have been conflated.

Within each issue of the magazine, we recognize stories and columns. None of these maps to a single file since all of them invoke *D-Lib*'s background color, bars, and buttons that enable users to navigate among the stories. But again, from the perspective of the user, the story that corresponds to the June editorial, "Too

FIGURE 2a. Contents page of *D-Lib Magazine*, June 1997

FIGURE 2b. Source for Contents page of *D-Lib Magazine*, June 1997

```
Source of: file:///D|/DLIB/06contents.html - Netscape

<HTML><HEAD>
<TITLE>D-Lib Magazine, June 1997</TITLE></HEAD>
<BODY background = "lgray_bg.gif" width = 700 height = 16>
<P>
<IMG src = "dlib_mag.gif" alt="D-Lib Magazine">
<H5>June 1997<BR>ISSN 1082-9873</H5>
<P>
<IMG src="edit_ba3.gif" ALT="Editorial"><P>
<A HREF="06editorial.html">
From the Editor</A>:  <I>Too Many Meetings?</I><BR>
<A href = "06messages.html">
To the Editor</A>:  <i>HyperNews</i><P>
<IMG src="stor_ba3.gif" ALT="Stories and Briefings"><P>
<a href = "06band.html"><I>Sui Generis</I> Database
Protection:  Has Its Time Come?</a><br>
Jonathan Band <br>
Jonathan S. Gowdy<br>
<I> Morrison & Foerster LLP</I>
<p>
<A HREF = "06lagoze.html">From Static to Dynamic
Surrogates</a>: Resource Discovery in the Digital
Age<br>
Carl Lagoze<br>
<i>Cornell University</i>
<p>
<a href = "metadata/06weibel.html">The 4th Dublin
Core Metadata Workshop Report</a>:
DC-4, March 3 - 5, 1997, National Library of
Australia, Canberra <br>
Stuart Weibel, <I>OCLC</I><BR>
Renato Iannella, <I>DSTC</I><BR>
Warwick Cathro, <I>National Library of Australia</I>
<p>
<A HREF = "zuno/06ferguson.html">
Paying Their Way</a>:  Commercial Digital Libraries
for the 21<SUP>st</SUP> Century<br>
Innes A. Ferguson<br>
Michael J. Wooldridge<BR>
<I>Zuno Ltd.</i>
<p></BODY></HTML>
```

FIGURE 2c. Directory/file structure of a monthly issue

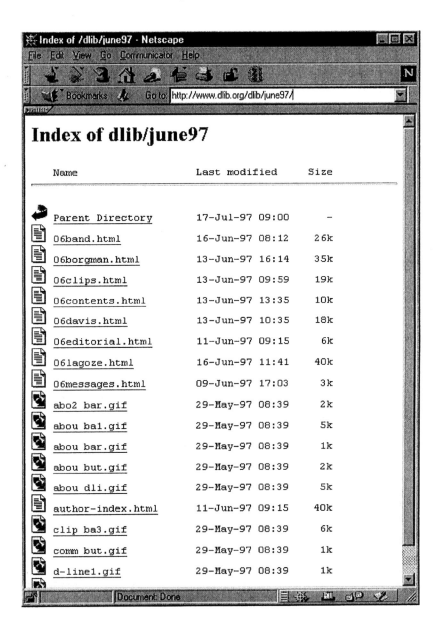

Many Meetings?", can be found via the URL: <http://www.dlib.org/ dlib/june97/06editorial.html> or the handle cnri.dlib/june97-editorial. (See Figures 3a and 3b.) The characteristic in these cases is that the principal content of the story is conveyed by a single file <06editorial. html>; the contributing images and buttons are boiler plate or standard across stories. So, although the editorial and the "Clips" col-

FIGURE 3a. Display of June 1997 editorial

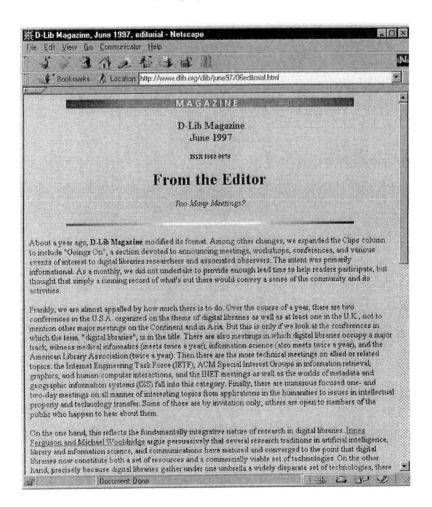

FIGURE 3b. Source of June 1997 editorial

```
Source of: file:///DI/DLIB/06editorial.html - Netscape          _ □ X

<HTML><HEAD>
<TITLE>D-Lib Magazine, June 1997, editorial</TITLE></HEAD>
<BODY BACKGROUND="lgray_bg.gif">
<P><P><CENTER><IMG SRC="mag_bar1.gif"></CENTER><p>
<H3><CENTER>D-Lib Magazine<BR>June 1997</CENTER></H3><p>
<H6><CENTER>ISSN 1082-9873</CENTER></H6><p>
<H1><CENTER>From the Editor <BR></CENTER></H1><p>
<CENTER>
<I>Too Many Meetings?</I><p><img src = "d-line1.gif"><p>
</CENTER><p>
About a year ago, <b>D-Lib Magazine</b> modified its format. Among
other changes, we expanded the Clips column to include "Goings On",
a section devoted to announcing meetings, workshops, conferences,
and various events of interest to digital libraries researchers and
associated observers.  The intent was primarily informational. As a
monthly, we did not undertake to provide enough lead time to help
readers participate, but thought that simply a running record of
what's out there would convey a sense of the community and its
activities.
<p>
Frankly, we are almost appalled by how much there is to do. Over
the course of a year, there are two conferences in the U.S.A.
organized on the theme of digital libraries as well as at least
one in the U.K., not to mention other major meetings on the
Continent and in Asia.  But this is only if we look at the
conferences in which the term, "digital libraries", is in the
title.  There are also meetings in which digital libraries occupy
a major track, witness medical informatics (meets twice a year),
information science (also meets twice a year), and the American
Library Association (twice a year). Then there are the more
technical meetings on allied or related topics: the Internet
Engineering Task Force (IETF), ACM Special Interest Groups in
information retrieval, graphics, and human-computer interactions,
and the INET meetings as well as the worlds of metadata and
geographic information systems (GIS) fall into this category.
Finally, there are numerous focused one- and two-day meetings on
all manner of interesting topics from applications in the
humanities to issues in intellectual property and technology transfer.
Some of these are by invitation only; others are open to members
of the public who happen to hear about them.
<p>
On the one hand, this reflects the fundamentally integrative
nature of research in digital libraries.
```

umn are technically sets of objects, to the *user*, they work as a single entity.

The basic principle of identifying components in terms familiar to users may be modified for contributed stories. When an author sends us a straight text file to which we only add our boiler plate display material, that story is treated as part of the top level of the issue; an example is Carl Lagoze's story in the June 1997 issue. This story is identified as <http://www.dlib.org/dlib/june97/071agoze.html> or cnri.dlib/june97-lagoze. This ensures that Lagoze's intellectual content is to some degree recognized, if not protected, by the file structure although the display includes items that do not "belong" to him, any more than the display in print contains only the intellectual work belonging to the author. Indeed it does not; the typeface, color of the paper, and other similar items are generic to the artifact or instantiation and are separate from the work for which a given author may hold the rights.

However, if any author sends us several files, whether text or images, then the "story" is assigned a subdirectory within the monthly issue. Thus, the story by Stuart Weibel, Renato Iannella, and Warwick Cathro in the June 1997 issue, "The 4th Dublin Core Metadata Workshop Report: DC-4, March 3-5, 1997, National Library of Australia, Canberra," was contained within a sub-directory as were the stories by Henry Gladney and Innes Ferguson and Michael Wooldridge. To start the metadata workshop story, users either point to <http://www.dlib.org./dlib/june97/metadata/06weibel.html>, or they can use the handle: cnri.dlib/june97-weibel. The story is seamless thereafter to the user. But the set of objects that embodies the story, in fact, is best understood as the sub-directory: june97/metadata together with the boiler plate images taken from a parent directory. (See Figures 4a, 4b, and 4c.)

So much for what we do. From a cataloging perspective, the questions are two: "What is the work?" and "What is the item, that is, the individual representation that the user will retrieve?" The work, admittedly an abstraction, seems straightforward enough; if we operate only at the serial level, then there exists *D-Lib Magazine* with many of the features that we are used to seeing in the print world.

However, there is a major difference in the digital world: the

FIGURE 4a. Display of 06weibel.html

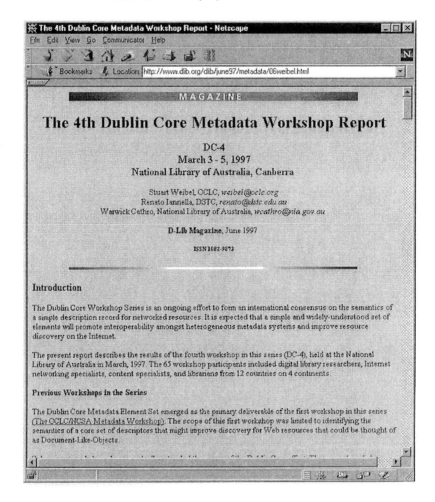

display that the user sees (which may not be identical across platforms) appears coherent in a way that the underlying file organization is patently not, and the internal file naming and structure itself may be a function of legacy systems and configurations. Moreover, *D-Lib* with the address <www.dlib.org> can be moved and the data internally re-structured in ways that would not necessarily affect the

FIGURE 4b. Display of source for 06weibel.html

```
Source of: file:///DI/DLIB/06weibel.html - Netscape                    _ □ ×

<HTML>
<HEAD>
<TITLE>The 4th Dublin Core Metadata Workshop Report</TITLE>
<META NAME = "DC.creator" CONTENT = "Stuart Weibel">
<META NAME = "DC.creator" CONTENT = "Renato Iannella">
<META NAME = "DC.creator" CONTENT = "Warwick Cathro">
<META NAME = "DC.subject" CONTENT = "metadata, conference,
workshop, dublin core element set">
<META NAME = "DC.date" CONTENT = "1997-06-16">
<META NAME = "DC.description" CONTENT ="Summary of the
Results of the  fourth Dublin Core Workshop">
</HEAD>
<body background = "../lgray_bg.gif" width = 700 height = 16><P>
<center> <img src = "../mag_bar1.gif"> </CENTER><p>
<CENTER>
<h1>The 4th Dublin Core Metadata Workshop Report</h1><h3>DC-4<BR>
March 3 - 5, 1997<BR>National Library of Australia, Canberra </h3>
</center><p><center>
Stuart Weibel, OCLC, <I>weibel@oclc.org</I><BR>
Renato Iannella, DSTC, <I>renato@dstc.edu.au</I><BR>
Warwick Cathro, National Library of Australia,
<I>wcathro@nla.gov.au</I></center><P>
<center><b>D-Lib Magazine</b>, June 1997<p>
<h6>ISSN 1082-9873</h6><p>
<img src = "../d-line1.gif"> </center> <p>
<h3>Introduction</h3>
<p>
The Dublin Core Workshop Series is an ongoing effort to form an
international consensus on the semantics of a simple description
record for networked resources. It is expected that a simple and
widely-understood set of elements will promote interoperability
amongst heterogeneous metadata systems and improve resource
discovery on the Internet.</p>
<p>
The present report describes the results of the fourth workshop in
this series (DC-4), held at the National Library of Australia in March,
1997. The 65 workshop participants included digital library
researchers, Internet networking specialists, content specialists, and
librarians from 12 countries on 4 continents.</p>
<h4>Previous Workshops in the Series</h4>
<p> The Dublin Core Metadata Element Set emerged as the primary
deliverable of the first workshop in this series
```

FIGURE 4c. Directory of june97/metadata

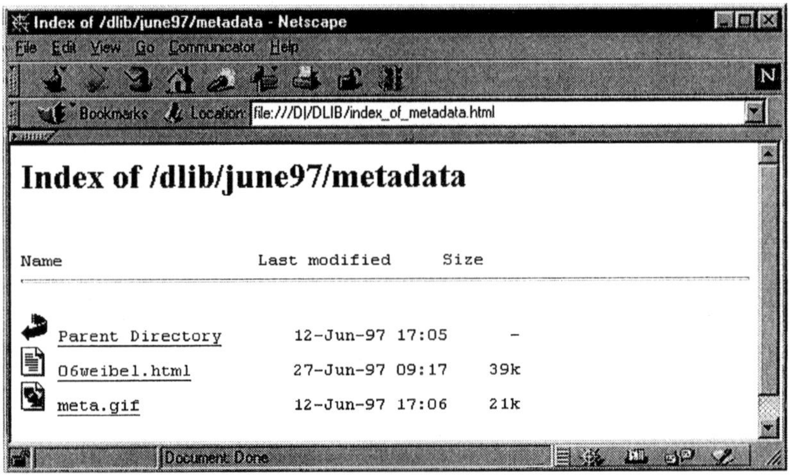

display. Thus, finding *D-Lib* on the Web is not equivalent to wandering up to stacks where the entire run of *Technology Review* may be neatly bound and shelved. We have chosen to organize the magazine as a series of hierarchical directories and sub-directories; with adjustments in naming of files that would not display to the user we could have decided to organize the whole thing as a single list (see Table 1). Instead of a sub-directory called august95/, for example, we could simply name a contents page (e.g., "august95contentspage. html") and then provide links to the relevant stories all in the same directory. So long as the links were correct, the display would be indistinguishable to the user, but we would lose the directory/sub-directory structure as a means of helping us understand the organization of the issues and their contents.

Both the hypothesized scenario and the existing organization assume that all of the information that is presented to the user is consolidated, or saved, on a single server. In a distributed system, it is not difficult to display an issue that seems to represent one set of stories which are physically stored on machines in different places. For example, in the July/August 1997 issue, we have thumbnails of images, files physically stored in Virginia, that point to large versions of the same images, files physically stored in California. But to the user, it is all point-and-click.

TABLE 1. Hypothetical organization of *D-Lib*'s files as a single Directory

```
august95contentspage.html

august95story1.html

august95story2.html

august96contentspage.html

august96story1.html

august96story2.html

dlib-banner.gif

homepage.html

lgray-background.gif

november95contentspage.html

november95story1.html

november95story2.html

november95story2-figure1.gif

november96contentspage.html

november96story1.html

november96story1-figure1.jpg

november96story3.html

october95contentspage.html

etc.
```

How then do you identify the item, that is, the digital representation of the work? Consider, for purposes of the example, that we wanted to catalog at the story level. Using the handle or one of the other persistent identifiers might, in this case, be much more useful in cataloging than the URL since resolving the handle would retrieve the set of objects that constitute the story while the URL <http://www.dlib.org/dlib/june97/metadata> would presently retrieve a directory from which the user would, we hope, select the file which starts the story. Under the handle scenario, the management issues associated with organizing files and updating them as files are moved around from server to server or directory to directory and off-loaded to a second service. The user and the cataloger need only know the persistent name, in *D-Lib*'s case, the handle.

On the other hand, *D-Lib Magazine* currently "lives" in a URL world and the relative links within the contents page are URLs. *D-Lib* registers its handles in anticipation of a world in which URLs would not be sufficient to find the relevant material. However, that solution, which relies on concurrent systems, would not necessarily be sufficient now in the MARC environment. It might well be appropriate for serials catalogers looking for compatibility with MARC as well as interoperability with other systems to consider using several fields for the same story. That is, a field that captures the persistent name, e.g., the handle, cnri.dlib/june97-weibel for the metadata story, as well as a field containing the URL that *starts* the story, <http://www.dlib.org/dlib/june97/metadata/06weibel.html> and hence in today's networked world would invoke a display familiar and useful to readers.

For at the end of the day, what matters is accurate representation of the author's work to the user–now and in the future. Thus, we keep faith with both reader and writer.

NOTES

1. The Digital Libraries Initiative <http://www.cise.nsf.gov/iris/DLHome.html> is a four-year program supported by three agencies of the federal government: National Science Foundation (NSF), Defense Advanced Research Projects Agency (DARPA), and National Aeronautic and Space Administration (NASA). Cooperative agreements with six major universities, each of which has many corporate, industrial, and professional partners, were signed in 1994. The grants are due to expire in 1998.

D-Lib is funded by the U.S. Defense Advanced Research Projects Agency (DARPA) under Grant No. MDA972-95-1-0003. The views and opinions expressed herein are those of the Author and do not necessarily reflect those of the Corporation for National Research Initiatives (CNRI) or the Government.

2. Arthur Plotnik, *The Elements of Editing: A Modern Guide for Editors and Journalists* (New York: Macmillan General Reference, 1982), 25.

3. For a summary of the technical issues associated with naming, see "Uniform Resource Names," *D-Lib Magazine*, February 1996. Available at: http://www.dlib.org/dlib/february96/02arms.html

4. William Y. Arms, Christophe Blanchi, Edward A. Overly, "An Architecture for Information in Digital Libraries," *D-Lib Magazine*, February 1997. Available at: http://www.dlib.org/dlib/february97/cnri/02arms1.html

5. Ibid.

6. H.M. Gladney and J.B. Lotspiech, "Safeguarding Digital Library Contents and Users Assuring Convenient Security and Data Quality," *D-Lib Magazine*, May 1997. Available at: http://www.dlib.org/dlib/may97/ibm/05gladney.html

Scandinavian University Press's Role as a Publisher in the Digital Future

Harald Joa

SUMMARY. The traditional system of scholarly communication has emerged over a period of hundreds of years and is now well-established regionally as well as internationally. This article attempts to identify whether there are specific characteristics with regard to new ways of disseminating scientific results in the Scandinavian region, and looks into practical experiences from the development of electronic journals.

The level of activity among libraries and publishers in Scandinavia with regard to electronic journals is relatively low. However, the interest in and discussions of this subject are widespread and it is on almost everybody's agenda. Some electronic journals are considered, including the *Nordic Journal of Philosophical Logic*, and several pilot projects are also presented and discussed.

There are considerably more initiatives in the international arena, and one important conclusion is that the development of electronic versions of scientific journals makes the world "smaller," that is, it is less difficult for the regional publisher to reach the international community of scientists. Many of the challenges that publishers face in the world of e-journals are considered, including copyright, fair use, one-stop-shopping, access control, printing, pricing and licensing. *[Article copies available for a fee from The Haworth Document Delivery Service: 1-800-342-9678. E-mail address: getinfo@ haworth.com]*

KEYWORDS. Publishing, electronic journals, Scandinavian scholarly communication, new media

Harald Joa is General Manager, Sivilokonom Harald Joa, Elgefaret 64, N-1347 Hosle, Norway (email: harald@joa.no).

[Haworth co-indexing entry note]: "Scandinavian University Press's Role as a Publisher in the Digital Future." Joa, Harald. Co-published simultaneously in *The Serials Librarian* (The Haworth Press, Inc.) Vol. 33, No. 1/2, 1998, pp. 21-43; and: *E-Serials: Publishers, Libraries, Users, and Standards* (ed: Wayne Jones) The Haworth Press, Inc., 1998, pp. 21-43. Single or multiple copies of this article are available for a fee from The Haworth Document Delivery Service [1-800-342-9678, 9:00 a.m. - 5:00 p.m. (EST). E-mail address: getinfo@haworth.com].

INTRODUCTION

In the autumn of 1996 I had the pleasure of presenting a paper at the 3rd European Serials Conference in Dublin, Ireland. The title of this paper was "A Case Study in E-journal Development: the Scandinavian Position." At that conference I was approached by Kerstin Fridén, and on behalf of Kibic Karolinska Institutet Library and Information Center she invited me to give a similar presentation at a conference in Stockholm, Sweden, entitled "Science Without Journals?!" This article is based on the papers presented in Dublin and Stockholm. It is an attempt to put electronic publishing into perspective, trying to identify the role of the publisher–in this case, Scandinavian University Press–in the digital future, taking into consideration the marketplace for scientific communication.

The article was written while I was Marketing and New Media Manager of Scandinavian University Press, but the thoughts and views are my own. I would like to thank my colleagues at the Press, who have given me the opportunity to work in this very interesting field of publishing. Finally, I would like to express my gratitude to my "network on the Internet"; taking part in and "lurking" on a number of news and discussion groups have given me immediate access to information that probably would have taken a lifetime to collect by traditional means.

DOCUMENT DELIVERY

In April 1993 the management of the journals division at Scandinavian University Press held a seminar, the objective of which was to work out a strategic plan to meet the challenges facing the publishing industry as a consequence of the ever-increasing demand for document delivery. The starting point for the discussions was Karen Hunter's article "Document Delivery: Issues for Publishers,"[1] which appeared in *Rights*. Karen Hunter is probably best known for the excellent job she does as manager of the Elsevier Science TULIP project (The University Licencing Program). In her article she sets forth ten decisions to be made by any publisher who wants to take part in the document delivery business:

1. Decide on a basic attitude or policy
2. Decide what you want to authorize
3. Decide to whom you want to authorize
4. Decide what you are going to charge
5. Decide how you are going to collect the money
6. Decide what else you want besides money: what information from the market
7. Decide if you want to be a document supplier yourself
8. Decide if you want to stimulate demand for your articles
9. Decide how to put this into a financial context
10. Decide to defend your rights[2]

With the knowledge we had at that time, we answered the questions and produced a strategic plan. Perhaps the most interesting aspect of the seminar was the collective anxiety for the future that arose at a certain point in the second day—is there room for publishers in a document-based marketplace? Well, the publishing houses are still here, and Scandinavian University Press has signed agreements with UnCover, UMI (University Microfilm International), ISI (Institute for Scientific Information), and many more. We decided how we are going to collect the money, but this has not created a significant amount of work for the accounts department of the Press.

According to statistics from FIDDO (Focused Investigation of Document Delivery Options),[3] there are 36 different commercial document delivery services; in addition there are 14 different development projects in this field. A very comprehensive overview of this market is available in reports from FIDDO.

The publishing industry is now once more facing more or less the same challenges as we did with document delivery, this time in a slightly different context. On the agenda is electronic dissemination of journals and journal articles, and the question of document delivery is only a small part of this.

The collective fear of the future that we experienced in April 1993 was that we would cease to exist. Scandinavian University Press wants to take part in the future. We want to identify the role of the publisher in this "brave new world." Only time will tell whether our strategies are consistent with the expectations in the marketplace, whether there is room for publishers in the digital future and, finally, whether there is a demand for electronic journals. In the discussion of how to face the digital future it is rather important to realize that different publishers will have different plans; to a large extent this is because there are many categories of presses.

SCANDINAVIAN UNIVERSITY PRESS

Scandinavian University Press is one of the largest publishers of non-fiction in Scandinavia and publishes academic books and textbooks as well as academic and professional journals. The head office is located in Oslo, Norway, with editorial branch offices in Stockholm and Copenhagen; there are also offices in Oxford and Boston. Although we have customers worldwide, Scandinavia is the main market.

Scandinavian University Press published 500 new and revised book titles in 1996. The Press also publishes 110 different journals, of which 65 are in English. We publish journals in several areas, mainly within medicine, social sciences and humanities. We also publish a few specialized magazines, for example within sports and music and–naturally–the oil industry. The Press publishes several CD-ROMs, mainly for the Norwegian and Scandinavian markets. At the time of writing, we are online with one electronic journal: *The Nordic Journal of Philosophical Logic* (see below).

Scandinavian University Press has been on the Internet since early 1995. Detailed information about the Press and its publications is available on the World Wide Web.[4] In 1996 these pages had an average of between 40,000 and 50,000 visitors monthly, and the number is increasing.

A GLASS OF WATER AND SOMEWHERE TO WHINGE

In the 1996 Christmas edition of the *British Medical Journal* there is an interesting discussion on the subject "Rights, Wrongs, and Journals in the Age of Cyberspace."[5] The first contributors in the discussion are Ronald E. LaPorte, one of the authors of "The

Death of the Biomedical Journals,"[6] and Bernard Higgins. This time LaPorte and Higgins are using the Beatles' song "Revolution" to once again predict the end of biomedical journals. Stating that "We all want to change the world," LaPorte and Higgins attack the journals: "Journals thus end up owning very valuable intellectual property that they barely contributed to making. . . ."[7] The best solution according to LaPorte and Higgins is "self-publishing." At the end LaPorte and Higgins refer to the Global Health Network, an Internet-based project which aims to promote alternative publishing models. One of the main contributions is a story called "Scientists Assassinate Journals"–and the assassination is expected to take place on 31 December 2001.

The first commentator to the LaPorte and Higgins article is Richard Smith, editor of *British Medical Journal*. He describes a journal as "A glass of water and somewhere to whinge."[8] Smith continues and makes a distinction between journals from "minimalist publishers" and journals that really add value to the content. Being convinced that minimalist journals will disappear, Mr. Smith states that reading a quality, value-added journal is "drinking from a glass rather than from a fire hydrant."[9]

According to Mr. Smith the value-added elements of a journal are as follows: independent legitimization, first-class peer review, good design, technical editing, commentaries that set scientific papers in context, an audience, marketing, a voice for a community, a forum for debate, education, an introduction to subjects you never thought important, a means to campaign, up-to-the-minute news, evidence-based advice, a place to tell your friends you are dead, somewhere to whinge, a source of after-dinner stories, and somewhere to wrap up fish and chips. Traditional journals that want to survive will also utilize the possibilities inherent in the networks: speed, links to other material, customization and interactivity.

The debate in the *British Medical Journal* is very interesting and is worth reading. The following are the main conclusions of the other contributors:

> Richard Horton, editor of *Lancet*, says that journals do not have a monopoly on scientific communication, "but we do not force researchers to send the Lancet over 6000 papers and 5000 letters each year."[10]

Georg D. Lundberg, editor of *Journal of the American Medical Association*, says "content is king". Furthermore he is very concerned with the quality aspect of the biomedical publishing: "real doctors use this information to help decide how to take care of real patients every day."[11]

Frank Davidoff, editor of *Annals of Internal Medicine*, describes the efficiency of and need for a marketplace for scientific communication. And despite a number of deficiencies and negative aspects, the scientific journal is for the time being working as such a marketplace.[12]

To summarize, there is a considerable divergence of opinion between the different commentators in the discussion of the journal as "threatened species." As a publisher, Scandinavian University Press is committed to entering the digital future, and we intend to do this in close collaboration with the editors, owners and societies that we currently serve.

Pieter S. H. Bolman, president of Academic Press, is correct when stating that "In science publishing, however, we are continuing to build on foundations constructed in the past and are dependent on them: A clean break, without taking care of building bridges from the old to the new, could lead to discontinuities and mismatches in the fabric of scientific literature that could be very difficult to remedy, if allowed to fester."[13]

Finally, we must be aware of the market mechanisms; it is in the marketplace that decisions are made. The scientist, the librarian, the societies, the readers, the buyers, the publishers—all have major input to the question as to whether journals are to be considered dinosaurs or not. Public authorities (e.g., governments, the US, the European Union) are increasingly taking part in the discussion in form of "green papers" and "white papers" (policy papers stating different points of view and action plans).

WHAT IS ELECTRONIC PUBLISHING?

We shall now consider the electronic publishing activities of Scandinavian University Press. But before doing so, let us have a look at the definition of electronic publishing.

Kjersti Rustad and Vidar Ringstrøm of the Norwegian National Library gave an introduction to electronic journals at the 4th Nordic ISSN/Union Catalogue meeting in Helsinki, Finland, on 8 and 9 September 1994.[14] After discussing news groups, discussion groups, file transfer protocol, gopher, bulletin board systems and the World Wide Web, Rustad and Ringstrøm propose the following definition of an electronic journal: "An electronic journal is a periodical–regular or irregular–and moderated unit made available in an electronic format, either on a static medium or via computer networks."[15] "Moderated" implies that the publication is subject to editorial control. An electronic journal can be made available both on paper and in electronic format or only electronically.

Scandinavian University Press's *Nordic Journal of Philosophical Logic* is one of twenty journals that constitute a pilot group on the subject of legal deposit of electronic journals at the Norwegian National Library. In the invitation to participate, the Library states: "The challenges concerning legal deposit of electronic journals are comprehensive. One thing is certain; networked documents are lost once they are removed by the publisher. At the same time it is important to preserve documents from the 'youth' of a medium to facilitate the researchers with the option of tracing the development from the start until it is a part of everyday life."[16] In other words, public authorities' concerns are (a) editorial control (in the current system of scientific publishing this is the peer-review), and (b) archiving so that the scientific results are available for future generations (for print publications, this is the role of libraries).

ELECTRONIC PUBLISHING ACTIVITIES AT SCANDINAVIAN UNIVERSITY PRESS

At Scandinavian University Press electronic journals and discussions about electronic publishing are part of the daily agenda and are becoming more and more important. During the last few years we have taken particular care to keep up with electronic trends and developments in the journals market. We discuss this with our colleagues in publishing and with the other important players in the market: the academics and the librarians. We are negotiating and collaborating with several companies and organizations.

We believe that 1997 will be the year when we will be "going live" with several electronic journals. During 1995 and 1996 we have mainly carried out tests and experiments. As mentioned earlier, however, we also launched our first electronic journal in May 1996: *Nordic Journal of Philosophical Logic*.

FOKUS PÅ FAMILIEN
(THE SCANDINAVIAN FAMILY THERAPY JOURNAL)

One of our test projects involved converting two issues of *Fokus på familien* to HyperText Markup Language (HTML) and Adobe Acrobat Portable Document Format (PDF). The journal, which is published in the Scandinavian languages, was made available free of charge on the World Wide Web.[17] The pilot project was carried out in collaboration with VTT Information Service in Finland. The reason for having the pilot journal in two electronic formats was to test whether the users regard page fidelity as an important factor: should the electronic version preserve the look and feel of the original publication? Another aim was to learn readers' opinions regarding the development of an electronic journal.

An important aspect of this pilot project was to gain hands-on experience with electronic publishing and to see how the different areas of the Press's Journals Department could handle a project like this. We have learned a great deal, and we are now in a much better position to see what training our staff need and the organizational changes we must make as a consequence of making journals available electronically. As Sandra M. Whisler at the University of California Press states: "The publishers' task is to prepare their staff and their organizations to live in constant change during these transitional years."[18]

The opinions of the online readers of the journal were surveyed by a questionnaire placed on the same Web page as the journal issue. Unfortunately, the response was low: it may be that the core readers of the journal are not yet very active Internet users. The low response is, of course, also a reflection of the general difficulty of getting information and feedback. A few interesting findings may be worth consideration, however. Readers seem to be willing to pay 20% in addition to the regular subscription price to gain access to the online version. They also seem to prefer the HTML version; this may be because the Acrobat PDF is rather time-consuming in the downloading process. These findings must be taken with a grain of salt, as the number of respondents was rather low.

One of the end results of the project is that practical recommendations about how to create Web publications were composed. There are five steps you have to go through. First you should decide upon the design–second you should identify and select tools; the next step involves testing the publication. Step 4 is the announcement in order to create traffic and readers, and finally–never forget to maintain your Web publication! For those who are interested, the entire cookbook is available on the World Wide Web.[19]

THE NORDIC JOURNAL OF PHILOSOPHICAL LOGIC

In 1995 we were approached by three young academics from the University of Oslo who were in the process of launching a new electronic journal called *Nordic Journal of Philosophical Logic*.[20] They wanted us to be the publisher of the paper version, while they would assume responsibility for the electronic version themselves.

These academics are of the new generation: they are used to and exploit the full potential of the new electronic media. In several meetings we made them aware of the full range of services, support and value-adding work the publisher may offer. A successful collaboration emerged, and in May 1996 we launched the first issue of the journal both in paper and electronically on the World Wide Web.

The University of Oslo and the National Research Council entered into the project with active support. This is thus also an example of how the scientific community may take interest in these new ways of communicating scientific results.

As publisher we developed electronic format guidelines for authors, providing requirements for articles to be published in the journal. The journal is typeset using LaTeX, as this provides a convenient way of producing the many special characters within the closely related fields of mathematics, computer science and logic. It is also easy to produce both print and hypertext documents for the World Wide Web, based on LaTeX's ability to produce PostScript files.

The Internet is used not only for publishing but, naturally, also for submission of articles, and for the peer-review process. The journal will be freely available on the World Wide Web for two years (until 1998), but users have to register to access the articles. The intention is also to make the journal a "living site" with discussion groups, links to related sites, and so forth.

We look forward to the continuous evaluation of this project, as we believe it will provide important user behavior information in the new market for scholarly communication. So far approximately 3,000 people have visited this specialized journal. When the period of free access comes to a close, we will evaluate the level of pricing we may introduce.

THE NORWEGIAN HEALTH NETWORK

Medicine and health constitute one of the fastest growing fields on the Internet. We see an enormous increase in the services, mainly in the form of different web sites. Scandinavian University Press is one of the partners in a project called the Norwegian Health Network. The idea is to offer a twofold service: one for the general public, which has already been launched as a "Health Encyclopedia on the Internet";[21] the other, for health-care professionals–service organizations, pharmaceutical companies, and many other parties that have an interest in meeting and serving the health care community.

This is a very good example of regional initiatives, because differences in medical legislation make it difficult to have an international perspective. As publishers we will evaluate using this channel as a supplemental means of distributing journals within health and medicine. But our participation depends on the presence of health-care professionals.

ISI ELECTRONIC LIBRARY PROJECT

Scandinavian University Press participates in the Institute for Scientific Information's Electronic Library Project. ISI is trying to persuade 350 publishers of 1350 journals in *Current Contents/Life*

Sciences to take part. At present some 500-600 journals are participating. Ten universities and companies in the USA and UK have been chosen to make the journals available to on-site users via local area networks (LAN). It is up to the different institutions to choose the core journals to be delivered in a digitized form. The rest will be made available for the institutions on a document delivery basis.

After long discussions, we worked out a price and access model for unlimited viewing, which essentially means subscribers pay the same whether or not they take the print version. Thus, if they already subscribe to the print version, there is a supplementary charge of 20%; if not, they pay a fee that is 120% of the print subscription price. There is no extra charge for making up to ten printouts per issue. Above that figure there is a charge, but the cost per copy decreases as the number of copies increases. We do not allow unlimited printing of articles. For document delivery there is a discount of 25% for the electronic subscriber.

IBM developed the software, and the project is "up and running," but there are no definite user data to report; however, there is a lot of activity, especially at Purdue University in Indiana. The aim of the project is to test user behavior, such as: how do they use the electronic access? How many printouts are produced? Does the price model work? Is the technical solution appropriate?

ADONIS

When describing electronic publishing activities one easily forgets ADONIS, a service that has been around for years. ADONIS is a document delivery service that scans bitmap images of journals pages and distributes them on CD-ROMs through a network of computers with CD-ROM jukeboxes. Scandinavian University Press participates with 13 journals. In the complete ADONIS system there are 640 journals from 60 publishers.

At the 1996 Frankfurt Book Fair ADONIS launched a new concept labeled "The best off-line online service." Trying to benefit from the advantages of the new technology, ADONIS is using PDF and comprehensive search tools. However, ADONIS will continue to distribute via CD-ROM, but now to LANs. ADONIS is not prepared to go online, partly because of the current slowness of the

Internet, and partly because the PDF technology is extremely time-consuming. Scandinavian University Press is in the process of evaluating the system, and as long as it fits with our overall strategy, and our partners want to, we are prepared to participate in the new ADONIS system.

OPINIONS FROM THE MARKET PLACE

It is always of great value to get input from users about their view on the development of a new service. We have found that it is not necessarily easy to get feedback from the marketplace; here, however, we will take a closer look at the information that we have gathered.

Multimedia Questionnaire

In 1996 Scandinavian University Press carried out a multimedia study in collaboration with Oxford University Press. We sent out a questionnaire to the individual member-subscribers to four journals, two from O.U.P (*Human Reproduction* and *Nephrology Dialysis Transplantation*) and two from Scandinavian University Press (*European Journal of Surgery* and *Scandinavian Journal of Gastroenterology*). The focus of the study was to determine how the researchers identify information today, and how they evaluate the different new ways and media (CD-ROM, online, World Wide Web) for information identification. We made a number of interesting findings.

Let us first take a closer look at the respondents–they appeared to constitute a middle-aged male universe. Half of the respondents were between 40 and 49 years of age, and very few were women. The majority were clinicians, with research and education as extra jobs. More than half considered the subscription model the best solution, but a considerable group favored a "pay as you go" model. A rather surprising fact was that only approximately 50% of the group were unwilling to give credit card details via the Net. A less surprising finding was that everybody wanted to have free access to everything from anywhere.

Most of the respondents spent four hours per week identifying relevant information, and another two to six hours per week absorbing the identified information. MEDLINE is much used, and search by keywords is the most common.

This group split almost 50-50 regarding online versus CD-ROM when asked to give preferences for electronic formats. The slow speed of the networks, and the fear of an ever-increasing telephone bill, are considered the disadvantages of online access. There seems to be a demand for electronic journals, but the quality must be improved, especially the quality of illustrations. There is also a growing demand for new multimedia features, such as sound and video. The most important demand is faster access and transfer of information.

Discussion Group Mini-Questionnaire

A number of electronic news and discussion groups follow developments in the electronic publishing market. In January 1997 I posed a question to a number of these groups (VPIEJ-L, ARL-EJOURNAL, WEB4LIB, SERIALST), asking for feedback about how people evaluate the role of the publisher in the digital future. I got a lot of answers, some comprehensive, others "quick and dirty." The shortest reply came from a librarian in Kansas, who wondered if "publishers would have ANY role in the digital future given the fact that almost all seem blind to the economic realities of library budgets."[22]

Here is a very brief summary of the input that was received:

- cost; the librarian's key concern, what will be the cost of electronic access to journals?
- archive; who will be responsible for the preservation of electronic journals?
- peer-review; how do we perform quality control and quality assurance in this new world?
- indexing; how is the digital library indexed?
- technical user-support; very important, but not good enough in the systems that are "live" today!
- loss of the generalist; the system opens for "over-specialization."

- loss of accidental discovery; users do not browse as they do in traditional print journals.
- prestige; not communication–that is what traditional journals are all about, in other words, "publish or perish."

One of the responses was from Joshua Lederberg, geneticist and Nobel Prize winner. In addition to presenting his views, he directed us to two related articles that he had written. The first of them was "Options for the Future," a presentation given at an ICSU/UNESCO symposium regarding electronic publishing in February 1996, in which Ledeberg did not look favorably on publishers, thinking rather that societies should take a greater part in the publishing of scientific results. It is interesting, though, to read his view of the journal: "So, if we had never heard of the Scientific Journal in its print form, and were just watching the manifestation of this communication as it is operating today on the net, I think we would very quickly come to the conclusion we had better invent something like a peer-review journal in order to provide some modicum of order and of discipline in that medium."[23]

The other article Lederberg mentioned was entitled "Communication as the Root of Scientific Progress." In this article he describes the scientific process, and also looks at the role of the publisher and editor. Mr. Lederberg remarks that the "potential for re-aggregation stands just after mechanized search and tempo of availability as the greatest advantage that these new kinds of media can offer."[24]

THE ORGANIZED MARKET
FOR ELECTRONIC PUBLISHING

Lederberg makes us aware of the fact that what gave us journals was the letter-based communication between scientists. At a certain moment in time, these letters were collected, went though a quality control, and were than wrapped up as journals. Today, the informal communication between scientists is growing; electronic mail is perhaps the most important form, but we also see an increase in preprints and off-prints. This communication is supplementing journals publishing. We must expect this form of communication to increase. Electronic publishing gives us an opportunity to organize this communication, in connection with legitimate and respected journals.

The current market for electronic publication is, in turn, becoming organized, and may be divided into the following:[25]

A. Those with comprehensive subject coverage:
- Inside (British Library Document Supply Centre)
- OCLC (Online Computer Library Center) FirstSearch Electronic Journals Online
- Blackwell's Electronic Journal Navigator
- SwetsNet, Swets electronic journals service
- EBSCOhost (EBSCO Subscription agent)
- EPSILON-Dawson
- PICA's Webdoc
- The CARL Corporation/Uncover

B. Specific subject-based information services:
- SCIFinder (Current Awareness Service)
- Entrez (National Library of Medicine)
- BioMedNet
- Bioline
- Ei Village
- ISI's Electronic Library Project
- Ovid Core Biomedical Collection

C. Publisher or product-related
- STeaMline (Bath Information and Data Services, BIDS), renamed Journals Online
- CatchWord
- ADONIS
- ScienceDirect (Elsevier)
- IDEAL (Academic Press)
- SuperJournal
- Red Sage
- SilverPlatter
- UMI ProQuest Direct

CHALLENGES IN THE DEVELOPMENT
OF ELECTRONIC PUBLISHING SERVICES

Before looking into some of the specific plans for electronic publishing at Scandinavian University Press, let us take a look at the challenges that we continually face in the development of quality online products.

Quality–Peer Review

In the presentation of scientific publishing in "Options for the Future" Lederberg states the role of the publisher: "the producers, the publishers and the editors, of course, have had their very important part to play, and their role in quality improvement and quality control has been indispensable. They have established the mechanisms for editorial review on which we rely."[26] Scandinavian University Press is aware of this fact, and we take it very seriously and will, of course, continue to do so in the digital future.

Copyright

Copyright, intellectual property rights, fair use–this is a "mine field." The problems concerning protection of copyright are by no means easier to resolve in the digital realm; it has never been easier to copy and re-distribute information. The author's rights must be taken care of, and we are following the discussions on regulation of this area with great interest. There are a number of interesting projects, perhaps the most interesting being a concept for electronic clearing of rights. On the other hand, we have to rely on people's morals and attitude, while informing users of the copyright concept. The music industry has survived the massive copying to cassette-tapes and the film industry has survived the videocassette, so as publishers we have an optimistic view.

Archives

Scandinavian University Press sees the development of systems that assure future generations access to the scientific memory as a collective responsibility. Librarians are very concerned about this, and it is difficult to imagine that electronic journals will ever come to be accepted into the library as long as the archive question remains unanswered. On the Internet it is a problem that URLs move or are being deleted, without a reference to an alternative location.

Economy-Investments-Price-Price Policy

No matter how you look at it, the Internet is not free. America Online doubled its price and offered unlimited use instead of charging users for the actual time they are on the Net. Today America Online is facing a court case that may end up costing them US$ 150 million. The reason for the lawsuit is bad service: the users were very often unable to connect due to lack of lines.

If we want the Internet and electronic publishing to succeed, we have to make considerable investments on a macro level; the current infrastructure simply is not good enough. Publishers, on the micro level, are facing investments in both hardware and software. To be able to invest and reinvest, there must be profits; this again requires charging for services. Elsevier Science is launching Science-Direct and estimates that they will have to spend US$ 25-30 million to make 1200 scientific journals available electronically.

Site License

Academic Press has with great success presented their IDEAL/APPEAL concept. This is based on site license, and they do not allow document delivery. Having a site license gives the participating library unlimited access to all Academic Press journals.

Site license is also the pillar of the interesting HEFCE (Higher Education Funding Council for England) project. Blackwell Science, Academic Press and the Institute of Physics are among the participants. All reports from this project are positive; users get access to an increasing number of journals, and publishers get funding for new investments and developments.

One-Stop Shop

At the Online Information '96 symposium in London in December 1996 Helge Clausen of the Danish National Library presented a paper entitled "Looking for the Information Needle in the Internet Haystack";[27] he said that "the Internet is for people who have enough time to browse through irrelevant information in search of pearls. But for business librarians this browsing becomes more like ploughing."[28]

Professor Peter Gärdenfors of Lund University in Sweden has renamed the information superhighway the "electronic drainage system." He is definitely not a fan of "net surfing," which he thinks is more like "swimming against the information drainage."[29] A number of one-stop shops, combining publications from different sources and publishers in an orderly manner and containing good search engines and indexes, may be the optimal solution to Clausen's and Gärdenfors's problems.

Production

Scandinavian University Press is setting up systems for the production of electronic journal articles. An important aspect is the fact that each and every article must be able to live its life separate from the journal. The reasons for this are, among others, indexing, identification and localization (from what location is an article available?). The PII, Publisher Item Identifier, giving the article a unique identity, seems to be one of the systems that will evolve into a standard in this field. At a more in-depth level there is the DOI, Digital Object Identifier, which may make the article live its life on its own, without the connection to a publisher. We are building the in-house capability to digitize the articles and journals, but we rely on printers for the production of SGML files and PDF files.

Distribution

From the start, one of our major concerns has been the market coverage. Currently we have large segments within libraries, institutions, societies and individuals. To be in a position where we can supply these traditional market segments in an efficient manner, Scandinavian University Press's intention is to use several channels. In the selection of distribution channels we also have to consider geographical location, because of the lack of speed on the Internet.

Technology

In principle, we are not particularly interested in technology for its own sake, but having experienced the rapid rate of change in this field, we realize that we have to keep up with developments. As an example, we can mention that initial discussions about electronic publishing of our journals with OCLC was based on an entirely different technological platform than what was finally presented on the market in the spring of 1997.

Another interesting observation is the development within browser software. Our first homepage was built for a "Mosaic community," and almost overnight everybody switched to Netscape. This meant a redesign of the pages. Today we are experiencing the power of Microsoft and their "war" to make Explorer the number one browser.

We try to produce homepages that are compatible with the largest segments of browsers, but find it alarming that the two biggest suppliers are developing their software in different directions. In the end, this may cause problems for information suppliers.

SCANDINAVIAN UNIVERSITY PRESS'S STRATEGY FOR ELECTRONIC PUBLISHING

As publishers we realize that one of the keys to success for electronic journals is that the user can easily access a comprehensive collection of quality journals from many different publishers within his/her field of interest. We believe that in the end the users are in favor of the one-stop shop concept. If every single publisher creates its own database, these have to be linked together, for example, within medicine in MEDLINE, *Current Contents* and so forth. We believe there will be several shops that present journals collections to large user groups. Thus, one possible scenario for us might be:

- Journals for the libraries: ISI, OCLC, CatchWord, ADONIS and so forth
- Journals directly to academics: BioMedNet, ChemWeb and other dedicated services
- Our own database: the Publisher's Database

On our way towards developing this scenario we have read innumerable pages of proposals, studied endless suggestions for formal agreements, and evaluated very many different concepts, and we have discussed them internally as well as with competitors, STM (Scientific-Technical-Medical) colleagues and several secondary publishers. There is a lot of activity around, involving three main interest groups:

- librarians working within the digital library;
- secondary publishers and agents trying to build electronic collections;
- publishers figuring out the best ways to publish electronically.

EVOLUTION–NOT REVOLUTION

At the Online Information '96 symposium in London in December 1996 C.J. Hildyard and B.J. Whittaker presented the paper "Chemical Publishing on the Internet: Electronic Journals–Who Needs Them?"[30] One of their conclusions was: "A properly refereed electronic journal, in particular one which has a respected printed version already in existence, has a good chance of becoming a respectable medium for publication. Whether electronic journals will continue to come out as purely parallel versions of their paper equivalents depends upon the attitudes of authors to this novel publishing medium. This in turn depends on the attitude of the scientific community in general."[31]

Nicholas Negroponte from the MIT Media Lab has described journals and books publishing as "squeezing ink onto dead trees."[32] Scandinavian University Press has no special interest in printing and distributing paper copies of journals; the production and distribution bills make up a major proportion of the total costs. But we realize that traditional journal publishing does have qualities that need to be conserved; medical publishing is both a transfer of knowledge as well as personal promotion. In a number of learned societies, the journal constitutes a primary source of income, and in many cases it is a major reason the members stay with the society.

Electronic publishing is here to stay, and we expect it to develop on the basis of the principles of the traditional paper-based academic publishing. John Peters, in his article "The Hundred Years War Started Today: An Exploration of Electronic Peer Review," describes electronic publishing as a "Type 1 Innovation."[33] In this kind of innovation there are changes in the format but no substantial changes in content: we are dealing with an evolution–not a revolution.

This view does not contradict the predictions of Charles Clark of the International Publishers Copyright Council, who puts it thus: "The possibilities inherent in the merger of the most advanced technologies from three different industries; cable, computer and telephone, are revolutionary. . . . If you add the impact of multimedia CD's and the Internet and its successor networks, the sheer scale of deliverability is revolutionary."[34]

At Scandinavian University Press we aim to enter our collection of scientific journals into this evolving system in a way that ensures the future of scholarly communication. We believe that academics will continue to send their best works to quality journals based on peer review and that the readers of these journals know that the articles have had a great deal of value added, having undergone corrections and modifications before they reach their desk. As a publisher we will continue to develop our products and services to this very quality-conscious community.

CONCLUSION

Still more questions than answers remain; we are at the very beginning of a new era in publishing; we believe in an evolution– not a revolution. We are testing and entering into non-exclusive agreements and arrangements with a number of players. We realize that there will be many changes–players will leave and new ones will arrive–but it is in the marketplace, with the end users, that the decisions of the electronic future will be made.

We are convinced that close collaboration among the author, the academic community, the library community, the subscription agents, the secondary publishers and publishers is the key to a new and successful electronic future. Public authorities–governments and the bureaucracy–may also increasingly enter into this collaboration.

The world is getting smaller, which makes it possible for a regional publisher to reach new interesting markets. We do treat the Scandinavian market as our home-market, but as an STM publisher of international academic serials, we do have an international perspective on electronic publishing. In the words of Pieter S. H. Bolman of Academic Press: "Science is a truly international endeavor and the scientific community forms one of the few true international markets currently in existence."[35]

NOTES

1. Karen Hunter, "Document Delivery: Issues for Publishers," *Rights* 6, no. 2: 9-12.

2. Ibid., 10-12.

3. FIDDO, "Commercial Document Delivery Services." Available: http://dils2.lboro.ac.uk/fiddo/providers.html

4. Available: http://www.scup.no/

5. "Rights, Wrongs, and Journals in the Age of Cyberspace," *British Medical Journal* 313 (1996), 1609-1612.

6. R. E. LaPorte, E. Marler, S. Akazawa, F. Sauer, C. Gamboa, C. Shenton et al., "The Death of Biomedical Journals," *British Medical Journal* 310 (1995).

7. R. E. LaPorte and Bernard Higgins, "We All Want to Change the World," *British Medical Journal* 313 (1996), 1609.

8. Richard Smith, "A Glass of Water and Somewhere to Whinge," *British Medical Journal* 313 (1996), 1609-1612.

9. Ibid., 1611.

10. Richard Horton, "A Colourless Conveyor Belt?" *British Medical Journal* 313 (1996), 1611-1612.

11. George D. Lundberg, "A Christmas Fairy Tale," *British Medical Journal* 313 (1996), 1612.

12. Frank Davidoff, "To Market, To Market," *British Medical Journal* 313 (1996), 1612.

13. Pieter S. H. Bolman, "Journals Face the Electronic Future," *LOGOS* 7, issue 1, 90.

14. Kjersti Rustad and Vidar Ringstrøm, "Electronic Journals in the National Library." Available: http://rosa.nbr.no/etids/e-tids.html

15. Ibid.

16. Rigmor Sjøvoll, letter to Scandinavian University Press, 16 Dec. 1996.

17. Available: http://www.scup.no/journals/fokus/fokus.html

18. Sandra M. Whisler, "Electronic Publishing and the Indispensability of Publishers," *LOGOS* 7, issue 1, 122.

19. Available: http://www.vtt.fi/inf/nordep/projects/webpilot/cookbook/

20. Available: http://www.hf.uio.no/filosofi/njpl/

21. Kristin G. Nicolaysen, "HelseNett-et helseleksikon på Internett," *Tidsskrift for den Norske Lægeforening* 116, nr. 26 (1996): 3154.

22. Barbara Steward, email to author, 7 Jan. 1997.

23. Joshua Lederberg, "Options for the Future," in *Electronic Publishing in Science: Proceedings of the Joint ICSU Press/Unesco Expert Conference* (Paris: Unesco, 1996).

24. Joshua Lederberg, "Communication As The Root Of Scientific Progress," *The Scientist* 7, no. 3 (Feb. 8, 1993).

25. "Electronic Dissemination Projects," *Scholarly Communications Report* no. 1 (Sept. 1996), 10-11.

26. Lederberg, "Communication."

27. Helge Clausen, "Looking for the Information Needle in the Internet Haystack," *Online Information 96*, 115-123.

28. Ibid., 121.

29. Peter Gärdenfors, *Lunds Universitet Meddelar* 11 (1995).

30. C.J. Hildyard and B.J.Whittaker, "Chemical Publishing on the Internet: Electronic Journals–Who Needs Them?" in *Online Information 96*, 143-150.

31. Ibid., 148.

32. Nicholas Negroponte, "Being Digital–What's the Next Big Thing?" *The Big Issue*, Dec. 2, 1996. Available: http://www.forbes.com/asap/120296/html/ nicholas_negroponte.htm

33. John Peters, "The Hundred Years War Started Today: An Exploration of Electronic Peer Review," *Journal of Electronic Publishing* 3, issue 1. Available: http://www.press.umich.edu/jep/works/PeterHundr.html

34. Charles Clark, "The Copyright Environment for the Publisher in the Digital World," 6th updated version (International Publishers Copyright Council, Mar. 1996).

35. Pieter S. H. Bolman, "Journals Face the Electronic Future," *LOGOS* 7, issue 1, 87.

Electronic Journals and Their Roles
on the Internet

Edward J. Valauskas

SUMMARY. Electronic, peer-review journals provide the clearest examples of the value of the Internet as a medium for serious scholarship, a counterpoint to whinings over digital disinformation and knowledge fragmentation. However, digital journals, like any other medium, battle for readers, contributors, and editors, in order to prove their efficiency and intellectual vitality. Electronic scholarship demands an awareness of both the similarities and differences of the medium from traditional printed journals, in order to truly achieve any measure of success. *[Article copies available for a fee from The Haworth Document Delivery Service: 1-800-342-9678. E-mail address: getinfo@haworth.com]*

KEYWORDS. Electronic journals, attention, reading, scholarship

THE IMPORTANCE OF ATTENTION

Electronic peer-review journals have been ballyhooed as one of the most vital components in a technological revolution in scholar-

Edward J. Valauskas is Chief Editor, *First Monday*, http://www.firstmonday.dk/, P.O. Box 87636, Chicago, IL 60680-0636, USA, and Principal of Internet Mechanics. He is a member of the Board of Directors of the Library and Information Technology Association (LITA) and the Professional Board of the International Federation of Library Associations and Institutions (IFLA) (email: ejv@uic.edu).

[Haworth co-indexing entry note]: "Electronic Journals and Their Roles on the Internet." Valauskas, Edward J. Co-published simultaneously in *The Serials Librarian* (The Haworth Press, Inc.) Vol. 33, No. 1/2, 1998, pp. 45-54; and: *E-Serials: Publishers, Libraries, Users, and Standards* (ed: Wayne Jones) The Haworth Press, Inc., 1998, pp. 45-54. Single or multiple copies of this article are available for a fee from The Haworth Document Delivery Service [1-800-342-9678, 9:00 a.m. - 5:00 p.m. (EST). E-mail address: getinfo@haworth.com].

ship, the greatest advance in intellectual discourse since the invention of the printing press.[1] Swayed by seductive fantasies of global networked academic communities, hard-wired together, busily tackling the most obscure problems of a discipline with supercharged workstations, electronic journals are seen as the catalyst for a new kind of scholarly utopia, an ultimate democracy of ideas.[2] Reality, however, paints an entirely different picture of reticent professors ignoring their computer accounts, of entire academic communities unconnected thanks to dysfunctional infrastructures.[3] Reality ultimately tells us that electronic journals depend–just like other more traditional printed journals–on readers: readers as commentators, readers as advertisers, readers as potential contributors. Electronic journals, like their print relatives, depend on attention.

What do we mean by attention? What is attention? Most dictionaries will tell us that attention means simply "the ability to observe carefully," to "notice." We need to expand on this definition to fit our own needs when we act as digital editors, authors, and researchers, taking advantage of networked resources and computerized media. Attention in the terabytic world of the Internet means an ability to first of all take note of a given site or server; to examine its information in an exploratory fashion; to assess its value to personal interests and professional projects; to retain some sense of a given resource's location; and, in the highest form of a digital compliment, to refer others to a given site or server.

This sort of Internet-defined attention is very important to peer-review electronic journals. These journals, as relatively new tools for communication, find themselves vying for attention from scholars in a rich, complex, and altogether new jungle of media. In the terabytic world of the Internet, and in the diverse mass-mediated everyday world, attention–that deceptively simple practice of careful observation–is incredibly valuable. Why?

The Internet is just one medium among many by which researchers circulate and test their ideas and discoveries. Although printed scholarly journals and books are still primary dissemination vehicles, mass media channels–newspapers, high-circulation magazines, television, radio–race to announce the latest spectacular discovery, say a new stew of antiparticles concocted in physicists' pressure cookers such as Fermilab and CERN.[4] Although some academics may express their displeasure with "media exploitation," this form of attention earns value in the eyes of funding bodies, institutional alumni, and the public.[5] In competition for attention with massively distributed and highly diffused media, electronic journals literally do not stand a chance.

Electronic journals also find themselves competing for attention with those well-known and oft-abused warhorses of scholarship—printed academic journals, which have existed as conduits of ideas for centuries. With their well-developed reputations, dedicated audiences, exacting editors and boards, and conservative publishers, they will continue as entities well into the next century. No electronic journal will ever overwhelm the *Natures*, *Sciences*, *Physical Reviews* in the sciences, and few digital journals will dream of ever reaching the status of mainline print journals in the humanities and the social sciences. Electronic journals, more than ever, have to carefully cultivate their audiences, attracting them to the essential benefits of Internet communication (in the absence of the "revolutionary" hype of agitators for digital academic scholarship).

Why is attention on the Internet so special? In essence, attention makes the Internet go 'round.[6] The most dedicated scholar, working in the most exotic speciality–say, analyzing the color patterns of trilobites–still needs to communicate research results to a small circle of colleagues.[7] More importantly, that small cadre of color-centric trilobite specialists needs to evaluate new discoveries, and fit a new finding into the totality of a discipline. Publishing in an electronic journal, say a newly founded peer-review digital journal entitled fancifully *Neon Trilobitomorpha*, will make it possible for this scholar to communicate quickly to compatriots, and more importantly learn of their approval or disapproval of the findings in much less time than in a print journal such as the *Journal of Paleontology*.

Attention is necessary for electronic journals to sustain their potential as laboratories for multimedia experiments, although I must admit that few electronic journals dare to strike out in new directions. Attention is also vital because the abundance of information on the Internet makes peer-review electronic journals perhaps the ultimate bastions for verified truth, edited readability, and logical discourse.

The meanings of "truth" and "measured discourse" are naturally defined by editors, contributors, and the state of a discipline at a given point in time. Each electronic journal creates its own sense of reality for a discipline, a different and yielding medium for expression for its followers, editors, and contributors, just as their printed counterparts do; the advantage for an electronic journal exists in time and space. Without the need for paper or postage, an electronic journal can develop its contents faster and reach its targeted audience quicker than any printed journal. Nevertheless, for many scholars, paper carries its own weight of authority, its very special solid aura that grants to each and every article a halo of acceptance and permanence; no electronic journal has this effect and none ever will.

WHY ELECTRONIC JOURNALS NEED TO BE READ

This lack of respect for digital scholarship parallels the Internet's own faulty reputation, a knock for the digital neighborhood that is difficult to erase. In the last 24 months, this marvelous mythology has taken on a life of its own about the Internet and its information—or actually the Internet's misinformation and disinformation.

Those professionally dependent on information—especially librarians, journalists, lawyers, scientists—saw a rapid evolution in Internet-based resources in the past decade and witnessed a sharp decline in the reputations of Internet-based information in the last half decade, as hoi polloi rushed to connect to this medium. Librarians were among the first to spot the defects of a few but (gratefully) not all Internet resources. For journalists, Internet-based information became double-edged, some falling prey to the sirenian call and allure of easy factoids. Columnist Clarence Page complained that Matt Drudge is just a "merry prankster cyber-geek," unconcerned "for anything dull and wussy as facts," with his digital newsletter entitled the *Drudge Report*.[8] Columnist Mary Schmich discovered the meaning of Internet fallacies when her words in a story were "morphed" on the Internet into a graduation speech by

Kurt Vonnegut.[9] The *New York Times*, to some, has been leading a one-newspaper crusade against the evils of Internet information.[10] All of these concerns point out the necessity for tested, evaluated, and substantiated Internet-based information.

Peer-review scholarly electronic journals provide a counterpoint to this image of the Internet as a collage of fables, impressions, and out-right lies.[11] Thanks to the peer-review process, scholarly digital journals provide their own filtering mechanism, separating the info-chaff, discarding it in advance for readers. Editors work to bring many an article up to a readable standard, so that almost anyone can understand an author's findings and arguments. In addition, editors check sources, both traditional and electronic; there is nothing more frustrating for a reader than to try to track an article with an incomplete citation or to point a browser to an extinct URL. Indeed, peer-review journals may already be working on a more holistic scale on the Internet in raising the overall quality of information, encouraging veracious reporting, inspiring would-be Net publishers to test their suppositions in advance of posting. Still, even if the quality of the articles in a given journal is impeccable, readers are needed and attention needs to be drawn to survive as an acceptable medium.

HOW TO SECURE ATTENTION AND REMAIN SERIOUS

Attention depends on finding ways to pull a reader into an electronic text, which at first blush is much easier to say than do. Electronic text does not work like print. Our eyes do not work with computer monitors, compared to paper; some studies indicate that readers of electronic text lose up to 40% of the information displayed with a monitor. Readers of electronic text digest the displayed word up to 25% to 30% more slowly than they do paper.[12] As editors of electronic journals, we have to think of these handicaps that our readers endure to examine the contents of our magazines. To secure someone's attention for text on the Internet simply requires more work in comparison with print.

We have to realize that different and unexpected factors will attract readers to our journals, factors that we might stumble upon.

With *First Monday*, we found that many visitors to the site remarked on what they called the unusual name of the journal, *First Monday*. Others were attracted to the logo for the journal, which uses a rich variety of different letters and symbols to spell out First Monday. Still others were attracted by the editorial roster, Esther Dyson, Vint Cerf, Ed Krol, among others. Some ignored all of these factors and simply read the articles!

Why? Unusual characters in a logo and a catchy name may have more than just graphical appeal working for them. Researchers analyzing brain activity, for example, have found that unusual and odd combinations of words and symbols stimulate the brain, that is, increase brain activity as recorded on an electroencephalogram (EEG).[13] Increased brain activity means–in one way or another–attention.

Once you attract readers to a site, it's important to bring them back. This return of your readers may be possible with a steady stream of exciting and stimulating (remember those EEGs) articles. With *First Monday*'s editorial team, it's been possible to find those sorts of articles for a peer-review journal, such as John Seely Brown's article on the social life of documents in the first issue in 1996 or Michael Goldhaber's article on the attention economy this year.[14] Finding ways to draw readers back every issue to the journal reinforces consciously or unconsciously for readers the reputation of a journal as a quality resource. Indeed, this sort of electronic reinforcement correlates to findings that indicate that it takes five to six hours for new skills–like remembering the URL of *First Monday*–to move from temporary storage in the front of the brain to permanent storage in the back.[15]

Attracting and keeping readers is an issue for publishers of all sorts of electronic magazines, journals, and newsletters. The mass-market *Utne Reader* discovered in 1995 the problems in making great expectations for readership and advertisers. Initial projections estimated for the electronic magazine were 100,000 hits per month, as well as the income from advertising to support a significant portion of the budget. Three months after its initial release, the number of hits measured only 25% of the projected level, with only one advertiser signing up. *Utne* decided that it needed to take advantage of the medium to draw in both more readers and advertisers and opened late in 1995 an online conferencing site called Café Utne.[16] The Café now draws in 48,000 hits a month but advertising–on a scale first anticipated in planning–has never followed. The publishers found other ways to support the digital magazine, including compact disk sales and subscriptions to the print equivalent.[17] Even though the *Utne Reader* is not a scholarly journal, there are lessons for every editor of a "serious" journal in *Utne*'s application of flexibility, creativity, diversity, and patience.

CONCLUSION

There is a "perversity" in the economics of scholarly publishing, as noted by Andrew Odlyzko.[18] This perversity is dependent on the decisions by scholars to contribute their works to journals which they view as being the most prestigious in a given field and which in turn reach the largest number of their professional colleagues, carrying, under the imprimatur of a given title and editorial board, the weight of authority. No electronic journal has yet passed into this sanctum sanctorum of scholarship, where academics will flood editorial digital mail boxes with manuscripts in the hopes of safe passage through the rough rapids of blind review and peer judgement. Indeed, to many scholars, electronic peer-review journals are mere digital will-o'-the-wisp, in comparison to their print complements. The true face of scholarship will change only when the many experiments in electronic publication finally yield a journal that meets the "perverse" demands of academics, libraries, and publishers.

Acting as oases for the information-thirsty on the Internet, digital academic journals have an alternative role to play as proof of the viability of networked information. These oases will exist only if creators of electronic journals understand the vital differences of the electronic medium from paper, and the necessity of attracting readers on a sustained level to their virtual pages. In this age of information overabundance, it is no longer mere words and the reputations of authors and editors that matter. Readers hold the power of electronic life or death for many with their modems and keyboards in hand.

NOTES

1. " . . . advocacy of electronic publishing sometimes takes on more strident tones. According to some, nothing less than a full revolution is taking place among humans, one that may dwarf anything we have seen so far. Cyberspace and global networks, in this perspective, are the signs of profound upheavals that promise to catapult humanity to some unprecedented level." From Jean-Claude Guédon, "The Seminar, the Encyclopedia, and the Eco-museum as Possible Future Forms of Electronic Publishing," in Robin P. Peek and Gregory B. Newby (eds.), *Scholarly Publishing: The Electronic Frontier* (Cambridge, Mass.: MIT Press, 1996), p. 72.

2. Digital communities, pursuing ideas, hypotheses, and allusions on a global scale have been part of the landscape of some recent fiction, such as David Brin's 112 million members of the Worldwide Long Range Solutions Special Interest Group, dealing with global ecology in the year 2040. For one communication from this fictional group, see David Brin, *Earth* (New York: Bantam, 1991), p. 68. I find it difficult to imagine moderating anything with 112 million components! The entire issue of scholarly fantasies with technology is examined in Rob Kling and Roberta Lamb, "Analyzing Alternate Visions of Electronic Publishing and Digital Libraries," in Robin P. Peek and Gregory B. Newby (eds.), *Scholarly Publishing: The Electronic Frontier* (Cambridge, Mass.: MIT Press, 1996), p. 28.

3. Contrast the remarks of Sven Birkerts:

I've been to the crossroads and I've seen the devil there. Or is that putting it too dramatically? What I'm really saying is that I've been to the newsstand, again, to plunk down my money for *Wired*. . . . *Wired* gives us our old planet repackaged as a weightless environment, more dream than matter–information moving through cyberspace at the speed of thought (intelligent thought) . . . Yes, I've been to the crossroads and I've met the devil . . . the sorcerer of the binary order, jacking in and out of terminals, booting up, flaming, commanding vast systems and networks with an ease that steals my breath away. (Sven Birkerts, *The Gutenberg Elegies: The Fate of Reading in an Electronic Age* [Boston: Faber and Faber, 1994], pp. 210-211)

to Nicholas Negroponte:

Information space is by no means limited to three dimensions. An expression of an idea or train of thought can include a multidimensional network of pointers to further elaborations or arguments, which can be invoked or ignored. The structure of text should be imagined like a complex molecular model. Chucks of information can be ordered, sentences expanded, and words given definitions on the spot. . . . (Nicholas Negroponte, *Being Digital* [New York: Knopf, 1995], p. 70)

or compare Clifford Stoll's idea of the digital library:

I claim that this bookless library is a dream, a hallucination of online addicts, network neophytes, and library-automation insiders. (Clifford Stoll, *Silicon Snake Oil: Second Thoughts on the Information Highway.* [New York: Doubleday, 1995], p. 176) to that of Raymond Kurzweil:

. . . the library of the future will be a network of knowledge systems in which people and machines collaborate. Publishing will be actively transformed. Authors may bypass text, adding their increment to human knowledge directly to knowledge structures. (Raymond Kurzweil, *The Age of Intelligent Machines* [Cambridge, Mass.: MIT Press, 1990], p. 328)

These remarks reflect a very real dichotomy in assessing the current state of digital discourse and its future.

4. A flurry of media "attention" fell on CERN in Geneva in the spring of 1996 over its antimatter creation, more publicity than CERN ever earned in 1989 over the development of the World Wide Web. For the media, antimatter easily translates into Star Trek and other science fictional diversions; the Web in 1989 for the media had no fictional parallel. For a useful overview of antimatter, see Nickolas Solomey, *The Elusive Neutrino: A Subatomic Detective Story* (New York: Scientific American Library, 1997), pp. 101-106.

5. Value in this case may mean increased donations from alumni to a college or university and increased opportunities for awards and grants from funding bodies (especially those seeking publicity for their financial support of research). For the general public, the mass media translates obscure research into reality, or into fantasies developed in other components of the media (so the discovery of antiparticles will be reduced to the mere pantoscopic Star Trek pseudoscience).

6. See the arguments of Michael Goldhaber, "The Attention Economy and the Net," *First Monday* 2, no. 4 (Apr. 1997). Available: http://www.firstmonday.dk

7. Color patterns in trilobites have been described at least on four occasions, according to H. J. Harrington, "General Description of Trilobita," in Raymond C. Moore (ed.), *Treatise on Invertebrate Paleontology. Part O. Athropoda 1* (New York; Geological Society of America; Lawrence: University of Kansas Press, 1959), p. 107.

8. The *Drudge Report* can be found at http://www.drudgereport.com/; see also Clarence Page, "A Wealth of Misinformation in Cyberspace," *Chicago Tribune* (Aug. 13, 1997), sec. 1, p. 21, and, James Warren, "Abuse Charge Against Clinton Aide a Bit of Skull-Drudgery," *Chicago Tribune* (Aug. 17, 1997), sec. 2, p. 2.

9. Mary Schmich might have benefited from the following:

"Many discussions in cyberspace seem to be mental gymnastics–exercises designed to sharpen the minds of the participants. . . . logical fallacies are likely to be used to bolster arguments . . . there is no shortage of fallacious reasoning in cyberspace" (David B. Whittle, *Cyberspace: The Human Dimension* [New York: W. H. Freeman, 1997], p. 76). Mary's digital misquotation has earned her at last count some 1,400 e-mail messages of sympathy and far wider publicity for her column than ever expected; for a summary, see Mary Schmich, "Her Last Web Word Might Be 'Rosewater'," *Chicago Tribune* (Aug. 8, 1997), sec. 2, p. 1.

10. On the *New York Times*, see "What Have They Been Smoking?", *Wired 5*, no. 9 (Sept. 1997), pp. 53-56.

11. "Internet newcomers who expect to find the world's collection of the best books and magazines are often mildly surprised to discover that to get to any 'good,' substantial stuff, they often have to wade through an inordinate amount of useless, off-the-subject material first" (*Child Safety on the Internet* [Upper Saddle River, N. J.: Prentice-Hall, 1997], p. 141).

12. Edward J. Valauskas, "Reading and Computers–Paper-based or Digital Text: What's Best?" *Computers in Libraries* 14, no. 1 (Jan. 1994), pp. 44-47.

13. Summarized in George A. Miller, *The Science of Words* (New York: Scientific American Library, 1991), p. 251.

14. John Seely Brown and John Duguid, "The Social Life of Documents," *First Monday* 1, no. 1 (May 1996). Available: http://www.firstmonday.dk/; for Michael Goldhaber, see note 6 above.

15. Bob Condor, "Brain Boost," *Chicago Tribune* (Aug. 14, 1997), sec. 5, p. 3.

16. Available: http://www.utne.com/cafe/

17. Robert W. Buchanan, Jr. and Charles Lukaszewski, *Measuring the Impact of your Web Site* (New York: Wiley, 1997), pp. 285-287.

18. Andrew Odlyzko, "The Economics of Electronic Journals," *First Monday* 2, no. 8 (Aug. 1997). Available: http://www.firstmonday.dk

PRICING

Online Journal Pricing

Bill Robnett, MS, MLIS

SUMMARY. Many commercial, association, and university press publishers have transferred the two-tier subscription plan into the online journals environment. First-copy costs are generally charged to institutional and nonmember subscribers. Some associations are permitting access to electronic and print formats for the price of the print subscription. Others charge a relatively modest add-on cost for access to the online version. A few associations are charging significantly greater subscription prices for online access and plan to eventually eliminate the print format. Many online reference serials are priced according to the number of simultaneous users required. Some electronic journal aggregators have adopted this pricing scheme for their services. *[Article copies available for a fee from The Haworth Document Delivery Service: 1-800-342-9678. E-mail address: getinfo@haworth.com]*

Bill Robnett is Director of the Central and Science/Engineering Libraries, Vanderbilt University, 419 21st Avenue South, Nashville, TN 37240, USA (email: robnett@library.vanderbilt.edu).

[Haworth co-indexing entry note]: "Online Journal Pricing." Robnett, Bill. Co-published simultaneously in *The Serials Librarian* (The Haworth Press, Inc.) Vol. 33, No. 1/2, 1998, pp. 55-69; and: *E-Serials: Publishers, Libraries, Users, and Standards* (ed: Wayne Jones) The Haworth Press, Inc., 1998, pp. 55-69. Single or multiple copies of this article are available for a fee from The Haworth Document Delivery Service [1-800-342-9678, 9:00 a.m. - 5:00 p.m. (EST). E-mail address: getinfo@haworth.com].

55

KEYWORDS. Online journal pricing, member subscription price, institutional subscription price, simultaneous user increments, aggregators

In the 1991 premier edition of the Association of Research Libraries' *Directory of Electronic Journals, Newsletters and Academic Discussion Lists*, only two of the twenty-seven journals and eighty-three newsletters listed required paid subscriptions–*Journal of the International Academy of Hospitality Research* and *Tetrahedron Computer Methodology.*[1] Since then the number of online journals and newsletters has grown almost exponentially. Subscribers to *NewJour-L*, an electronic journal announcement list, see the numbers increase daily. By midsummer 1997 the announcement service exceeded 4,000 titles.[2] While many of these continue to be free, the entry of more commercial, university press, and society publishers into the electronic journal arena means that many titles require paid subscriptions.

All players in the serials industry at one time anticipated that online journals would be the panacea for the pricing crisis. However, it is now very clear that both profit and not-for-profit publishers require capital to experiment with electronic publishing. The American Chemical Society estimates that first-copy costs of a high quality electronic journal represent 82% to 86% of total journal production cost, and its CD-ROM journals cost 25% to 33% more than the print journal counterparts, due to additional expenses associated with search software.[3] The American Institute of Physics believes that its expenses will be ten to fifteen times greater in producing both Web and print journals.[4] The experience of society publishers is corroborated by reports from university presses developing online delivery of their journals. Janet Fischer of MIT Press reports that the overall costs for the *Chicago Journal of Theoretical Computer Science (CJTCS)* are quite comparable to those of the press's print journals. Marketing and overhead for *CJTCS*, which are two-thirds of the total production expense compared to one-third for print journals, counterbalance any economies of the electronic medium. The lack of back-issue sales and permission/subsidiary rights income as well as mailing list rental and advertising revenues further negates any savings.[5]

Publishers, as much as libraries, are confronted by the pricing conundrum resulting from the economic downward spiral in which all parties are ensnared. As publishers raised journal prices over the past years to keep pace with inflation, subscriptions were canceled to the point that the one action precipitated the other. Publishers recognize that they must temper their pricing, although it may be at the expense of limited page increases.[6] Costs associated with the first copy continue to be charged back to non-members and institutions, so that many electronic journal publishers preserve the significant differential between personal and library subscription prices for both print-plus-electronic and electronic-only formats. Yet, there is still much uncertainty about the best way to support these online journal production costs.

One analysis of the necessity of perpetuating the two-tier pricing scheme is offered by Hal Varian. Writing in *D-Lib Magazine* he describes the economic phenomenon of inducement of self-selection among certain subscribers to association or society serial publications when offered electronically. Individuals must be enticed to maintain their subscriptions (memberships) by receiving something more attractive than what they can access through the library's electronic subscription. Varian suggests that in order to maintain society revenues, inconvenience, that is, making the library copy accessible only within the library, or added value, for example, hypertext links to cited articles, early access to forthcoming articles, enhanced images, and so forth will stimulate individuals to maintain their personal subscriptions.[7] However, to date there appear to be no significant differences between online journals available to institutions compared to those accessible by the membership, or—in cases in which some publishers have begun to offer added-value versions to their members—those differences have not been discovered.

Price, at one time a relatively simple concept that implied institutional or individual subscription costs occasionally increased by added volumes, now also encompasses tiered licenses under which various numbers of simultaneous users are permitted access according to the agreed-upon price, particularly for the electronic abstracting and indexing services. While most electronic journals are not priced according to number of simultaneous users, gateways to those journals, such as OCLC's Electronic Collections Online

(ECO), have adopted the simultaneous-user approach, and the add-on costs must be considered. A variant of the simultaneous-user approach is access to electronic serials priced according to user population size. Pricing is made additionally complex when libraries enter into consortial agreements, in which multiple institutions combine their purchasing power to attain what they hope will be a reduced cost per institution for access to the electronic publications.

The products, services, and companies cited in the examples below are not intended to be an exhaustive listing, but rather are examples of pricing schemes available from an ever-growing number of publishers in the online serials domain.

ONLINE REFERENCE SERIALS

Electronic indexing and abstracting and data resources are vended through multiple distributors or intermediates, including UMI, EBSCO, SilverPlatter, Information Access Corporation (IAC), OCLC's FirstSearch, and Ovid. Many of these online serials are the digital counterparts of long-standing print publications, such as the *MLA Bibliography*, the various Wilson indexes, *Sociological Abstracts*, *Psychological Abstracts*, *Index Medicus*, and others. Some products offer discounts when libraries continue subscribing to the print format, for example, *Biological Abstracts*, *International Political Science Abstracts*, *PsycLIT*, and so forth.

There are often two different annual prices for a single-user subscription when access is through a stand-alone versus a networked workstation. Using SilverPlatter's price guide information as an example, the 1997 *GPO* subscription on a stand-alone workstation is $630, whereas that for a single-user license on a networked terminal/workstation is $788; for the *MLA International Bibliography*, the single user stand-alone price is $1,995, but $2,993 when available to one user on a network.[8] The rationale for this dual pricing scheme, the end result of both being one user accessing the product at a given time, is unclear. Current network software can control the access according to the license agreement, and when stipulated by the license more than one user at the same network simply cannot gain access.

In a networked environment in which more than one user per title is the intent, reference serials are usually priced according to the number of simultaneous users. For example, SilverPlatter typically establishes its simultaneous user bands (increments) of two to four, five to eight, nine to twelve, and thirteen or more or thirteen to twenty, depending upon the producer. Some databases vended by SilverPlatter have an additional user band of twenty-one plus, and some collapse the first two bands into two to eight simultaneous users. As a comparison, Ovid generally prices access by groups of one, up to five, up to ten, occasionally fifteen, and twenty. This variation compounds the difficulty of comparing various vendor prices for the online reference serials.

An interesting pricing structure is represented by *PsycLIT* and *PsycINFO*, again using SilverPlatter and Ovid comparisons as examples. To further complicate matters, *PsycINFO* is different in coverage from *PsycLIT*. The former indexes journals, dissertations, and technical reports from 1984 to date and covers books and chapters beginning in 1987. The latter includes journal indexing and abstracting from 1974 to date, as well as the book and chapter indexing and abstracting beginning in 1987. In addition *PsycLIT* is available only as a CD-ROM installation.

Through SilverPlatter, *PsycLIT* licenses are available for five to eight users at $8,990, while from Ovid, the pricing allows up to 6 users at $6,095 according to its 1997 database catalogs. These prices assume the library continues to subscribe to *Psychological Abstracts*. There is an additional levy of $900 ($655 if for a single user) when there is no active subscription to the print abstracts.

When additional simultaneous users are required above the eight, SilverPlatter stipulates that a subscription then be established for *PsycINFO* for which there is no limit on the number of simultaneous users. The subscription price, however, increases to $19,995. The CD-ROM format is not available; access is through SilverPlatter's ERL (Electronic Reference Library) gateway or over the Internet. Ovid prices access to *PsycINFO* at $18,500. For both vendors' versions the *PsycINFO* backfile (1967 through 1983) must be purchased separately for a one-time charge. In 1997 SilverPlatter's *PsycINFO* backfile was $12,000, and $13,000 through Ovid.

Other online indexing and abstracting service vendors have similar pricing schemes. OCLC's FirstSearch establishes three database packages: a Base Package of thirteen databases including *WorldCat*, Custom simultaneous logons in which libraries can subscribe to one or more databases of choice, and add-on databases to the Base Package. Pricing for the Base Package ranges from $5,840 for one user to $84,400 for 20 simultaneous users. For Custom simultaneous logons, the range is $3,400 to $68,000.[9]

AGGREGATORS OF ONLINE SERIALS

The first type of aggregator (an organization which contracts with the journal providers on behalf of several or many libraries[10]) considered is one that is evolving from the online indexing and abstracting services, such as UMI's ProQuest Direct; EBSCO's *Academic Abstracts FullTEXT* and *Academic Abstracts FullTEXT 1,000*; IAC's SearchBank; and Ovid's *Biomedical (Core and II-IV)*, *Mental Health*, and *Nursing Collections*. Libraries negotiate subscriptions directly with these aggregators, who provide common gateways to online periodicals of many publishers.

The individual article is the unit of delivery, leading some to question whether these are actually amalgamations of texts and images or are online periodicals. However, for the purposes of this article such compilations will be considered, as these are becoming commonplace in the digital environments of academic, special, school, and public libraries and can have one of the more complex pricing structures currently available.

Multiple formats are available, including citation, citation with abstract, ASCII text of the article including abstract and citation, page image, and page image with enhanced graphics. Access can be based on a subscription price or cost per transaction. For example the article image through *ProQuest Direct* is priced at $9.50, and the citation is $0.50 on a transaction basis. Blocks of images can be purchased to reduce the cost per article, or page image availability can be part of the negotiated subscription price. Additional charges are levied when patrons wish the search results to be delivered to their institutions, for example, by fax when laser printers are not available for printing page images. IAC prices access to all formats only and does not provide subscriptions to format subsets of the database, for example, citation or citation with abstract. Their price is based on either the stipulated number of simultaneous users or on unlimited access.

In the previous category, pricing is negotiated directly with the aggregator. There is a second type of aggregator which also brokers access to online serials of many publishers through a common interface, such as Blackwell's Electronic Journal Navigator and OCLC's ECO. (Elsevier will also host other publishers' titles through its ScienceDirect.[11]) The noteworthy feature of this type of aggregator is that the subscribing library negotiates the price of the online periodical subscription directly with the publisher or through a subscription agent. The cost of the gateway service must then be considered in the price of access to online serials. As users have access to citations for all publications available through the services, independent of subscription, there is added value that may justify the cost of using the services of the aggregator.

OCLC has developed a price matrix for its Electronic Collections Online, ranging from $80 (in addition to the negotiated subscription price between library and publisher) for one simultaneous user with access to one journal title, to $200,000 for 100 simultaneous access with access to 500 journals.[12] Blackwell's Navigator service is priced at $3,950 annually, which permits an unlimited number of users, and offered an "early adopter" discount for libraries committing to Navigator in 1997. Blackwell's can serve as aggregator for orders placed through its own subscription service or for those through other vendors.[13]

JSTOR[14] is a unique case in the online serials arena. Originally funded by the Mellon Foundation and now moving toward self-support through development and annual access fees to subscribers, JSTOR purchases copyright of back issues of periodicals and is mounting these as bit-mapped images with searchable text files of the contents. Only backfiles are available, and generally there is a five-year rolling time period between the current year and the first available year of a journal title from JSTOR. A major feature is its goal of building absolutely complete backfiles of the journal titles selected for digitization.

Phase I is a three-year period during which 100 journals in ten to fifteen fields are to be made available. Subscribing libraries and qualified consortia were offered a 25% charter discount on the database development and annual access fees, if paid by April 1, 1997. Renewals after the first phase will be in one-year increments.

Table 1 gives the four tiers of pricing for charter-member libraries and regular pricing for libraries committing after the April 1, 1997 deadline.

ONLINE ASSOCIATION PERIODICALS

At an ever-increasing rate commercial and society journal publishers are making their periodicals available online. A most welcome variation on pricing schemes comes from society and association publishers who are not charging for access to their online journals when an individual and/or a library subscribes to the paper format. Examples of such societies are the Association for Comput-

TABLE 1. Comparison of four-tier pricing structure for JSTOR charter-member libraries and regular member libraries (those committing after Apr. 1,1997)

Library Size[1]	Large	Medium	Small	Very Small
Database Development Fee/Charter[2]	$30,000	$22,500	$15,000	$7,500
Database Development Fee/Regular	$40,000	$40,000	$20,000	$10,000
Annual Access Fee/Charter[2]	$3,750	$3,000	$2,250	$1,500
Annual Access Fee/Regular	$5,000	$4,000	$3,000	$2,000

[1]Large: Carnegie Research I & II, Doctoral I & II with some exceptions; Medium: Masters I & II with some exceptions; Small: Bachelors I & II; Very Small: All Masters and Bachelors colleges with enrollments below 1,000.

[2]Available only through April 1,1997.

ing Machinery (ACM), the Institute of Physics (IOP), the American Institute of Physics (AIP), the Australian Academy of Science (AAS) with the Commonwealth Scientific and Industrial Research Organization (CSIRO), and the American Physical Society. The IOP suite of thirty-three titles also permits non-subscriber access to featured articles selected by the editor because of timeliness or popularity. The AAS/CSIRO online journals are publicly accessible during 1997 but will be available only to members in the following year. The ACM offers public access to its article citations in the form of tables of contents, abstracts, and reviews, but only members can access the full-text electronic versions of journals for which they have current paper subscriptions through their memberships. They have also recently established not-for-profit institutional pricing for their Digital Library: Core Package (all ACM journals and magazines) is $2,957, Master Special Interest Group (SIG) Package is $2,250, and the Conference Series is $1,650. These prices include both print and electronic subscriptions, including a Core Package six-year online archive. When more than three simultaneous users are required, there is an additional charge of $175 per added user.[15]

Other societies offer subscriptions to the online journal and the print format at different prices and levy a modest surcharge, comparatively speaking, to subscribe to both formats. For example, the American Mathematical Society (AMS) supplies both formats at 15% above the cost of the paper, while the price of the online format only is 90% of the paper format cost.[16] The Society of Industrial and Applied Mathematics (SIAM) offers electronic access at approximately 90% of the institutional print price and at a flat rate of $35 to personal members in 1997 and 1998.[17]

The American Chemical Society (ACS) and the American Society for Biochemistry and Molecular Biology (ASBMB), however, have established pricing guidelines for their online periodicals that are in no way modest, compared to many other societies. The ACS Electronic Editions currently consist of the *Journal of Physical Chemistry (JPC), Biochemistry, Environmental Science and Technology (ES&T), Journal of the American Chemical Society*, and the *Journal of Organic Chemistry*. The latter two titles are free to institutional subscribers through December 31, 1997. The 1997 site license costs for the *JPC* combined format add $900, or 46%, to the

$1,995 nonmember institution print subscription, and $900, or 48%, to the *Biochemistry* print price of $1,870. When there is no print subscription, the site license charges increase to $2,200 for *JPC* and to $2,100 for *Biochemistry*. For *ES&T* there is a $500 charge for online access to research articles only if there is a print subscription; there is no stand-alone online version, as in the case of the other two titles.[18]

Highwire Press and the ASBMB surprised many libraries with their 1997 online version price of $1,100 for the *Journal of Biological Chemistry (JBC)*, a significant increase from the $200 partial-year charge for 1996. A subscription to both paper and online formats for 1997 totals $2,500. Robert Simoni, Associate Editor of *JBC*, explained that his association is committed to moving toward the online version and ceasing the print format. Their reasoning is to avoid the appearance of merely adding a supplemental fee to the cost of the print subscription to gain access to the online format. Simoni acknowledged that subscribers, including some on the *JBC* editorial board, are reluctant to convert solely to the electronic format. He also recognizes that a subscription to both formats does put smaller institutions in a bind, because the electronic format is priced to be a stand-alone publication and not as an add-on fee.[19]

The genesis of this publishing partnership reflects what librarians had both hoped for and urged to help hold down ever-increasing periodical prices, that is, the collaboration of a research library and a professional society in an online publishing venture. However, the press and the association missed a prime opportunity to educate and inform subscribers about their pricing approach in the case of *Journal of Biological Chemistry*. Information on subscriptions to the other fourteen currently available Highwire Press journals, including *Science* from the American Association for the Advancement of Science, is available at the press's homepage.[20]

The Ecological Society of America (ESA) launched its quarterly electronic journal, *Conservation Ecology*, on June 15, 1997. The society anticipates charging modest prices for the journal beginning in 1998 ($25 for individuals and $75 for institutions). The information on the ESA development plan for the Conservation Ecology Program and the role of journal revenues is the information that librarians need in advance to make fiscally responsible decisions regarding online journals.[21]

ONLINE COMMERCIAL PERIODICALS

Academic Press's IDEAL, Elsevier's ScienceDirect (Web access to titles mounted on Elsevier's host server) and Electronic Subscriptions (EES, locally mounted online journals), Blackwell Science, and Springer LINK represent developments in the provision of online journals with established paper versions from major commercial publishers. Springer has not yet determined what it will charge for access to its electronic titles and will make them available free through the remainder of 1997 and 1998.[22] Blackwell charges 90% of the print subscription price for access to the online version only, and approximately 130% for access to both formats.[23]

The cost of Elsevier's EES journal package is calculated by determining a library's Elsevier holdings at the 1997 journal prices plus an annual surcharge of 7.5% in year one (6% if the contract was signed before July 1, 1997), and 9.5% above the 1997 print plus online costs for the second and third year, respectively. A single year's subscription for EES entails a 15% surcharge above the print price.[24] Through ScienceDirect, Elsevier also plans to have document delivery to non-subscribed titles, both Elsevier's and those of other publishers using their gateway, toward the end of 1997. The pricing structure of ScienceDirect has not yet been established.[25]

Academic Press (AP) has made the marketing decision to license access to library consortia only. AP's IDEAL, International Digital Electronic Access Library, has a pricing structure similar to that of Elsevier's EES, that is, an electronic surcharge levied for its 176 titles for a three-year period followed by yearly adjustments to the price. The Academic Press license (APPEAL) stipulates that the fee for electronic access is 110% of the base price, defined as the total of the amount members of the consortium would pay if the constituents continued their Academic Press print subscriptions plus new serials to be included the license. There is a $1,000 minimum base price per consortium member, which gives the small members a very significant advantage. Academic library consortia are also eligible for a 20% discount. There is a local server premium of 20% that is usually only applicable where achieving adequate response time would require establishing a mirror site. The base price increase in subsequent years is to be contained at 10% plus inflation, which AP defines as the Consumer Price Index-Urban for the previous twelve months. Annual increases, while capped at 10%, cover growth and other cost increases which are primarily those associated with increases in the number of articles across the AP journal list. Costs associated with adding new consortia members and/or adding Academic Press publications are also accommodated under the terms of APPEAL.[26]

Renewals after the initial three-year period will be annual only, and the press has no plans to develop document delivery. According to Taissa Kusma, Director of Electronic Product Development for Academic Press, the situation will be assessed after the initial three-year contracts are complete in order to determine what market niches might still remain.[27]

There is an additional benefit to participating in IDEAL. Print subscriptions to Academic Press journals are discounted according to their Deep Discount Price schedule, which averages about 75% of the full institutional rate.[28]

Neuroscience-Net has taken the approach of charging the authors rather than charging users for subscriptions, to support production of the journal. Authors are assessed reprint charges of $650 for storage and transfer of the published articles. For additional charges staff will digitize images, sound, and video associated with the articles. There is no print counterpart to the journal.[29] Charging authors may be a more acceptable means of online journal support in the biomedical and other fields where there is relatively plentiful grant funding. For this same reason it is a concept that may find less acceptance in the humanities and social sciences.

ONLINE UNIVERSITY PRESS JOURNALS

Project Muse of the Johns Hopkins University Libraries and the Johns Hopkins University Press (JHUP) is the leader in the field of university press electronic journals. The press has developed a complex pricing scheme for single campuses/libraries/institutions (including special libraries), consortia and multi-campus systems, public library systems, and high school systems. Two titles are currently available for the individual subscriber. There is incentive to maintain dual formats in that JHUP print journal prices are reduced by 60% if a single campus or a consortium subscribes to all their electronic titles. For consortia/multi-campus institutions there is also a potentially significant discount for the complete electronic journal package, the size of which depends upon the number of subscribing members within the group. It is noteworthy that JHUP acknowledges that it may not be possible to discount print titles placed through subscription agencies, unless all members of the consortium place orders through the same agency.[30]

Compared to the Johns Hopkins University Press, the development of online serials by other university presses is relatively nascent. SCAN, Scholarship from California on the Net, a joint project of the University of California Press, the University Libraries at Berkeley, Irvine, and Los Angeles, and the Division of Library Automation of the Office of the UC System President, has a growing list of online titles. Currently *Nineteenth-Century Literature* and *Classical Antiquity* are available, with *Pacific Historical Review, The Public Historian,* and *Agricultural History* to be added in 1998. The online versions of *Nineteenth-Century Literature* and *Classical Antiquity* are priced at 80% of the paper subscription cost and 120% of the same price when both formats are desired. These two online journals are also available as part of SCAN's *Nineteenth-Century Studies Database* ($62 for print and electronic, $42 electronic only, 1997 price) and *Classical Antiquity Database* ($83 for print and electronic, $55 electronic only, 1997 price), which will include the full text of selected UC Press monographs beginning in 1997.[31]

Other university presses that presently publish online serials include the University of Chicago Press, publisher of *The Astrophysical Journal,* provided free to institutional subscribers of the paper format.[32]

THE FUTURE OF PRICING ONLINE SERIALS

The complexities of online serial pricing may increase as more publishers enter the electronic publishing market. Libraries may ultimately long for the relatively simple two-tier pricing scheme that many publishers have carried over from the print medium. Pricing by transaction, already available through some services such as ProQuest Direct and in development in ScienceDirect, may eventually dominate the online serials domain. How such pricing ultimately affects the seriality of scholarly and research reporting remains to be seen. One consideration is that serials budgets will be redefined, as libraries purchase access in units of articles, an open-ended concept quite different from the now-prevalent subscription. Whatever the unit of transaction, it is almost a certainty that libraries will remain major players in the electronic serials publishing industry and will continue to acquire research literature to provide access for their users.

NOTES

1. Association of Research Libraries, *Directory of Electronic Journals, Newsletters, and Academic Discussion Lists* (Washington, DC: Association of Research Libraries, 1991).

2. Available: http://gort.ucsd.edu/newjour/

3. Robert H. Marks, "The Economic Challenges of Publishing Electronic Journals," *Serials Review* 21, no. 1 (spring 1995): 85-88.

4. Tom Abate, "Publishing Scientific Journals Online," *Bioscience* 47, no. 3 (Mar. 1997): 175-179. Available: http://www2.aibs.org/aibs/bioscience/vol47/mar97abate.html

5. Janet H. Fisher, "The True Costs of an Electronic Journal," *Serials Review* 21, no. 1 (spring 1995): 88-90.

6. Abate, "Publishing," p. 177.

7. Hal Varian, "Pricing Electronic Journals," *D-Lib Magazine*, June 1996. Available: http://www.dlib.org/dlib/june96/06varian.html

8. SilverPlatter Information, Inc., *SilverPlatter Information Price Guide, Second Quarter 1997* (Norwood, MA: SilverPlatter Information, Inc.).

9. OCLC Online Computer Library Center, Inc., *FirstSearch Annual Subscription Pricing–February 10, 1997* (Dublin, OH: OCLC, Inc.).

10. N. Gilbert, "Aggregators of Electronic Journals," *Liblicense-L*, 6 Mar. 1997. Available: email LIBLICENSE-L@pantheon.yale.edu

11. George S. Machovec, "Electronic Journal Market Overview in 1997: Part I–The Publishers," *Information Intelligence, Online Libraries, and Microcomputers*, 1-6. Available: UMI/ProQuest Direct.

12. OCLC Online Computer Library Center, Inc., *Pricing and Billing for the Electronic Collections Online Access Account–February 21, 1997* (Dublin, OH: OCLC, Inc.).

13. S. McKay, email to author, 7 May 1997.
14. Available: http://www.jstor.org/
15. Available: http://www.acm.org/membership/institutional/
16. Available: http://www.ams.org/
17. Available: http://www.siam.org/eaccess/prices.htm
18. Available: http://pubs.acs.org/acselec/jrn_pricing/electj-pr2.html
19. Abate, "Publishing," p. 175-178.
20. Available: http://highwire.stanford.edu/
21. Available: http://www.consecol.org/Journal/editorial/case-study.html#journal
22. Jerry Curtis, announcement during discussion period, "Electronic Publishing: Between Two Poles" (annual meeting of NASIG, Ann Arbor, Mich., 1 June 1997).
23. Available: http://www.blackwell-science.com/online/default.htm
24. J. Tagler, Elsevier response to Rouse article, *Newsletter on Serials Pricing Issues* 181, 22 May 1997. Available: email PRICES@listserv.oit.unc.edu
25. Elsevier Science, "ScienceDirect™ Entering Early Release Phase," 13 June 1997. Available: http://www.sciencedirect.com/science/page/static/splash_latest_news.html#2. See also Karen Hunter, "ScienceDirect™," in this volume, 287-297.
26. Available: http://www.apnet.com/www/ap/genlay.htm
27. Taissa Kusma, telephone conversation with author, 13 June 1997.
28. Available: http://www.apnet.com/www/ap/ddpa-c.htm
29. Available: http://www.neuroscience.com/
30. Available: http://muse.jhu.edu/
31. Available: http://sunsite.berkeley.edu:8080/scan/absc.html#scan
32. Available: http://www.journals.uchicago.edu/ApJ/

COPYRIGHT

On Beyond Copyright

Erika Linke

SUMMARY. The focus of discussions about copyright and electronic publishing centers on the access to the text, recompense to the publisher and unauthorized transmission. A formal initiative to clarify fair use began in 1994 under the aegis of the Conference on Fair Use (CONFU). At the present time, no formal guidelines have been endorsed by the CONFU participants and unresolved issues remain. Librarians should use this hiatus as an opportunity to reeducate themselves about copyright law and electronic publishing. *[Article copies available for a fee from The Haworth Document Delivery Service: 1-800-342-9678. E-mail address: getinfo@haworth.com]*

KEYWORDS. Copyright, CONFU, fair use

BACKGROUND: THE PAST AND THE PRESENT

The importance of copyright to the framers of the U.S. Constitution is evidenced by its inclusion in the Constitution. Specifically,

Erika Linke is Acting University Librarian, Carnegie Mellon University, 5000 Forbes Avenue, Pittsburgh, PA 15213-3890, USA (email: erika.linke@cmu.edu).

[Haworth co-indexing entry note]: "On Beyond Copyright." Linke, Erika. Co-published simultaneously in *The Serials Librarian* (The Haworth Press, Inc.) Vol. 33, No. 1/2, 1998, pp. 71-81; and: *E-Serials: Publishers, Libraries, Users, and Standards* (ed: Wayne Jones) The Haworth Press, Inc., 1998, pp. 71-81. Single or multiple copies of this article are available for a fee from The Haworth Document Delivery Service [1-800-342-9678, 9:00 a.m. - 5:00 p.m. (EST). E-mail address: getinfo@haworth.com].

"the Congress shall have the power . . . To promote the Progress of Science and useful Arts, by securing for limited Times to Authors and Inventors the exclusive Right to their respective Writings and Discoveries. . . . " It established the importance of encouraging the development of science and the arts and securing the rights to the creators. Since 1790, this premise has not altered. Encouraging, stimulating and promoting science and the useful arts are essential in fostering new ideas and fertilizing the seeds of change. The exchange of ideas and the capacity to build on them are the source from which progress in the arts and sciences springs.

Publishers have played an important role in the dissemination of writings and discoveries by producing and distributing the printed work of the content creators. Today some authors assign rights to the publisher without taking into account future use in other endeavors and media. Many authors of journal articles simply assign the rights to the publisher in order to expedite the publication of the work without reserving for themselves (the authors) rights to future use in their classroom or for their reserve readings. Recompense to the author seldom occurs for journal articles in scholarly, academic or scientific and medical publishing. In fact, there are instances when an author subsidizes the publication of his article in these fields. With the advent of computing and new technology, new opportunities for disseminating journal literature have arisen.

The literature describing the electronic publication process has burgeoned and participants in the discussion about all facets of academic electronic journals have grown and broadened to include authors, publishers, librarians, lawyers and computer professionals. The relationship between copyright and electronic journals has been the focus of many articles (both printed and electronic) and conferences. Authors, publishers, librarians, the legal profession and computing professionals have all taken an interest regarding copyright of electronic journals, focusing on fair use and the economic ramifications of the new technology. Authors want to protect and preserve the rights that are conferred on creation of a work. Publishers have a professional and a financial stake in the manner in which the academic community chooses to exploit and cope with electronic publications.

Within the digital community, some advocate for major changes in copyright. Nicholas Negroponte, Director of the Media Lab at the Massachusetts Institute of Technology, asserts, "Copyright law is totally out of date. It is a Gutenberg artifact. Since it is a reactive process, it will probably have to break down completely before it is corrected."[1] Furthermore, information itself is changing radically with the result that the relationship between information and intellectual property demands to be examined with a fresh eye.[2]

The impact of computing and technology on the publishing and distribution process has resulted in the re-examination of copyright legislation and concomitant guidelines established in concert with the Copyright Law of 1976. The technology which permits the reproduction of a work pleases the scholar or scientist as a user; concerns the scholar, scientist, author or publisher as a rights holder; vexes the librarian as champion of the public and fair use; and challenges the technologists and software engineers and engages the legal profession in sorting out the laws, amendments and case law. The rapid and accurate transmission and re-transmission and distribution with no regard to copyright, with no permissions, with no fees paid, appears to be at the heart of the copyright discussion and debate.

Acknowledging the impact of new technology, the Conference on Fair Use (CONFU) was convened in 1994. Its mission was to develop guidelines for fair use in a networked environment. Areas in which guidelines were to be developed include interlibrary loan, electronic reserves, visual images and distance education. During the course of deliberations, guidelines for multimedia were also considered. What began as a few interested parties grew as participants expanded to include more publishers and representatives from the scholarly, business and educational arenas. Over a series of regularly scheduled meetings, the participants came together and grew apart. In May 1997, the final meeting was held with no guidelines in any area supported by a majority of participants. This meeting was to have concluded the CONFU discussions. Instead, a plenary meeting of participants has been scheduled for May 18, 1998, to see if any additional progress on guidelines could be achieved within the year.[3]

FORCES OF CHANGE

The copyright law, imbedded in the Constitution, is being influenced by technology that was barely imagined in 1976. But technology is not the only factor influencing the course of copyright dialogue. Looking at the pressures in the public and private sectors, one realizes that other factors are changing the environment and may well shape the dialogue about copyright and electronic journals in unanticipated ways.

Changing levels of governmental support to public institutions, changing priorities of higher education and reductions in federal funding for research converge on higher education. Arthur Levine (president of the Teachers College, Columbia University) asserts that "American higher education has become a mature industry."[4] In his view higher education must begin to address the change in its status and to make the hard decisions necessary to ensure the relevance and vitality of higher education in the future. Institutions of higher education are asking hard questions about their future and mission, and changing operations and priorities. Reduced federal funds not only affect the coffers of institutions but also influence institutional priorities. Highly attractive retirement packages and incentives are offered as a means to reduce the size of the faculty or to stimulate faculty retirement so that younger faculty and untenured faculty can be hired, usually at lower salaries. Utilizing business techniques and practices, institutions are trying to cut or control their largest expenses in an effort to remain fiscally sound and intellectually vital.

Simultaneously as institutions try to control costs, they are also seeking new ways to deliver education, to broaden their base in the market and to generate additional income. Institutions look closely at distance education as an opportunity to build and expand to a new market to meet the needs of new consumers, to build a new model of delivering education and to maintain a distinct presence in the education marketplace. Expanding the market also includes specialized courses for the retiree, summer workshops for educators, and expansion of evening and weekend programs focusing on business and management professionals. Finding and developing niches in the educational marketplace become important.

In this volatile and changing marketplace, institutions must control costs by any means they can. Institutions value the importance of the work developed at the institution. Faculty development of electronic courseware may be one arena that institutions may view as an opportunity to improve delivery of education both locally and remotely, with the possibility of expanding into new arenas. Transferring technology to the corporate sector or supporting faculty start-up or spin-off enterprises can be serious business in academe.

The interest in technology transfer and the establishment of procedures for commercializing work signify how highly these economic possibilities are regarded. Academic institutions are no longer committed to the status quo but are interested in change and in ensuring their future stability and growth. This institutional imperative to manage the bottom line will affect all of the academy and will likely influence the course and development of academic libraries.

Some institutions have considered having faculty assign copyright for articles to the institution rather than to publishers. Whether this notion can gain a significant following is not clear. Related to this issue of copyright assignment is the notion that institutions need to take control of copyrights as a means of cost control. As the number and costs increase, and as the funds available to support journals do not rise at the same rate, institutions of higher education consider whether taking over the means of production can achieve meaningful cost savings. Efforts to do just that have begun, but whether this is a trend that will continue is uncertain.

Lest it be thought that change is afoot only in the library community, publishers too are faced with change in the digital environment. The increased utilization of technology in manuscript submission and in all phases of production and storage requires an investment in software and equipment infrastructure, and a sufficient financial return is needed to support and upgrade the environment to keep pace with technological progress. Commercial publishers must grow or at least maintain their position in the marketplace and focus on their balance sheets to ensure that their products are viable and priced to secure the future of their firm and an attractive return to their investors and stockholders. As demands for electronic distribution to users increase, the investment in the infrastructure grows and so does the concern for appropriate reimbursement. Like everyone in the information chain, publishers too are subject to pressures and forces both within and outside their control.

The use of licensing to replace copyright law became widespread as institutions sought to obtain digital access to copyrighted information, be it on tape, on CD-ROM, by licensed remote access or in the form of full-text journals. When a license is signed to afford use of an electronic journal, the contract, not copyright law, governs uses of the text. Thus, the contents of the license must be scrutinized and reviewed by knowledgeable staff before signing. Because a license is governed by contract law, an institution should have its signatories be higher level administrators or legal counsel. It must not be overlooked that licensing, because it outlines the terms of use, can negate fair use in any form. Each institution must manage this process according to local norms and desires. Understanding the terms of the license and consulting with knowledgeable authorities provide the best protection for the institution and users by setting up the most favorable license possible.[5]

TECHNOLOGY CHALLENGES

Technology and computing have enabled publishers to begin using technology to compose, set and print the publications delivered to subscribers. By expanding and reusing electronic files received, a publisher can transform a publication from an exclusively printed document to an exclusively digital form or to some combination.

Many users are eager to be the recipients of electronic texts, both for the convenience of desk-top delivery and for the potential speed and currency of the delivered material. But it is this ease of transmission that so worries publishers. Illegal retransmission could lead to insufficient recompense and profits and a perilous future for publishing as it is currently conceived. Publishers and researchers are presently engaged in developing technological means to track and to identify the origin of electronic texts. In September 1996, the Association of American Publishers (AAP) selected a team to develop a Digital Object Identifier (DOI). The DOI is a first step in developing a workable scheme for electronic or digital copyright management. The DOI is being developed by a team from R.R. Bowker (part of Reed Elsevier) and the Corporation for National Research Initiatives (CNRI).[6] This copyright management information system will enable ready identification of digital materials. This identification will be achieved by developing a number system to be used by the publisher to uniquely identify each digital work or object. An agency for assigning publishers' numbers will be created along the lines of the ISBN assignment (currently under the umbrella of R.R. Bowker). Lastly, a directory will be created to link publishers with their digital output or objects. CNRI will develop the network and R.R. Bowker will create the agency. Though created under the auspices of the AAP, it should be recognized that the development of the DOI is not yet international and is not necessarily championed by all AAP members.[7]

Another technological enhancement under development is digital watermarking.[8] This technology focuses on images and media and can be utilized for electronic texts and images. This technology will potentially provide publishers and rights holders with a means to monitor usage for the purpose of copyright revenue, as well as to track unauthorized use.[9] The technology also has the potential means to control access to documents and to identify users. Publishers could use this technology to find evidence of illicit copying and dissemination. Its pervasive nature might also be a deterrent to users, so that they would be more cautious about redistributing copyrighted works and more careful about duplication. Both these technologies have the potential to provide the publisher community with powerful tools to track not only what is being used electronically but also who is using it. The capability to control access is inherent in the technology. The relative anonymity in which researchers and scholars can pursue their investigations and research may be challenged in the digital environment. Just the possibility of electronic surveillance in this fashion could prove to have a chilling effect on academic investigation, research and free inquiry.

WHAT TO DO NOW

With CONFU having produced no guidelines, with deliberations continuing beyond 1997 and with new copyright management technology and watermarking on the horizon, what can librarians do now to position themselves, their institutions and their users for the future?

1. Take the time to learn about the copyright issues in a digital environment. (See Appendix.)
2. Educate users about copyright and the importance of adhering to copyright laws.
3. Work to establish best practice scenarios through professional societies and organizations on the state local and national level.
4. Identify your campus and local experts and work with them to plan information meetings and seminars on copyright.
5. Track technological changes such as the DOI, copyright management system innovation and watermarking.
6. Monitor the licenses for electronic materials and modify them for the benefit of the institution.
7. Track federal legislation about copyright and intellectual property. Monitor the various listservs and Web sites that follow these issues.
8. Bookmark good copyright sites and visit them for changes.
9. Create a copyright Web page site for your institution if appropriate.

NOTES

1. Nicholas Negroponte, *Being Digital* (New York: Alfred A. Knopf, 1995), p. 58.
2. John Perry Barlow, "The Economy of Ideas: A Framework for Rethinking Patents and Copyrights in the Digital Age (Everything You Know about Intellectual Property is Wrong)," *Wired* 2, no. 3 (Mar. 1994): 84-90, 126-129). Available: http://wwww.wired.com/wired/2.03/features/economy.ideas.html
3. David Green, "CONFU Continues? Is it Time to Regroup?" *ARL Newsletter*, no.192 (June 1997): 4-5. This issue of the *ARL Newsletter* is devoted to copyright and the latest information about digital environments and CONFU. It also reprints the "National Humanities Alliance Basic Principles for Managing Intellectual Property in the Digital Environment."
4. Arthur Levine, "Higher Education's New Status as a Mature Industry," *Chronicle of Higher Education*, Jan. 31, 1997: A48.
5. An excellent source for learning about licensing issues is the Web site on licensing maintained at Yale: http://www.library.yale.edu/~llicense/index.shtml.

In addition, Ann Okerson of Yale has written several thoughtful articles and made presentations on this topic.
    6. Calvin Reid, "Bowker, CNRI to Develop Digital Identifier System," *Publishers Weekly*, Sept. 16, 1996: 15.
    7. Calvin Reid, "AAP Unveils DOI at PSP Confab: Publishers Interested but Wary," *Publishers Weekly*, Feb. 24, 1997: 11.
    8. Jian Zhao, "Look, It's Not There." *BYTE (International Edition)* 22, no. 1 (Jan. 1997). Available: http://www.byte.com/art/9701/sec18/art1.htm
    9. H. Berghal and L. O'Gorman, "Protecting Ownership Rights Through Digital Watermarking," *Computer* (USA) 29, no. 7 (July 1996): 101-103.

APPENDIX

Some selected articles and Web sites to begin an exploration about copyright issues in the digital environment.

SELECTED MONOGRAPHS

Bruwelheide, Janis H. *The Copyright Primer for Librarians and Educators*. Chicago: American Library Association; Washington, DC: National Education Association, 1995.
Gasaway, Laura N. *Libraries and Copyright: a Guide to Copyright Law in the 1990s*. Washington, DC: Special Libraries Association, 1994.
Scholarly Publishing: the Electronic Frontier. Cambridge, Mass.: MIT Press, 1996.
Strong, William S. *The Copyright Book: a Practical Guide*. Cambridge, Mass.: MIT Press, 1993.

SELECTED ARTICLES

Ardito, Stephanie C. "Electronic Copyright Under Siege." *Online* 20, no. 5 (Sept./Oct. 1996): 83-88.
Bennett, Scott B. "The Copyright Challenge: Strengthening the Public Interest in the Digital Age." *Library Journal* 119 (Nov. 15, 1994): 34-37
Cox, John E. "Publishers, Publishing and the Internet: How Journal Publishing Will Survive and Prosper in the Electronic Age," *Electronic Library*, 15, no. 2 (Apr. 1997): 125-131.
Coyle, Karen. "Copyright in the Digital Age." Available: http://www.dla.ucop.edu/~kec/sfpltalk.html

Erickson, John S. "Can Fair Use Survive Our Information-Based Future?" Available: http://picard.dartmouth.edu/~oly/FairUseInfoFuture.html

Gasaway, Laura N. "Scholarly Publication and Copyright in Networked Electronic Publishing," *Library Trends* 43, no. 4 (spring 1995): 679-700.

Gasaway, Laura. "The White Paper, Fair Use, Libraries and Educational Institutions." *The Serials Librarian* 31, no. 1/2 (1996): 211-220.

Harper, Georgia. "Will We Need Fair Use in the Twenty-First Century?" Available:http://www.utsystem.edu/ogc/IntellectualProperty/fair_use.htm

Risher, Carol. "The Great Copyright Debate: Electronic Publishing Is Not Print Publishing–Vive la Différence" *The Serials Librarian* 31, no. 1/2 (1996): 205-210.

Risher, Carol. "Libraries, Copyright and the Electronic Environment," *Electronic Library* 14, no. 5 (Oct. 1996): 449-452. (Also appeared in *Publishing Research Quarterly*, 12, no. 4 [winter 1996/97]: 50-56.)

Samuelson, Pamela. "The Copyright." *Wired* 4, no. 1 (1996): 134-138. Available: http://www.wired.com/wired/whitepaper.html

Samuelson, Pamela. "Regulation of Technologies to Protect Copyright Works." *Communications of the ACM* 39, no. 7 (July 1996): 17-22.

Schockmel, Richard B. "The Premise of Copyright, Assaults on Fair Use, and Royalty Use Fees." *Journal of Academic Librarianship* 22, no. 1 (Jan. 1996): 15-25.

Weiner, Robert S. "Copyright in a Digital Age," *Online* 21, no. 3 (May/June 1997): 97-102.

SELECTED WEB SITES

Copyright Clearance Center.
http://www.copyright.com/
Information about the services of the Copyright Clearance Center.

Cornell University. Legal Information Institute. Copyright Law Materials.
http://www.law.cornell.edu:80/topics/copyright.html
Links to federal statutes, treaties, regulations and court decisions as well as key Internet resources.

Digital Copyright Protection & Digital Watermarking Technology (Jian Zhao)
http://www.igd.fhg.de/~zhao/copyright.html.
Links to many useful sites about digital copyright protection and digital watermarking technology.

IFLA Information Policy: Copyright and Intellectual Property.
http://www.nlc-bnc.ca/ifla/II/cpyright.htm
IFLA site with a rich array of links to copyright organizations, electronic journals, etc. Includes an extensive bibliography of articles on copyright in the digital age. Well worth reviewing.

Indiana University Purdue University Indianapolis. Copyright Management Center.
http://www.iupui.edu/it/copyinfo/
Active copyright management center with assorted links to other sites including a page of links to alternative views of intellectual property.

Stanford University Libraries. Copyright and Fair Use.
http://fairuse.stanford.edu/
Rich Web source with links to many useful topics, such as coursepacks and multimedia.

University of Texas System. Crash Course in Copyright.
http://www.utsystem.edu/ogc/intellectualproperty/cprtindx.htm
Links to articles on copyright and includes what is termed a "crash course on copyright."

ACQUISITIONS
AND COLLECTION DEVELOPMENT

Beyond Print:
Revisioning Serials Acquisitions
for the Digital Age

Ellen Finnie Duranceau, AB, MA, MLS

SUMMARY. Electronic serials, especially Web-based serials, present new challenges as well as new opportunities for serials acquisitions departments. Web-based serials require an entirely new workflow, one that is no longer a series of linear and standardized steps, but is rather a complex, cyclical, labor-intensive, variable, and team-based process. License negotiation and compliance demand an entirely new set of skills to be added to the serials acquisitions repertoire. The impact of Web-based serials on every area of serials

Ellen Finnie Duranceau is Assistant Acquisitions Librarian for Digital Resources, Massachusetts Institute of Technology Libraries, Room 14E-210, Cambridge, MA 02139-4307, USA (email: efinnie@mit.edu). She was formerly Associate Head, Serials and Acquisitions Services, MIT Libraries (1991-1996), and has worked as a cataloger, gifts librarian, reference librarian, and indexer/abstractor.

[Haworth co-indexing entry note]: "Beyond Print: Revisioning Serials Acquisitions for the Digital Age." Duranceau, Ellen Finnie. Co-published simultaneously in *The Serials Librarian* (The Haworth Press, Inc.) Vol. 33, No. 1/2, 1998, pp. 83-106; and: *E-Serials: Publishers, Libraries, Users, and Standards* (ed: Wayne Jones) The Haworth Press, Inc., 1998, pp. 83-106. Single or multiple copies of this article are available for a fee from The Haworth Document Delivery Service [1-800-342-9678, 9:00 a.m. - 5:00 p.m. (EST). E-mail address: getinfo@haworth.com].

83

acquisitions has been dramatic, from ordering through receipt and claiming. This is apparent from an examination of the MIT Libraries' serials acquisitions process as a case study. Staffing patterns have begun to shift in the face of these new demands. Serials librarians are uniquely positioned to meet these demands by leveraging their experience with print serials to carve out a niche in the world of the Web. *[Article copies available for a fee from The Haworth Document Delivery Service: 1-800-342-9678. E-mail address: getinfo@ haworth.com]*

KEYWORDS. Serials acquisitions, Web-based serials, digital resources, workflow, staffing, licensing

INTRODUCTION

Serials acquisitions work is not what it was a mere two years ago. The proliferation of electronic resources, particularly Web resources, has dramatically altered the daily lives of serials librarians. The issues they face, the work they do, and the skills required to do it–all have shifted focus.

The identity crisis in serials acquisitions engendered by the Web is only a reflection of the more sweeping identity crisis facing academic–and particularly research–libraries. On the larger scale, we must ask ourselves what a research library *is* when it is becoming more gateway than repository. On the smaller scale, we must ask what a serials acquisitions department *is* when more and more materials are not being "acquired" but pointed to, when these materials render checkin meaningless, and when the concept of claiming (at least in the traditional manner based on issue-level receipt records) no longer applies.

In the face of the dramatic shift in information delivery patterns the Web has created, serials acquisitions needs to seek a new role if it hopes to continue to be an essential link in the information chain. This is a particular challenge, since serials acquisitions departments must find their own new role while their parent library systems are still redefining theirs. This dual challenge is significant indeed, especially given that serials is a branch of librarianship that brought a pre-existing identity problem into the electronic era, one that seems even more profound than the identity problem widespread in librarianship. While acquisitions and serials librarians have debated endlessly what it means to be an acquisitions professional, or if, in fact, there is such a thing, the ground has shifted under us so dramatically that any earlier conclusion has to be reconsidered. Our role–and our professionalism–must be revisioned.

The digital revolution demands, but also offers, a defining moment to serials librarians. We have a new opportunity to demonstrate our value, for electronic serials ask us to do more and to be more: electronic serials are more complex to buy, more complex to bring into the library, more complex to provide access to, more complex to regulate, and more complex to renew. Their pricing structures are more difficult to understand and interpret, and their purchase process is not standardized. These products are licensed, and license review and negotiation demand an entirely new set of activities and skills of those involved in the purchase process. If we can take advantage of this defining moment, it will be an opportunity for growth in the profession. If we cannot or do not, we will have a more restricted future as purveyors of print publications only, a subset of material that will represent a smaller and smaller piece of the serials pie as time goes on.

The MIT Libraries' serial purchasing patterns indicate that the print portion of the serials pie is shrinking at a rapid rate. While MIT may differ somewhat from other research libraries given its emphasis on science and engineering, the facts are nevertheless telling: of the total number of serial orders for paid titles placed by the MIT Libraries during the six months from January through June 1997, a full 23%, or almost one quarter, were for electronic serials. What is more, electronic serials represented 85% of the dollars expended for new serial orders in the same period. Of the entire list of MIT's currently committed serials, only 0.7% of the titles, or 4% of the serial dollars, are electronic. Thus it is clear that advent of Web-based serials, which have been on the market in substantial volume only since late 1996, has resulted in an explosion of electronic serial orders, at least at MIT. For serials acquisitions, these orders represent the future.

The good news is that the same Web-based resources whose complexities and market prominence are forcing a redefinition of serials acquisitions are also making the redefinition a fairly organic process. Serials librarians are uniquely positioned to create a niche in the digital world. Our skills, nourished and extended naturally, can serve us well in the new environment. We have skills as negotiators, built from years in establishing the best deals with our vendors for print material. These skills will serve us well in license negotiation. We have pricing savvy, developed after years of reading the *Newsletter on Serials Pricing Issues* and following the heated debates between libraries, publishers, and vendors, about what pricing models are fair and how we can influence pricing. In trying to check in through the cumbersome serials modules of various integrated library systems, we've already had to ask ourselves what checkin is for and why we do it. Faced with the frustrations of fulfillment houses, we have already had to address the issue of whether claiming always make sense. We've dealt with the mind-numbing paperwork involved in purchases and the intricate communications that must exist between public service staff, technical service staff, vendors, and publishers. We are positioned as well as–or better than–other librarians to play an essential role as mediators, negotiators, procurers, and implementation facilitators in the digital environment. But we need to create our niche, not wait for it to be offered to us.

A case study of how serials acquisitions has changed at one ARL library, the MIT Libraries, may help to demonstrate the kind of revolution that is underway, and what role serials librarians can play in it.

WORKFLOW COMPARISON: WHY NETWORKED ELECTRONIC SERIALS CANNOT BE TREATED "JUST LIKE THE PRINT"

Networked, Web-based electronic serials break the mold. Procedures designed to order, receive, and check in print serials worked–with some awkwardness–for serials arriving on floppy disks or CD-ROMs, but there is simply no way to use a print-based acquisitions model for Web-based serials. The two formats place entirely different demands on the system and present entirely different problems to solve.

The workflow in the print universe, which seemed challenging while it was our only model, looked (and still looks) something like this at MIT (see Table 1).[1]

The basic characteristics of this process are that an order is passed along a linear path of six steps, with one person working independently on it at any given time. An order is requested, placed, and entered into our databases; then a piece is received, cataloged, and shelved.

For a Web-based serial, the workflow bears little, if any, resemblance to the print process (see Table 2).[2]

TABLE 1. Workflow: Print Serial Acquisition

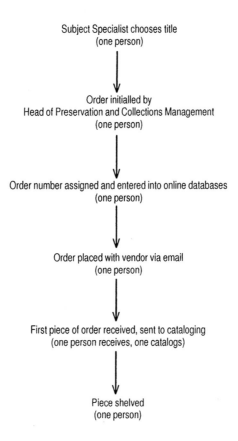

Subject Specialist chooses title
(one person)

Order initialled by
Head of Preservation and Collections Management
(one person)

Order number assigned and entered into online databases
(one person)

Order placed with vendor via email
(one person)

First piece of order received, sent to cataloging
(one person receives, one catalogs)

Piece shelved
(one person)

TABLE 2. Workflow: Networked Serial Acquisition

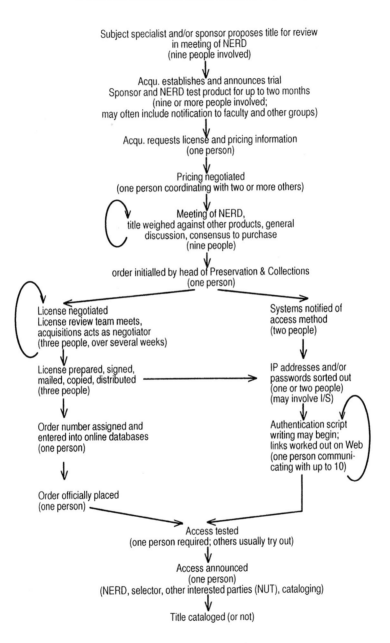

In the case of a networked serial, the process is considerably more complicated, involves an entirely different set of players, and is not a linear process. Unlike the print serial order, which is handled by one person at a time, the networked serial requires a team-based approach from the outset. Because many Web titles are very costly or interdisciplinary, it is no longer appropriate for one subject specialist to decide whether or not to order these titles.

At MIT, a subject specialist proposes a title for review in a larger standing committee, created expressly because of the demands of purchasing digital resources. This committee, the Networked Electronic Resources Discussion Group (or "NERD"), consists of the collection managers and reference coordinators from each divisional library, the Head of Acquisitions, the Assistant Acquisitions Librarian for Digital Resources, and the Head of Preservation and Collections Management. This group of nine librarians, two of whom are department heads and all of whom are above entry level, reviews products and makes collective decisions about what to buy.

Once NERD has decided to pursue a given product, the digital resources librarian sets up a trial for it, obtains the license, and begins to negotiate price. When the trial is complete and the pricing information stabilized, NERD makes a final purchase decision. The order request is prepared and initialled (in the only step that mirrors the print world) and then the license review process begins. (Note that the order is not placed at this stage, since we cannot commit to a purchase before determining that we can agree with the vendor on license terms.)

License review at MIT involves another expensive team, this time a group of three librarians, including one Department Head and one Associate Director. This team currently meets weekly with a representative from MIT's in-house legal counsel to review licenses and discuss licensing issues. The license review process begins a series of negotiations carried out by the digital resources librarian over weeks or days. The team may have to revisit the terms of the license several times during the negotiation, and it can take anywhere from five hours in one round of discussion, to several weeks or months with four or five rounds of discussion, to achieve resolution.

Simultaneously with license negotiation, systems assessment and implementation begin. The systems office is notified of the impending arrival of the product, and access methods, whether IP- or password-based, are discussed and worked out. Communication with MIT's Information Systems (I/S) office and/or the vendor may be necessary. Authentication script-writing to ensure that only MIT community members can access the product occurs just as, and after, the order is being placed.

Once access is available, it is tested, and the product is announced to NERD, the sponsor, all subject specialists, and a special group composed of systems staff and staff from MIT's I/S group. The title then may, or may not, be cataloged. (We are still assessing and defining our cataloging policy for electronic resources.

It is clear from comparing these workflows that the purchase of a networked serial requires an entirely different level of staff-wide commitment and involvement. The characteristics of the two processes, far from being comparable, are almost diametrically opposed.

Table 3 summarizes the differences in the two workflows.[3]

The print world is linear and involves a mix of low- and higher-level staff; the process is standardized, and rarely varies. In six steps, the work is done. Little, if any, communication or coordination is needed. Most of the time delay is in waiting for the first piece to appear. The print purchase process is a short, straight garden path.

The digital world is cyclical, and involves high-level staff almost exclusively; the process is different each time and is completely unstandardized. Communication, coordination, and team effort is required at almost every stage. More than twice as many players are involved, and non-library staff may be involved. In a minimum of fifteen steps, many involving extensive documentation, the purchase process is a long, complex, winding dirt road filled with potholes.

From the outset, the purchase process is team-based, cooperative, and expensive. It rests heavily in the hands of high-level, expensive staff. The MIT Libraries have also felt the need to create a new role of "sponsor" to accommodate the large number of expensive, interdisciplinary digital resources. Our print purchase model allocated a

TABLE 3. Comparison of Characteristics: Print vs. Networked Serial
Acquisition Process

PRINT:	NETWORKED:
Characteristics of process:	**Characteristics of process:**
One person works at a time on each step.	Team-based
Requires mix of support and librarian staff	Requires high-level librarian staff
Little coordination is needed	High demand for communication and coordination
Linear process	Cyclical, not linear process
Documentation limited (copy of PO)	Documentation-intensive (lots of paper!)
Little variation	Great variation
Total number of individuals involved: 6	**Total number of individuals involved:** 15 for an "average" networked title.
Two are support staff whose operations take only a few minutes.	All are high-level staff Director must sign each license
No staff outside Libraries involved	I/S staff needed at times.
	MIT legal counsel may need to be consulted
Total number of steps: 6	**Total number of steps:** 15, some repeated
Timeframe: Order request to order: one week or less. Order to receipt: weeks or months.	**Timeframe:** Order request to order: weeks or months. Order to receipt: one day to one week.

certain budget figure to each of hundreds of funds in ten decentral-
ized public service locations, with a subject specialist in charge of
purchases for each fund. High-cost interdisciplinary titles do not
lend themselves to this model, since the subject funds are inadequate and a broader constituency needs to review a product that
covers many disciplines.

Adding the sponsor and the standing committee NERD has
slowed and complicated the purchase process. The same could be
said for the increased number of consortial purchases, driven by
lower prices available to groups and the new format's ability to
avoid the question that has plagued the print world: "but who will
get to house it?" These consortial purchases further complicate the
picture by adding players, constraints, and timelags (as well as
added time pressure in some cases) to the process. But while the
team-based model has lengthened, complicated, and increased the
scope of the collections decision and purchase process, it has fos-
tered wise decisions and productive new relationships both inside
and outside the MIT Libraries.

STAFFING

Clearly these dramatic differences in workflow–in which the
print purchase process bears no resemblance at all to its '90s counterpart, the digital purchase process–have broad and deep implications for staffing in serials acquisitions. Broad, because many roles
and jobs are affected; deep, because the changes required are profound.

In the MIT Libraries, we responded to the demands of the digital
world by carving out a new position from an existing vacancy in
another department. We created the Assistant Acquisitions
Librarian for Digital Resources. This position is charged to assume
primary responsibility for the acquisition of digital resources as
follows:

- Maintaining an awareness of development of electronic products;
- Acting as a resource for staff on trends in product development;

- Facilitating the acquisition process, including defining access options, equipment requirements, and arranging tests and demo sessions;
- Managing license review, negotiation, and compliance;
- Collaborating with subject specialists and systems office staff; and,
- Contributing to ongoing planning for the management of digital resources in the MIT Libraries.

We perceived a need for this position because the demands of the digital products were so great that we did not feel that they could be met by an "add-on" to another position. In addition, an integrated workflow seemed impossible at this stage, given the drastically different characteristics of the print and digital purchase processes. Clearly, however, it was costly to create this position. And in times of downsizing and fiscal constraint, creating a new position is extremely costly to any organization.

Many library systems seem to be feeling the same pressure we felt at MIT and have–despite the costs–created new positions to cope with new demands. An informal survey over the listserv Serialst in June 1997 revealed that many institutions have created positions over the past few years. While these positions address a common need, they also reflect a range of approaches, including what might be called "systems-intensive" roles and "collections-intensive" roles as well as "acquisitions-intensive" roles.

For example, Brigham Young added an "Electronic Access" librarian whose responsibilities include planning for electronic journals, developing systems to monitor usage of electronic resources, and chairing an electronic resources committee that helps implement new products and reviews licenses of all electronic products. This position is also deeply involved in planning and developing new electronic products and services.[4] Vanderbilt has a new "Electronic Resources Librarian" who coordinates reviews of software and hardware, writes documentation, designs interfaces, and sets information technology objectives.[5] These two institutions have designed what seem to be relatively systems-intensive positions.

Yale has advertised for an "Electronic Publications and Collections Specialist" who will support electronic collections development and deployment, create "strategic partnerships between the Yale Library and information producers . . . in order to develop successful electronic publications" and serve as a "collections resource for the Library's electronic consortial activities."[6] Yale's position is collections-based but also contains systems development responsibilities.

North Carolina State University (NCSU) is advertising for a "Scholarly Communications Librarian" who will grapple with intellectual property issues.[7] NCSU is seeking a candidate with the JD as well as the MLS. This position seems to be the first to address the growing demand for understanding how digital resources can and will be used, and is a harbinger of how the licensing concerns facing all libraries will unavoidably raise complex copyright and intellectual property issues. While this position is not within NCSU's acquisitions department, it could be.

University of California at San Diego has a new "Electronic Resources Unit" in the Acquisitions Department.[8] This unit contains two positions, and between them they order all electronic resources for UCSD libraries, communicate with the vendors, and monitor licenses for compliance. Like the new MIT position, this new staff allocation offers an acquisitions-intensive perspective on how to cope with the new demands.

Many other institutions have tried to tack these responsibilities onto other jobs, often acquisitions jobs. This is the case at George Washington University, where the Acquisitions Librarian is now responsible for negotiating licenses, working along with the electronic reference coordinator.[9] At American University, the position of serials librarian was redefined and recreated as the "Serials/Electronic Resources Librarian." The position now includes traditional serials activities, but also is responsible for providing "access, bibliographic control, maintenance, and user support for serial electronic resources." As Claire Dygert, who holds this position, notes, she must "sometimes function as a systems librarian, sometimes as a serials librarian, sometimes as a cataloger, sometimes as a public service librarian, sometimes with a legal eye."[10]

What is suggested by Dygert's comments and by these anecdotal examples is that digital resources have driven the creation of new roles while causing the traditional lines between public and technical service to blur. In this new digital world, the lines between acquisitions, collections, and systems work seem particularly fluid and unclear. If someone needs to worry about implementation, access, copyright, and quality control, it is not always clear who, as these many examples demonstrate. This blurring of roles means confusion, ambiguity, and the potential for turf wars, but also . . . opportunity. Different institutions have chosen different places to add a position; yet they all seem to address a similar demand and achieve similar goals: getting *someone* to focus on the unique demands of digital material. Acquisitions and serials librarians, if they hope to have a future at the center of research libraries, need to make clear to their libraries why *they* are prepared to take on many of the key tasks involved in bringing these resources to the library.

CHECKIN AND CLAIMING IN THE DIGITAL WORLD

When pointing to a remote Web site, no real checkin of issues is necessary or even possible. Nothing is received, therefore there is nothing to check in.

However, the fundamental goal of checkin remains the same as in the print world: serials acquisitions needs to be able to ensure that we get what we pay for and that we are making resources that have been chosen for our collections available to our community in a timely and effective manner.

In the digital world, this means link checking and maintenance, and checking holdings of remote sites. In the print world, we do not have to continually verify that something we received several years prior is still available. In the digital world, we have to monitor Web sites to be sure that they are live and being added to on schedule, but also that the entire run of holdings we expect access to is still present.

This sounds simple, but represents a very substantial commitment of labor, so much so that here in the MIT Libraries we have not yet developed link maintenance workflows. Link checking software exists to determine if a URL is still live, but someone still has to analyze the results of such software to separate real and temporary problems, and make link changes as necessary. To be certain that the library is getting what it pays for, someone needs to visit each remote site and verify both that the site is being added to regularly and that holdings have not been dropped.

While these activities fall naturally to serials acquisitions as the direct counterparts of checkin and claiming in the print world, they require new higher-level skills, new procedures, and more time than the print counterparts. The alternative is for an organization to decide that it can no longer afford to claim or check in Web resources. This is not as radical as it may sound, since, as noted above, such decisions have been made in the print world for certain categories of materials in certain libraries. Some libraries, for example, do not claim titles from fulfillment houses, since it involves fruitless effort. They simply purchase the issue on a newsstand or leave the issue as a gap in the collection. Other libraries, such as MIT, do not check in and claim certain technical reports, but prepare orders when a user notices a gap and makes a request. For digital material, the economics may turn out to be similar: it costs so much to check the sites that it is more cost-effective to depend on user feedback to resolve access problems, at least for sites that are expected to be dependable, stable, and committed to archiving. Quality assurance in the Web world is an area wide open for creative solutions and innovation. Once again, serials acquisitions is poised to find these solutions and implement them.

LICENSING

Licensing offers a crucial case study for how and where acquisitions can add value in the new digital purchase process. The license review and negotiation process has fallen to many serials librarians by default; it builds upon known skills, but also presents new challenges. Again, it may be useful to offer the MIT Libraries as a case study to demonstrate how the acquisitions department here has developed skills in the licensing arena.

The first challenge we faced was understanding the legal terminology in licenses. This problem has been addressed by the outstanding Web resource "Lib-license." Created by a team of library and legal professionals, Lib-license describes itself much too modestly as "a useful starting point towards providing librarians with a better understanding of the issues raised by licensing agreements in the digital age." This resource offers definitions of the major legal terms used in licenses, explains the key licensing issues, and, most importantly, presents clauses from actual licenses in each key licensing area with a discussion of the issues raised by the clauses.[11]

The MIT Libraries' license review group has found that the issues raised in Lib-license are indeed those we have to grapple with in negotiations over and over again. The key issues for MIT and for any campus tend to be: definition of the user population; location from which users will want to access the information; definition of authorized uses of information (including quotations, copying, and printing); and whether or not the institution can technically comply with restricted access provisions.[12]

All of these issues have presented problems for us in one guise or another. We pay particular attention to the following issues during our reviews of licenses (this is not a complete list of issues we negotiate; it is rather a list of key issues we must commonly address):

- *Authorized Users:* does the definition of "authorized user" include patrons physically present in the library (walk-ins), faculty, staff, students, visiting scholars, and affiliated researchers? We almost invariably need to request that one or more of these user categories be added to the definition of "user."

- *Authorized Use:* We have tried to ensure that something approximating fair use as defined for materials in section 107 of the US copyright law (P.L. 94-553) applies to our digital products. We ask for revisions to language that prohibits all copying, downloading, and sharing, asking that such activities in support of education and research be considered acceptable, as long as they are not systematic.

- *Policing Use:* Perhaps our most important issue in negotiations is avoiding responsibility for the actions of individual members of our user community. Many–if not most–licenses will ask that the licensee (the MIT Libraries) ensure that there will be no unauthorized use or unauthorized users on the system. We always request a rewording to suggest that we can make only "reasonable efforts" to ensure this.

- *Venue/Governing Law:* Our legal counsel has advised us to avoid all clauses that would cause a law suit to be carried out in another state or under another state's laws.

- *Indemnification and Liability:* We try to be sure that the providers are not asking us to indemnify them (that is, to "take financial responsibility for damages that the [information provider] may suffer"[13]) and guarantee that they have not infringed intellectual property rights in creating their product. We also attempt to negotiate an exception from any cap on damages for cases involving intellectual property infringement.

We have learned a great deal in a short time, simply by working on these licenses. Each one presents a new opportunity to advance our understanding and skills. To give just one example of many: In the case of one society publisher, the original license read "You may not copy, modify, upload, download, transmit, (re)publish, or otherwise distribute any Code or Content from this site unless expressly permitted. . . . " During negotiations, this provider agreed that the clause as it stood essentially prevented use of the product, and modified the language. The negotiation process thus becomes a two-way education, usually to the benefit of both parties.

Since negotiating licenses is relatively new for most serials librarians, managing license compliance is perhaps the least developed aspect of the new serials chain. We have simply not been through many cycles of negotiating, signing, renewing, and managing compliance in an ongoing way. Some libraries have developed strategies to assist in getting the word out about what the terms of the agreement are, which is an essential first step in ensuring compliance. One library, the University of California at San Diego, is planning to scan licenses onto their Web so everyone on the staff can easily refer to these documents.[14] The MIT Libraries plan to do the same. This will allow all library staff to have quick access to the terms, which will be more effective and efficient than distributing print copies, given the number of licenses and the number of people who need to be concerned with the terms.

Some license agreements demand user sign-off sheets to inform users of the authorized uses of the product. While we try to avoid this extra administrative and logistical burden, these sign-off sheets are sometimes unavoidable, as when user rules are particularly stringent and/or when licenses demand that libraries make efforts to educate each user about the use restrictions. In these cases, user sign-off sheets become an essential component of license compliance. Someone (and it naturally falls to those who negotiated the license) needs to be sure the sign-off sheets express the use rules properly, are maintained, and that copies are available at appropriate service points.

Any unusual arrangements (such as the need to include certain phrases in publicity for library patrons, which has arisen in at least one of MIT Libraries' agreements, or the need for user sign-off sheets, as noted above) must be recorded in a central location, but also communicated to all relevant parties. This kind of storing and distributing of information also falls naturally to the serials acquisitions staff, which has been stockpiling and distributing serials pricing and policy information for years. In the MIT Libraries, we have developed a database to help cope with the large array of details that must be tracked for electronic serials, from request of a license agreement, through negotiation, distribution of copies (or mounting on the Web), and raising awareness about special terms (see Table 4). This database will act as a trigger for managing compliance and anticipating renewals and will ensure that no title gets lost in the labyrinthine process of testing, negotiating a license, and implementing the product locally.

RENEWALS

Before the 1997 conference of the American Library Association, an advertisement was circulated regarding a discussion on whether electronic serials require special handling. As was noted throughout this discussion, there is simply no area of handling for electronic serials that does *not* require some special additional process or skill. The issue of renewals is no different.

TABLE 4. Sample Record from Electronic Serials Titles Database: American Institute of Physics Online Journal Service

Field Name: Contents of field: [description of field]

ORDER	S23524	[purchase order number]
FUND	PHYS	[fund code]
TYPE	J	[serial type; here, J for Journal]
FUNC	E	[designator that serial is electronic]
VENDOR	AMINPHYS	[vendor code]
COST	0.00	[cost]
COMEON	AIPPRT	[does title come as result of another title?]
TITLE	AM. INST. OF PHYSICS ONLINE JOURNAL SERVICE	
CTY	US	[country of publication]
PUBLISHER	AM. INST. OF PHYSICS	
LIBRARY	S	[library at MIT who purchased]
PRODUCER		[if purchased by an intermediary, this field would name the actual producer.]
FORMAT	WEB	[format of title: CDROM v. WEB, etc.]
ACCNTRL	IP ADDRESS	[how is access controlled?]
ORDRECD	01/01/97	[date order request received]
ORDENT	01/01/97	[date order entered]
LICRECD	01/01/97	[date license received]
LICREVD	01/01/97	[date license reviewed]
NEGSTART	01/22/97	[date license negotiations started]
NEGNOTES		[notes about negotiation, if any]
NEGDONE	02/04/97	[date negotiation complete]
SIGNED	02/04/97	[date license signed]
MAILED	02/04/97	[date license mailed]
ACCESS	/ /	[date access became available]
NOTIFY	/ /	[date selectors, etc., notified access available]
TERMS		MUST INCLUDE SPECIFIED LANGUAGE ABOUT USE RESTRICTIONS IN EMAIL PROMOTION TO FACULTY [notes about special license terms]
USERS		[number of simultaneous users, if licensed that way]
COPIED	02/04/97	[date license copied and distributed]
TERMMEMO	memo	[more lengthy notes about license terms, if any]
TOCAT	05/01/97	[date cataloging notified]
CATDONE	/ /	[date cataloging completed]
SPONSOR	CHRIS S	[product's sponsor]
URL	www.aip.org/ojs/entry.html	

In the print world, most academic libraries in the US allow all their titles to be renewed each year unless there is a cancellation project underway. This practice is so fundamental to the print serials world that European serial vendors generally offer their services on a "'til forbid" basis, meaning that they assume a library wants a title until special notice is sent contradicting this assumption.

In the digital world, serials acquisitions must be much more proactive and anticipatory about renewals. Deals, options, interfaces, and products change so rapidly that it is no longer sufficient to assume a product purchased the prior year is still the best way to deliver a certain set of information to a given community. In the MIT Libraries, we are intending to use our digital title database to trigger product and license review several months prior to renewal. We also attempt to remove "automatic renewal" clauses from licenses. Along with these efforts to prevent titles from renewing without review, we intend to implement a market assessment process to determine whether a given product still meets our needs, or whether the information is now available in a more desirable way. We expect this to be a frequently complex process in which a team of public and technical service staff must evaluate whether a given database, for example, is best received in an OCLC FirstSearch package, or purchased separately; if purchased separately, it may be necessary to select from the interfaces provided by several different intermediaries. Pricing models change rapidly, as do the prices themselves, and these must be reviewed freshly prior to renewal. We may need to reconsider the terms of the license if new groups of users have access to our campus network, or if we require more simultaneous users; we may have learned that certain use restrictions do not work for us and want to renegotiate certain points in the license. While these issues are truly collection management issues, serials acquisitions is now in a new position of needing procedures that prevent automatic renewal, so that these issues can be evaluated regularly. For the MIT Libraries, this means generating creative work-arounds in the integrated library system's serials module to prevent renewal invoices from being automatically paid upon receipt, which is yet another exception to the print workflow.

THE ROLE OF THE VENDOR
AND THE ARCHIVING QUESTION

Another major shift in focus that has resulted from an emphasis on digital resources is that the vast majority of interactions for digital products are direct with publishers, not with vendors. In the print world, a majority of orders are placed with vendors, and a large portion of our problem-solving is through major vendors. Managing vendor relationships and managing allocation of titles among vendors is a big feature on the map of serials acquisitions in the print model. In the digital world, at least for now, vendors play a very small role (if any) in purchase and implementation. Because license agreements are nonstandard and complex and raise issues that are specific to a given institution, discussions of these issues must take place between the library and the provider if the process is to be as efficient as possible. While vendors develop gateways to electronic journals (notably Blackwell's Electronic Journals Navigator (EJN)) or act as aggregators of electronic versions of journals (for example, EBSCO's full-text services)–products that may ultimately change the way libraries access electronic serials–at this early stage in the market's development, the vendor role in the order process is not clear, at least at MIT, where we find we need direct communication with the provider to implement Web-based resources.

Vendors, of course, are searching for and creating their own new roles in the digital environment. Some are committed to archiving at least some titles (as is the case for a subset of the Blackwell's EJN). The question for libraries is whether they want to abdicate their historical archiving role to a commercial entity such as a vendor. The current economics of academic libraries may promote this, but in the long run, libraries must consider if it is in their best interest, or in the best interest of the worldwide scholarly community, to accept such a model.

While an exploration of archiving digital resources is well beyond the scope of this discussion, any analysis of serials acquisitions in the digital age must at least address the archiving issue tangentially, for serials acquisitions has always been about creating holdings and making sure they are complete. At this time, responsibility for archiving seems to be falling to vendors and aggregators such as OCLC and Blackwell's EJN. It seems too costly, time-consuming, and redundant for libraries to take on this role, although some are trying. For example, Stanford University Libraries' Highwire Press offers twelve full-text, archived journals at the time of this writing.[15] According to a survey of ARL libraries performed by Barbara Hall of the University of Southern California, Stanford is not typical. Her survey shows that 75% of libraries are not archiving ejournals locally. Most of those which do archive, archive "only a handful" which are typically "produced by the local organization."[16]

The archiving issue will not go away, and while it may be expedient in the short run to rely on vendors and other commercial enterprises to step into the archiving breach, in the long run libraries will lose a key role, a role historically theirs, if they allow the commercial market to take over the archiving function entirely. How libraries can fund and manage digital archives remains to be worked out, but one feasible model is to have serials acquisitions departments as central players in the logistics of consortial arrangements among libraries to archive key resources.[17]

RELATIONSHIP OF SERIALS ACQUISITIONS TO CATALOGING

Electronic, remote-access serials challenge our cataloging philosophy and practice. While the particulars of cataloging issues, like those of archiving, lie outside the scope of this discussion, cataloging issues do affect serials acquisitions as well. As indicated by the last line of the digital serial workflow diagram (Table 2), at MIT there is no longer an assumed path to cataloging after acquisition of a remotely accessed title, as there has been for all but a tiny subset of print material. There is no piece received to trigger cataloging, and not all remote resources are cataloged. This means redesigned workflows. The MIT Libraries are in the process of designing a unique form for digital resources that will collect needed information for the acquisitions staff as well as the catalogers, such as number of simultaneous users, URL, technical access issues, and extensive notes on components of complex packages.

In this case, as in all serials procedures, the question that needs to be asked is not "do we need special handling?" but "how do we create efficient workflows for electronic serials?"

CONCLUSION

Buying digital resources is like buying a used car.[18] You feel anxious throughout the deal (is someone else getting a better price?); you wonder whether you are getting what you're paying for (what will this purchase mean five years, or even one year, from now?); you wish a slightly different model were available; and the pressure to sign immediately can be intense. However, such ambiguity makes the purchase process more educational and more interesting than purchasing another print serial. On good days, we can exult in that knowledge, and be thankful that our subprofession is being offered a new arena in which to demonstrate its value. For as serials librarians, we did not choose a field of great glamour or global impact, or even one that presented the sustained challenge of continual change. However, as John Lennon is supposed to have said, life–in this case, life in serials–is what happens while you're making other plans.[19] The digital revolution is upon us and the choice is ours: like all professions, we will grow or we will die. When every assumption we've built on for at least fifty years is now being challenged, when every role is up for grabs, we need to be our own advocates.

One might reasonably ask why it is important for serials librarians to take a central role in the new arena. After all, as service professionals, we are trained to care first and foremost about the end users. If their needs are being met, why does it matter who meets them? Whether it is a Fortune 500 company, the collections staff of a library, or a group of serials librarians? Yet why *shouldn't* serials librarians vie for their piece of the pie? If we don't establish a role for ourselves, we will be relegated to processors of a shrinking print collection. Someone else will do the new, exciting, more challenging stuff. If that "someone" is a corporation, rather than a library, the entire structure of access to scholarly archives could shift from nonprofit to a profit-seeking model with all its attendant losses for scholars. If research libraries are to maintain a central role in the scholarly community–and this discussion presupposes that as a valid goal–it is logical that serials librarians play a central part. The skills required are a very natural extension of our skills base.

Serials librarians can position themselves to be fundamental in the digital resources world, surveying the marketplace, arranging demos and trials with vendors, and negotiating prices and licenses. We can track access and maintain quality control mechanisms. We are uniquely positioned to fulfill these essential roles. In the MIT

Libraries, we have tried to position ourselves to do so, but it is a long road and we are only taking a first few faltering steps. Whether electronic serials are "old wine in new bottles" or "new wine in new bottles"[20] remains open to debate, but one thing is clear: the new bottles are so thoroughly redesigned that the serials acquisitions workflow does not need to be tweaked, but retooled and recreated, if it is to work efficiently. Certainly there are analogies from the print serials world to the digital, but these analogies only give us frameworks to help us think about our work; they don't help us negotiate licenses well, manage compliance and renewal, keep up with the market, or create team-based structures out of linear ones. It is up to us in serials acquisitions to use our role in the print world as a strength to position ourselves to contribute in the new digital environment.

NOTES

1. This workflow diagram was developed originally for a presentation: Ellen Duranceau, "Buying a Used Car Every Day: The Implications of the Digital Revolution for Serials Acquisitions at MIT" (ACRL New England Chapter Serials Interest Group Panel Discussion: "From Overdrive to Cyberdrive: The Impact of Technology on Technical Services," Gutman Library, Harvard University Graduate School of Education, Cambridge, MA, May 7, 1997).

2. Ibid.

3. Ibid.

4. Keith Sterling, email message to author, 10 June 1997.

5. Theresa Trawick, email message to author, 9 June 1997.

6. Cynthia Crooker, email message to author, 8 June 1997.

7. Eleanor Cook, email message to author, 6 June 1997.

8. Karen Cargill, email message to author, 6 June 1997.

9. Marifran Bustion, email message to author, 9 June 1997.

10. Claire Dygert, email message to author, 19 June 1997.

11. Ann Shumelda Okerson et al., "Lib-License: Licensing Digital Information." Available: http://www.library.yale.edu/~Llicense/index.shtml

12. Patricia Brennan, Karen Hersey and Georgia Harper, *Licensing Electronic Resources: Strategic and Practical Considerations for Signing Electronic Information Delivery Agreements* (Washington, DC: Association of Research Libraries, 1997).

13. Okerson, example clause 8, "Warranties, Indemnities and Limitations of Liability," in Lib-license. Available: http://www.library.yale.edu/~llicense/warrcls.shtml

14. Cargill.

15. Judy Luther, "Full Text Journal Subscriptions: An Evolutionary Process," *Against the Grain* 9, #3, (June 1997): 20.

16. Barbara Hall, "Archiving Electronic Journals: Current Practices and Policies in Academic Research Libraries." Available: http://www-lib.usc.edu/Info/Acqui/research.html

17. Ellen Duranceau et al., "Electronic Journals in the MIT Libraries: Report of the 1995 E-Journal Subgroup," *Serials Review* 22, no. 1 (spring 1996): 60.

18. In a conversation with the author in winter 1997, Jennifer Banks compared the purchase of digital resources to "buying a used car every day." I first elaborated on this analogy in my presentation "Buying a Used Car."

19. Remark attributed to John Lennon in *The Harper Book of Quotations* (New York, Harper & Row, 1988), 344.

20. Ellen Duranceau, "Balance Point: Old Wine in New Bottles? Defining Electronic Serials," *Serials Review* 22, no. 1 (spring 1996): 69.

Collection Development for Online Serials: Who Needs to Do What, and Why, and When

Cindy Stewart Kaag, MLS

SUMMARY. Once you have finally decided to incorporate online serials into your collection, set your policies, and selected your titles, are you done? Far from it. Online serials bring their own unique questions and problems to the collection development-acquisition-cataloging process, and it is vital that the right people be involved at the right point in the procedure. *[Article copies available for a fee from The Haworth Document Delivery Service: 1-800-342-9678. E-mail address: getinfo@haworth.com]*

KEYWORDS. Collection development, online serials, selection, acquisition, cataloging

Cindy Stewart Kaag earned her MLS from the University of Wisconsin-Madison in 1975. Since January 1997 she has been Head of the George Brain Education Library, Washington State University, Pullman WA 99164-2112, USA (email: kaag@wsu.edu). Before that she was Head of Collections for the WSU Owen Science and Engineering Library. She was chair of the Collection Development and Evaluation Section of the Reference and User Services Division of ALA 1996-97.

The author wishes to thank her WSU colleagues who worked on the Access to Electronic Information and Online Utilities (AEIOU) committee: Joy Suh, John Webb, Christy Zlatos.

[Haworth co-indexing entry note]: "Collection Development for Online Serials: Who Needs to Do What, and Why, and When." Kaag, Cindy Stewart. Co-published simultaneously in *The Serials Librarian* (The Haworth Press, Inc.) Vol. 33, No. 1/2, 1998, pp. 107-122; and: *E-Serials: Publishers, Libraries, Users, and Standards* (ed: Wayne Jones) The Haworth Press, Inc., 1998, pp. 107-122. Single or multiple copies of this article are available for a fee from The Haworth Document Delivery Service [1-800-342-9678, 9:00 a.m. - 5:00 p.m. (EST). E-mail address: getinfo@haworth.com].

INTRODUCTION

If you want to include online serials in your collection, but haven't yet, or have had troubles making them accessible to users, this article offers a sample procedure detailing who in the library needs to be involved at which points in the selection/acquisition/ cataloging process. These are by no means the only issues and questions pertaining to online serials. There is already a considerable body of professional literature covering pricing, archiving, copyright, cataloging and bibliographic control, selection policies, etc.: a sampling of these is included in the bibliography following.

This article offers a template, adaptable to your institution, for making sure the necessary people are involved at the right time.

WHO NEEDS TO BE INVOLVED IN GETTING ELECTRONIC PRODUCTS UP AND RUNNING?

Selections: they're not just for collection development librarians anymore. Before an online serial can be made available to users, a great deal of consultation and communication among library personnel has to take place. Leaving people out of the process, or not consulting key players at the right stage, can hold up access. Each library needs to determine who will be involved in making online serials available to users and at what points in the process they should be contacted.

Assume you are responsible for collection development in the field of general science and you are interested in adding the Journal of Unnecessary and Pretentious Gobbledygook to your collection. Depending on your local practice, you might normally: (1) evaluate the product, make a decision, send the order to the acquisitions unit; or (2) evaluate the product, consult with colleagues in your unit, make a decision, send the order to the acquisitions unit; or (3) evaluate the product, consult with your head of collections, make a decision, send the order to the acquisitions unit; (4) some combination of these and/or other steps. It's not that easy with online serials.

Suppose it's the online version of the Journal of Unnecessary and Pretentious Gobbledygook you want. Immediately new questions arise: do you have the technology to make the online version available to users? Do you have someone in your unit who is coordinator or head for electronic products who can find out what the product requires and compare it to available hardware and software, or do you have to do that yourself? Are you talking about a locally loaded tape, or Internet access, or some other access permutation? If you choose Internet, will it be through your OPAC or some other interface? Will passwords be necessary, or will the user's IP address suffice for identification? Will your license agreement allow you to fill interlibrary loan requests? And can your users download, print, and/or email the text? Can they do it from office and home, or only from within the library? Who in your library is in charge of online systems? It won't do you any good to send a purchase order to your acquisitions unit until these questions are answered.

Once an order has gone to the acquisitions unit, consultation and coordination are still needed. Acquisitions personnel may have to order a specific type of software, pay attention to backfile restrictions and charges, specify the subscription period, and most especially make sure the licensing agreement is signed by both the vendor and the purchaser, and that a copy of it is received and *filed* by the library, whether that file is kept in the acquisitions unit or elsewhere. The order should specify that the signed license agreement be returned within a set time period. This is an area where vendors are notoriously lax; once they have your money and your signature, signing themselves and sending a copy back to you is not a high priority. If the vendor does not respond within whatever timeframe you set, claim the license just as you would claim an unfilled order. The license file is just one of the new requirements of online serials, but it is one of the most important.

When the signed license agreement and passwords (if any) are received, the cataloging unit can take over, but here too there are questions to answer unique to online serials. Will your OPAC reflect the journal title only, and give its Internet address in lieu of a local location, or will the user be directed to a separate file of online journals, or will the record be hotlinked to the full text? It is perfectly possible that all these options, and others, will be incorporated by your library for different titles with different license restrictions. Options need to be explored in consultation with the cataloging unit ahead of time, so clear instructions on what to do with the title in hand can be included with the original order. Obviously, unless you are the sole collections-systems-acquisitions-cataloging librarian yourself, you are going to have to talk to a number of people to determine the best process for your organization. It will undoubtedly be useful to find out what (if anything) has been done about handling online products in the past, talk to those who will be involved in the future, and draw up draft guidelines to circulate for comment. Because change can be scary, or at least bothersome, it's important to give everyone involved a chance to make suggestions about how to go about adding an online serial. It's especially important to make sure everyone understands that guidelines are not writ in stone, that change is inevitable and improvement is expected, and that the important thing is to get a process in place and adapt that process as experience teaches.

SAMPLE COVER LETTER AND GUIDELINES

Possibly the most important part of adding online serials to your collections is preventing panic. Library staff and users alike may feel overwhelmed by the newness of the approach and the changes it brings. The first step to helping your users is to help your staff realize that this is essentially no different from what they already do so ably: get the material to the user.

When you have drafted a set of guidelines for online serials, it will help if everybody gets to see the whole document, and not just a part of it. To that end, sending out a draft copy should serve two purposes: it will answer many questions, and it will generate many more! Even if you think you've covered all contingencies, someone will surely think of another. That's exactly the purpose of a draft–to refine, revise, rethink, and reforge.

Following is a draft cover letter sent along with the guidelines to library personnel; it was written to emphasize the malleable nature of the process.

Sample Cover Letter

"This is a draft of interim guidelines for obtaining/accessing electronic products, such as online serials. For the past few years library units have dealt with these issues piecemeal in response to questions as they arose. These guidelines bring together elements from individual unit practices into a cradle-to-grave overview of what needs to happen for the Libraries to make an electronic product available to users. Keep in mind that:

• Procedures will change over time.
• Procedures will change as more efficient practices evolve.
• Not all products will require all steps set forth in this draft.
• Not all possible permutations are addressed by this draft.
• Adjustments and exceptions are expected."

Sample Guidelines

Guidelines for Selecting, Processing and Accessing Electronic Resources

This is a guide for the decision-making process involved in acquiring electronic resources. Electronic resources include online serials, CD-ROMs, database products, Internet sites and software accessible to the public through public workstations or the online library catalog. This guide addresses who should participate at which stage in obtaining and handling electronic resources materials. There will be exceptions to these guidelines.

1. Initial Material Review

   a. Selector checks reviews of electronic resources under consideration, based on the criteria listed on "Guidelines for Electronic Resource Selection" (Appendix I).
   b. Selector gathers necessary information on candidate products to facilitate decision making. Information may include system requirements, search engine, costs, networking restrictions, dates of coverage, etc.
   c. Selector submits this information to or consults with appropriate colleagues (electronic resources librarian, faculty, systems personnel, collection development head, etc.).
   d. If the product requires system-wide access or a state-wide consortium, selector recommends the product to the head of

the unit (or others as appropriate), who coordinates soliciting the necessary information from other participants.

e. If the product is the online version(s) of existing paper resources, the license agreement is sent to the appropriate library unit to be checked for acceptability.

2. Checking Technical Accessibility and Licensing

a. The selector may check the usefulness of products by setting up a trial period.

b. The electronic resources librarian determines what is needed to make the product work with the current configuration of the library system and determines the best suitable access method/location for the product (stand alone workstation, LAN, or loading on the online catalog, etc.) after consulting with appropriate public and technical service personnel (including other units such as ILL).

c. The electronic resources librarian forwards recommendations for the access location and licensing information (prices, number of users, etc.) to the systems office.

d. If the product is to be loaded onto the online catalog, the selector(s) and/or the electronic resources librarian(s) forward the issue to the body in charge of the catalog for evaluation and approval.

3. Arranging a Sample Trial Period

a. If appropriate, the collection development head of the unit, the subject specialist(s), and electronic resources librarian(s) may arrange a trial period of a sample version for librarians and users to review the product.

4. Purchase Decision

a. The unit collection development head and the electronic resources librarian make a purchase decision after evaluating all criteria above. If the product requires system-wide access, they report a purchase recommendation as appropriate.

b. Both the unit collection development head and the electronic resources librarian must sign off on purchase requests, except in the case where the source of funding comes outside of the unit, such as the university itself or a state-wide consortium. In the latter case, the library director will sign along with the unit collection development head of the unit and/or the appropriate electronic resources librarian.
c. The unit fills in the Electronic Product Purchase Request (Appendix II) and forwards it to the systems office.

5. Systems responsibilities

a. When the person in charge of the library systems receives licensing information, he/she will consult with appropriate librarians, including the selector, electronic resource librarian, head of interlibrary loans, and if necessary the library's attorney, on the terms of the license. S/he will send any proposed amendments to the vendor for approval.
b. After the library and the vendor agree to license terms, systems personnel make the amendments, add needed technical information relating to the local network, and send the document(s) to the acquisitions unit.
c. Systems personnel notify the interlibrary loan office of the titles and any license restrictions, and the Webmaster of any titles to be added to the library homepage.
d. If the license covers multiple titles, the selector notifies the acquisitions and systems office of any changes in titles covered. Systems personnel notify interlibrary loans and the Webmaster of the changes.
e. The systems office develops and maintains a file of licenses, including information about use restrictions. This is a temporary deliberate redundancy with the acquisitions file, and will be phased out in a couple of years once procedures are well established.
f. Except in extraordinary circumstances, the process above does not apply to single-user, stand-alone, products with so-called shrink-wrap licenses. These usually do not require

negotiation, and access is normally limited to the walk-in users of the library.

6. Acquisitions responsibilities

   a. Purchase requests come to the acquisitions unit from the systems office, complete with payment information, signed license, address of vendor, and full user/location information in the order form.

   b. Acquisitions personnel create an interim record and send order with completed license, requesting return of counter-signed license. All electronic products are ordered on a "rush" basis. Items (and signed licenses) will be claimed in 30 days if not received. Acquisitions personnel maintain the official license file for items in the collection (not for hardware and software) and send a copy of the completed license to the systems office with a list of the resources covered by the license.

   c. Serials are shipped to appropriate unit. EXCEPTION: Subscription program software, e.g., Lexis-Nexis, is sent to the person designated on the purchase request.

   d. Monographs are shipped to the acquisitions unit, which sends them on to the cataloging unit.

7. Cataloging responsibilities

   a. Paperwork is sent to the cataloging unit from the acquisitions unit, along with the physical item if any. Cataloging personnel process the product and notify the systems office and the unit/electronic resources librarian as applicable when the item is available for public use.

8. Post-purchase

   a. Products may be reviewed at any time and should be reviewed for cost, usage, uniqueness, and importance at least yearly.

   b. Terminations or changes in avenues of access need to be reported to:

- Webmaster
- cataloging
- unit head of collections
- electronic resources librarian
- subject specialist.

CONCLUSION

As convoluted as this procedure seems, you will find it better to be sure everybody is involved early on than to have access delayed because an essential step along the way was skipped. Once you have some experience in choosing and processing online serials, you will be able to simplify the process. Remember: you are still doing what librarians do best, bringing together the user and the information. The fundamental facts remain as time goes by.

BIBLIOGRAPHY

RECENT ARTICLES RELEVANT TO COLLECTION MANAGEMENT OF ONLINE SERIALS

Accessing

Donnice Cochenour and Elaine F. Jurries, "An idea whose time has come: the Alliance Electronic Journal Access Web site," *Colorado Libraries,* 22 (Summer 1996), 15-19.

"Electronic journals: trends in World Wide Web (WWW) Internet access," *Information Intelligence, Online Libraries, and Microcomputers,* 14, no. 4 (1 April 1996), 1.

Stephen P. Harter and Hak Joon Kim, "Accessing electronic journals and other E-publications: an empirical study," *College and Research Libraries,* 57, no. 5 (Sept. 1996), 440-443, 446-456.

Les Hawkins, "Network accessed scholarly serials," *The Serials Librarian,* 29, no. 3-4 (1996), 19-31.

Martha Hruska, "Remote Internet serials in the OPAC?" *Serials Review,* 21 (Winter 1995), 68-70.

Thomas Moothart, "Providing access to E-journals through library home pages," *Serials Review,* 22 (Summer 1996), 71-77.

Pamela Pavliscak, "Trends in copyright practices of scholarly electronic journals," *Serials Review*, 22 (Fall 1996), 39-47.

Acquiring and Processing

"Acquiring electronic journals," *Library Technology Reports*, 32, no. 5 (1996), 636.

Robert D. Cameron, "To link or to copy? Four principles for materials acquisition in Internet electronic libraries." Available: http://fas.sfu.ca/0/projects/ElectronicLibrary/project/papers/e-lib-links.html

CIC Electronic Journals Collection. Available: http://ejournals.cic.net

Tim Collins, "EBSCO's plans for handling electronic journals and document delivery," *Collection Management*, 20, no. 3-4 (1996), 15-18.

Cynthia M. Coulter, "Electronic journals: acquisition and retention issues," *Technical Services Quarterly*, 14, no. 2 (1996), 75.

Anthony W. Ferguson, "I am beginning to hate commercial E-journals: ten commandments for acquiring electronic journals," *Against the Grain*, 8 (Sep. 1996), 86.

Clifford A. Lynch, "Technology and its implications for serials acquisitions," *Against the Grain*, 9 (Feb. 1997), 34+.

Gail McMillan, "Technical processing of electronic journals," *Library Resources and Technical Services*, 36, no. 4 (Oct. 1992), 470-477.

NewJour: Electronic Journals and Newsletters. Available: http://gort.uscd.edu/newjour/

Sara von Ungern-Sternberg and Mats G. Lindquist, "The impact of electronic journals on library functions," *Journal of Information Science*, 21, no. 5 (1995), 396-401.

Hazel Woodward, "Electronic journals: issues of access and bibliographic control," *Serials Review*, 21, no. 2 (Summer 1995), 71-78.

Cataloging and Archiving

William C. Anderson and Les Hawkins, "Development of CONSER cataloging policies for remote access computer file serials," *Public-Access Computer Systems Review*, 7, no. 1 (1995), 6-25.

Margy Burn, "Electronic journals: the issues for libraries," *LASIE*, 26 (July/Dec. 1995), 28-33.

Ellen Finnie Duranceau, "Cataloging remote-access electronic serials: rethinking the role of the OPAC," *Serials Review*, 21 (Winter 1995), 67-77.

Ellen Finnie Duranceau, "Naming and describing networked electronic resources: the role of uniform resource identifiers," *Serials Review*, 20, no. 4 (1994), 31-44.

Wayne Jones, "We need those E-serial records," *Serials Review*, 21 (Winter 1995), 74-75.

Wayne Jones and Young-Hee Queinnec, "Format integration and serials cataloguing," *The Serials Librarian*, 25, no. 1-2 (1994), 83-95.

Wim C. Luijendijk, "Archiving electronic journals: the serial information providers perspective," *IFLA Journal*, 22, no. 3 (1996), 209-210.
Eric Lease Morgan, "Adding Internet resources to our OPACs," *Serials Review*, 21 (Winter 1995), 70-72.
Eric Lease Morgan, "Mr. Serials revisits cataloging: cataloging electronic serials and Internet resources," *The Serials Librarian*, 28, no. 3-4 (1996), 229-238.
Judith Wusteman, "Electronic journal formats," *Program*, 30 (Oct. 1996), 319-343.

Overall

John H. Barnes, "One giant leap, one small step: continuing the migration to electronic journals," *Library Trends*, 45, no. 3 (Winter 1997), 404-415.
Donnice Cochenour, "CICNet's electronic journal collection," *Serials Review*, 22 (Spring 1996), 63-68.
Ellen Finnie Duranceau, "Old wine in new bottles? Defining electronic serials," *Serials Review*, 22 (Spring 1996), 69-79.
Ellen Finnie Duranceau, "Electronic journals in the MIT libraries: report of the 1995 E-journal subgroup," *Serials Review*, 22 (Spring 1996), 47-56+.
Thomas B. Hickey, "Present and future capabilities of the online journal," *Library Trends*, 43 (Spring 1995), 528-543.
Stella Keenan, "Electronic publishing: a subversive proposal, and an even more subversive proposal, and a counter argument," *Online*, 20, no. 2 (Apr. 1996), 93-94.
Bonnie MacEwan and Mira Geffner, "The CIC electronic journals collection project," *The Serials Librarian*, 31, no. 1-2 (1996), 191.
Bonnie MacEwan and Mira Geffner, "The Committee on Institutional Cooperation electronic journals collection (CIC-EJC): a new model for library management of scholarly journals published on the Internet," *Public-Access Computer Systems Review*, 7, no. 4 (1995), 5-15.
Thomas E. Nisonger, "Collection management issues for electronic journals," *IFLA Journal*, 22, no. 3 (1996), 233-239.
J. F. B. Rowland, "Electronic journals: delivery, use and access," *IFLA Journal*, 22, no. 3 (1996), 226-228.
The Serials Librarian, 30, no. 3-4, entire issue and 31, no. 1-2, entire issue. These issues are devoted to the proceedings of NASIG's 11th annual conference.
Carol Tenopir, "Managing scientific journals in the digital era," *Information Outlook*, 1 (Feb. 1997): 14-17.
S. W. Weibel, "The World Wide Web and emerging Internet resource discovery standards for scholarly literature," *Library Trends*, 43, no. 4 (1995), 627-644.
Hazel Woodward et al., "Electronic journals: myths and realities," *Library Management*, 18, no. 3-4 (1997), 155.
Hazel Woodward, "Electronic journals in an academic library environment," *Serials: the journal of the United Kingdom Serials Group*, 10, no. 1 (1997), 53.

Pricing

Eyal Amiran, "The rhetoric of serials at the present time," *The Serials Librarian*, 28, no. 3-4 (1996), 209-221.

Ellen Finnie Duranceau, "The economics of electronic publishing," *Serials Review*, 21, no. 1 (1995), 77-90.

Jack Meadows, David Pullinger and Peter Such, "The cost of implementing an electronic journal," *Journal of Scholarly Publishing*, 26, no. 4 (Jul. 1995), 227-233.

APPENDIX I: Guidelines for Electronic Resource Selection

The best single source is the site developed by the Collection Development Policies Committee of the Collection Development and Evaluation Section (CODES) of the Reference and User Services Association. This site includes Core Policy Elements for electronic formats in general, an annotated bibliography, and selected policy statements. Paper copies are available on interlibrary loan from ALA.

http://academic.uofs.edu/organization/codes

Following is an abbreviated guideline to serve as a starting point for developing your own:

POLICY FOR SELECTING ONLINE RESOURCES

Content

1. Content should be relevant to the information needs of the community served.
2. Coverage should be comparable or superior to other electronic or print products in the same subject.
3. Content should include a significant amount of material not already available in other locally accessible resources. If another version/format of the item is owned, cancellation should be considered.
4. Accuracy and completeness should be judged as for any other item under purchase consideration.
5. Bibliographic databases should be updated on a schedule reflecting the nature of the data and needs of users.

Cost

1. Cost must be competitive with other electronic versions of the information, if any. Considerations include: cost per use, backfiles

to purchase, network fees, discounts for retaining or savings from canceling other formats, costs of necessary new software and equipment.

2. Maintaining hardcopy and electronic versions of an item must be justified. Considerations: no archival coverage with electronic version, content differs between formats, license restricts printing, downloading, multiple users, etc., graphics are not comparable.

Software

1. Software should be largely intuitive for the user. Considerations: appealing screen design, both free text and indexed searching, boolean and proximity searching, save search feature, speed, search engine appropriate for material, display modifications possible, printing and downloading capabilities, onscreen help that is really helpful, compatibility with existing systems and equipment, ease of maintenance.

Access

1. Resource should meet networking standards even if financial or legal constraints limit initial networking.
2. Resource should meet international data standards.
3. Multiple simultaneous use agreements are preferred.
4. If competing products have comparable costs, preference will go to the product with no added networking charges.
5. Preference will go to products which enhance access to materials currently unavailable or which maximize use of existing resources.

Additional Considerations

1. Cost should not be the overriding consideration for core resources. Non-core resources should meet one or more of the following criteria: unique access, inexpensive, improved service to users from improved staff efficiency.
2. Owning is preferable to leasing.
3. Staff resources should be considered.
4. A sample version or trial period before purchase is recommended. As with any other item, reviews are useful.

APPENDIX II: Electronic Product Purchase Request Form

Date _____

Title _____
_____

Producer/Publisher _____
_____

Fund to be charged _____

Price _____

Order Type: (see list below) _____

Media Type _____

URL (if applicable) _____

APPROVAL INFORMATION:

Selector approval _____

Unit Collection Development Head approval _____

Electronic Resources Librarian _____

Systems Approval _____

ACCESS INFORMATION:

Access method _____

Location _____

License Restrictions _____

Interlibrary Loan? _____ yes _____ no

Number of simultaneous users: _____

Additional Resources Required for Use _____

_____

_____

Passwords _____

_____

TRACKING INFORMATION:

Date License Due from Vendor _____

Date Information/Item Sent to Cataloging _____

Date Webmaster Notified: _____

SEND AVAILABILITY NOTIFICATION TO: _____

_____

Notes _____

_____

_____

_____

Form should be filled out as completely as possible.

Order Types: MONO

    STO
    REPLACEMENT
    SERIAL SPECIAL
    OTHER

Media Types: CD-ROM

    DATATAPE
    MULTI
    INTERNET
    OTHER

URL is mandatory for all Internet resources.

Unit approval needed for new purchases initiated from library units. Broad-based purchases (e.g., FirstSearch) or electronic versions of items for which there is a print counterpart (e.g., e-journals) wouldn't normally require unit approval.

Systems approval normally required for multiuser CD-ROM and Internet licenses. (Single user, shrink-wrapped licenses do not need negotiation in most cases.)

License restrictions typically include access (who uses?), use (printing, downloading allowed? as well as, interlibrary loan), number of simultaneous users, and additional resources required for use (e.g., PDF files require Adobe Acrobat software).

Typically, when the license returns from the vendor, the item (or just the paperwork in the case of Internet resources) is given to cataloging at the same time that the Webmaster is notified. Thus, the license return date is an important date which must be noted.

When cataloging is finished, the cataloging unit will notify the name(s) listed on the NOTIFICATION line.

CATALOGING AND METADATA

Serials Published
on the World Wide Web:
Cataloging Problems and Decisions

Les Hawkins

SUMMARY. An annotated list of serials published on the World Wide Web is presented to point out features important in making cataloging decisions. Problem areas such as title and file format changes are noted, as well as features such as article based delivery and dispersal of issue content into searchable databases. *[Article copies available for a fee from The Haworth Document Delivery Service: 1-800-342-9678. E-mail address: getinfo@haworth.com]*

KEYWORDS. Cataloging, article-based delivery, databases

Les Hawkins is a cataloger at the U.S. ISSN center, National Serials Data Program, Library of Congress, 101 Independence Avenue, Washington, DC 20540-4160, USA (email: lhaw@loc.gov).
The views expressed in this paper do not necessarily reflect those of the Library of Congress.

[Haworth co-indexing entry note]: "Serials Published on the World Wide Web: Cataloging Problems and Decisions." Hawkins, Les. Co-published simultaneously in *The Serials Librarian* (The Haworth Press, Inc.) Vol. 33, No. 1/2, 1998, pp. 123-145; and: *E-Serials: Publishers, Libraries, Users, and Standards* (ed: Wayne Jones) The Haworth Press, Inc., 1998, pp. 123-145. Single or multiple copies of this article are available for a fee from The Haworth Document Delivery Service [1-800-342-9678, 9:00 a.m. - 5:00 p.m. (EST). E-mail address: getinfo@haworth.com].

123

INTRODUCTION

This annotated listing of World Wide Web-based serials is intended to demonstrate some of the cataloging problems and design features of online serials that influence cataloger decisions for bibliographic description. It is structured in broad categories and there are some serials that share features of several categories. These examples were culled from requests for the International Standard Serial Number (ISSN) received by the National Serials Data Program (NSDP), through an interactive ISSN application form mounted on NSDP's Web page. The examples are a few of the approximately 200 requests for network-based serials received by NSDP through this route (other applications are received through regular mail) from May 1996 to May 1997. CONSER-level records were adapted or created on OCLC. The listed examples were last viewed by the author on July 31, 1997.

There is also an Appendix of associated CONSER-level OCLC records as they existed in September 1997. They are given for the purpose of illustrating some of the problems encountered in creating or adapting records for World Wide Web-based serials. They reflect a range of evolving cataloging practice and style over the period covered and are therefore not intended to be model cataloging examples for 1998 and beyond.

World Wide Web authors and publishers use semantic models from the real world (e.g., neighborhoods or rings of related material) to provide a familiar semantic interface for users. Publishers have similarly maintained elements of the paper serial as a model for delivery on the World Wide Web. Such features include titles that are indicative of a serial (e.g., journal, newsletter, zine) and a table of contents to guide readers through the Web site, issues, or articles.

While publishers have retained many features of paper serials as a model for World Wide Web publishing, there are differences in how serials appear online. The Web has allowed publishers to emphasize article delivery through a database format rather than to rely on single issues as a means of organizing content. It is sometimes difficult to locate the first issue as a source for description if earlier issues are dispersed into an archive without retaining issue numbering. There are examples below that demonstrate this emphasis on article delivery and its effects on issue numbering and access to back issues. There are also examples of the table of contents as a navigational tool. A contents listing structure has become a primary collocating device for article titles of individual issues in some online serials. Though it is sometimes discarded when articles are later archived into a database, it is frequently a source of bibliographic information at the time of cataloging. Sometimes only the content listing for the current issue is available for cataloging because of this.

The ability to format an online serial in a frames or tables style is also becoming a common device to enhance navigation. Publishers increasingly also allow readers the option of viewing the serial in some combination of text-based, HTML, tables, frames, nonframes, or floating frames versions. This allows access to low- and high-end browsers. Sometimes Web-specific design features such as these present additional bibliographic elements and add to the complexity of citing sources of information in the catalog record. There are examples throughout the list that show such features and variations in presentation of bibliographic information.

The online environment also allows publishers to update and reformat material easily. Some of the examples below demonstrate problems caused by publishers making changes to previously released issues that involve the title chosen for the title proper in a catalog record. Others demonstrate the multiplicity of file formats available.

There are a few cases where bibliographic information about the various version formats differs, e.g., the ASCII version and HTML version of a single issue present a slightly different title. Part of this is a result of publishers reformatting documents earlier encoded in ASCII into HTML or other formats.

Another set of examples is given to show the relationships between paper and online serials. These include cases where the paper serial ceases entirely and is continued only in electronic form and cases of simultaneous paper and online serials.

A final category includes World Wide Web sites that provide access to two or more serials that appear to be related, including a different language version.

SERIAL PARTS AND DATABASE DELIVERY
OF ARTICLES

The first group of examples is given in three general categories. The first of these is article-based delivery where issue content is dispersed into a database. The serials are often updated with new articles on a continuous basis and sometimes have maintained annual volumes to which new articles are added until the volume is closed. The second category shows examples of several ways of handling back issues, dispersing them into subject areas, providing access to a limited number of back issues, and open-ended issues. The third demonstrates the use of table of contents as a navigational device.

Article/Database Journals

1. Alzheimer's disease review. Available: <http://www.coa.uky.edu/ADReview> Sanders-Brown Center on Aging, University of Kentucky. ISSN 1093-5355.

Access to articles is through volume table of contents. The articles of the two volumes that have been published as of July 1997 are available from the same contents page. There is combined issue numbering for the contents of the current volume, no. 1/2 (June 1997), but no issues are identified for the first volume. The OCLC record for this title cites volume 1, no. 1/2 (spring/summer 1996) as the first issue, so the issue numbering appears to have been dropped after the first volume was complete. The issue numbering in the current volume appears to act as an indication of how current the articles are. The articles in both volumes are continuously paginated for the volume. The article citations (in the articles and abstracts) include the page numbering. Peer reviewed.

2. Frontiers in bioscience. Available: <http://www.bioscience.org> ISSN 1093-4715.

Offered with frames, floating frames, or no-frame formats. The frames format provides a readily available table of contents while viewing text of the articles. Manuscripts are added to annual volumes as they are finally accepted; no issue numbering is used.

Manuscripts each have a hypertext table of contents and a search engine. A variety of resources and services are offered by the associated virtual library. Peer-reviewed journal.

3. Advances in environmental research. Available: <http://www.sfo.com/~aer/> ISSN 1093-7927.

Peer-reviewed journal in environmental science, engineering and technology. Issue table of contents provides access to articles. Volume and issue numbering are used. Accepted articles are published first online (HTML and PDF) and later organized into a quarterly paper version. Articles in the paper version are identical to the PDF formats, according to the publisher.

Access to Back Issue Contents

4. Refermation. Available: <http://www.clrc.org/referm.htm> Central New York Resources Council. ISSN 1090-3070.

Only the current 6 months worth of issues are maintained on the Web.

5. Pif. Available: <http://www.dimax.com/pif/> ISSN 1094-2726.

Designation on current issue only. Archives disperses back issue content into four categories: Artwork, Fiction, Poetry, Rhetoric. Back issues aren't maintained whole, though one can determine which issue a particular piece of artwork, article, etc., came from.

6. eNetDigest. Available: <http://www.enetdigest.com/> ISSN 1090-3054.

Environmental, natural resources, and agricultural Internet resources. Weekly review of new Internet sites, Subject index breaks back issue content into six types of site categories: Agricultural sites, Environmental sites, Natural resources sites, General and Government sites, Mailing lists, Web tools. Weekly back issues also maintained in whole for 1996 and 1997. Also contains search engine for issue database, keywords indexed to issues. (For example, searching the word "lead" retrieved a list of issues which contained the word; the next step is to move to particular whole issues containing the term.)

7. *(re)soundings.* Available: <http://www.millersv.edu/~resound> ISSN 1091-8728.

An interactive hypermedia periodical in the humanities. "Readers are invited to participate in the forum by adding their comments (utilizing print, graphic, music, and other text formats) to the discussion initiated by the peer reviewed articles." Makes use of frames, encourages reader comments and displays discussion/interaction from readers. Current issue remains "open" for six months; articles are added continuously, after which issues, comments/discussion are archived.

Examples of Access to Back Issues Through Table of Contents Screens

8. *Ethnomusicology online.* Available: <http://umbc.edu/eol/> ISSN 1092-7336.

Articles are added to the current issue as they are ready. Also contains sound files in some articles.

9. *Hmong studies journal.* Available: <http://www.tc.umn.edu/nlhome/ g450/vueb0001/HER/HSJ.html> ISSN 1091-1774.

Each issue has a table of contents screen for article access; there is a title variant on the journal home page.

10. *Newyorske listy.* Available: <http://www.columbia.edu/ ~js322/nyl/nyl.html> ISSN 1093-2887.

Czech-language publication. Access to issues through table of contents. Current-year issues maintain monthly table of contents; past year issues are dispersed into a topically organized list designated by year.

TITLE CHANGES

These three examples include a case of the publisher entirely reformatting an earlier title, a case where earlier issues with the former title are archived in whole, and a case where design changes over the years and multiple title sources have resulted in catalogers creating separate records for essentially the same serial.

11. Lexica. Available: <http://lexica.inherent.com> ISSN 1092-4094.

Title change from *LawMagNet*. Issues with the former title are no longer available. The earlier title, numbered volume 1, no. 1, is now referred to by the publisher as a "proof of concept" issue and its contents are being converted to the new title format.

12. Textual reasoning. Available: <http://web.bu.edu/mzank/Textual_ Reasoning> ISSN 1094-3447.

Title change from *Postmodern Jewish Philosophy Bitnetwork*. It also appears that some issues were called *Postmodern Jewish Philosophy Network*. Earlier title issues are maintained at the primary site and also at a separate archive site.

13. The Mississippi review: MR. Available: <http://sushi.st.usm.edu/mrw> Center for Writers. ISSN 1093-5347.

Appears to have gone through several title changes and perhaps reformatting. As of July 1997 there were several OCLC records based on the same early issues which cited different titles. The earlier titles no longer appeared prominently on the sources of title cited. Access to earlier issues is through a screen showing contents for all back issues. The journal's home page or introductory screen shows current "cover" artwork with the current issue date and the title *MR*. Frames-based structure supports viewing of a contents list, at all times in a banner.

ELECTRONIC FILE FORMATS

File format options for viewing and printing are a necessity in the World Wide Web. Problems such as limited bandwidth impede handling of diverse file formats (e.g., motion picture formats) easily. In addition, servers are incapable of making distinctions when sending special format files to low- and high-end clients. Many of the serials below are limited in the type of files they provide access to. Mainly they are text, simple image files, and downloadable print formats (e.g., PDF).

One of the file format examples below is intended to illustrate the importance of a systems requirement note to explicitly mention additional software needs in cases where a serial is issued in unique file formats. The Chinese title listed here is available in different formats for viewing Chinese characters, which requires readers to use or download appropriate viewing software.

14. *Agent news webletter.* Available: <http://www.cs.umbc.edu/agentnews/> or <ftp://ftp.cs.umbc.edu/pub/agents/agentnews/> ISSN 1090-3062.

Covers software agents, intelligent information systems, knowledge sharing, and information retrieval. Issues maintained in ASCII (for emailing and FTP access) and HTML formats; some of the ASCII issues have a different title: *Agentnews service.* The same issues in HTML format have the title *Agentnews webletter* or *UMBC agentnews webletter.*

15. *Scout report.* Available: <http://www.cs.wisc.edu/scout/report> or <http://rs.internic.net/scout/report> ISSN 1092-3861.

A project of InterNIC and the Computer Science Department of the University of Wisconsin. Provides weekly list of Internet sites of interest to researchers and educators. Published in email, PDF, and HTML formats.

16. *About this particular Macintosh.* Available: <http://www.atpm.com> ISSN 1093-2901

Current issue is HTML-encoded; back issue archives include HTML and downloadable DOCMaker format issues.

17. *The Rock.* Available: <http://www.paintedrock.com/memvis/rockmag/rockmag.htm> Painted Rock Writers and Readers Colony. ISSN 1094-3471.

Poetry, art, literary magazine. Older back issues available only in PDF; a few recent back issues are in ASCII only; current issues are in HTML and ASCII only.

18. *Zhong-guo yu shi jie.* Available: <http://www.chinabulletin.com> Publisher: China and the World. ISSN 1091-9562.

Issued in GB, BIG5, and HZ formats for downloading full issues with Chinese text. Though tables of contents contain Chinese characters viewable online in GIF format, viewing software is necessary to view the full issue with Chinese characters.

PAPER TO ONLINE, SIMULTANEOUS PAPER AND ONLINE PUBLISHING

The first set of examples is of online serials that have replaced the paper entirely. The next group represents serials published in simultaneous paper and online formats. In such cases, the cataloger also must make decisions about how to show when the online version began. If the publisher has plans to digitize back issues of the paper serial, should the record contain a formatted MARC field 362, with the beginning designation of the first available issue online, or should it show a description based on note citing the earliest available online (a suggestion that earlier paper issues may be digitized later)?

Change from Paper to Online Format

19. *Selected new acquisitions.* Available: <http://CAS.calacademy. org/~library/newacq> California Academy of Sciences Library. ISSN 1089-5337.

Changed to online format in 1995; only digital issues from that time to the present are maintained online.

20. *Cosmic current news online.* Available: <http://www.netport.com/ rainey/index.html> ISSN 1091-3114.

Changed to online format in 1996 and began numbering of the online serial with #1.

Simultaneous Paper and World Wide Web Versions

21. *Systematic biology (Online).* Available: <http://www.utexas.edu/ ftp/ depts/systbiol> Society of Systematic Biologists. ISSN 1076-836X.

Online issues begin with volume 44. The cataloger was uncertain about the intention of the publisher to digitize back issues and used a description based on note, rather than indicating the first issue available online.

22. Arid lands newsletter. Available: <http://ag.arizona.edu/OALS/ALN/ALNHome.html> Office of Arid Lands of the University of Arizona. ISSN 1092-5481.

Online versions begin with number 35. A discussion with the publisher indicated that there was no intention of digitizing paper back issues, so the OCLC record indicates that this is the first issue of the online version.

23. REDI: resources for environmental design index. Available: <http://oikos.com/redi> ISSN 1089-1897.

Paper version was issued as an online directory or catalog. Most recently, the online version provides only a searchable database with an "updated" date rather than successive parts or issues. This perhaps was a candidate for single record treatment, using a MARC field 856 on the record for the print version.

Multiple Serials Issued at a Single Site: Serials Within Serials or Just Links?

24. The weekly bookmark. ISSN 1091-6202.

25. The weekly bookmark. Plus. ISSN 1091-6210. Both available: <http://www.weeklyb.com/>

The weekly bookmark is a site that provides access to a title issued in two sections. They are offered in ASCII or HTML and can be delivered by email or downloaded through FTP. They provide links and annotations to new general-audience Web resources.

26. The Internet tourbus. Available: <http://www.tourbus.com> Bob Rankin and Patrick Crispin, publishers. ISSN 1094-2238.

Issue archive also offered in Spanish at the same site.

APPENDIX

OCLC Records

1.
```
OCLC:  36168140          Rec stat:    c
Entered:   19970107      Replaced:    19970909      Used:     19970708
Type:  m    ELvl:         Srce:  d    Audn:          Ctrl:        Lang:  eng
BLvl:  s    File:  d      GPub:                      MRec:        Ctry:  kyu
Desc:  a                               DtSt:  c      Dates: 1996,9999
 1  010        sn97-3897
 2  040        EYM $c EYM $d CAS $d NSD
 3  006        [sqr1p       0   a0]
 4  007        c $b r $c u $d c $e n $f u
 5  012        $1 1
 6  022  0     1093-5355
 7  030        ADREFN
 8  042        nsdp $a lcd
 9  082 10     616 $2 12
10  090        $b
11  049        NSDP
12  210  0     Alzheimer's disease rev.
13  222  0     Alzheimer's disease review
14  245 00     Alzheimer's disease review $h [computer file].
15  260        Lexington, KY : $b Sanders-Brown Center on Aging, University
of Kentucky, $c c1996-
16  310        Quarterly
17  362  0     Vol. 1, no. 1/2 (spring/summer 1996)-
18  500        Title from homepage.
19  510  0     Chemical Abstracts $x 0009-2258
20  516  8     Electronic serial in HTML and PDF formats
21  538        System requirements: Adobe Acrobat Reader for viewing and
printing PDF files.
22  538        Mode of access: World Wide Web (URL:
http://www.coa.uky.edu/ADReview/).
23  650  0     Alzheimer's disease $x Periodicals.
24  710  2     Sanders-Brown Research Center on Aging.
25  856  7     $u http://www.coa.uky.edu/ADReview/ $2 http
26  936        Vol. 1, no. 3/4 (fall/winter 1996) LIC
```

2.
```
OCLC:  36722732          Rec stat:    c
Entered:   19970411      Replaced:    19970715      Used:     19970715
Type:  m    ELvl:  7      Srce:  d    Audn:          Ctrl:        Lang:  eng
BLvl:  s    File:  d      GPub:                      MRec:        Ctry:  flu
Desc:  a                               DtSt:  c      Dates: 1996,9999
 1  010        sn97-3859
 2  040        NSD $c NSD $d NLM $d NSD $d CAS
 3  006        [s x1        0   a0]
 4  007        c $b r $d c $e n $f u
 5  012        $1 1
 6  022  0     1093-4715
 7  030        FRBIF6
 8  037        $b S. Tabibzadeh, MD Dept of Pathology Moffitt Cancer Center,
12902 Magnolia Drive, Tampa, FL 33612 $c Free
 9  042        nsdp $a lcd
10  082 10     570 $2 12
11  090        $b
12  049        NSDP
13  210  0     Front. biosci. $b (Online)
14  222  0     Frontiers in bioscience $b (Online)
15  245 00     Frontiers in bioscience $h [computer file].
16  260        Tampa, FL : $b [s.n., $c 1996-
17  310        Irregular
18  362  0     Vol. 1 (1996)-
19  500        Title from title screen.
20  510  0     Chemical Abstracts $x 0009-2258
21  510  1     Index medicus $x 0019-3879 $b Jan. 1996-
22  515        Articles are continuously added to each annual volume.
```

```
23   516     HTML encoded text, graphics, and video (electronic journal)
24   530     Also available in paper and CD-ROM formats.
25   538     Mode of access: World Wide Web.
26   776  1  $t Frontiers in bioscience (Print) $x 1093-9946 $w (DLC)sn
97004044
27   776  1  $t Frontiers in bioscience (CD-ROM) $x 1094-3935 $w (DLC)sn
97004227
28   856  7  $z US: $u http://www.bioscience.org $2 http
29   856  7  $z Israel: $u http://bioinfo.weizmann.ac.il/bioscience $2
http
30   856  7  $z France: $u http://genome.eerie.fr/bioscience $2 http
31   856  0  moffitt.usf.edu $h tabibzadeh
```

3.
```
OCLC:  36835262          Rec stat:    n
Entered:   19970501      Replaced:    19970501      Used:    19970501
Type:  m     ELvl:  7    Srce:  d     Audn:         Ctrl:         Lang:  eng
BLvl:  s     File:  d    GPub:                      MRec:         Ctry:  cau
Desc:  a                              DtSt:  c      Dates: 1997,9999
  1  010      sn97-3965
  2  040      NSD $c NSD
  3  006      [sqr1p        0   a0]
  4  007      c $b r $d c $e n $f u
  5  012      $1 1
  6  022  0   1093-7927
  7  037      $b Nelson & Commons Communications, 1620 Acton Street,
Berkeley, CA 94702
  8  042      nsdp $a lcd
  9  082  10  333 $2 12
 10  090      $b
 11  049      NSDP
 12  130  0   Advances in environmental research (Online)
 13  210  0   Adv. environ. res. $b (Online)
 14  222  0   Advances in environmental research $b (Online)
 15  245  00  Advances in environmental research $h [computer file].
 16  260      Berkeley, CA : $b [s.n., $c 1997-
 17  310      Quarterly
 18  362  0   Vol. 1, no. 1-
 19  500      Title from title screen.
 20  516      Text (electronic journal)
 21  538      Mode of access: World Wide Web.
 22  776  1   $t Advances in environmental research
 23  856  7   $u http://www.sfo.com/%7Eaer $2 http
```

4.
```
OCLC:  35253263          Rec stat:    c
Entered:   19960816      Replaced:    19970909      Used:    19970909
Type:  m     ELvl:  7    Srce:  d     Audn:         Ctrl:         Lang:  eng
BLvl:  s     File:  d    GPub:                      MRec:         Ctry:  nyu
Desc:  a                              DtSt:  c      Dates: 1996,9999
  1  010      sn96-4417
  2  040      NSD $c NSD
  3  006      [smx1p        0   a0]
  4  007      c $b r $d c $e n $f u
  5  012      $1 1
  6  022  0   1090-3070
  7  037      $b Central New York Library Resources Council, 3049 E Genesee
St, Syracuse, NY 13244 $c free on Web
  8  042      nsdp $a msc
  9  082  10  021 $2 12
 10  090      $b
 11  049      NSDP
 12  130  0   Refermation (Online)
 13  210  0   Refermation $b (Online)
 14  222  0   Refermation $b (Online)
 15  245  00  Refermation $h [computer file] / $c CLRC.
 16  260      Syracuse NY : $b Central New York Library Resources Council,
$c [1996-
 17  310      Ten no. a year
 18  362  0   July-Aug. 1996-
 19  538      Mode of access: World Wide Web.
 20  500      Title from title screen.
 21  516      HTML (electronic journal)
```

```
22  710 2    Central New York Library Resources Council.
23  776 1    Central New York Library Resources Council. $t Refermation $x
0034-2920 $w (DLC)sn 81006194
24  856 7    $u http://www.clrc.org/referm.htm $2 http
```

5.

OCLC: 37134414	Rec stat:	c

Entered:	19970617	Replaced:	19970909	Used:	19970909
Type: m	ELvl: 7	Srce: d	Audn:	Ctrl:	Lang: eng
BLvl: s	File: d	GPub:		MRec:	Ctry: hiu
Desc: a			DtSt: c	Dates: 1995,9999

```
 1  010    sn97-4200
 2  040    NSD $c NSD
 3  006    [sqrlp        0    a0]
 4  007    c $b r $d c $e n $f u
 5  012    $l 1
 6  022 0  1094-2726
 7  037    $b Pif, P.O. Box 893162, Mililani, Hawaii 96789-0162
 8  042    nsdp $a lcd
 9  082 10 808 $2 12
10  090    $b
11  049    NSDP
12  130 0  Pif (Honolulu, Hawaii)
13  210 0  Pif $b (Honol. Hawaii)
14  222 0  Pif $b (Honolulu, Hawaii)
15  245 00 Pif $h [computer file].
16  260    Honolulu, Hawaii : $b Richard Luck,
17  310    Quarterly
18  362 1  Began in 1995?
19  500    Description based on: spring 1997; title from journal home
page.
20  516    Text, graphic, and sound files (electronic magazine)
21  538    Mode of access: World Wide Web.
22  856 7  $u http://www.dimax.com/pif/ $2 http
23  856 0  $u mailto:pif@dimax.com $i Subscribe
```

6.

OCLC: 35253111	Rec stat:	n

Entered:	19960816	Replaced:	19960816	Used:	19960816
Type: m	ELvl: 7	Srce: d	Audn:	Ctrl:	Lang: eng
BLvl: s	File: d	GPub:		MRec:	Ctry: wau
Desc: a			DtSt: c	Dates: 1996,9999

```
 1  010    sn96-4419
 2  040    NSD $c NSD
 3  006    [swrlp        0    a0]
 4  007    c $b r $d c $e n $f u
 5  012    $l 1
 6  022 0  1090-3054
 7  037    $b 1075 Bellevue Way NE, Suite 314, Bellevue, WA 98004 $c No
Charge
 8  042    nsdp $a lcd
 9  082 10 333 $2 12
10  090    $b
11  049    NSDP
12  210 0  eNetDigest $b (Bellevue Wash.)
13  222 0  eNetDigest $b (Bellevue, Wash.)
14  245 00 eNetDigest $h [computer file].
15  260    [Bellevue, Wash.] : $b Kathy E. Gill, $c c1996-
16  310    Weekly
17  362 0  1.1 (7 Jan. 1996)-
18  538    Mode of access: World Wide Web and Internet email.
19  500    Title from title screen.
20  516    HTML (World Wide Web) and ASCII (email)
21  856 7  $u http://www.enetdigest.com/ $2 http
22  856 0  halcyon.com $h kegill $z Send message to editor with the word
subscribe in subject field and in the body of the message type: subscribe
enetdigest [your email address]
```

7.

OCLC: 36006539	Rec stat:	c

Entered:	19961127	Replaced:	19970909	Used:	19970722
Type: m	ELvl: 7	Srce: d	Audn:	Ctrl:	Lang: eng
BLvl: s	File: d	GPub:		MRec:	Ctry: pau
Desc: a			DtSt: c	Dates: 1996,9999

```
 1  010    sn96-3674
```

```
 2  040      NSD $c NSD
 3  006      [sfr1p       0    a0]
 4  007      c $b r $d c $e n $f u
 5  012      $1 1
 6  022 0    1091-8728
 7  042      nsdp $a lcd
 8  082 10   001 $2 12
 9  090      $b
10  049      NSDP
11  210 0    (Re)soundings $b (Millersv. Pa.)
12  222 0    (Re)soundings $b (Millersville, Pa.)
13  245 00   (Re)soundings $h [computer file].
14  246 3    Resoundings
15  260      [Millersville, Pa.] : $b (Re)Soundings, $c c1996-
16  310      Semiannual
17  362 0    Vol. 1, no. 1-
18  500      Title from title screen.
19  515      Articles are added to issues on a continuous basis and are
complete after six months.
20  516      Text (electronic journal)
21  538      Mode of access: World Wide Web.
22  856 7    $u http://www.millersv.edu/%7Eresound $2 http
```

8.

OCLC: 36374735	Rec stat:	c			
Entered:	19970212	Replaced:	19970909	Used:	19970805
Type: m	ELvl:	Srce: d	Audn:	Ctrl:	Lang: eng
BLvl: s	File: m	GPub:		MRec:	Ctry: mdu
Desc: a			DtSt: c	Dates: 1995,9999	

```
 1  010      sn97-3763
 2  040      NSD $c NSD $d IUL $d NSD
 3  006      [s x1       0    a0]
 4  007      c $b r $d c $e n $f u
 5  012      $1 1
 6  022 0    1092-7336
 7  042      nsdp $a lcd
 8  082 10   780 $2 12
 9  090      $b
10  049      NSDP
11  210 0    Ethnomusicol. online
12  222 0    Ethnomusicology online
13  245 00   Ethnomusicology online $h [computer file] : $b EOL.
14  246 30   EOL
15  260      [Baltimore, Md.] : $b EOL, $c 1995-
16  310      Irregular
17  362 0    No. 1 (2 Nov. 1995)-
18  500      Title from introductory screen.
19  516      HTML encoded online journal
20  530      "Accepted submissions ... published on the Web from EOL's
server and its mirror site, and on CD-ROM"-- author guidelines and help
screen.
21  538      System requirements: World Wide Web browser software capable
of displaying graphics and playing audio and video files.
22  550      Hosted by: University of Maryland, Baltimore County.
23  710 2    University of Maryland, Baltimore County.
24  856 7    $u http://umbc.edu/eol $2 http
25  856 7    $z Mirror site: $u http://www.wiu.edu/eol $2 http
```

9.

OCLC: 35684447	Rec stat:	c			
Entered:	19961004	Replaced:	19961127	Used:	19970218
Type: m	ELvl: 7	Srce: d	Audn:	Ctrl:	Lang: eng
BLvl: s	File: d	GPub:		MRec:	Ctry: mnu
Desc: a			DtSt: c	Dates: 1996,9999	

```
 1  010      sn96-4741
 2  040      NSD $c NSD
 3  006      [suu1p       0    a0]
 4  007      c $b r $d c $e n $f u
 5  012      $k 1 $1 1
 6  022 0    1091-1774
 7  037      $b Hmong Studies Journal, 1171 East Sixth Street, St. Paul,
MN 55106
 8  042      nsdp $a lcd
 9  082 10   959 $2 12
```

```
10  090      $b
11  049      NSDP
12  210 0    Hmong stud. j.
13  222  0   Hmong studies journal
14  245 00   Hmong studies journal $h [computer file].
15  246 1    $i Title on journal home page: $a HSJ
16  260      St. Paul, Minn. : $b Robin Vue-Benson, $c c1996-
17  362 0    Vol. 1 (Oct. 1996)-
18  500      Title from title screen.
19  516      HTML encoded text (electronic journal)
20  538      Mode of access: World Wide Web.
21  856 7    $u http://www.tc.umn.edu/nlhome/g450/vueb0001/HER/HSJ.html $2
http
10.
OCLC:  36623972           Rec stat:    c
Entered:    19970325      Replaced:   19970326      Used:      19970326
Type:  m      ELvl:  7    Srce:  d    Audn:        Ctrl:      Lang:  cze
BLvl:  s      File:  d    GPub:                     MRec:      Ctry:  nyu
Desc:  a                              DtSt:  c     Dates: 1996,9999
  1  010      sn97-3684
  2  040      NSD $c NSD
  3  006      [smrlp      0   b0]
  4  007      c $b r $d c $e n $f u
  5  012      $l 1
  6  022 1    1093-2887
  7  037      $b Newyorsk e Listy, 549 Riverside Drive, New York NY 10027
$c free
  8  042      nsdp $a lcd
  9  090      $b
 10  049      NSDP
 11  130 0    Newyorsk e listy (Online)
 12  222  0   Newyorsk e listy $b (Online)
 13  245 00   Newyorsk e listy $h [computer file].
 14  246 1    $i Title on journal home page: $a New York herald
 15  260      [New York, N.Y.] : $b J. Schrabal,
 16  310      Monthly
 17  362 0    Began in 1996.
 18  500      Description based on: led. 1997; title from issue menu
screen.
 19  515      Issues for 1996 are only available as individual articles,
organized topically.
 20  516      HTML encoded text (electronic serial)
 21  538      Mode of access: World Wide Web.
 22  856 7    $u http://www.columbia.edu/%7Ejs322/nyl/nyl.html $2 http
11.
OCLC:  36223169           Rec stat:    c
Entered:    19970117      Replaced:   19970909      Used:      19970909
Type:  m      ELvl:  7    Srce:  d    Audn:        Ctrl:      Lang:  eng
BLvl:  s      File:  d    GPub:                     MRec:      Ctry:  mau
Desc:  a                              DtSt:  c     Dates: 1997,9999
  1  010      sn97-3369
  2  040      NSD $c NSD
  3  006      [sbrlp      0   a0]
  4  007      c $b r $d c $e n $f u
  5  012      $l y
  6  022 0    1092-4094 $y 1089-2222
  7  037      $b Inherent.Com, Inc., 75 Leonard Rd., Boxborough, MA 01719-
1019
  8  042      nsdp $a lcd
  9  082 10   340 $2 12
 10  090      $b
 11  049      NSDP
 12  210 0    Lexica $b (Waltham Mass.)
 13  222  0   Lexica $b (Waltham, Mass.)
 14  245 00   Lexica $h [computer file].
 15  260      Waltham, MA : $b Inherent.Com, Inc., $c c1997-
 16  310      Bimonthly
 17  362 0    Vol. 2, issue 1-
 18  500      Title from title screen.
 19  516      HTML source files stored in .zip, .tar, and .sit formats for
PC, Unix and Macintosh machines
 20  538      Mode of access: World Wide Web.
```

```
21  780 00  $t LawMagNet $x 1089-2222 $w (DLC)sn 96004119
22  856 7   $u http://lexica.inherent.com/ $2 http
12.
OCLC:   36709415           Rec stat:     c
Entered:    19970409       Replaced:    19970909      Used:     19970409
Type:  m        ELvl:       Srce:  d     Audn:         Ctrl:   Lang:  eng
BLvl:  s        File:  u    GPub:                      MRec:         Ctry:  mau
Desc:  a                                 DtSt:  c      Dates: 1996,9999
  1  010       sn97-4201
  2  040       BUF $c BUF $d NSD
  3  006       [suu1        0    a0]
  4  007       c $b r $c u $d c $e n
  5  012       $j 0 $l 1
  6  022 0     1094-3447
  7  042       nsdp $a msc
  8  082 10    296 $2 12
  9  090       $b
 10  049       NSDP
 11  210 0     Textual reason. $b (Online)
 12  222 0     Textual reasoning $b (Online)
 13  245 00    Textual reasoning $h [computer file].
 14  260       Madison, NJ : $b Postmodern Jewish Philosophy Network, $c
c1996-
 15  362 0     Vol. 5, no. 2 (July 1996)-
 16  500       Title from caption.
 17  500       Published: Boston, Mass., Nov. 1996-
 18  516 8     Electronic serial in ASCII text
 19  530       Also available in paper version.
 20  538       Mode of access: Internet. Host: web.bu.edu/ Available at URL:
http://web.bu.edu/mzank/Textual reasoning/
 21  538       For email subscription, send a request to the journal's
editorial address: mzank@bu.edu.
 22  650 0     Judaism $x Periodicals.
 23  710 2     Postmodern Jewish Philosophy Network.
 24  776 1     $t Textual reasoning (Print) $x 1094-5954 $w (DLC)sn 97004316
 25  780 00    $t Postmodern Jewish philosophy bitnetwork $w (OCoLC)31492357
 26  856 0     bu.edu $h mzank $m Michael Zank $z Editorial email address
 27  856 7     $u http://web.bu.edu/mzank/Textual Reasoning $2 http
 28  936       Vol. 5, no. 4 (Dec. 1996) LIC
13.
OCLC:   36786937           Rec stat:     c
Entered:    19970423       Replaced:    19970528      Used:     19970528
Type:  m        ELvl:  7    Srce:  d     Audn:         Ctrl:   Lang:  eng
BLvl:  s        File:  d    GPub:                      MRec:         Ctry:  msu
Desc:  a                                 DtSt:  c      Dates: 1995,9999
  1  010       sn97-3896
  2  040       NSD $c NSD
  3  006       [smn1p       0    a0]
  4  007       c $b r $d c $e n $f u
  5  012       $l 1
  6  022 0     1093-5347
  7  037       $b The Mississippi Review Online Ed., Box 5144, Hattiesburg,
MS 39406-5144
  8  042       nsdp $a lcd
  9  082 10    810 $2 12
 10  090       $b
 11  049       NSDP
 12  130 0     Mississippi review (Online ed.)
 13  210 0     Miss. rev. $b (Online ed.)
 14  222 4     The Mississippi review $b (Online ed.)
 15  245 04    The Mississippi review $h [computer file] : $b TMR.
 16  246 1     $i "About MR" screen contains the title: $a Mississippi
review Web
 17  246 1     $i Document source title: $a Mississippi review Web ed.
 18  246 30    TMR
 19  250       Online ed.
 20  260       Hattiesburg, MS : $b The Center for Writers, University of
Southern Mississippi, $c c1996-
 21  310       Monthly, except Aug.
 22  362 0     Vol. 1 no. 1 (Apr. 1995)-
 23  500       Title from back issues table of contents screen.
 24  516       HTML encoded text and image files (electronic journal)
```

```
25  530      Print version: Mississippi review.
26  538      Mode of access: World Wide Web.
27  710 2    University of Southern Mississippi. $b Center for Writers.
28  776 1    $t Mississippi review $x 0047-7559 $w (DLC)    72620236
29  856 7    $u http://sushi.st.usm.edu/mrw $2 http
```

14.
```
OCLC:  35253209             Rec stat:    c
Entered:    19960816        Replaced:    19960816    Used:    19960816
Type:  m    ELvl:  7        Srce:  d     Audn:       Ctrl:        Lang:   eng
BLvl:  s    File:  d        GPub:                    MRec:        Ctry:   mdu
Desc:  a                                 DtSt:  c    Dates: 1996,9999
 1  010      sn96-4418
 2  040      NSD $c NSD
 3  006      [serlp        0    a0]
 4  007      c $b r $d c $e n $f u
 5  012      $1 1
 6  022 0    1090-3062
 7  042      nsdp $a msc
 8  082 10   005 $2 12
 9  090      $b
10  049      NSDP
11  210 0    Agentnews weblett.
12  222 0    Agentnews webletter
13  245 00   Agentnews webletter $h [computer file] / $c UMBC Laboratory
for Advanced Information Technology.
14  246 1    $i ASCII format issues v. 1, no. 1-v. 1, no. 6 have the
title: $a Agentnews service
15  246 1    $i Some issues (HTML and ASCII) have the title: $a Agentnews
webletter and mailing lists
16  246 1    UMBC agentnews webletter
17  246 30   Agentnews
18  260      Baltimore : $b The Laboratory, $c c1996-
19  310      Biweekly
20  362 0    Vol. 1, no. 1 (Jan. 1, 1996)-
21  538      Mode of access: World Wide Web and Internet email.
22  500      Title from title screen.
23  500      HTML issues for July 6, 1996-   have at head of title: UMBC.
24  516      HTML, PostScript and ASCII formats
25  710 2    University of Maryland, Baltimore County. $b Laboratory for
Advanced Information Technology.
26  856 7    $u http://www.cs.umbc.edu/agentnews/ $2 http
27  856 0    cs.umbc.edu $h MAJORDOMO $i subscribe agentnews
28  936      Vol. 1, no. 12 (Aug. 12, 1996) LIC
```

15.
```
OCLC:  32864544             Rec stat:    c
Entered:    19950724        Replaced:    19970909    Used:    19961203
Type:  m    ELvl:           Srce:  d     Audn:       Ctrl:        Lang:   eng
BLvl:  s    File:  d        GPub:                    MRec:        Ctry:   wiu
Desc:  a                                 DtSt:  c    Dates: 199u,9999
 1  010      sn97-3375
 2  040      EYM $c EYM $d OCL $d EYM $d NSD
 3  006      [swrlp        0    a0]
 4  007      c $b r $d c $e n $f u
 5  012      $1 1
 6  022 0    1092-3861
 7  042      nsdp $a msc
 8  082 10   025 $2 12
 9  090      $b
10  049      NSDP
11  130 0    Scout report (InterNIC Information Services)
12  210 0    Scout rep. - InterNIC Inf. Serv.
13  222 0    Scout report - InterNIC Information Services
14  245 04   The scout report [computer file] : $b a service to the
Internet community provided by the InterNIC.
15  246 1    $i List name: $a SCOUT-REPORT
16  260      [Herndon, Va.] : $b InterNIC,
17  310      Weekly
18  500      Description based on printout of online display of: Apr. 28,
1995; title from caption.
19  516 8    Electronic serial in ASCII, HTML, and pdf formats
20  538      Mode of access: Electronic mail and World Wide Web.
21  550      Published: Madison (Wis.) : Net Scout Services, Dec. 1, 1995-
```

```
22  650  0   Internet (Computer network) $x Periodicals.
23  710  2   InterNIC Information Services.
24  710  2   Net Scout Services.
25  856  0   $z Email subscription-- ASCII version: $a lists.internic.net
$f SCOUT-REPORT $h listserv $i subscribe
26  856  0   $z Email subscription-- HTML version: $a lists.internic.net
$f SCOUT-REPORT-HTML $h listserv $i subscribe
27  856  7   $u http://rs.internic.net/scout/report/ $2 http
28  856  7   $u http://www.cs.wisc.edu/scout/report/ $2 http
29  936      Jan. 10, 1997 LIC
```

16.

OCLC:	36630727	Rec stat:	c		
Entered:	19970326	Replaced:	19970909	Used:	19970909
Type: m	ELvl:	Srce: d	Audn:	Ctrl:	Lang: eng
BLvl:	File: d	GPub:		MRec:	Ctry: xxu
Desc: a			DtSt: c	Dates: 1995,9999	

```
 1  010      sn97-3677
 2  040      NSD $c NSD
 3  006      [smrlp      0    a0]
 4  007      c $b r $d c $e n $f u
 5  012      $1 1
 6  022  0   1093-2909
 7  037      $b ATPM, 14 Gates Road, Etna, NH 03750 $c Free
 8  042      nsdp $a lcd
 9  082  10  004 $2 12
10  090      $b
11  049      NSDP
12  210  0   About part. Macintosh
13  222  0   About this particular Macintosh
14  245  00  About this particular Macintosh $h [computer file] : $b ATPM.
15  246  30  ATPM
16  260      [U.S.] : $b R.D. Novo : $b Only Boy Productions,
17  310      Monthly
18  362  1   Began in 1995?
19  500      Publisher: MT/RPL Production, Oct. 26, 1996-
20  500      Description based on: Vol. 2, no. 5 (May 22, 1996); title
from title screen.
21  516      Macintosh DOCMaker and HTML (electronic serial)
22  538      Mode of access: World Wide Web.
23  856  7   $u http://www.atpm.com $2 http
24  856  0   atpm.com $h subscribe
25  936      Oct. 26, 1996 LIC
```

17.

OCLC:	37134791	Rec stat:	n		
Entered:	19970617	Replaced:	19970617	Used:	19970617
Type: m	ELvl: 7	Srce: d	Audn:	Ctrl:	Lang: eng
BLvl: s	File: d	GPub:		MRec:	Ctry: alu
Desc: a			DtSt: c	Dates: 1996,9999	

```
 1  010      sn97-4202
 2  040      NSD $c NSD
 3  006      [smrlp      0    a0]
 4  007      c $b r $d c $e n $f u
 5  012      $1 1
 6  022  0   1094-3471
 7  037      $b The Rock, P.O. Box 240, Waverly, AL 36879-0240 $c Free
 8  042      nsdp $a msc
 9  082  10  808 $2 12
10  090      $b
11  049      NSDP
12  130  0   Rock (Waverly, Ala.)
13  210  0   Rock $b (Waverly Ala.)
14  222  0   The rock $b (Waverly, Ala.)
15  245  04  The rock $h [computer file].
16  260      Waverly, AL : $b Painted Rock Writers and Readers Colony, $c
c1996-
17  310      Monthly
18  362  0   Vol. 1, no. 1 (July 1996)-
19  500      Title from title screen.
20  516      Current issue is available in HTML and ASCII text format;
back
issues for July 1996-Mar.-Apr. 1997 are available only in pdf format; back
issues for May 1, 1997-  are available only as ASCII text
```

```
21  538     Mode of access: World Wide Web.
22  710  2  Painted Rock Writers and Readers Colony.
23  856  7  $u http://www.paintedrock.com/memvis/rockmag/rockmag.htm $2
http
24  856  0  $u mailto:prock-on@mail-list.com $i Text version available by
email request
```

18.
```
OCLC:  36035717            Rec stat:   n
Entered:   19961205        Replaced:   19961205      Used:    19961205
Type: m      ELvl:  7      Srce:  d    Audn:         Ctrl:      Lang:  chi
BLvl: s      File:  d      GPub:                     MRec:      Ctry:  ilu
Desc: a                                DtSt:  c      Dates: 1996,9999
 1  010     sn96-3732
 2  040     NSD $c NSD
 3  006     [smr1p     0   e0]
 4  007     c $b r $d c $e n $f u
 5  012     $l 1
 6  022  0  1091-9562
 7  037     $b China and the World, 5006 S. Blackstone Ave., #302,
Chicago, IL 60615
 8  042     nsdp $a msc
 9  082 10  951 $2 12
10  090     $b
11  049     NSDP
12  210  0  Zhong-guo yu shi jie
14  245 00  Chung-kuo y u shih chieh $h [computer file].
15  246  1  $i Title appears in English on journal homepage: $a China and
the world
16  260     [Chicago, Ill.] : $b China and the World, $c c1996-
17  310     Monthly
18  362  0  1996 nien ti 1 ch i-
19  500     Title from title screen.
20  515     Issues for ti 1 ch i-   called also tsung ti 1 ch i-
21  516     Available in GB, BIG5, and HZ formats for online viewing;
some issues also available in Postscript version for downloading and
printing offline
22  538     System requirements: downloadable software to view Chinese
characters in GB, BIG5 or HZ formats; postscript printer.
23  538     Mode of access: World Wide Web.
24  856  7  http://www.chinabulletin.com $2 http
```

19.
```
OCLC:  35014713            Rec stat:   c
Entered:   19960701        Replaced:   19970909      Used:    19960709
Type: m      ELvl:         Srce:  d    Audn:         Ctrl:      Lang:  eng
BLvl: s      File:  e      GPub:                     MRec:      Ctry:  cau
Desc: a                                DtSt:  c      Dates: 1995,9999
 1  010     sn96-4229
 2  040     CAW $c CAW $d NSD
 3  006     [sqr1p  cb   0   a0]
 4  007     c $b r $d c $e n $f u
 5  012     $l 1
 6  022  0  1089-5337
 7  042     nsdp $a lcd
 8  043     n-us-ca
 9  082 10  500 $2 12
10  090     $b
11  049     NSDP
12  110  2  California Academy of Sciences. $b Library.
13  210  0  Sel. new acquis. - Calif. Acad. Sci., Libr. $b (Online)
14  222  0  Selected new acquisitions - California Academy of Sciences.
Library $b (Online)
15  240 10  Selected new acquisitions (California Academy of Sciences.
Library : Online)
16  245 10  Selected new acquisitions $h [computer file] / $c California
Academy of Sciences Library.
17  246  1  $i HTML source title: $a CAS Library acquisitions
18  246  2  California Academy of Sciences Library selected new
acquisitions
19  260     [San Francisco, Calif. : $b The Library, $c 1995-
20  310     Quarterly
21  362  0  Jan.-Mar. 1995-
22  538     System requirements: Computer with modem or direct Internet
```

```
connection; World Wide Web browser.
  23  538     Mode of access: Internet World Wide Web. URL:
http://CAS.calacademy.org/%7Elibrary/newacq/
  24  500     Title from title screen.
  25  516     Electronic journal in HTML format
  26  580     With Apr.-June 1995 supersedes print publication of same
title.
  27  610 20  California Academy of Sciences. $b Library $x Catalogs $x
Periodicals.
  28  650  0  Natural history libraries $z California $z San Francisco $x
Catalogs $x Periodicals.
  29  650  0  Natural history $x Bibliography $x Catalogs $x Periodicals.
  30  655  7  Computer network resources. $2 local
  31  780 10  California Academy of Sciences. Library. $t Selected new
acquisitions $x 1065-7703 $w (DLC)sn 92006095 $w (OCoLC)26731912
  32  856  7  $u http://CAS.calacademy.org/%7Elibrary/newacq/ $2 http

20.
OCLC:   35750874              Rec stat:    c
Entered:     19961017         Replaced:    19970909      Used:     19970909
Type:  m     ELvl:  7         Srce:  d     Audn:         Ctrl:        Lang:  eng
BLvl:  s     File:  d         GPub:                      MRec:        Ctry:  cau
Desc:  a                                   DtSt:  c      Dates: 1996,9999
  1  010       sn96-4896
  2  040       NSD $c NSD
  3  006       [s x1         0   a0]
  4  007       c $b r $d c $e n $f u
  5  012       $l 1
  6  022 0     1091-3114
  7  037       $b Al Rainey, 38300 30th St. East #465, Palmdale, CA 93550
  8  042       nsdp $a lcd
  9  082 10    291 $2 12
 10  090       $b
 11  049       NSDP
 12  210 0     Cosm. curr. news online
 13  222  0    Cosmic current news online
 14  245 00    Cosmic current news online $h [computer file].
 15  260       Palmdale, CA : $b Al Rainey, $c c1996-
 16  310       Irregular
 17  362 0     #1-
 18  500       Title from title screen.
 19  516       HTML encoded text and image files (electronic newsletter)
 20  538       Mode of access: World Wide Web.
 21  780 00    $t Cosmic current news $x 1043-0180 $w (DLC)sn 89006279
 22  856  7    $u http://www.netport.com/rainey/index.html $2 http

21.
OCLC:   34872116              Rec stat:    c
Entered:     19960605         Replaced:    19960605      Used:     19960620
Type:  m     ELvl:  7         Srce:  d     Audn:         Ctrl:        Lang:  eng
BLvl:  s     File:  d         GPub:                      MRec:        Ctry:  txu
Desc:  a                                   DtSt:  c      Dates: 19uu,9999
  1  010       sn96-4080
  2  040       NSD $c NSD
  3  006       [sqr1p        0   a0]
  4  007       c $b r $d n $e n
  5  012       $l 1
  6  022 0     1076-836X
  7  037       $b Society of Systematic Biologists, c/o D. Cannatella, Texas
Memorial Museum, 2400 Trinity, University of Texas, Austin, TX 78705
  8  042       nsdp $a lcd
  9  082 10    572 $2 12
 10  090       $b
 11  049       NSDP
 12  130 0     Systematic biology (Online)
 13  210 0     Syst. biol. $b (Online)
 14  222  0    Systematic biology $b (Online)
 15  245 00    Systematic biology $h [computer file].
 16  260       [Austin, Tex.] : $b Society of Systematic Biologists,
 17  310       Quarterly
 18  538       Mode of access: World Wide Web.
 19  500       Description based on: Vol. 44, no. 1 (Mar. 1995); title from
title screen.
 20  530       Contains articles issued in the print version: Systematic
```

```
biology.
 21  710 2   Society of Systematic Biologists.
 22  776 1   $t Systematic biology $x 1063-5157 $w (DLC)   92641595
 23  856 7   $u http://www.utexas.edu/ftp/depts/systbiol $2 http

22.
 OCLC:  34060720              Rec stat:    c
 Entered:   19960122          Replaced:    19970909     Used:    19970707
 Type:  m      ELvl:          Srce:  d     Audn:        Ctrl:        Lang:  eng
 BLvl:  s      File:  d       GPub:  s                  MRec:        Ctry:  azu
 Desc:  a                                  DtSt:  c     Dates: 1994,9999
  1  010       sn95-15561
  2  040       AGL $c AGL $d OCL $d DLC $d NSD
  3  006       [sfr1p     s0    a0]
  4  007       c $b r $d c $e n $f u
  5  012       $l 1
  6  022  0    1092-5481
  7  042       lcd $a nsdp
  8  070  0    S612.A7532
  9  072  0    B200
 10  082  10   333 $2 12
 11  090       $b
 12  049       NSDP
 13  130  0    Arid lands newsletter (Online)
 14  210  0    Arid lands newsl. $b (Online)
 15  222  0    Arid lands newsletter $b (Online)
 16  245  00   Arid lands newsletter $h [computer file].
 17  246  1    $i Home page title: $a Aridlands newsletter
 18  260       Tucson, Ariz. : $b Office of Arid Lands Studies, University
of Arizona, $c 1994-
 19  310       Semiannual
 20  362  0    No. 35 (spring/summer 1994)-
 21  500       Title from title screen.
 22  516       Text (electronic journal)
 23  520       International newsletter for exploring events and issues of
interest to arid lands researchers, resource managers, and policy makers.
 24  530       Also available in paper.
 25  538       Mode of access: World Wide Web and Internet email.
 26  650  0    Arid regions $x Periodicals.
 27  710  2    University of Arizona. $b Office of Arid Lands Studies.
 28  776  1    $t Arid lands newsletter $x 0277-9455 $w (DLC)sn 81004117 $w
(OCoLC)5041908
 29  850       DNAL
 30  856  7    $u http://ag.arizona.edu/OALS/ALN/ALNHome.html $2 http
 31  856  0    ag.arizona.edu $h majordomo $i subscribe aridlands-nl
 32  936       No. 38 (fall/winter) 1995 LIC

23.
 OCLC:  34910227              Rec stat:    c
 Entered:   19960611          Replaced:    19970909     Used:    19970909
 Type:  m      ELvl:  7       Srce:  d     Audn:        Ctrl:        Lang:  eng
 BLvl:  s      File:  d       GPub:                     MRec:        Ctry:  oru
 Desc:  a                                  DtSt:  c     Dates: 1996,9999
  1  010       sn96-4149
  2  040       NSD $c NSD
  3  006       [smr1p       0    a0]
  4  007       c $b r $d c $e n $f u
  5  012       $l 1
  6  022  0    1089-1897
  7  037       $b Iris Communications, Inc., PO Box 5920, Eugene OR 97405 $c
$49.00
  8  042       nsdp $a lcd
  9  082  10   691 $2 12
 10  090       $b
 11  049       NSDP
 12  210  0    REDI $b (Eugene Or.)
 13  222  0    REDI $b (Eugene, Or.)
 14  245  00   REDI $h [computer file].
 15  246  2    Resources for environmental design index
 16  260       Eugene, OR : $b Iris Communications, Inc.,
 17  362  1    Began in 1996.
 18  538       Mode of access: Internet via World Wide Web.
 19  500       Description based on: June 7, 1996; title from title screen.
 20  515       Issues for June 7, 1996-  also called: 96-
```

```
21  516     Text (electronic journal)
22  856  7  $u http://oikos.com/redi/ $2 http
```

24.
```
OCLC:  35869624         Rec stat:    c
Entered:   19961108     Replaced:    19970723    Used:     19970723
Type:  m    ELvl:  7    Srce:  d     Audn:       Ctrl:     Lang:  eng
BLvl:  s    File:  d    GPub:                    MRec:     Ctry:  ilu
Desc:  a                             DtSt:  c    Dates: 1995,9999
 1  010     sn96-3795
 2  040     NSD $c NSD
 3  006     [scrlp      0    a0]
 4  007     c $b r $d c $e n $f u
 5  012     $l 1
 6  022  0  1091-6202
 7  042     nsdp $a lcd
 8  082 10  051 $2 12
 9  090     $b
10  049     NSDP
11  210  0  Wkly. bookmark, Stand.
12  222  4  The weekly bookmark. Standard
13  245 04  The weekly bookmark. $p Standard $h [computer file].
14  246  1  $i Title on table of contents screen: $a WBS
15  260     [DeKalb, Ill.] : $b Matt Alberts, $c [1995-
16  310     Semiweekly
17  362  0  V1.01 (Sept. 18, 1995)-
18  500     Title from title screen.
19  516     Text (electronic serial)
20  538     Mode of access: World Wide Web.
21  856  7  $u http://www.weeklyb.com/ $2 http
22  856  0  weeklyb.com $h majordomo $i subscribe wbs
```

25.
```
OCLC:  35869653         Rec stat:    c
Entered:   19961108     Replaced:    19970723    Used:     19970723
Type:  m    ELvl:  7    Srce:  d     Audn:       Ctrl:     Lang:  eng
BLvl:  s    File:  d    GPub:                    MRec:     Ctry:  ilu
Desc:  a                             DtSt:  c    Dates: 1996,9999
 1  010     sn96-3793
 2  040     NSD $c NSD
 3  006     [scrlp      0    a0]
 4  007     c $b r $d c $e n $f u
 5  012     $l 1
 6  022  0  1091-6210
 7  042     nsdp $a lcd
 8  082 10  051 $2 12
 9  090     $b
10  049     NSDP
11  210  0  Wkly. bookmark, Plus
12  222  4  The weekly bookmark. Plus
13  245 04  The weekly bookmark. $p Plus $h [computer file].
14  246  1  $i Title on table of contents screen: $a WBP
15  260     [DeKalb, Ill.] : $b Matt Alberts, $c c1996-
16  310     Semiweekly
17  362  0  Vol. 2, no. 26 (May 24, 1996)-
18  500     Title from title screen.
19  515     Volume numbering follows the numbering of: The weekly
bookmark. Standard.
20  516     Text (electronic serial)
21  538     Mode of access: World Wide Web.
22  856  7  $u http://www.weeklyb.com/ $2 http
23  856  0  weeklyb.com $h majordomo $i subscribe wbp
```

26.
```
OCLC:  37027575         Rec stat:    c
Entered:   19970606     Replaced:    19970909    Used:     19970909
Type:  m    ELvl:  7    Srce:  d     Audn:       Ctrl:     Lang:  eng
BLvl:  s    File:  d    GPub:                    MRec:     Ctry:  nyu
Desc:  a                             DtSt:  c    Dates: 199u,9999
 1  010     sn97-4132
 2  040     NSD $c NSD
 3  006     [scrlp      0    a0]
 4  007     c $b r $d c $e n $f u
 5  012     $l 1
 6  022  0  1094-2238
```

```
 7  037        $b Internet Tourbus, PO Box 39, Tillson, NY 12486
 8  041 0      engspa
 9  042        nsdp $a lcd
10  082 10     384 $2 12
11  090        $b
12  049        NSDP
13  210 0      Internet tourbus
14  222  4     The Internet tourbus
15  245 04     The Internet tourbus $h [computer file].
16  246 1      $i Some issue have the title: $a Tourbus
17  260        [Tillson, N.Y.] : $b Bob Rankin and Patrick Crispen,
18  310        Twice weekly
19  500        Description based on: Jan. 9, 1996; title from introductory
screen.
20  516        Text (ASCII) (email newsletter)
21  546        In English and Spanish.
22  538        Mode of access: Internet email; archived messages available
via World Wide Web.
23  856 7      $u http://www.tourbus.com $2 http
24  856 0      $u mailto:listserv@listserv.aol.com $i Send SUBSCRIBE TOURBUS
```

A Square Peg in a Round Hole:
Applying *AACR2* to Electronic Journals

Steven C. Shadle

SUMMARY. With the widespread use and acceptance of electronic journals, catalogers have been confronted with the problem of applying a paper-based cataloging code to the developing environment of the electronic serial. This article will review the problems inherent in applying *AACR2* to electronic journals and discuss the current policies and strategies the serials cataloging community has developed to address those problems. *[Article copies available for a fee from The Haworth Document Delivery Service: 1-800-342-9678. E-mail address: getinfo@haworth.com]*

KEYWORDS. Electronic journals, serials cataloging, Anglo-American Cataloguing Rules

INTRODUCTION

To some degree, it's been said the *Anglo-American Cataloguing Rules* (*AACR*) and the International Standard Bibliographic Description (ISBD) were written largely for a print, monograph world and that the descriptive bibliographic standards for serials

Steven C. Shadle is a Serials Cataloger, University of Washington Libraries, Box 352900, Seattle, WA 98195, USA (email: shadle@u.washington.edu).

[Haworth co-indexing entry note]: "A Square Peg in a Round Hole: Applying *AACR2* to Electronic Journals." Shadle, Steven C. Co-published simultaneously in *The Serials Librarian* (The Haworth Press, Inc.) Vol. 33, No. 1/2, 1998, pp. 147-166; and: *E-Serials: Publishers, Libraries, Users, and Standards* (ed: Wayne Jones) The Haworth Press, Inc., 1998, pp. 147-166. Single or multiple copies of this article are available for a fee from The Haworth Document Delivery Service [1-800-342-9678, 9:00 a.m. - 5:00 p.m. (EST). E-mail address: getinfo@haworth.com].

147

and for other physical formats are variations on those basic standards. Or if that is too strong a statement, one can at least say that there are certain principles, such as:

- transcription from an item can serve as the basis for bibliographic identification
- sources can be consistently identified on an item that can be used for transcribing bibliographic information
- an item's physical format is the basis for bibliographic description

that work relatively well for static, monographic items and have been applied to the cataloging of materials in all formats.

With the use of the Internet as a supplement to, or replacement for, the traditional publishing process, the flaws of a cataloging code developed for a different information environment are becoming more apparent. This article will examine some specific problematic areas in the current American cataloging code (*Anglo-American Cataloguing Rules*, 2nd ed. 1988 revision [*AACR2*]) that affect the bibliographic description of electronic journals and will discuss the current policies and practices that the serials cataloging community has developed as interim solutions to address those problems.

BACKGROUND

Anderson and Hawkins provide a good up-to-date overview of the developments in cataloging standards for computer files. These include the development of *AACR2* Chapter 9, developments in USMARC to accommodate Internet resources (specifically the 008, 256, 516 and 856 fields) and developments in CONSER policies which were the results of early efforts to catalog electronic serials.[1] The resulting CONSER policies have been formally developed as Module 31 of the *CONSER Cataloging Manual: Remote Access Computer File Serials.*[2] Many of the examples and the discussion presented in this article are taken from that source.

DEFINITION OF A SERIAL,
OR "WHAT EXACTLY IS A JOURNAL, ANYWAY?"

A serial, as defined in *AACR2,* is

A publication in any medium issued in successive parts bearing numeric or chronological designations and intended to be continued indefinitely. Serials include periodicals; newspapers; annuals (reports, yearbooks, etc.); the journals, memoirs, proceedings, transactions, etc., of societies; and numbered monographic series.[3]

There are three conditions to be met under this definition in order for a publication to be considered a serial:

- It must be issued in successive parts
- The successive parts must have some type of unique identification
- There must be an intention to continue publication indefinitely

In her discussion of cataloging electronic journals, Geller provides four examples of self-identified electronic journals, two of which fail to fit the *AACR2* definition of a serial because they are not issued in uniquely identifiable successive parts.[4] The *Journal of Electronic Publishing* (*JEP*) provides what appears to be volume and issue numbering. When users access the home page at http://www.press.umich.edu/jep/ they are presented with a page identified as "Volume 3 Issue 1" with a list of links to current articles *and* links to Volumes 1 and 2 of *JEP*'s backlist. Clicking on the Volume 1 backlist link sends the user to a page headed "Volume 1, issues 1 and 2, January and February 1995." The user is presented with three links for searching the volume 1 archives by subject, author or title. The corresponding indexes provide information about which issue the article was originally published in by listing the date after the article title (e.g., 1/95). The first issue *could* be recreated (to a certain degree) by identifying those articles appearing in that first issue and rebundling them in some way. This "unbundling" of articles from their original issue seems to be a common characteristic of many electronic journals. *JEP* follows an organization common to many electronic journals of identifying a "current" issue (often using some kind of standard issue numbering) and then providing an archival database of articles from earlier issues.

The other issue-less journal which Geller describes was a publication of the University of Arizona School of Library Science entitled *Olive Tree*. It described itself as "a cumulative publication to which new articles are periodically added." This description sounds like a Web page with no identifiable issues, only links directly to articles. The use of the past tense in describing this publication is quite appropriate as any trace of the *Olive Tree* has disappeared from the UA School of Library Science Web space. But many examples can still be provided which fit this model of electronic journal as Web page. The ones that have the most potential for confusion are those which call themselves the electronic version of a print journal. Examples of these include:

- *The PM Zone:* an electronic version of *Popular Mechanics* that provides the contents of the current issue, archives of selected previous editorial content (organized topically) and much original material tailored specifically for the World Wide Web. (http://popularmechanics.com)
- *Frontiers in Bioscience,* which (like *JEP*) provides a current issue and archives of earlier articles organized by volume. There is also additional material consistently available in the current issue which is not in the print version. (http://www.bioscience.org/)
- *Red Tape: The Official Newsletter of the Government Documents Round Table of Michigan.* Each issue of the print version consists of a series of titled columns. The online version is organized by column title, not by issue, so that the columns of individual issues are accessible, but there is no online issue corresponding to the entire print issue. (http://www.lib.msu.edu/harris23/red%5Ftape/red%5Ftape.htm)

According to *AACR2*, all of these examples would be considered monographs as they are nonserial items.

Even though "publishers do not consciously set out to create serials as defined by *AACR2*,"[5] the journal publication pattern of successive issues has been closely enough identified with the genre of the journal ("users recognize journals because of their intrinsic characteristics, i.e., an assemblage of articles on various topics, usually with some unifying purpose, subject, slant, or field of enquiry"[6]) that the use of the *AACR2* successive issuance serial definition to identify journals has worked relatively well in catalogs to date. However, following the letter of *AACR2* in the cataloging of these items introduces two inconsistencies into the catalog:

- some electronic journals will be cataloged as serials and some as monographs depending on whether they fit the *AACR2* definition of a serial
- print journals which are cataloged as serials may have their electronic versions cataloged as monographs

Philosophically, these discrepancies may or may not cause problems. Jones, and Graham and Ringler both make the case that electronic journals which aren't serials should not be treated as such since there is functionality built into the serial record (serials control, successive records, ISSN) which is not necessary for the electronic journal not distributed in successive issues.[7,8] However, Jones also points out that treating electronic journals as monographs can create problems for systems which

> segregate their catalog records by type of material and bibliographic level, so that some resources calling themselves "journals" will not be found in the serials file of such systems. And this is not desirable from the point of view of addressing user expectations in such a system.[9]

Even if systems don't store serials records in separate files, many systems still use the information from serial specific fields (such as Leader byte 06/07, 006 byte 00) to identify serials. In addition, users have been known to use other areas of the serial record such as frequency (310/321), or subject headings (650 $x Periodicals) to identify serials. In cataloging issue-less electronic journals as monographs, these markers to provide identification for this genre of material will be lost.

Catalogers have developed a variety of strategies to help identify the journal nature of these items regardless of whether they fit the

AACR2 definition of a serial. Catalogers at the University of Michigan are using the non-standard general material designator (GMD) [*electronic serial*] to help users identify the nature of the resource from brief catalog displays. The *CONSER Cataloging Manual* suggests the use of the Type of Computer File or Data Note (USMARC 516) to help identify these resources:

> 516 *Electronic journal available in ASCII, Acrobat, and Post-Script file formats.*

In addition, the newly approved International Standard Bibliographic Description for Electronic Resources (ISBD(ER)) will be using a wider variety of specific material designators (SMDs), including the use of the terms "computer journal" and "computer newsletter." The intent is that these SMDs may eventually be used in the Computer File Characteristics field (USMARC 256). Other libraries are providing additional identification of these resources through the local use of genre/form headings or subdivisions (USMARC 655, 650$v) such as "Computer network resources" or "Electronic journals" and at least one major subject heading system (Medical Subject Headings) has established the use of "electronic journal" as a form subject subdivision. Additionally, many libraries are cataloging these resources as serials even though they don't fit the *AACR2* definition of a serial.

PROBLEMS OF BIBLIOGRAPHIC DESCRIPTION

The developing environment of the Internet has produced information resources that differ from print publications in significant ways:

- they are organized differently, often in distributed files or databases
- they are mutable
- they often have additional functionality
- they don't follow the same standards for display of bibliographic information

This next section will discuss some specific problems of bibliographic description that are commonly encountered in the process of cataloging electronic journals.

Identification of a First Issue, or "Where Have You Gone, Joe DiMaggio?"

Both *AACR2* 12.0B1 and the *CONSER Cataloging Manual* Module 3.1 instruct the cataloger to use the chief source of the first or earliest available issue as the primary source of transcription of the title and statement of responsibility. One of the advantages to using the first issue as the basis for bibliographic description is that the description will remain unchanged over the life of a serial title. Changes which will not result in the creation of a new bibliographic record (e.g., changes in imprint) are recorded in notes. This works well in the print environment where the issue is what a subscriber receives in the mail every month. It even works relatively well for serially issued direct-access computer files as the physical piece (either diskette, CD-ROM or magnetic tape) is understood to be the issue. However, with the Internet the delivery of information is no longer tied to the delivery of a physical object. The result is that electronic journals no longer need to be organized in issues in order to provide articles to their readers. So how to identify a first issue when no issue exists? In some cases, individual articles will have some type of numbering or date that can be used to identify it, thereby turning the article into the "successive part" that was formerly the issue. As seen earlier, another common pattern is to see evidence of original issue numbering which is no longer used to organize articles on the Web site as the issues themselves have been unbundled. This appears to be the case in *JEP* where there is evidence from the archive page that there was originally a Volume 1, Issue 1 dated January 1995. Many catalogers are using this as a first issue and attempt to create a bibliographic description by transcribing information from the individual articles if possible.

The publications of Project Muse (http://muse.jhu.edu) present another case in point. The home page for a specific journal provides links to the tables of contents to specific issues. The tables of contents then provide links to the individual articles. In one respect, the issue consists of the table of contents of a specific issue and the individual articles which are linked to that table of contents. In many catalogers' judgment these pages would serve as the first issue and potentially the chief source for transcription. Generally in a print journal, an issue will have additional sources such as cover, masthead, colophon, editorial or publisher statements, etc., that are formal presentations of bibliographic information by the publisher. In print journals, the more formal presentations of title page, cover or masthead generally provide the basis for transcription. These additional sources are necessary in the print journal as the individual issues serve as a delivery mechanism and therefore must be identifiable. However, in electronic journals, this same information is provided in abbreviated form or not at all at the issue level, but instead is provided at a higher level, such as a journal home page. Many catalogers consider the presentation of bibliographic information at the home page to be the equivalent of the title page or cover of a journal (even though it isn't specific to an individual issue) and will cite this source as the chief source, instead of an issue-specific source.

One interesting development is that some resources which have previously been described as not providing distinct issues online (such as the *CONSER Cataloging Manual*'s reference to *Mother Jones*) are now providing access to articles through the use of distinctive issues. One can only hope that publishers have begun to recognize that the unique identification of successive parts (whether articles or issues) will help with article identification and citation.

Identifying the Chief Source, or "A Title Screen by Any Other Name"

This is another interesting example of applying a print analogy to a non-print medium. The chief source for print serials is the title page or title page substitute. The *AACR2* definition of a title page is:

> A page at the beginning of an item bearing the title proper and usually, though not necessarily, the statement of responsibility and the data relating to publication.[10]

In addition, the *CONSER Cataloging Manual* gives further guidance on what does *not* constitute a title page:

A title page is not: a page that contains text, tables of contents, or extensive editorial information, i.e., a page that has been designed to fulfill a different function.[11]

The title page is identified because its function is to provide the formal presentation of title and possibly statement of responsibility and publication information. This is an important point in cataloging print journals because so few journal publishers dedicate an entire page of a journal to provide a formal presentation of title, instead incorporating the presentation of the title into other sources (e.g., cover, masthead, table of contents, text). *AACR2* provides an ordered list of title page substitutes (analytic title page, cover, caption, masthead, editorial pages, colophon, other pages) to use in the case there is no title page.

Now, for computer files, the relevant rule from Chapter 9 (9.0B) states that the chief source of information for computer files is the title screen. The *AACR2* definition of a title screen is:

A display of data that includes the title proper and usually, though not necessarily, the statement of responsibility and the data relating to publication.[12]

Catalogers of direct-access computer files know exactly what a title screen is. On starting up a program, the title screen is usually the first or second screen that appears which briefly and formally displays the title and oftentimes a statement of responsibility or publication information. What truly identifies the title screen is that it appears for such a brief period of time, that the cataloger is required to reload the program several times in order to transcribe the appropriate information! As in the print model, the title screen is identified by its function of formally presenting the title. If this were not the case, then according to the strict definition of the term, any display of data that includes the title proper could be considered the title screen, resulting in a large number of sources, all of which could legitimately be called a title screen.

Unfortunately, electronic journals available over the Web generally follow the same practice as their print counterparts of not providing a display of data whose function is *solely* to provide a formal presentation of the title. Instead, there are a large number of possible sources for title transcription. These can include:

- the issue (if one exists)
- the home page or Web site of the journal
- source document metadata
- "about" or "readme" files
- links from other pages.

Unlike Chapter 12, Chapter 9 provides no additional guidance in choosing the title screen substitute other than:

In case of variation in fullness of information found in these sources, prefer the source with the most complete information.[13]

There is no ordered list of sources, so it is left to the cataloger's judgment to determine which source has the most complete information. An example of the kind of judgment required of a cataloger is illustrated in the cataloging of the newsletter of the Oregon Flora Project at: http://www.orst.edu/Dept/botany/herbarium/projects/ofn/index.html.

Figure 1 is the home page for the Project's newsletter. On this one screen there are several variant forms of title. "Oregon Flora Newsletter" is presented within the graphic at the head of the display. "Oregon Flora On-Line Newsletter" is presented formally as the title and is also tagged as the title in the source code. This is evident by the fact that it is appears in the window header. A look at the source code in Figure 2 will confirm that it has been marked-up as the title. "Oregon Flora Newsletter On-Line" is presented in the equivalent of a print journal masthead. In addition, the box which serves as a link to the top of the page has the title "Flora Newsletter."

Using a non-graphics based Web browser (such as Lynx) will produce the display seen in Figure 3. Note that the graphic which contained the title "Oregon Flora Newsletter" was replaced with the text "Welcome to the" which is grammatically connected to the formal title presentation "Oregon Flora On-Line Newsletter." A cataloger using this browser will not be aware of the other title presentation and would probably feel less ambivalent about the choice of title proper.

FIGURE 1. Home page of the *Oregon Flora Newsletter.*

The continuation of the original home page seen in Figure 4 provides the links to the individual articles. Note that the articles are organized into issues, but there is no page or source that serves as an actual issue. "OFN" is what appears as the title most closely associated with the issue itself at this point. In lieu of having an actual issue, should this link be chosen as the chief source?

Clicking on the first article of the first issue produces the display seen in Figure 5.

On what appears to be the first page of the first issue, there are only two title presentations. Although this presentation is similar to the home page presentation, the masthead title "The Oregon Flora Newsletter On-line" doesn't appear. It does appear that this banner is meant solely for the purpose of formally presenting the title. The *AACR2* definition of title screen talks about a "display of data" not about a "screen of data." Can this formal presentation be considered a separate display so that the use of the phrase "title screen" is appropriate to describe it? Or is this analogous to the case of a print

FIGURE 2. Source code of *Oregon Flora Newsletter* home page.

```
<html>

<body bgcolor=#FFFFFF>

<p align=center>

<IMG border=2 SRC="../../images/OFN_title.GIF" ALT="Welcome to

the">

</P>

<TITLE>Oregon Flora On-Line Newsletter</TITLE>

<H2 align=center>Oregon Flora On-Line Newsletter</H2>


The <cite>Oregon Flora Newsletter On-line</cite> is published three

times a year

and is a publication of the<A HREF="../OFP/ofp.html">Oregon Flora

Project</A> news. It

is edited by Rhoda Love and put on-line by Douglas Linn.<P>
```

newsletter, that the banner title is considered a caption title because it is given at the beginning of the first page of text? Library of Congress Rule Interpretation 12.0 states:

> If a serial lacking a title page has a title (the same title or different titles) on more than one source in the item, choose as the title page substitute the source that appears first in the preferred order of sources listed in the rule. *Use the entire page from which the title was taken as the title page substitute, not just the caption area, masthead area, etc.*[14] (author's emphasis)

By analogy, does this same concept apply to Web pages so that the entire Web document is considered a single source and the function

FIGURE 3. Home page of *Oregon Flora Newsletter* using a non-graphics browser.

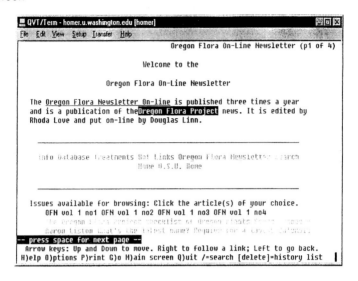

FIGURE 4. Continuation of home page of *Oregon Flora Newsletter.*

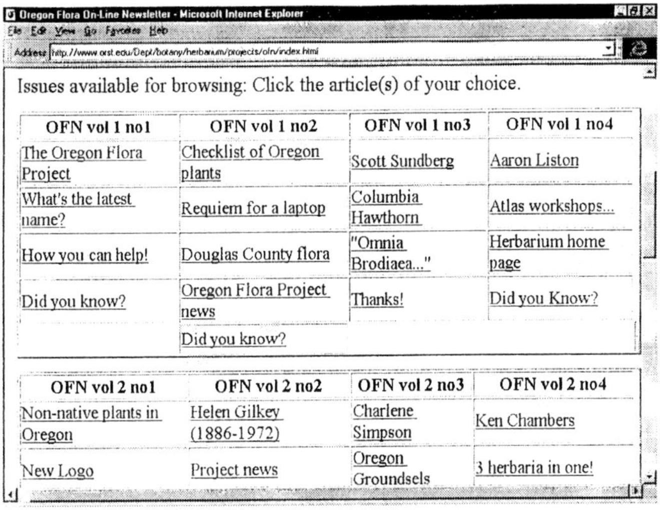

FIGURE 5. First article of first issue of *Oregon Flora Newsletter.*

of the entire document is considered to determine whether a source is a "title screen" or "home page"? And is it still appropriate to examine the issue to identify chief source, or is it more appropriate to examine formal presentations of the title which are not associated with a specific issue (e.g., home page) to identify the publication? The problems with the cataloging code that these questions have raised are:

- First issue may not be an appropriate chief source for identification and description of electronic journals.
- Just as with print journals, an ordered list of potential sources may help with inter-cataloger consistency.
- Chapter 9 needs to be updated to reflect the nature of the Web. This includes the introduction of Web terminology and changing concepts such as "title screen" which still work relatively well for direct-access computer file, but don't apply in the Web environment.

Additionally, Hirons and Graham recommend that the concept of chief source needs to be examined and possibly replaced with the concept of "source of title" which would allow for "greater flexibility in the selection of title within the parameters of the prescribed sources."[15]

General strategies for coping with this proliferation of titles and lack of specificity in the catalog code include:

- Always citing the source of title proper (this is required per *AACR* 9.7B3) and citing a specific source rather than "Title screen" unless the source primarily serves the specific function of a title screen. Users of text-based browser software may understand why the title that is cited in a bibliographic record isn't displayed if they know the title was taken from a graphic element.
- Generously using title added entries, so that other catalogers and users will be able to retrieve the catalog record no matter which title is considered *the* title.

Multiple File Formats, or "You Say Tomato. . . ."

Neither *AACR2* nor the Library of Congress Rule Interpretations (LCRIs) adequately address the reality that the same journal can be made available in a variety of formats which may differ. Are these different editions that require separate catalog records, or can one catalog record adequately describe several formats? *AACR2* is unclear as 9.2B generally refers to updated versions of files (e.g., Rev. ed., Version 5.20) and not to differing file formats (ASCII, PostScript, HTML). *AACR2* 9.2B3 cites as an optional addition providing an edition statement if one version is known to contain "significant changes" (e.g., changes in content, programming, or the addition of sound or graphics). This would imply that an ASCII version would be cataloged separately from its HTML version if the HTML version included illustrations. However, *AACR2* 9.2B4 states not to treat a version as a new edition if the differences are minor changes such as corrections, or changes in the arrangement of contents, in the output format or in the display medium.

With input from meetings and online discussion, CONSER decided to use a single-record approach for multiple file formats. Anderson and Hawkins cite the opinion that creating and maintaining a single record is more efficient both for catalogers and for catalog users. They also cite some potential disadvantages including "more complex records, less detailed information in the records, and greater difficulty in identifying the specific version made available at a specific site."[16]

Generally this information is recorded in the Type of Computer File or Data Note (USMARC 516):

> *516 Electronic journal available in ASCII, Acrobat, and Post-Script file formats.*

This information can also be represented by using multiple Electronic Location and Access fields (USMARC 856):

> *856 0 $z Email subscription: $a netsurf.com $f nsdigest-html (for the HTML version) $f nsdigest-text (for the ASCII version) $h nsdigest-request $i subscribe*

> *856 7 $z ASCII version: $u ftp://ftp.netsurf.com/pub/nsd/README $2 ftp*

> *856 7 $z HTML version: $u http://www.netsurf.com/nsd/index.html $2 http*

Mutability of Materials, or "All Is Flux, Nothing Stays Still"

In the world of *AACR2* title changes (specifically 21.2), works are either successively serial, single-part monographs which change from one edition to the next, or multi-part monographs which change from one physical part to the next. There is no allowance in the cataloging code for the mutable, single-part work. Hirons and Graham cite this as a problem in the current cataloging code that affects all ongoing publications which don't fit the *AACR2* serial definition whether they are loose-leaf publications, databases, Web sites or unnumbered series.[17] In their examination of serials cataloging principles, they cite several which don't lend themselves well to mutable, single-part works. Two that specifically have to do with the changing nature of these materials are:

- *Description based on earliest issue.* Bibliographic description based on the first issue is not practical for mutable, single-part works in which the earlier version of the chief source has completely disappeared. They recommend the retention of description based on earliest issue for publications issued successively, and description based on latest iteration for updated, single-part works. In the meantime, serials catalogers are still attempting to identify a date or numbering that can be used in a formatted 362 or a "description based on" note for electronic journals without issues.
- *Successive entry.* When all traces of an earlier title disappear, what is the purpose of creating or maintaining a bibliographic record for a nonexistent earlier title? Hirons and Graham recommend following a successive entry approach for successively issued publications and a latest entry approach for updated, single-part works. Some catalogers have experimented with this approach both locally and nationally by using "Title history" or "Previous title" title added entries, thus providing access for users who may find citations for a Web site or electronic journal under its previous title. However, CONSER policy as represented in the *CONSER Cataloging Manual* is to create a new record when a change in title or main entry occurs.[18]

Online Versions of Printed Serials, or "They Walk Alike, They Talk Alike. . . . "

As a final point, the CONSER interim policy to represent both a print serial and its online version with a single bibliographic record will be discussed. This policy allows for the noting of the existence and electronic location of the online version in the record for the printed serial by:

- Noting the availability of the online version in field 530;
- Identifying its electronic location in field 856.

Figure 6 shows that the only additions made to the print record are the additions of the 530 and 856 fields. This is very clearly *not* a multiple versions record as there is information specific to the

FIGURE 6. CONSER record for print version used to catalog the electronic version.

```
Type:   a     ELvl:         Srce:  d    GPub:        Ctrl:
Lang:  eng
BLvl:   s     Form:         Conf:  0    Freq:  m     MRec:
Ctry:  be
S/L:    0     Orig:         EntW:       Regl:  r     ISSN:
Alph:
Desc:   a     SrTp:  p      Cont:       DtSt:  c     Dates:
1996,9999
1   010       sn97-46009
2   040       MIA $c MIA $d PIT $d WAU
3   012       $i 9702
4   037       $b EUR-OP (Information Society News) 2, rue
Mercier (MER 193-195), L-2985, Luxembourg
5   042       lcd
6   043       e------
7   090       HE8081 $b .E875
8   090       $b
9   049       WAUW
10  110 2     European Commission. $b Information Society
Project Office.
11  245 10    Information Society news / $c ISPO.
12  246 10    IS news
13  246 13    ISPO Information society news
14  260       Brussels : $b ISPO, $c 1996-
15  300       v. : $b ill. ; $c 30 cm.
16  310       Monthly
17  362 0     No. 1 (Apr. 1996)-
18  530       Also available on the Internet via the World Wide
Web.
19  650  0    Telecommunication $z European Union countries $x
Periodicals.
20  650  0    Telecommunication policy $z European Union
countries $x Periodicals.
21  650  0    Information technology $z European Union
countries $x Periodicals.
22  610 20    European Commission. $b Information Society
Project Office $x Periodicals.
23  856 7     $z Online issues: $2 http $u
http://www.ispo.cec.be/ispo/newsletter/
24  850       PPiU $a WaU
25  936       No. 9 (Jan. 1997) LIC
```

online version (such as computer file characteristics) which is not noted in this record. *AACR2* requires that separate records would be created for versions in different physical formats. However, CONSER members may experiment with the one-record approach for versions for which they feel a separate record is not necessary. These are generally digital reproductions of print journals, online versions whose continued publication is questionable or online versions that may be difficult to separately catalog for whatever reason. Feedback so far has generally been good as it allows for the creation of separate records by those institutions which, for local reasons–such as subscription control or catalog access–are required to create separate records, yet it provides enough information on the print record so that users can access the electronic version of the resource. It can be a useful approach for many of the electronic journals cited in this article, for which the application of current cataloging practices can be problematic.

CONCLUSION

Many libraries have, with varying degrees of success, integrated electronic journals into their catalogs and Web catalogs are providing direct access to these journals. This paper has investigated those aspects of the current cataloging code which are not easily applicable to the environment of the electronic journal published and distributed on the Internet. Changes in the cataloging code will be required in order for the cataloging community to better integrate electronic journals into library catalogs and collections. A much more detailed and principled discussion of many of these same issues is available in "Issues Related to Seriality," a paper presented by Jean Hirons and Crystal Graham at the International Conference on the Principles and Future Development of *AACR*. The paper is currently available from the *AACR* Joint Steering Committee Website at: http://www.nlc-bnc.ca/jsc/confpap.htm.

NOTES

1. Bill Anderson and Les Hawkins, "Development of CONSER Cataloging Policies for Remote Access Computer File Serials," *The Public-Access Computer Systems Review* 7, no. 1 (1996): 8-12. Available: http://info.lib.uh.edu/pr/v7/n1/ande7n1.html

2. Melissa Beck, "Remote Access Computer File Serials," in *CONSER Cataloging Manual*, ed. Jean Hirons (Washington, DC: Library of Congress, 1996), Module 31. Available: http://lcweb.loc.gov/acq/conser/module31.html

3. *Anglo-American Cataloguing Rules*, 2nd ed., 1988 rev., eds. Michael Gorman and Paul W. Winkler (Ottawa: Canadian Library Association; Chicago: American Library Association, 1988), p. 622.

4. Marilyn Geller, "A Better Mousetrap is Still a Mousetrap," *Serials Review* 22, no. 1 (spring 1996): 72.

5. Ed Jones, "Serials in the Realm of the Remotely-Accessible: An Exploration," *Serials Review* 22, no. 1 (spring 1996): 77.

6. Jean Hirons and Crystal Graham, "Issues Related to Seriality" (paper presented at the International Conference on the Principles and Future Development of AACR, Toronto, Canada, Oct. 23-25, 1997), p. 18. Available: http://www. nlc-bnc.ca/jsc/confpap.htm

7. Jones, "Serials in the Realm," p. 78.

8. Crystal Graham and Rebecca Ringler, "Hermaphrodites & Herrings," *Serials Review* 22, no. 1 (spring 1996): 76.

9. Jones, "Serials in the Realm," p. 78.

10. *Anglo-American Cataloguing Rules*, p. 624.

11. *CONSER Cataloging Manual*, Module 3, p. 10.

12. *Anglo-American Cataloguing Rules*, p. 624.

13. *Anglo-American Cataloguing Rules*, p. 222.

14. *Library of Congress Rule Interpretations*, 2nd ed., ed. Robert M. Hiatt (Washington, D.C.: Cataloging Distribution Service, Library of Congress, 1989), 12.0B1, p. 1.

15. Hirons and Graham, "Issues Related to Seriality," p. 32-33.

16. Anderson and Hawkins, "Development of CONSER Cataloging Policies," p. 16.

17. Hirons and Graham, "Issues Related to Seriality," p. 30-35.

18. Beck, "Remote Access Computer File Serials," Module 31.19.

A Meditation on Metadata

Gregory Wool, MA, MLS

SUMMARY. Metadata, or "data about data," have been created and used for centuries in the print environment, though the term has its origins in the world of electronic information management. The close relationship between traditional library cataloging and the documentation of electronic data files (known as "metadata") is presented, showing that cataloging is changing under the influence of information technology, but also that metadata provision is essentially an extension of traditional cataloging processes. *[Article copies available for a fee from The Haworth Document Delivery Service: 1-800-342-9678. E-mail address: getinfo@haworth.com]*

KEYWORDS. Metadata, cataloging, definition, relationship, decision-making

INTRODUCTION

In the last few years the term "metadata" has become a buzzword in the realm of online information access. The word figures prominently in discussions of how to improve electronic data

Gregory Wool is Associate Professor and Monographs Cataloger at the Iowa State University Library, 209TS Parks Library, Ames, IA 50011, USA (email: gwool@iastate.edu).

The author wishes to thank Crystal Graham, Gerry McKiernan, and Kristin Gerhard for their comments and suggestions.

[Haworth co-indexing entry note]: "A Meditation on Metadata." Wool, Gregory. Co-published simultaneously in *The Serials Librarian* (The Haworth Press, Inc.) Vol. 33, No. 1/2, 1998, pp. 167-178; and: *E-Serials: Publishers, Libraries, Users, and Standards* (ed: Wayne Jones) The Haworth Press, Inc., 1998, pp. 167-178. Single or multiple copies of this article are available for a fee from The Haworth Document Delivery Service [1-800-342-9678, 9:00 a.m. - 5:00 p.m. (EST). E-mail address: getinfo@haworth.com].

retrieval. The Institute of Electrical and Electronics Engineers (IEEE) organizes conferences devoted entirely to metadata. At the same time Clifford Lynch has advised at least one audience of library catalogers that if they tell their directors they create metadata, they could improve their chances for a higher salary.[1]

This paper was written to help show how metadata can be applied to online serials. Its specific task, however, is to establish (with apologies to the late short-story writer Raymond Carver):

WHAT WE TALK ABOUT WHEN
WE TALK ABOUT METADATA

There are two overlapping but somewhat contradictory definitions of metadata worth considering. The first is from Priscilla Caplan, Assistant Director for Systems at the University of Chicago Library and a participant in the discussions which produced the Dublin Core metadata standard:

> Metadata really is nothing more than data about data; a catalog record is metadata; so is a TEI header, or any other form of description.[2]

The second is from the International Federation of Library Associations and Institutions (IFLA) "Metadata Resources" home page:

> Metadata is data about data. The term refers to any data used to aid the identification, description and location of networked electronic resources.[3]

Caplan's definition is preferable, because it encompasses the print as well as the online environment. It also reassures us that metadata are not something new and strange, but have been created and used for centuries, by publishers as well as librarians. At the same time, the more restrictive IFLA definition contributes to our understanding of the topic by reminding us of the term's origins in the world of digital information. It implies that metadata can take many forms, exist on many levels, and be manipulated in many ways in order to fulfill their stated purpose. It also implies that new approaches to metadata are not only possible but necessary.

So just as online serials represent a familiar document type with new characteristics and possibilities, metadata are essentially the cataloging and other identifying data that librarians (and other information workers) have always recorded and used–but with new forms and capabilities in the online environment. In addition–to the extent technology has allowed–such data have always been borrowed, adapted, and further distributed in the interests of promoting the efficient use of information. As such, metadata are the special province of librarians, who have a vital interest in ensuring that the right metadata are created, preserved, and put to optimal use. To alter slightly the old folk rhyme prescribing what a bride should wear on her wedding day for good luck, metadata are something old, something new, something borrowed, something we (i.e., librarians) "do."

METADATA AS SOMETHING OLD

The catalog record, usually containing such identifying information as title, author, publisher, subject categories, and physical description, is (to librarians at least) the most obvious metadata application in the print environment. Such "document surrogates" have been created probably as long as there have been libraries (and certainly since the Middle Ages) as components of a catalog–the authoritative record of a library's holdings, which functions as both a management tool and a finding aid for the library's users. For much of this century, bibliographic records from various libraries have been collected and published in "union catalogs" as well. Publishing firms also issue catalogs, listing for potential customers the titles they offer, usually with brief identifying data and perhaps tables or summaries of contents. Subject bibliographies have a long history, and their contents, too, are metadata.

Printed documents usually contain their own metadata, in the form of title pages, cover information, colophons, tables of contents and indexes. Such information, besides being transcribed in catalogs and bibliographies, is compiled and organized for access in periodical indexes and other reference databases. Metadata have long been used to locate not only books and journals, but also individual articles, chapters of books, and concepts within documents. Indexes and concordances employ words from the text itself as metadata.

Finally, metadata include the various sorts of information libraries keep about their serials for internal management purposes. Such items of interest as subscription cost, vendor used, issues checked in, binding status of volumes, and retention policies, while not bibliographic in nature, are just as surely "data about data" and warrant appropriate consideration in any metadata strategy.

Many of the metadata applications we see in the online information environment are extensions of techniques long used in the print domain, enhanced with uniquely online capabilities. Perhaps the most obvious is OCLC's Intercat project, which provides a hypertext link within a catalog record for an Internet resource for direct access to that resource.[4] This functionality can also be found in many of the new metadata schemes consciously or unconsciously modelled on library cataloging standards. Hotlinked subject "webliographies" and search engines matching natural-language queries to words or phrases in file headers serve as less obvious examples.

METADATA AS SOMETHING NEW

Though in many ways the forms and functions of metadata remain substantially the same in the online environment, and for online information objects, as with their print counterparts, the technology has brought structural innovations. These can be classified as new elements, new functionalities and new paradigms.

New Elements

The new elements actually result from the new technologies of data objects rather than those of information management systems. A good information manager will make available all the types of metadata necessary to answer common questions about a resource. Not surprisingly, electronic resources have a number of characteristics not found in printed materials. Moreover, there are multiple electronic resource formats (e.g., numeric data files, Websites,

CD-ROMs), each with its peculiar set of characteristics, and a new format seems to come along every few months. (Thus we have serials catalogers learning to record Uniform Resource Locators– URLs–for Web-based journals and required machine specifications for CD-ROMs.) Library standards such as *AACR2* and MARC have been scrambling to keep up, but with their need for general applicability, they cannot provide the level of detail for specialized formats their user groups demand. Hence there is a proliferation of metadata schemes for such resource types as geographic information system (GIS) coverages and humanities text files.

New Functionalities

Some of the new functionalities have been referred to already. The hotlinking of metadata elements in a catalog record, a title list, or elsewhere, accomplished through the use of Hypertext Markup Language (HTML), creates a direct link for the searcher from externally produced metadata to the item itself.[5] Through algorithms using such techniques as relevance ranking and concept mapping, search engines generate metadata on the fly while mimicking the performance of human indexers. Perhaps more significantly, the growing use of HTML and other applications of SGML (Standard Generalized Markup Language) creates a class of metadata that govern or facilitate retrieval and display while remaining hidden from the user.[6] Catalog and database search software can be configured to conceal metadata as well, whether for brief record displays or for natural-language search assistance.

New Paradigms

The development of computer storage and networked retrieval of information has resulted in at least two new paradigms for metadata which make it seem like a new phenomenon rather than the ancient art of cataloging in a new environment. One might be called the Database Paradigm. In it, metadata associated with a data object are recorded as attributes with values; the attributes are registered with definitions in a data dictionary. (This contrasts with the tagless, citations-with-annotations approach typical of catalog cards.) The metadata are stored in a record, which could display in full or in any possible subset (e.g., brief entries in a catalog or list of search results) depending on what choices are programmed. Metadata shared by several data objects may reside in a separate record linked to the objects' metadata records, especially if the metadata have cross references (for example, an author's name known in several forms).[7] Each metadata item is autonomous, depending only on its definition in the data dictionary and the identifier of the data object for its meaning, not on the other metadata; thus it can be displayed in a variety of sequences and tagging schemes without loss of meaning.

Online library catalogs using the MARC formats mimic the Database Paradigm, but critically lack an effective data dictionary, as records are still created using rules set up for a structured prose-like citation-with-annotations scheme (the International Standard Bibliographic Description, or ISBD), and then "translated" by the catalog software into a list of attributes and values. The redundancy, inflexibility, potential for confusion, and two-dimensionality that result are well-documented elsewhere.[8]

The Markup Paradigm involves the embedding of metadata in the data object, usually by tagging the data using an SGML document type definition. Typically SGML tagging is used to control the display of data, rather than describe the data object, but by marking data elements crucial to identification, it can index a data object and facilitate its direct retrieval. In addition, such tagging can be used to automatically generate catalog records. By contrast, printed books and serials contain metadata (on a title page, cover, or elsewhere) with either unstandardized or no tagging, making their interpretation by a trained cataloger necessary for future identification and retrieval. Perhaps the greatest potential for the Markup Paradigm involves the encoding of relationships within a body of data for use in data mining applications and precision retrieval systems based on artificial intelligence.[9]

METADATA AS SOMETHING BORROWED

At least since the invention of title pages, metadata have been attached to information objects by their creators or publishers and later adapted for catalog records and other third-party reference or management applications. The extent to which such information has been altered or used unchanged varies with the type of metadata as well as the metadata scheme being used. It has also varied over time; a look at North American cataloging standards over the past century reveals a trend, not so much away from interpretation and toward faithful transcription, as toward the recording of parallel versions of the same metadata: one transcribed verbatim from the item being described, a second altered as necessary to enable collocation with other records bearing the same characteristic (e.g., association with a particular person or corporate body), perhaps a third in encoded form. But an element of interpretation is always present in the reuse of author/publisher-supplied metadata, even when selecting the data to transcribe.[10]

With the growth in the number (and variety) of information objects outstripping that of the resources available for their management, interest in expanding the role of authors and publishers in creating metadata is greater than ever (as is, of course, interest in sharing metadata among libraries). Nearly a decade ago Maurice Line, a library consultant who had previously been an administrator of the British Library, proposed the creation of an "all-through system" whereby library catalog records would be produced by book publishers and sent to libraries along with the books.[11] While that has not yet materialized, many book jobbers and subscription vendors now offer catalog-ready records, whether created in-house or derived from a bibliographic utility, for the materials they supply. Increasingly, access to "virtual collections" on the Internet such as the Government Information Locator Service (GILS) and the National Engineering Education Delivery System (NEEDS) is built upon the use of metadata templates, with the producers of data objects filling in the values for a predefined list of attributes.[12] The Text Encoding Initiative (TEI) header standard is a more elaborate version of such a template (as well as one created and used more from a librarian's perspective), but its use of SGML also allows the same set of metadata to function as both a title page and a catalog record.[13]

Inevitably, though, increasing reliance on what might be called "source" metadata in the library environment (including Internet-based "digital libraries") raises the question of how such unstandardized metadata can be managed to improve retrieval effectiveness. Many players appear to be betting the farm on future breakthroughs in artificial intelligence, although human language (the very stuff of metadata) is notoriously resistant to machine comprehension. In the meantime, solutions mean finding the most effective ways to leverage the intervention of human organizers.

METADATA AS SOMETHING WE DO

If, then, people are to provide and manage the metadata needed to administer and maintain access to collections of recorded information, how does one get started? One ready answer might be, "Plug into an existing system." But which one? There are dozens. Next ready answer: "The one that best meets your needs." Ah, but what are those needs?

A few years ago I had the opportunity to build a prototype online catalog for remotely held (but not networked!) files of machine-readable databases and numeric data files. I found the following four-part question helpful in not only planning my work, but also explaining it to the agencies funding my project:

What kinds of information do you want to:

1. collect?
2. display?
3. label?
4. index?[14]

Seen as a decision model, this question has two underlying assumptions: first, each part represents a separate decision; second, the answer to each part determines the pool of choices for the next part. As may be surmised, this second assumption will not be entirely applicable to all metadata situations (e.g., one may want to index information but not display it in a record). Nonetheless the model can provide a useful framework for thinking about metadata because the question addresses not only the basic information need, but also the structure and use of the information.

Collect

This is the first cut. What sorts of information about your data objects will you want to make available, whether to an external audience or for internal management needs? Each type of information should be recorded for every data object as applicable. What will be done with the information is not at issue here. If it is not collected, it cannot be used.

Display

This refers to record displays for external users. Some things you may want to collect for internal use only. If there are multiple display formats (search results list entry, brief record, full record, in-between record, etc.) the decisions to be made are correspondingly multiplied.

Label

What separates this from the Display decision is that this puts the metadata into categories, at least for public display. (In relational database terms, it defines the attributes for which the metadata are values.) For example, you may choose to collect names of personal authors and of corporate authors, and to display them, but decide to use a single label for the two types of authors, thus creating a single category. For that matter, are editors "authors"? Here is where you would decide.

Index

Here you would decide what types of metadata users could search. In most online catalog systems, of course, several indexes are configured (typically for titles, authors/names, and subjects) and someone has to decide what types of data go into each one.

Some Added Wrinkles to the Decision-Making Process

With online catalog systems, of course, many of the decisions described above have been made during system configuration. On the other hand, in a client-server environment, the advent of clients that can search multiple database systems using the Z39.50 standard raises the possibility that searchers from remote sites will be able, through the configuration of their Z39.50 client, to make their own decisions regarding display, labeling, and indexing of your metadata.[15] This means that as far as possible, metadata should be recorded (and categorized) in a way that minimizes dependence on context for its meaning.[16]

CONCLUSION

The intent of this paper has been to demystify metadata for librarians by showing that cataloging and metadata collection are essentially the same task. It sets out to do so by emphasizing the broader definitions of both "cataloging" and "metadata," so that cataloging is seen to be more that just the creation of bibliographic records in libraries, and metadata, more than just the documentation of electronic datasets. In the process, two things should become apparent. One, cataloging is changing and will change further under the influence of online information technology. Two, the creation and maintenance of metadata for online serials are at most an extension of the processes used in online cataloging and catalog maintenance for their printed counterparts.

NOTES

1. Clifford Lynch, "Descriptive Cataloging Hits the Net: Metadata, Uniform Resource Identifier Systems and New Descriptive Requirements" (paper presented at "AACR2000: Toward the Future of the Descriptive Cataloging Rules," pre-conference institute sponsored by the Association for Library Collections and Technical Services, Chicago, Ill., June 22, 1995).
2. Priscilla Caplan, "You Call It Corn, We Call It Syntax-Independent Metadata for Document-Like Objects," *The Public-Access Computer Systems Review* 6, no. 4 (1995). Available: http://info.lib.uh.edu/pr/v6/n4/cap16n4.html
3. International Federation of Library Associations, *Digital Libraries: Metadata Resources*. Available: http://www.nlc-bnc.ca/ifla/II/metadata.htm
4. Cf. *Intercat: A Catalog of Internet Resources*. Available: http://orc.rsch.oclc.org:6990/
5. Cf. W3C, *Hypertext Markup Language (HTML)*. Available: http://www.w3.org/pub/WWW/MarkUp/MarkUp.html

6. Cf. David Seaman, "About SGML." Available: http://etext.lib.virginia. edu/sgml.html.

7. Proposals for this type of functionality in online catalogs can be found in Michael Carpenter, "Does Cataloging Theory Rest on a Mistake?" in *Origins, Content, and Future of AACR2 Revised*, ed. Richard P. Smiraglia (Chicago: American Library Association, 1992), 98-100; Michael Gorman, "After *AACR2R*: The Future of the Anglo-American Cataloging Rules," in *Origins*, 91-93; and Barbara B. Tillett, "Bibliographic Structures: The Evolution of Catalog Entries, References, and Tracings," in *The Conceptual Foundations of Descriptive Cataloging*, ed. Elaine Svenonius (San Diego, Calif.: Academic, 1989), 161-162.

8. Cf. Gregory H. Leazer, "An Examination of Data Elements for Bibliographic Description: Toward a Conceptual Schema for the USMARC Formats," *Library Resources & Technical Services* 36 (Apr. 1992): 189-208; Michael Heaney, "Object-Oriented Cataloging," *Information Technology and Libraries* 14 (Sept. 1995): 135-153; Gregory J. Wool et al., "Cataloging Standards and Machine Translation: A Study of Reformatted ISBD Records in an Online Catalog," *Information Technology and Libraries* 12 (Dec. 1993): 383-403.

9. "Data mining (also known as Knowledge Discovery in Databases-KDD) has been defined as 'the nontrivial extraction of implicit, previously unknown, and potentially useful information from data.' It uses machine learning, statistical and visualization techniques to discovery [sic] and present knowledge in a form which is easily comprehensible to humans." (Andy Pryke, "Introduction to Data Mining." Available: http://www.cs.bham.ac.uk/~anp/dm_docs/dm_intro.html). Cf. *Knowledge Discovery Mine*. Available: http://www.kdnuggets.com/; Andy Pryke, *The Data Mine*. Available: http://www.cs.bham.ac.uk/~anp/TheDataMine.html; Knowledge Discovery and Data Mining Foundation, *Knowledge Discovery & Data Mining*. Available: http://www.kdd.org/

10. Cf. Ben R. Tucker, "The Limits of a Title Proper; or, One Case Showing Why Human Beings, Not Machines, Must Do the Cataloging," *Library Resources & Technical Services* 34 (Apr. 1990): 240-245.

11. Maurice B. Line, "Satisfying Bibliographic Needs in the Future–From Publisher to User," *Catalogue & Index* no. 90-91 (autumn-winter 1988): 10-14. A revised version of this paper appears in *Aslib Proceedings* 42 (Feb. 1990): 41-49 under the title "Bibliographic Records for Users: From Disordered Superabundance to Cost-Effective Satisfaction."

12. Cf. *Government Information Locator Service (GILS)*. Available: http://www.usgs.gov/public/gils/; National Archives and Records Administration, *Guidelines for the Preparation of GILS Core Entries*. Available: http://www.dtic. dla.mil/gils/documents/naradoc/; *NEEDS: National Engineering Education Delivery System*. Available: http://www.needs.org/

13. Cf. David Seaman, "Guidelines for Text Mark-up at the Electronic Text Center." Available: http://etext.lib.virginia.edu/tei/uvatei4.html.

14. Iowa Policy and Planning Data Project, "Report, January 1, 1993 to March 31, 1993" (Ames, Iowa, 1993, photocopy), 2-7.

15. "What is Z39.50?" in *The ANSI/NISO Z39.50 Protocol: Information Retrieval in the Information Infrastructure*. Available: http://www.cni.org/pub/ NISO/docs/Z39.50-1992/www/50.brochure.part01.html

16. Gregory J. Wool, "Bibliographical Metadata; or, We Need a Client-Server Cataloging Code!" in *Finding Common Ground: Creating the Library of the Future Without Diminishing the Library of the Past*, ed. Cheryl LaGuardia and Barbara A. Mitchell (New York: Neal-Schuman Publishers, in press).

Metadata Conversion
and the Library OPAC

Amanda Xu

SUMMARY. This paper examines the metadata movement on the Internet and anticipates the need to establish a metadata repository for library collections. The library OPAC not only functions as a gateway for local and external metadata repositories, but also is equipped to extract, map, convert, and display all metadata. One of the benefits is that the newly integrated metadata can be accessed using the full functionality of the OPAC. *[Article copies available for a fee from The Haworth Document Delivery Service: 1-800-342-9678. E-mail address: getinfo@haworth.com]*

KEYWORDS. Metadata, metadata repository, metadata conversion, metadata conversion system, OPAC

INTRODUCTION

The number of scholarly information resources offered on the Internet has grown tremendously and will increase exponentially in the future. This development has pointed up the need for applying metadata to networked information resources, as it has been widely

Amanda Xu is a Serials Cataloger at the Massachusetts Institute of Technology, Room 14E-210A, 77 Massachusetts Avenue, Cambridge, MA 02139-4307, USA (email: zxu@mit.edu).

[Haworth co-indexing entry note]: "Metadata Conversion and the Library OPAC." Xu, Amanda. Co-published simultaneously in *The Serials Librarian* (The Haworth Press, Inc.) Vol. 33, No. 1/2, 1998, pp. 179-198; and: *E-Serials: Publishers, Libraries, Users, and Standards* (ed: Wayne Jones) The Haworth Press, Inc., 1998, pp. 179-198. Single or multiple copies of this article are available for a fee from The Haworth Document Delivery Service [1-800-342-9678, 9:00 a.m. - 5:00 p.m. (EST). E-mail address: getinfo@haworth.com].

accepted that resources with metadata attached or embedded have the potential to be more easily discovered and retrieved via the Internet.

This paper examines the metadata movement on the Internet, and anticipates the need to establish a metadata repository for library collections. It suggests using the OPAC as a gateway to access the metadata repository, whether it is located on the library Website, or on local databases mounted with specialized metadata formats.

The paper conceptualizes a metadata conversion system built into library OPACs for metadata integration and display. As a result, both locally created metadata and incoming metadata selected as part of the library collection can be captured via automatic metadata extraction, mapping, conversion, and integration. Consequently, the newly integrated metadata can utilize the full functionality of the library OPAC.

METADATA AND THE METADATA MOVEMENT ON THE INTERNET

Metadata, or representational data, is generally defined as data about data. It contains a set of data elements to describe the content and location of an information object and to facilitate its discovery and retrieval in the networked environment.

A library bibliographic record is one type of metadata. It differs from other metadata in that it uses *AACR* as rules for data modelling, USMARC for encoding schemes, and proprietary online systems for information retrieval.

Most metadata on the Internet do not have such long-established and well-regulated standards, encoding schemes, and systems to support the mission of networked resources discovery and retrieval. But this is changing, and we have to examine the impact on the library world.

The Necessity for Metadata

Metadata is important in global information retrieval on the Internet for the following reasons:

- It manages large amounts of data with low network bandwith: Metadata addresses the issue of indexing large quantities of data of various types without requiring enormous amounts of network bandwidth. What gets indexed is the representational data rather than the information object itself.
- It assists effective discovery and retrieval of networked information resources: Metadata facilitates more sophisticated and comprehensive searching of information as the metadata elements and structures are designed to analyze content of the data in depth.
- It shares and integrates heterogeneous information resources: Information resources exist in different formats with different features residing in heterogeneous databases. Standard metadata description permits the comparing, sharing, integrating and reusing of various types of data in a distributed networking environment. Metadata has thus become an important long-term approach for finding information in heterogeneous databases.
- It controls restricted-access information: Metadata can not only facilitate effective searching and retrieving of heterogeneous information resources, but it can also manage restricted-access information and services to users, e.g., billing, filtering and rating, privacy, and security. Metadata serves a gatekeeper function, an indispensable feature for ever-growing commercialized information resources.

Metadata Formats and the Creation of Metadata

The movement to utilize metadata to organize the content of information on the Internet is expanding. Metadata can be created at the authoring stage, when the author embeds metadata into the resource using HTML META-tags, SGML headers, and/or other metadata templates. It can also be generated on the fly by search engines. For instance, metadata in SOIF (Summary Object Interchange Format)[1] is generated by Harvest gatherers. And it can be constructed at the service stage as well: the metadata is located in a central or distributed databases with pointers to the resources it describes.

Metadata formats have proliferated, ranging from simple and

structured formats to rich formats, and moving from proprietary, emerging standards, to international standards. A comprehensive report documenting metadata description formats has been written by DESIRE (Development of a European Service for Information on Research and Education).[2]

Searching for Metadata

Not all resources with metadata attached will be discovered by search engines, because the types of metadata a search engine gathers depend largely on the types of metadata templates that are profiled.[3] For those "Internet accessible but non-HTML based resources,"[4] metadata can be accessed via protocols such as Whois ++,[5] LDAP (Lightweight Directory Access Protocol),[6] Z39.50,[7] or other proprietary search engines. One such proprietary search engine is Panorama.[8] It is the primary software available for searching SGML-based encoding schemes such as the TEI Header[9] and EAD (Encoded Archival Description)[10] records. OCLC's Site Search, though it claims to be able to search SGML documents with a Z39.50-based search form, cannot effectively handle long text documents such as finding aids.[11]

Mapping Metadata

To improve metadata interoperability, metadata mapping has been seriously considered by the various metadata players. The most frequently mapped metadata formats are: IAFA (Internet Anonymous FTP Archive) templates,[12] Dublin Core metadata sets,[13] USMARC, GILS (Government Information Locator Services),[14] SGML TEI Header, EAD,[15] and Z39.50 tag set G.[16] Among them, USMARC, TEI Headers, EAD, GILS, and Dublin Core can represent the center of metadata mapping.

By mapping the content, syntax, and data elements of various metadata models, correct metadata conversion between various syntaxes can be assured.[17] Sketchy records such as IAFA and Dublin Core records can be accurately upgraded during the migration so as to satisfy the needs of rich description records such as USMARC, TEI Header, and EAD. Ultimately, searching across metadata syntaxes and databases can be facilitated.

The very fact that metadata can be mapped indicates that most metadata models share characteristics in their metadata elements, structures, and level of complexity for description. The design of the various metadata schemes has been largely influenced by USMARC. Although the various schemes are complementary, each also has its own emphasis.

For instance, USMARC records, TEI Headers, and EAD can provide highly structured bibliographic descriptions of electronic resources. However, USMARC also provides for summary bibliographic descriptions of print and electronic resources. TEI Headers are used to provide bibliographic and non-bibliographic description of SGML-conformant text, though it can also be used for non-SGML-conformant text. EAD allows for detailed description of archives and manuscript collections. It is also used for library finding aids, as it allows inventory description of the full range of archival holdings in various media.

Metadata Architecture

How can the above overlapping, complementary, or even competing metadata schemes communicate with one another regardless of location and syntaxes? Specifically speaking, how can those "aggregated metadata objects"[18] such as USMARC bibliographic records, SGML metadata records, Dublin Core metadata records, GILS records, finding aids in EAD, and other future metadata records be organized in a consistent way so that they can be interchanged in a distributed networking environment?

A metadata architecture is necessary to address the issues. Web Collections,[19] PICS (Platform for Internet Content Selection),[20] and Warwick Framework[21] are examples of recent proposed metadata architecture derived from the need.

Metadata Repository

The metadata movement on the Internet points up the need for building a metadata repository. The repository should reside on the Internet. It should be extensive enough to incorporate many metadata formats into its databases and to be integratable with legacy systems such as library OPACs. The repository should be functional enough to facilitate portable metadata creation, sophisticated metadata searching, mapping and interchange, and easy updating and deletion.

It should also support the navigational and hierarchical architecture to (1) collocate different metadata types associated with an information object in diverse formats, and (2) maintain links from any of the metadata types to the object, as well as its related objects. Many types of information services should be supported at the interface level, for example information filtering, selecting, acquiring, organizing, delivering, billing, and so forth.

So what should this metadata repository be, from the library's perspective? How can we ensure good access to the repository?

THE LIBRARY METADATA REPOSITORY
AND THE LIBRARY OPAC

Library OPACs have long been regarded as information gateways. The databases such as bibliographic databases, citation databases, and finding aids in which OPACs are directly indexed or interfaced have served as library metadata repositories for years. So, can a library OPAC serve as a gateway to metadata repositories on the Internet as well as to its existing databases? The recent evolving technologies on the Web and the Internet, as well as in the computer industry, have promised such potential.

The Library OPAC as Gateway to Metadata Repositories

The typical library OPAC gateway under development now by library communities is Window-interfaced with Z39.50 search capabilities, and TCP/IP connections. It provides users with a single interface to access library bibliographic databases, networked CD-ROM databases, full-text databases, online services, and other remote Z39.50-compatible databases. SilverPlatter's WinSPIRS[22] is an example of such a system.

The system has also been extended to Web-to-Z39.50 gateways. Web browsers become the clients of Z39.50 servers. As a result, OPAC databases are integrated with a wide variety of internal Internet resources, as well as external Internet resources. Yale University's WWW Orbits Gateway[23] is an example.

Evidently, with the demand for seamless access to diverse resources, using such a system to interface the metadata repository on the Internet seems feasible.

The Library Web Site as a Metadata Repository

A typical library Web site nowadays is still the place where a number of selected Internet resources, electronic journal collections, full-text databases, vendor-supplied Web-interfaced databases, and other library-related resources are mounted.[24]

Some libraries have a search engine built into their Web servers so that users can have full-text search features. The majority of them, however, still maintain lists of Web resources arranged by subject, or classification. The first approach doesn't permit targeted searching. In other words, it has low precision. The second approach requires users to be familiar with the collections, and to browse the listing page by page. For subjects with which the user is unfamiliar, access to the full extent of the subject is limited.

With the explosion of electronic information on the Internet, a library Web site becomes the only location for library electronic resources and services. With the capability of the Web-to-Z39.50 gateway, the Web site is broadened to legacy resources as well. The library Web site is no longer a mirror of a library, but an electronic library for diverse resources and services. A systematic and standard approach to all of the library's resources is required. The limitations of full-text searching, and of simply browsing a list of Web resources on a Web site, point out the advantages of using metadata.

In addition, with the increasing use of metadata, more and more Internet resources will have metadata already attached. Accordingly, libraries are obligated to maintain a metadata repository for Web resources. A library OPAC gateway will therefore become a logical system to access the repository.

Locally Created Metadata on Local Databases as a Metadata Repository

Many libraries are using metadata already.[25,26,27,28] They have created EAD records for archival description and finding aids,

SGML TEI Headers for electronic text, Dublin Core for simplified description of networked resources, and GILS for Government Information Locator Services. Most of these metadata can be created with local word-processing or database systems, but retrieval technologies are still under development,[29] and as a result, no common interface is in place yet for all of these metadata formats. For instance, GILS records are currently searched via Z39.50 gateways, Dublin Core Metadata Sets via automatic search engines, and EAD and SGML TEI Headers via SoftQuad's Panorama. Developing library OPAC gateways as a common interface to the database seems the only way to go.

Limitations of Web-to-Z39.50 Gateways

If library OPACs are used as a common gateway to all of the above metadata formats, Z39.50 profiles have to be established for each of them. Currently only MARC, GILS, and some vendor databases have such profiles.

Evidently, Web-to-Z39.50 gateways are not flexible enough to handle all necessary data types and structures. Therefore, if library OPACs are used as gateways to access all the databases, including metadata repositories either on library Web sites or on local databases, a metadata conversion system built into the gateway is needed to ensure metadata interchange.

Web-to-Z39.50 gateways are session-oriented. Even with Z39.50 profiles extended to other commonly accessed metadata formats, users will still have the problem of large system overhead, as the server remembers each session initiated, but never knows when to delete unnecessary sessions. With diverse metadata to be searched simultaneously, the slow response time could be a critical problem for effective retrieval.

Therefore, due to the limitation of current technology, using one type of metadata that has been profiled and implemented with Z39.50 as the base format for all the other metadata formats seems to be a practical approach. A metadata conversion system is then needed to convert all the other metadata to the base format, currently USMARC, in any future SGML-based encoding scheme.

For libraries which don't have Z39.50 capabilities, and which need to incorporate records encoded with other metadata schemes into their OPAC databases, a library metadata conversion system is needed as well.

In short, when a library OPAC is used as a gateway to access metadata repositories on its Web site or on local databases, a metadata conversion system is essential for three reasons:

- to capture, upgrade, and convert selected incoming metadata into the OPAC;
- to integrate locally created metadata into the OPAC;
- to display metadata in a user-specified format.

A LIBRARY METADATA CONVERSION SYSTEM

Metadata Conversion

Metadata conversion for library resources means:

1. conversion of the selected incoming metadata into USMARC format;
2. conversion of locally created metadata into USMARC format, and;
3. conversion of metadata in metadata repositories into a user-specified format when records are being displayed.

Whether it is incoming or locally created, the metadata may be encoded in various formats. This paper deals only with recently proposed metadata standards for Internet resources, namely Dublin Core Metadata Sets, EAD, TEI Header, GILS, and the USMARC format. The conversion system will automatically remove the metadata from their heterogeneous encoding schemes, and convert them into a generic format–currently USMARC format–at the point of metadata integration.

The encoding level of both incoming and locally created metadata may differ as well. A lot of the literature has covered the metadata analysis aspects.[30,31,32] Too little meta-information will fail to meet the purpose of information discovery and retrieval. Too much meta-information is slow and costly to generate. Therefore, the essential metadata elements need to be defined for the conversion, and the conversion system must automatically verify these essential elements.

As most existing library resources have been encoded in USMARC format, a library metadata conversion system may still use the USMARC format as the basis for metadata description, storage, exchange, manipulation and retrieval. As a result, all metadata will be converted into USMARC format during integration and display. In this way, the existing bibliographic data can be preserved, and the full functionality of integrated library systems can be utilized.

Basic Functional Requirements

A library metadata conversion system must have the following basic functionalities (but not necessarily in this order):

Extract Metadata

The process is to capture metadata, and extract it when (A) metadata is already associated with the information object either via hyperlinks or attached to the object, and (B) highly structured information objects exist with no metadata attached.

In situation A, metadata can be extracted by automatically matching semantically similar elements and structures found in standard metadata format templates, namely the templates for Dublin Core Metadata Sets, EAD, TEI Header, GILS, and the USMARC format. If selected resources contain metadata that match with one of the templates, the metadata will be extracted and converted. If they do not match or just partially match with any of the templates, offline data mapping and modification are required. Li and Clifton's Semint is an example.[33]

Extracting metadata in situation B depends largely on the media and formats of the information object. Different media (such as text, images, and audio) and different formats (such as an HTML, SGML, PostScript, DVI, PDF, etc.) will require different programs to extract metadata automatically. Shklar et al.'s InfoHarness system is an example.[34] It is based on the fact that the lowest level of granularity of information is a logical unit of information, which they call an information unit (IU). The system includes an extraction program to recognize functional blocks (i.e., sections) within individual IUs, and then to encapsulate and index them.

Both Semint and InfoHarness have practical implications for automatic metadata extraction in library OPACs. Existing library databases are highly structured. They consist primarily of bibliographic databases with records in USMARC format. Selected Internet resources are usually in HTML or other structured file formats. Therefore, it is possible to extract metadata from the information object at the semantic level and information unit level, as in situations A and B respectively.

Map Metadata

This process finds corresponding attributes between extracted metadata and standard metadata templates. It occurs several times during the conversions:

- In the course of extracting, standard metadata templates are matched against metadata associated with selected Internet resources. The purpose is to identify content-bearing metadata elements, recognize metadata formats, and verify essential metadata attributes. Off-line adding and deleting data elements can also take place at this point.
- In the course of converting (see below), all extracted and verified metadata are mapped to a USMARC template, or a USMARC record is simulated into templates for other metadata formats. Each template contains essential data sets to describe information of various types, but the USMARC template serves as a common template for metadata comparison and exchange.

Convert Metadata

This process transforms metadata formats. A converter program takes the data elements from a newly extracted metadata record, and loads them into corresponding USMARC fields according to a specified USMARC template. Thus, a new USMARC record is created.

The same method can be used to convert a USMARC record into other metadata formats.

Integrate Metadata

This process resolves the differences when combining data values and data structures that reflect the same information for the same entity from multiple databases.[35] It is a continuing process, involving extracting, mapping, converting, and indexing metadata into existing databases.

Provide an Interface to Metadata

This process provides an interface to facilitate a metadata search of both metadata repositories and existing library resources, and to display the search results in a user-specified metadata format. Using a library OPAC as a metadata interface will preserve the sophisticated search features and powerful linking models of the library OPAC,[36] and will also provide integrated searching of heterogeneous information in various metadata formats.

A CONVERSION MODEL FOR THE LIBRARY OPAC

This model details the procedures of a metadata conversion system during the process of metadata extraction, mapping, conversion, and integration, in the three scenarios:

- For selected Internet resources which are to be integrated with existing OPAC databases, the incoming metadata on the repository (that is, the library Website) will be extracted in the following steps:

1. It identifies the hyperlink associated with the page and takes information on the page as an information unit (see the discussion of the IU above).
2. It maps semantically similar data elements and structures with standard metadata templates, e.g., Dublin Core, and expresses them as metadata.

3. It verifies the completeness of the data elements by mapping to its own template.
4. It loads the data elements into a USMARC template, converts them into a USMARC record, and integrates them into existing databases.
5. It searches the data elements using library OPACs.

- For locally created metadata on the repository (that is, specialized metadata mounted on local databases), the metadata conversion system will identify the content-bearing metadata elements, load them into a specified USMARC template, and convert and index them into existing databases;
- When a library OPAC is used as a gateway to access remote metadata repositories, a metadata conversion system will verify if the resources contain meta-information, load the data elements into metadata templates, confirm the metadata format and encoding level, and then display metadata in user-specified formats.

BENEFITS OF THE MODEL

The Internet contains various kinds of information in such diverse formats that it would take substantial *human* effort to create a metadata record, let alone to have it done automatically. This model therefore suggests building metadata extraction functions into the metadata conversion system, for three reasons:

- The model is intended for selected Internet resources which have metadata already attached. If these resources are selected as part of a library's collections, then those which have commonly used metadata attached could have that metadata captured, modified, converted, and integrated into the existing databases, either automatically or semi-automatically;
- The model is also designed for locally created metadata, such as finding aids in Dublin Core, EAD or SGML TEI Header formats. These metadata are often generated with human intervention. They tend to have high-quality data contents, elements, and structures. Extracting, converting and integrating

these metadata into the OPAC databases will ensure efficient metadata access;

- This model is applicable to Internet resources which lack metadata but which have highly standardized data attributes and structures. The system will identify a Web page and then extract meta-information from these attributes and structures, and thereby create a metadata record.

This model also suggests using the USMARC format as a common template for metadata comparison and exchange. One reason for this is that millions of existing library collections already use USMARC as the metadata encoding standard. Converting other metadata standards to the USMARC format allows integrated access to both the existing resources and newly selected resources.

Another reason for using USMARC as a common template is that the Electronic Location and Access (856) field has been added to USMARC, making it possible to connect USMARC records to their source data directly via sophisticated OPACs. In addition, the 856 field has been improved so as to accommodate Uniform Resource Names, to indicate file format type, and to indicate the relationship between the 856 and the resource which the record describes.[37] With a full Z39.50 connection, library OPACs become an ideal hub for information resources. Adding metadata conversion systems into the OPAC will further enhance interoperability among metadata repositories.

In addition, this model also handles metadata conversions in an integrated way. Other models deal with only one format at a time. This model can automatically detect which format to use by matching extracted metadata against a number of standard metadata templates simultaneously.

Furthermore, this model offers the library community the ability to choose a metadata standard that fits individual local needs. Catalogers can work with the metadata format which is easy for them to use, but later on have their records converted into another format which is compatible with their local databases.

Finally, this model will greatly increase the speed of adding filtered Internet resources into library bibliographic databases. Library users can obtain an accurate and complete picture of information on a given subject with a one-stop search on the library OPAC.

ISSUES FOR THE FUTURE

A number of issues still need to be addressed.

Semantic Differences

Whether extraction occurs at the data source level or metadata level, one of the biggest challenges for metadata extraction is semantic differences such as attribute naming, format, structure and identity conflicts. For example, attribute naming is problematic when data elements are conceptually the same but named differently, or named the same but conceptually different.[38] A 650 field in USMARC is named as LCSH, while in other metadata format it is named as keywords, key words, subject, subject headings, etc. Metadata naming standardization is a remedy.

Losing Metadata

During the metadata conversion, metadata elements in one format may not fit in another format. Vizine-Goetz, Godby and Bendig[39] and Xu[40] have done some studies on data element and data structure mapping among recently developed metadata standards such as the Dublin Core, TEI Header, and USMARC. They found that there were some overlapping data sets among these standards, but not all of them had one-to-one correspondent matches. For instance, the TEI Header contains some data elements that are impossible to convert into USMARC. A global system control number is needed to keep track of the format change of each metadata record. This would enable the system to trace the USMARC record back to its original metadata format.

Web-Interfaced OPACs

Building a metadata conversion system at the Web-interfaced OPAC level is essential. Most current library metadata conversion programs are built on the Web,[41,42] because that is where the resources reside (and should reside). A Web-interfaced OPAC will have the hyperlinking feature of the Web which connects the metadata and the information object. It also makes it possible for the conversion system to periodically and semi-automatically verify source data against extracted metadata.[43] The process will ensure that the metadata still accurately reflects the information object it describes. Another reason is that many conversion programs are available in CGI (Common Gateway Interface) scripts. It is time-saving to build the conversion systems upon existing programs. There are several projects involving automatic metadata conversion already underway.[44,45]

Conversion and Indexing

With today's technology, the OPAC armed with a metadata conversion system will surely increase the speed of metadata integration and display. Will future technologies such as IIOP (Internet InterORB Protocol),[46] CORBA (Common Object Request Broker),[47] Java, and new Z39.50 profiles offer the same capability without conversion?

AACR and USMARC were originally designed for static information objects with flat data structure. However, with the impact of the metadata movement, will they be replaced by newly emerging metadata designed for network use, such as Dublin Core,[48] Warwick Framework,[49] PICS,[50] and XML (Extensible Markup Language)?[51] What impact would these formats have on conversion?

With a variety of metadata and metadata sets integrated into the OPAC databases, what will be the best indexing strategies for the OPAC to ensure effective access? Should there be one index for all media? Or multiple indexes for all the various media? Or should both be allowed to exist?

CONCLUSION

By examining the metadata movement on the Internet, this paper points out the need to use the OPAC as the gateway to access to library metadata repositories. Within the context of these depositories, the paper analyzes a library metadata conversion system which will be able to extract selected incoming external metadata from Internet resources, convert it into USMARC format, and integrate it with existing library databases automatically. The model also suggests the possibility of transferring locally created metadata into the format that is the best to describe Internet resources, and then converting and integrating the resulting records into the OPAC databases. And finally, the metadata needs to be able to be displayed in a format which the user specifies.

With such a system in place, libraries would be able to expand their collections to incorporate a wide variety of information on the Internet with ease. They could share, re-use and integrate metadata repositories around the world. And library users could have access to a wealth of diverse information resources.

These theories and procedures on how to build this system still need to be tested and proved. This paper has attempted to propose a model, and to highlight the importance of a metadata conversion system in the library.

NOTES

1. "The Summary Object Interchange Format (SOIF)." Available: http:// harvest.transarc.com/afs/transarc.com/public/trg/Harvest/user-manual/node151.html

2. L. Dempsey and R. M. Heery, "A Review of Metadata: A Survey of Current Resource Description Formats," in *DESIRE-RE 1004*, May 28, 1997. Available: http://www.ukoln.ac.uk/metadata/DESIRE/overview

3. "META Tagging for Search Engines." Available: http://WWW.Stars.com/ Search/Meta/Tag.html

4. Willy Cromwell-Kessler and Ricky Erway (meeting report from Metadata Summit organized by the Research Libraries Group, Mountian View, Calif., July 1, 1997).

5. Network Working Group, "Architecture of the WHOIS++ Service." Available: ftp://ds.internic.net/rfc/rfc1835.txt

6. "Lightweight Directory Access Protocol." Available: http://www.umich. edu/~rsug/ldap/ldap.html

7. "International Standard Z39.50: Information Retrieval (Z39.50): Application Service Definition and Protocol Specification." Available: http://lcweb.loc.gov/ z3950/agency/

8. "SoftQuad's Panorama Publishing Suite." Available: http://www.sq.com/ products/panorama/

9. "The TEI Header," in *TEI Guidelines for Electronic Text Encoding and Interchange*. Available: http://etext.virginia.edu/bin/tei-tocs?div=DIV1&id=HD

10. "Encoded Archival Description (EAD) DTD." Available: http://lcweb. loc.gov/ead/

11. "Harvard/Radcliffe Digital Finding Aids Project: History and Project Report." Available: http://hul.harvard.edu/dfap/projectdescription.html

12. David Beckett, "IAFA Templates in Use as Internet Metadata." Available: http://www.w3.org/pub/Conferences/WWW4/Papers/52/

13. Stuart Weibel and Renato Iannella, "The 4th Dublin Core Metadata Workshop Report," in *D-Lib Magazine*, June 1997. Available: http://www.dlib.org/ dlib/june97/metadata/06weibel.html

14. "Government Information Locator Service (GILS)." Available: http://www. usgs.gov/public/gils/

15. "Development of the Encoded Archival Description Document Type Definition." Available: http://www.loc.gov/ead/eadback.html

16. Michael Day, "Metadata: Mapping Between Metadata Formats." Available: http://www.uloln.ac.uk/metadata/interoperability/

17. Rebecca Guenther, "Metadata, Dublin Core and USMARC: a Review of Current Efforts." Available: gopher://marvel.loc.gov/00/.listarch/usmarc/dp99.doc

18. Carl Lagoze, Clifford Lynch, and Ron Daniel Jr., "The Warwick Framework: A Container Architecture for Aggregating Sets of Metadata." Available: http://cs-tr. cs.cornell.edu:80/Dienst/Repository/2.0/Body/ncstrl.cornell%2TR96-1593/html

19. Yoelle Maarek and Dror Zernik, "Web Collections: A Mechanism for Grouping Web Documents and Site Mapping." Available: http://www-ee.technion.ac.il/ W3C/WebCollection.html

20. "Platform for Internet Content Selection." Available: http:// www.w3.org/ PICS/

21. Carl Lagoze, "The Warwick Framework: A Container Architecture for Diverse Sets of Metadata," in *D-Lib Magazine*, July/Aug. 1996. Available: http://www. dlib.org/dlib/july96/lagoze/071agoze.html

22. "Silverplatter World." Available: http://www.silverplatter.com/

23. "WWW Orbis Web-to-Z39.50 Gateway." Available: http://webpac.library. yale.edu/webpac5.htm

24. "MIT Libraries." Available: http://libraries.mit.edu/

25. "Encoded Archival Description (EAD) Sites on the Web." Available: http://www.loc.gov/ead/eadsites.html

26. "Development of Integrated Online Community Information Systems." Available: http://www.solinet.net/monticello/monticel.htm

27. Ibid.

28. Andy Powell, "Metadata Management." Available: http://www.ukoln.ac.uk/ metadata-june1997/ap/sld001.htm

29. "Z39.50 Profile for Access to Digital Library Objects: Fourth Draft." Available: http://lcweb.loc.gov/z3950/agency/profiles/dl.html

30. Rachel Heery, "Review of Metadata Formats," *Program* 30, issue no. 4 (Oct. 1996).

31. Eric Miller, "Monticello Electronic Library: Dublin Core Element Set Crosswalk." Available: http://www.oclcorg:5046/~miller/DC/crosswalk.html

32. "Digital Libraries: Metadata Resources." Available: http://www.nlc-bnc. ca/ifla/II/metadata.htm

33. Wen-Syan Li and Chris Clifton, "Semint: A System Prototype for Semantic Integration in Heterogeneous Databases," in *Proceedings of the 1995 ACM SIGMOD International Conference on Management of Data, May 23-25, 1995, San Jose, California,* (New York: Association for Computing Machinery, 1995).

34. Leon Shklar, Amit Sheth, Vipul Kashyap, and Kshitij Shah, "InfoHarness: Use of Automatically Generated Metadata for Search and Retrieval of Heterogeneous Information," in *Advanced Information Systems Engineering: 7th International Conference, CAiSE '95, Jyvèaskylèa, Finland, June 12-16, 1995: Proceedings* (New York: Springer, 1995).

35. Wen-Syan Li and Chris Clifton, "Dynamic Integration in Multidatabase Systems," *Journal of Database Management* 7, no. 1 (1996): 28-40.

36. Amanda Xu, "Hyperlinks in the WebPAC Systems: A Study of Hypertext Links to A Bibliographic Record in the Web Based OPACs," in *ISAL '96: Proceedings of the International Symposium on Academic Libraries in the 21st Century: Sept. 1-4 1996, Shanghai, China* (Shanghai: Shanghai Jiao Tong University Press, 1996).

37. See the *Guidelines for the Use of Field 856,* rev. Aug. 1997 (Washington, D.C.: Library of Congress, Network Development and MARC Standards Office). Available: http://www.loc.gov/marc/856guide.html

38. Stephanie Cammarata, Iris Kameny, Judy Lender, and Corrinne Replogle, "A Metadata Management System to Support Data Interoperability, Reuse and Sharing," *Journal of Database Management* 5, no. 2 (spring 1994): 30-40.

39. Diane Vizine-Goetz, Jean Godby, Mark Bendig, "Spectrum: a Web-Based Tool for Describing Electronic Resources," *Computer Networks and ISDN Systems* 27 (1995): 985-1001.

40. Amanda Xu, "Access Information on the Internet: Feasibility Study of USMARC Format and AACR2," in *Proceedings of OCLC Internet Cataloging Colloquium, San Antonio, Texas, January 19, 1996.* Available: http://www.oclc.org/ oclc/man/colloq/xu.htm

41. Robert Atkinson, Meta Access Query, intercat@oclc.org (12 July 1996).

42. Gerald S. Barton, "Multiple Metadata Formats from the NOAA Environmental Services Data Directory," in *Proceedings of the First IEEE Metadata Conference, April 16-18, 1996, Silver Spring, Maryland* (New York: IEEE, 1996).

43. Pamela Drew and Jerry Ying, "A Metadata Architecture for Multi-System Interoperation," in *Proceedings of the First IEEE Metadata Conference.*

44. Stanley Elswick, Gary McCone, and Paul M. Kuin, "Report on Possible Conversion From the DIF to the USMARC Format," *Library Hi Tech* 13, no. 1-2 (1995): 36-42.

45. Jackie Shieh, "Common Good: Cataloging Operations and Electronic Text Processing" (paper presented at Finding Common Ground Conference, Harvard College Library, Cambridge, Massachusetts, Mar. 30, 1996).

46. "CORBA 2.0/IIOP Specification: the Complete Formal, 97-02-25: CORBA 2.0/IIOP Specification." Available: http://www.omg.org/corba/corbiiop.htm

47. David Curtis, "Java, RMI and CORBA." Available: http://www.omg.org/news/wpjava.htm

48. Committee on Cataloging: Description and Access, Task Force on Metadata and the Cataloging Rules, "Dublin Core and the Cataloging Rules: Analysis Project." Available: http://www.libraries.psu.edu/iasweb/personal/jca/dublin/index.htm

49. Carl Lagoze, "Rethinking Metadata." Available: http://www2.cs.cornell.edu/lagoze/talks/austalk/index.htm

50. Philip DesAutels, "PICS and the Dublin Core" (paper presented at Seminar on International Metadata Development, Mar. 6, 1997). Available: http://www.nla.gov.au/niac/meta/desautel/desautxt.html

51. "Specification for XML-Data." Available: http://www/microsoft.com/standards/xml/xmldata.htm

Online Serials:
Preservation Issues

Michael W. Day, BA, MA

SUMMARY. The paper consists of a preliminary investigation of preservation issues related to scholarly online electronic serials. Some background issues are discussed relating to how preservation should be defined, types of electronic serials, the current and future development of scholarly communication and formats currently in use. The discussion of preservation that follows looks at media longevity, hardware and software dependence and obsolescence, data migration, authentication, copyright and ownership issues, legal deposit and the related problems of who should preserve and what should be preserved in the digital age. *[Article copies available for a fee from The Haworth Document Delivery Service: 1-800-342-9678. E-mail address: getinfo@haworth.com]*

Michael Day is a Research Officer at UKOLN The UK Office for Library and Information Networking, University of Bath, Bath BA2 7AY, United Kingdom (email: M.Day@ukoln.ac.uk).

UKOLN is funded by the Joint Information Systems Committee of the UK Higher Education Funding Councils and by the British Library Research and Innovations Centre, as well as by project funding from several sources. The views expressed in this paper do not necessarily reflect those of UKOLN or its funding bodies.

[Haworth co-indexing entry note]: "Online Serials: Preservation Issues." Day, Michael W. Co-published simultaneously in *The Serials Librarian* (The Haworth Press, Inc.) Vol. 33, No. 3/4, 1998, pp. 199-221; and: *E-Serials: Publishers, Libraries, Users, and Standards* (ed: Wayne Jones) The Haworth Press, Inc., 1998, pp. 199-221. Single or multiple copies of this article are available for a fee from The Haworth Document Delivery Service [1-800-342-9678, 9:00 a.m. - 5:00 p.m. (EST). E-mail address: getinfo@haworth.com].

KEYWORDS. Online serials, electronic journals, networks, digital preservation, archiving

INTRODUCTION

Digital preservation has interested the library and information communities since the viability of electronic publication was first noted in the 1970s. Serious problems have consistently been raised with ensuring the continued existence of electronic information, and these concerns led to the publication of a report on *Preserving Digital Information* by the Task Force on the Archiving of Digital Information commissioned by the Commission on Preservation and Access and by the Research Libraries Group in May 1996.[1] The recent growth in the production and use of online serials–electronic serials available over networks–demonstrates that the development of sensible preservation strategies for these items is essential to ensure the future of scholarly communication. This paper will look at the preservation implications of scholarly online serials, as well as discuss some background issues and outline the most important current digital preservation issues.

BACKGROUND ISSUES

Defining Preservation

The concept of preservation, when used with regard to electronic or digital information, can be difficult to define adequately. Some people prefer to use the word "archiving," which is used in a computing science context to mean the creation of a secure backup copy for a fixed period of time, but the term "preservation" will be used in this paper as it avoids confusion with the work of the archives community. The objective of preservation itself has been defined by John Feather as: "to ensure that information survives in a usable form for as long as it is wanted."[2] Preservation, therefore, is not just concerned with the conservation or restoration of artefacts, but includes all strategic considerations related to the survival of information over time. A distinction is often made between the preservation of the information embodied in a document (the informational content) and the conservation of the information carrier itself (the physical object).[3] This is especially relevant for digital information, including networked online serials, because the user does not even have to be aware of what particular physical object is being accessed. There may be a case for retaining physical objects–for example, in a museum of technology–but the preservation of informational content is much more important.

How long information should be kept is also another important, and often emotional, issue. It is often assumed that preservation should be permanent, often defined with reference to loaded terms such as "in perpetuity" and "indefinitely." In the context of archives, David Bearman has pointed out the absurdity of using concepts of permanence with regard to preservation and instead has proposed a more realistic concept of "retention for period of continuing value."[4] On similar lines, James O'Toole has pointed out that an acute conservation consciousness has meant that archivists have been lulled into a false sense of security about their collections, and have thus "lost sight of the larger purposes of their work–preserving over time information that is of benefit and use to society–and have restricted the available options for approaching that goal."[5] In consequence, this paper will assume that preservation is irrevocably linked to access and use, not to nebulous concepts of permanence.

Furthermore, a distinction has also to be made between digital preservation and digitisation for preservation, as the two are often confused. In the context of serials, back issues of important or rare serials are often digitised and made available over networks both to improve access to the information contained therein and sometimes to aid the preservation of the original item.[6] Examples of this type of operation are the Journal Storage Project (JSTOR) funded by the Andrew W. Mellon Foundation and the Internet Library of Early Journals (ILEJ) funded by the UK Electronic Libraries Programme (eLib).[7] Although these digitised versions of serials will need preservation themselves, they will not form the primary focus of this paper.

Types of Online Serial

While printed serials are a familiar part of the research library, there is more than one recognisable type of electronic serial. A preliminary survey of electronic information and serials collection management by Hazel Woodward in 1994 identified three major categories of electronic serial.[8]

- *Online*–full-text electronic serials available through online hosts such as DIALOG, usually available on a cost-per-access basis. Woodward has elsewhere noted that this type of online electronic journals are mostly "the electronic versions of existing printed journals."[9]
- *CD-ROM*–electronic serials distributed on CD-ROM, e.g., full-text newspapers or the ADONIS document delivery system.[10] Many of these are also electronic versions of printed serials. Serials published exclusively on CD-ROM will not, however, be discussed in this paper.
- *Networked electronic journals*–electronic serials available via networks, usually the Internet. These, as defined by Woodward, are normally only available in electronic form and include only those serials which have been peer-reviewed. They also tend to be non-commercial in nature. Serials of this type are listed in the *Directory of Electronic Journals, Newsletters and Academic Discussion Lists* published by the Association of Research Libraries (ARL).[11]

For the purpose of this paper, there is no reason to maintain a fixed distinction between online serials and networked electronic journals, as both are available online. The major differences are the type of publisher involved–commercial and learned society publishers on one side and non-commercial "network publishers" on the other–and whether the serial is an electronic version of a journal that already exists in printed form or is available only in electronic form.

The Development of the Online Serial

The electronic serial has been in development for about twenty years. Research projects in the 1980s first proved that electronic serials were technically feasible. The Electronic Information Exchange System (EIES) and the Birmingham and Loughborough Electronic Network Development (BLEND) demonstrated that systems could be developed for all stages of the production of an electronic serial, including article submission, peer-review processes, editing and distribution.[12] However, there was no major adoption of electronic serials as a result of these experiments largely because the necessary technological infrastructure–widespread access to computers and robust international networks–was not in place at that particular time.[13]

At about the same time as these technological shortcomings were being remedied, concern was also being raised over two significant problems of scholarly communication: the relatively long time it takes for a paper to be published in scholarly serials–particularly significant in the fields of Science, Technology and Medicine (STM)–and the "serials crisis"–a rapid growth in serial numbers and prices at the same time as research institutions and their libraries had entered an extended period of financial stringency.[14] It was felt that electronic publication would help speed up the publication time for serial articles and–crucially–might enable financial savings to be made to offset the effect of the serials crisis. Indeed, self publishing through electronic networks began to be seen in a new, more radical light–returning the responsibility of ownership and distribution of scholarship to its creators.[15] Widespread adoption of self-publishing through electronic networks would have a significant impact on the future viability of serials, whether available online or traditionally, and needs to be considered here with reference to preservation.

Andrew Odlyzko, a mathematician, has argued in an important article that traditional printed scholarly serials are likely to disappear within the next ten to twenty years.[16] He suggests that there are two main factors for this: the rapid growth of the scholarly literature; and the increasing availability and capability of electronic technology. Odlyzko thus predicts that scholarly publishing will soon move to electronic delivery mechanisms because of the "economic push of having to cope with increasing costs of the present system and the attractive pull of the new features that electronic publishing offers."[17] He is a supporter of recent developments in informal scholarly communication like bulletin boards and pre-print archives, but argues that there is also a need to build in reli-ability mechanisms, such as peer-review, so that scholars are able to build upon the accumulated knowledge.

The academic psychologist Stevan Harnad has similarly argued, with reference to what he calls "esoteric" literature (i.e., that origi-nating in specialised scholarly and scientific research and with no realistic market), that in the post-Gutenberg era there is no need to perpetuate the "Faustian bargain" made between authors and com-mercial publishers whereby authors trade the copyright of works in exchange for having them published.[18] He argues that this type of bargain made sense when publishing remained an exclusive and expensive domain, but has no relevance in the electronic era when scholars can publish their own papers at little or no personal cost. In addition to the benefits of improved accessibility, increased speed of publication and possible financial savings, Harnad suggests that network publication would enable authors to interact with their peers, for example, published articles could be open to immediate comment and response. This is what has been characterised by the term "scholarly skywriting."[19]

In order to facilitate the post-Gutenberg era, Harnad, Odlyzko and others have formulated what they refer to as a "subversive proposal" to bring down the "paper house of cards."[20] They sug-gest that all authors of "esoteric" works should make available the texts of all current papers on the Internet and readers would rapidly form the habit of accessing the free electronic version of a paper rather than a more expensive paper version published much later.[21] Harnad considers that publishers could respond to this challenge in one of three ways.[22] Firstly, they could invoke copyright law to attempt to force the removal of these papers from the Internet. Secondly, they could give up altogether the publication of "eso-teric" serials–leaving this task to the research communities them-selves who would have to implement the relevant quality control mechanisms. Thirdly, publishers could adopt an economic model where the publication cost and profit could be recovered by means of page-charges, paid for as part of a research grant or by the author's institution. Distribution would then be electronic and free of charge to the user.

The most commonly cited example of the "subversive proposal" in action is Paul Ginsparg's "e-print archive" established at the Los Alamos National Laboratory.[23] The original service, which went online in August 1991, gave electronic access to pre-prints in Ginsparg's own subject area: high-energy physics. The most remarkable thing about this service was that it very quickly became the primary means of scholarly communication in its subject area. An academic physicist was quoted in 1994 as saying that the archive had completely changed the way people in the field exchanged information: "the only time I look at the published journals is for articles that predate the Los Alamos physics databases."[24]

Odlyzko, Harnad and their supporters are correct in supposing that scholarly communication methods are being changed significantly by network publishing. The use of electronic bulletin boards, mailing-lists and pre-print servers has already had a profound effect on the way research is carried out. The evidence of successive editions of the *ARL Directory* also demonstrates that scholarly electronic serials are increasingly available on the Internet. In addition, there are signs that quality control mechanisms are being applied to these serials. Many of the first scholarly serials available online were newsletters or non-refereed journals but there is today an ever-increasing number of refereed journals.[25] Despite this, however, there is no evidence that commercial scholarly serials are in terminal decline. Indeed, many papers deposited in pre-print archives will eventually find their way through peer-review and into the printed journal literature. The reason for this is that online serials have not been able to replicate all of the functions currently carried out by traditional printed serials.

Cliff McKnight has pointed out that for an electronic serial to be completely acceptable to users, it must allow them to do at least what can be done with traditional paper serials, and preferably more.[26] Fytton Rowland, summarising the work of others, has described the main functions of traditional scholarly serials as follows.[27]

- The dissemination of information
- Quality control
- The canonical archive
- Recognition of authors

Network publication already fulfills the important function of dissemination–indeed it could be claimed to be a better (faster and cheaper) dissemination medium than print. Quality control processes such as peer-review can be added to electronic publications, as can strategies for the recognition of authors' contributions to them. This is why online serials are increasingly being used for the publication of scholarly output. There is not the same level of confidence, however, that any electronic publication–including network publication–will contribute much to the canonical archive.

While Harnad and others have been arguing for the widespread adoption of network publication of "esoteric" works, professional publishers from the commercial sector and learned societies themselves have not neglected to investigate the potential of electronic publication of their own serials.[28] The publisher-led ADONIS experiment in document delivery was an early example of this, and this has been followed by initiatives such as the Chemical Journals Online (CJO) service whereby the American Chemical Society (ACS) has made its scholarly journals available over the international Scientific and Technical Network (STN). Professional publishers have also showed themselves willing to co-operate with libraries in experiments such as The University Licensing Program (TULIP), in which journals in the subject area of materials science from the Elsevier/North Holland/Pergamon group were delivered to participating US research libraries to investigate the technical, legal and economic issues associated with electronic serials and user behaviour.[29] Another example of publisher and library co-operation is the ELVYN project involving the Institute of Physics Publishing, a team at Loughborough University and others.[30] In the UK a major reason for the recent increased visibility of the online serial is the Higher Education Funding Council for England (HEFCE) pilot site initiative which has given universities online access to serial articles originating from professional publishers such as Academic Press, Blackwell Science and Institute of Physics Publishing.[31] The UK eLib Programme, funded by the Joint Information Systems Committee of the higher education funding councils, has also funded some projects relating to electronic serials. The result of all this activity is a growing number of scholarly online serials, distributed in several different ways and in several different formats.

Distribution Methods and Formats Currently in Use

In 1994 David Pullinger suggested that there are three possible models for the network publishing of serials.[32] In the first, the "publisher" distributes copies of contents pages, abstracts, articles or whole issues to subscribers over the Internet usually in the form of e-mail. Many of the earliest non-commercial network serials were distributed in this way, based on electronic mailing-list software such as LISTSERV, which enabled serial contents pages and abstracts to be sent out to a centrally held list of subscribers who then could request the system to deliver particular articles.[33] Pullinger's second model relies on serials being made available through local networks such as Campus Wide Information Systems—as used in the ELVYN project. In the third model, serial issues/articles are held on a central host where users can browse and download relevant items. This seems to be the currently favoured model—largely because of the influence of the World Wide Web—and is used for both network publication and for the commercial distribution of scholarly serials.

Electronic serials are also available in a variety of formats. Until comparatively recently the most popular format was plain ASCII text or bit-mapped page images. ASCII is fine for articles comprised largely of text, but is inadequate for representing the visual complexity of STM literature. ADONIS, with this in mind, scanned the paper copy of the journal and distributed the pages as bit-maps on CD-ROM.[34] ASCII and bit-mapped images are still used to distribute electronic journal articles, but a variety of other formats is emerging and growing in popularity.

STM serials have been described as the most difficult (and expensive) to produce in any format because, according to Hitchcock, Carr and Hall, they contain "specialised terminology, they frequently include detailed mathematics and often have complex artwork and tabular data."[35] For these reasons online STM serials tend to use formats which retain the features of print journals. The most popular of these formats are PostScript and its more flexible relation, Adobe's Portable Document Format (PDF).[36] PDF's popularity has been enhanced by the free distribution of Adobe's Acrobat viewer and Acrobat's integration with Web browsers such as

Netscape Navigator. PDF is particularly good for use in situations where electronic versions of printed serials are being made available online, as the pages will look the same as in the printed version. Its strong position in the field of online serials is attested by the fact that all the serials included in the UK HEFCE's pilot site licence initiative are currently made available in PDF.

The other popular format currently used for the distribution of online serials is the HyperText Markup Language (HTML). Online serials use HTML because they want to take advantage of the hypertextual and multimedia features of publishing on the Web rather than just replicate print. For example, the UK eLib-funded journal *Internet Archaeology* has published a paper on Roman Amphorae found in Britain which contains "clickable" maps and timelines.[37] Many online serials previously distributed in ASCII form by LISTSERV are now also available in HTML on the Web. HTML is not always an ideal format for STM serials as it has limitations in encoding some special characters and relies on inline graphics or helper applications for the full display of illustrations.[38] Accordingly, HTML is often used to create an interface for the viewing of other formats. The International Digital Electronic Access Library (IDEAL) service from Academic Press contains contents page information and abstracts in HTML while the full-text of the article itself is available in PDF. A similar approach is taken in giving online access to the journals published by the Johns Hopkins University Press in Project Muse.

Naturally, there is interest in other formats–SGML being the obvious example. Project ELVYN, for example, had first considered PostScript to be the best delivery format for the journal *Modelling and Simulation in Materials Science and Engineering*, but it was eventually delivered in SGML so that it could be converted to HTML for viewing on a Web browser.[39] The Chemistry Online Retrieval Experiment (CORE), which gave access to American Chemical Society (ACS) serials, converted data from the format used by the ACS to a variant of the SGML Document Type Definition (DTD) produced by the Association of American Publishers for their Electronic Manuscript Standard.[40]

Online serials differ from printed serials in their publication and use. For example, there is no essential requirement for serials to be published in regular issues as this is a constraint of printing processes which make it cheaper and more convenient to bundle articles together for distribution. For this reason, online serials often issue individual articles as soon as they have cleared peer-review. In a similar way, the use of online serials is going to be more orientated towards individual articles rather than issues or volumes—meaning that organisations giving access to such serials are going to have much more in common with document delivery services than they do at the moment. There will be more emphasis upon resource discovery through searching rather than browsing. In addition, scholarly online serials are partly moving away from the position where electronic serials merely replicate the functionality–and sometimes the appearance–of printed serials. An electronic serial can be a dynamic document including multimedia, active links to related publications or data, and can be regularly updated to take account of comments made by scholars in reviews or other publications. Experiments with dynamic types of online journal include the eLib-funded *Internet Archaeology* and the CLIC[41] electronic journal project. For example, CLIC has attempted to include ways in which users can acquire three-dimensional molecular data in digital form through electronic journals to act as a starting point for their own exploration of the content.[42] These new publication models will present a severe challenge for preservation. As the CLIC researchers themselves ask: "how long should any given data be expected to reside in automatically accessible form on the Internet?"[43] Also, can data be preserved in such a way that it is able to be retrieved in the future using mechanisms developed at the present time?

PRESERVATION ISSUES

Technological Preservation Issues

The root of the digital preservation conundrum is technological. Digital information has to be interpreted by a machine before it becomes intelligible to human users. There are problems associated with three aspects of digital information technology: the digital medium itself and its associated hardware and software.

Media Longevity

Ten years ago, the digital preservation literature had a lot to say about media longevity.[44] In the 1980s this was often seen as the key technological problem with what was then called machine-readable information. It is still important. Digital media, both magnetic and optical, have short lifetimes in comparison with media such as paper and microfilm. Margaret Hedstrom argues that the threat posed by magnetic and optical media is "qualitatively different" in that the media are reusable and they deteriorate in a matter of years, not decades.[45] The technological response to media longevity is known as "digital refreshing," the periodic recopying of the data onto a new medium. The focus has in recent years, however, moved away from media longevity issues, not because the problems have been solved to any extent, but because there is a greater awareness of significant technological problems associated with hardware and software obsolescence.

Hardware Obsolescence and Software Dependence

John Mallinson noted in 1987 that one of the most serious problems with preserving electronic information is the rapid obsolescence of electronic hardware.[46] Brichford and Maher sum up this problem when they say that a "twenty-year life for the plastic backing material used for computer tapes and disks is irrelevant if the tape or disk drives on which they were recorded become obsolete and unavailable after ten years."[47] In addition, digital information is increasingly stored in formats which are dependent upon particular software to interpret them correctly. This is known as software dependence. We have already noted that online serials are currently made available in several different ways and in a large number of different formats, and this is likely to get worse rather than better in the future as delivery mechanisms and formats change and increase in complexity. One possible answer to the problem of software dependence is to preserve all software together with the information itself, although it is debatable whether this would be a long-term solution. As an alternative, Jeff Rothenberg has suggested preserving metadata that would adequately describe systems so that future generations could build emulators to mimic the behaviour of obsolete hardware and software.[48] A more realistic answer, in the short term at least, is the concept that has replaced refreshing– data migration.

Migration

The Task Force on the Archiving of Digital Information defined migration as "the periodic transfer of digital materials from one hardware/software configuration to another, or from one generation of computer technology to a subsequent generation."[49] Migration differs from refreshing in that it takes account of the hardware/software obsolescence problem. There is no point in making an exact copy onto a new medium if the software and hardware necessary to interpret it no longer exist. The point of migration is to transfer to new formats while, wherever possible, preserving the integrity of the information.

The simplest migration strategies would involve transfer to universal formats such as ASCII text or flat-file data which are (relatively) software independent. Indeed, this might be the best solution for online serials primarily consisting of textual information, but would probably result in a considerable loss of functionality for most STM online serials or those publications which have tried to incorporate dynamic features. An alternative strategy would be to migrate records to a small number of "standard" formats such as PDF or particular applications of SGML. This strategy would simplify the migration process itself while helping to maintain some of the important characteristics of the original.[50] In any case, migration strategies used should be recorded as metadata and preserved together with the original item so that future users are aware of significant changes made to a document during the preservation process.

Despite their intractability, technological problems are probably not the most significant factor in the preservation of online serials. Digital information can be preserved if it is identified early enough, although, as Lesk notes, "preservation means copying, not physical preservation."[51]

Intellectual Preservation Issues

Authenticity

Digital information is easy to change and update. Indeed this is one of its major advantages over paper and print. However, with preservation in mind, this malleability becomes problematic. It becomes very difficult to prove that digital information has not been accidentally or deliberately corrupted at some time. This is as true of online serials as any other digital information. Corruption is not the only issue: online serial articles could be frequently updated to take account of new research and the comments of other scholars. This is not in itself a problem, but it is important that users of electronic serials are sure that the version that they are referring to is the version that they want to see. This is taken for granted in the print world where citations refer to the "canonical archive" of publications. This concern with data integrity is characterised by Peter Graham as intellectual preservation.[52]

Archivists also have an interest in data integrity and a project based at the University of British Columbia has stressed the importance of the concepts of "reliability" and "authenticity." In an archival context, Luciana Duranti has defined both of these terms as follows:[53]

- Reliability refers to the authority and trustworthiness of a record as evidence.
- Authenticity proves that the document is what it claims to be.

In archives, reliability is exclusively linked to record creation. Reliability would similarly be guaranteed for an online serial by editing, peer-review and other quality control processes. Authenticity, on the other hand, ensures that a record "is protected and guaranteed through the adoption of methods that ensure that the record is not manipulated, altered, or otherwise falsified after its creation."[54] With relation to online serials, authenticity could be promoted by the adoption of techniques based on cryptographic theory. Graham himself has suggested adopting something like digital time-stamping (DTS) which uses one-way cryptographic hashing techniques,[55] but recognises that there are likely to be other solutions.[56] Other relevant initiatives might include the Digital Signature Initiative (DSig) of the World Wide Web Consortium (W3C) which is concerned with the development of trust mechanisms for the Web.[57] The importance of intellectual preservation for the future of scholarly communication cannot be over-emphasised. Without some way of ensuring authenticity over time, it is possible that networks will ultimately be unable to support serious scholarly communication.

Administrative Preservation Issues

There are technical solutions to the digital preservation of online serials, and there is some interest in problems concerning intellectual preservation. However, there remain a large number of unresolved issues. These relate to administrative or legal matters, and may actually be the most difficult problems to solve. The questions regarding copyright and ownership are the most intractable, so will be dealt with first.

Copyright and Ownership

The growth in provision and use of electronic information resources (including online serials) has resulted in fundamental changes in the way information is owned.[58] The information embodied in traditional printed serials is normally purchased by subscription, either directly from publishers or through subscription agents. This remains the case, even when most users of this information will obtain it through an intermediary such as a library or document supply service. The organisation or individual that purchases a serial will then retain physical custody of an artefact–a volume or issue–for as long as it is required. Assuming that this artefact is kept in a reasonably good environment and safeguarded against disaster (fire and flood), it should last a long time. Given the fact that printed serials will normally be subscribed to by more than one organisation, a distributed "canonical archive" of scholarly serials will be built up in this way. Long-term preservation (and access) is essentially a by-product of this process and does not require specific initiation.

The situation of electronic information resources is quite different. The "purchaser" of an electronic resource, unless it is an artefact such as a CD-ROM, does not necessarily retain "physical custody" over it. Concerns over copyright mean that the current practice is for commercial publishers to licence the use of information to customers, thus ensuring that the use of this information is governed by contract law rather than copyright law.[59] A licence for a commercial online serial might give the "subscriber" only specific rights over use of a particular serial or group of serials for a limited amount of time. This is where the position becomes problematic. What happens when the subscribing institution decides to cancel its subscription? Will all access rights to that journal, including "volumes" already "paid for," be removed? What would happen if the serial ceases publication or the publisher goes out of business? Research organisations and libraries might find that they have no direct control over which particular online serials would be preserved as part of the "canonical archive." Publishers, especially network publishers, currently seem to be happy to actively encourage browsing, downloading and copying of online serial articles for personal use and also permit the distribution of copies for research purposes,[60] but may have to be persuaded that ensuring long-term access and preservation of their online serials is a desirable objective and that co-operation with other stakeholders (e.g., research libraries or data archives) may be the best way to do this. After all, authors may be reluctant to contribute articles to serials that may not exist very far into the future. In the short term, at least, solutions to these problems will have to be worked out with co-operation between publishers and libraries.[61]

Management Issues

Who Should Preserve?

In the past, preservation has been the responsibility of organisations (such as libraries and archives) that give access to information rather than the producers of that information themselves. Two broad approaches are possible, one a centralised repository model, the other a radical decentralised "non-custodial" model.

National libraries have traditionally conformed to the centralised model using legal deposit legislation to ensure that all relevant published works are collected and preserved. A few have success-fully extended legal deposit legislation to cover electronic publica-tions, but this does not usually include online publications. The British Library, for example, has recently requested the extension of legal deposit to electronic media, but specifically excluded online publications because of their problematic nature.[62] One exception is the National Library of Canada's experimental Electronic Publica-tions Pilot Project, which has been identifying and making copies of Canadian online serials, texts, etc., with the co-operation of publish-ers. Despite this, it is clear that the physical transfer of online publications to central repositories is not going to be a cost-effec-tive solution. It is likely that online publications will require a more decentralised model.

This model originates from ideas promoted by David Bearman (and others) for archives.[63] They have argued that record-creating organisations should retain responsibility for their electronic records while centralised archival repositories would take these over only as a last resort to ensure their preservation. The Task Force on the Archiving of Digital Information, following this argu-ment, proposed that digital information creators, providers and owners should have the initial responsibility for archiving while certified digital archives should be given the right and duty to exercise an aggressive fail-safe rescue function.[64] This sort of approach is attractive for online serials because most publishers will have an interest in maintaining access over time and will migrate the information themselves until such time as the serial is no longer of interest or economic value. Hardware will be periodically upgraded, sometimes formats will change, but the serial need not go "out of print." The crucial time will come when publishers no longer have any interest in keeping a serial going, or cease to exist. It is at that time that fail-safe mechanisms should be activated. The role of central repositories would, thus, be reduced but it would also emphasise the need for leadership and co-ordination from informa-tion professionals.[65] The role of organisations such as the Commis-sion on Preservation and Access in the US and the National Pres-ervation Office in the UK will be crucial in co-ordinating activity in this general area.

What Should Be Preserved?

Deciding what needs to be preserved is another problem. The temptation will be, with digital storage devices becoming cheaper and more compact, to keep everything. However, preservation of digital information is still likely to be expensive–continuous migration will be time-consuming and requires technical expertise–and as the amount of digital information grows, it is likely to remain so. Therefore, some kind of selection before preservation will be necessary.

For scholarly online serials, this process will be made easier by the reliability mechanisms that exist. Peer-reviewed serials will be obvious candidates for preservation as will less formal, newsletter-type publications issued by learned societies and research organisations. It may be harder to assess articles "published" in electronic pre-print archives or the products of scholarly "skywriting." If Odlyzko's vision of an integrated system–combining informal methods of communication (such as electronic bulletin boards) with formal (such as peer-reviewed online serials)–comes to fruition, there may be a case for preserving some information that has not been peer-reviewed or subject to any other quality control processes. This could build either upon appraisal techniques developed for records selection by the archives community or upon the quality selection criteria being adopted by some Internet subject services.[66]

The nature of digital information also means that such appraisal will have to take place very early in its life-cycle. It will not be possible to wait until the information has become unavailable or "out-of-print" before preservation, or no copies may be in existence to be preserved. Instead, the identification of relevant items will have to be made almost at the time of "publication" and rights for its long-term preservation will have to be negotiated. It would be an additional advantage if these processes of selection and appraisal were continuous, indeed with migration as the preservation strategy there will be regular opportunities to reassess the value of the information being migrated.

CONCLUSION

This paper has attempted to outline some of the problems which will need to be confronted to ensure the continued existence and accessibility of the information embodied in the scholarly online serial. Other important issues exist which have not been discussed here, most notably the economic implications of digital preservation. Many of these issues are currently being investigated by librarians, publishers, computer scientists and other stakeholders in digital preservation, but it is important to realise that many of the problems will only be solved with practical experience of ensuring the preservation of digital information and with practical co-operation.

It is easy to become despondent when considering the magnitude of the challenge that digital preservation poses to scholarly communication and those organisations that currently support it, but there are grounds for a cautious confidence in our ability to make the information embodied in online serials available for future generations of scholars.

One more point needs to be considered. In the past, preservation was an activity considered only by specialists within the library and information professions. With the advent of digital preservation, it might become the primary function of the digital research library. All other activities, including resource discovery and access, may ultimately become dependent upon digital preservation.

REFERENCES

1. Task Force on the Archiving of Digital Information, *Preserving Digital Information* (Washington, D.C.: Commission on Preservation and Access, 1996).

2. John Feather, *Preservation and the Management of Library Collections* (London: Library Association Publishing, 1991), 2.

3. Charles M. Dollar, *Archival Theory and Information Technologies: the Impact of Information Technologies on Archival Principles and Methods* (Ancona, Italy: University of Macerata, 1992), 66.

4. David Bearman, *Archival Methods*, Technical Report, vol. 3, no. 1 (Pittsburgh, Pa.: Archives and Museum Informatics, 1989), 17-27.

5. James M. O'Toole, "On the Idea of Permanence," *American Archivist* 52, no.1 (Winter 1989): 10-25.

6. Michael Alexander, "Virtual Stacks: Storing and Using Electronic Journals," *Serials* 10, no. 2 (July 1997): 173-178.

7. Michael Breaks, "The Digitisation of Journal Literature: Towards Sustainable Development," *Serials* 10, no. 2 (July 1997):164-172.

8. Hazel Woodward, "The Impact of Electronic Information on Serials Collection Management," *IFLA Journal* 20, no. 1 (1994): 35-45.

9. Hazel Woodward, "Electronic Journals in Libraries," in *Project ELVYN: an Experiment in Electronic Journal Delivery*, ed. Fytton Rowland, Cliff McKnight and Jack Meadows (London: Bowker-Saur, 1995): 51.

10. Robert M. Campbell and Barrie T. Stern, "ADONIS: a New Approach to Document Delivery," *Microcomputers for Information Management* 4, no. 2 (1987): 87-107.

11. *ARL Directory of Electronic Journals, Newsletters and Academic Discussion Lists*, 6th ed. (Washington, D.C.: Association of Research Libraries, 1996).

12. Brian Shackel, *BLEND-9: Overview and Appraisal*, British Library Research Paper, 82 (London: British Library, 1991).

13. Fytton Rowland, "Recent and Current Electronic Journal Projects," in *Project ELVYN: an Experiment in Electronic Journal Delivery*, ed. Fytton Rowland, Cliff McKnight and Jack Meadows (London: Bowker-Saur, 1995): 15-36.

14. Dennis P. Carrigan, "Research Libraries Evolving Response to the 'Serials Crisis'," *Scholarly Publishing* 23, no. 3 (Apr. 1992): 138-151.

15. Ann Okerson, "Publishing through the Network: the 1990s Debutante," *Scholarly Publishing* 23, no. 3 (Apr. 1992): 170-177.

16. Andrew M. Odlyzko, "Tragic Loss or Good Riddance? The Impending Demise of Traditional Scholarly Journals," *International Journal of Human-Computer Studies* 42 (1995): 71-122.

17. Odlyzko, "Tragic Loss," p. 83.

18. Stevan Harnad and Jessie Hey, "Esoteric Knowledge: the Scholar and Scholarly Publishing on the Net," in *Networking and the Future of Libraries 2: Managing the Intellectual Record*, ed. Lorcan Dempsey, Derek Law and Ian Mowat (London: Library Association Publishing, 1995): 110-116.

19. Stevan Harnad, "Scholarly Skywriting and the Prepublication Continuum of Scientific Inquiry," *Psychological Science* 1 (1990): 324-343.

20. Ann Okerson and James O'Donnell, eds., *Scholarly Journals at the Crossroads: a Subversive Proposal for Electronic Publishing* (Washington, D.C.: Association of Research Libraries, 1995).

21. Harnad and Hey, "Esoteric Knowledge," 114-115.

22. Stevan Harnad, "Electronic Scholarly Publication: *Quo Vadis?*" *Serials Review* 21, no. 1 (1995): 70-72.

23. Paul Ginsparg, "First Steps towards Electronic Research Communication," *Computers in Physics* 8, no. 4 (July/Aug. 1994): 390-396.

24. Steven B. Giddings, quoted in: Gary Stix, "The Speed of Write," *Scientific American* 271, no. 6 (Dec. 1994): 72-77.

25. Jack Meadows, David Pullinger and Peter Such, "The Cost of Implementing an Electronic Journal," *Journal of Scholarly Publishing* 26, no. 4 (July 1995): 227-233.

26. Cliff McKnight, "The Human Factors of Electronic Journals," in *Project ELVYN: an Experiment in Electronic Journal Delivery*, ed. Fytton Rowland, Cliff McKnight and Jack Meadows (London: Bowker-Saur, 1995): 37-47.

27. Fytton Rowland, "Print Journals: Fit for the Future?" *Ariadne* 7 (Jan. 1997): 6-7. Available: http://www.ariadne.ac.uk/issue7/fytton/

28. Fytton Rowland, "Recent and Current Electronic Journal Projects," in *Project ELVYN: an Experiment in Electronic Journal Delivery*, ed. Fytton Rowland, Cliff McKnight and Jack Meadows (London: Bowker-Saur, 1995): 15-36.

29. Jaco Zijlstra, "The University Licensing Program (TULIP): a Large Scale Experiment in Bringing Electronic Journals to the Desktop," *Serials* 7, no. 2 (1994): 169-172.

30. Fytton Rowland, Cliff McKnight and Jack Meadows, eds., *Project ELVYN: an Experiment in Electronic Journal Delivery* (London: Bowker-Saur, 1995).

31. Bahram Bekhradnia, "Pilot National Site Licence Initiative for Academic Journals," *Serials* 8, no. 3 (Nov. 1995): 247-250.

32. David Pullinger, "Journals Published on the Net," *Serials* 7, no. 3 (Nov. 1994): 243-248.

33. Cliff McKnight and John Richardson, "The Impact of New Publishing Media," in *The International Serials Industry*, ed. Hazel Woodward and Stella Pilling (Aldershot: Gower, 1993): 89-105.

34. Barrie T. Stern and Henk C. J. Compier, "ADONIS: Document Delivery in the CD-ROM Age," *Interlending and Document Supply* 18, no. 3 (1990): 79-87.

35. Steve Hitchcock, Leslie Carr and Wendy Hall, "A Survey of STM Online Journals, 1990-95: the Calm before the Storm," in *ARL Directory of Electronic Journals, Newsletters and Academic Discussion Lists*, 6th ed. (Washington, D.C.: Association of Research Libraries, 1996): 7-32. Available: http://journals.ecs.soton.ac.uk/survey/survey.html

36. Judith Wusteman, "Electronic Journal Formats," *Program* 30, no. 4 (Oct. 1996): 319-343.

37. Paul Tyers, "Roman Amphoras in Britain," *Internet Archaeology* 1 (1996). Available: http://intarch.ac.uk/journal/issue1/tyers_index.html

38. Richard Entlich, Lorrin Garson, Michael Lesk, Lorraine Normore, Jan Olsen and Stuart Weibel, "Testing a Digital Library: User Response to the CORE Project," *Library Hi Tech* 14, no. 4 (1996): 99-118.

39. Cliff McKnight, Jack Meadows, David Pullinger and Fytton Rowland, "ELVYN: Publisher and Library Working towards the Electronic Distribution and Use of Journals," in *Digital Libraries '94: Proceedings of the First Annual Conference on the Theory and Practice of Digital Libraries, June 19-21, 1994–College Station, Texas*. Available: http://csdl.tamu.edu/DL94/paper/mcknight.html

40. Michael E. Lesk, "Electronic Chemical Journals," *Analytical Chemistry* 66, no. 14 (15 July 1994): 747A-755A.

41. CLIC is the acronym for the four organisatons involved in the project: Cambridge Site of the Royal Society of Chemistry; Leeds University; Imperial College of Science, Technology and Medicine, University of London; Cambridge University.

42. David James, Benjamin J. Whitaker, Christopher Hildyard, Henry S. Rzepa, Omer Casher, Jonathan M. Goodman, David Riddick and Peter Murray-Rust, "The Case for Content Integrity in Electronic Chemistry Journals: the CLIC Project," *New Review of Information Networking* (Dec. 1995). Available: http://www.ch.ic.ac.uk/clic/video.html

43. Omer Casher, Gudge K. Chandramohan, Martin J. Hargreaves, Christopher Leach, Peter Murray-Rust, Henry S. Rzepa, Roger Sayle and Benjamin J. Whitaker, "Hyperactive Molecules and the World-Wide-Web Information System," *Journal of the Chemical Society: Perkin Transactions* 2, no. 1 (Jan. 1995): 7-11.

44. Michael W. Day, *Preservation Problems of Electronic Text and Data* (Loughborough: EMBLA Publications, 1990).

45. Margaret Hedstrom, "Preserving the Intellectual Record: a View from the Archives," in *Networking and the Future of Libraries 2: Managing the Intellectual Record*, ed. Lorcan Dempsey, Derek Law and Ian Mowat (London: Library Association Publishing, 1995), 180.

46. John C. Mallinson, "On the Preservation of Human- and Machine Readable Records," *Information Technology and Libraries* 7 (1988): 19-23.

47. Maynard Brichford and William Maher, "Archival Issues in Network Electronic Publications," *Library Trends* 43, no. 4 (spring 1995): 701-712.

48. Jeff Rothenberg, "Ensuring the Longevity of Digital Documents," *Scientific American* 272, no. 1 (Jan. 1995): 24-29.

49. Task Force on the Archiving of Digital Information, *Preserving Digital Information*, 6.

50. Margaret Hedstrom, "Preserving the Intellectual Record," 185.

51. Michael Lesk, *Preservation of New Technology: a Report of the Technology Assessment Advisory Committee of the Commission on Preservation and Access* (Washington, D.C.: Commission on Preservation and Access, 1992).

52. Peter S. Graham, *Intellectual Preservation: Electronic Preservation of the Third Kind* (Washington, D.C.: Commission on Preservation and Access, 1994).

53. Luciana Duranti, "Reliability and Authenticity: the Concepts and their Implications," *Archivaria* 39 (spring 1995): 5-10.

54. Luciana Duranti and Heather MacNeil, "The Protection of the Integrity of Electronic Records: an Overview of the UBC-MAS Research Project," *Archivaria* 42 (fall 1995): 46-67.

55. Hashing techniques use algorithms which convert the arrangement of all characters, symbols, graphics, etc., within a particular document into a unique hash value which can be stored and retrieved as metadata. Any change (however small) to the document will produce a different hash value when it is converted using the same algorithm. The process is described as "one-way" because there is no means of recreating the original document from its hash value.

56. Peter S. Graham, "Long-Term Intellectual Preservation," in *Digital Imaging Technology for Preservation*, ed. Nancy E. Elkington (Mountain View, Calif.: Research Libraries Group, 1994): 41-57.

57. World Wide Web Consortium, *Digital Signature Initiative*. Available: http://www.w3.org/Security/DSig/

58. Ann Okerson, "What Academic Libraries Need in Electronic Content Licenses," *Serials Review* 22, no. 4 (winter 1996): 65-69.

59. Okerson, "What Academic Libraries Need," 65.

60. Pamela Pavliscak, "Trends in Copyright Practices of Scholarly Electronic Journals," *Serials Review* 22, no. 3 (fall 1996): 39-47.

61. Ann Okerson, "Some Economic Challenges in Building Electronic Libraries: a Librarian's View" (paper presented at IFLA Congress, Beijing, Aug. 1996). Available: http://www.library.yale.edu/~okerson/ifla.html

62. British Library Research and Innovation Centre, *Proposal for the Legal Deposit of Non-Print Publications* (London: British Library, 1996), Section 2D. Available: http://www.bl.uk/services/ric/legal/legalpro.html

63. David Bearman, "An Indefensible Bastion: Archives as Repositories in the Electronic Age," in *Archival Management of Electronic Records*, ed. David Bearman, Technical Report, no. 13 (Pittsburgh, Pa.: Archives and Museum Informatics, 1991): 14-24.

64. Task Force on the Archiving of Digital Information, *Preserving Digital Information*, 21.

65. Margaret Hedstrom, "Electronic Archives: Integrity and Access in the Network Environment," in *Networking in the Humanities*, ed. Stephanie Kenna and Seamus Ross (London: Bowker-Saur, 1995): 77-95.

66. Gregory F. Pratt, Patrick Flannery and Cassandra L. D. Perkins, "Guidelines for Internet Resource Selection," *College and Research Libraries News* 57, no. 3 (Mar. 1996): 134-135.

LOCAL, NATIONAL
AND INTERNATIONAL PROJECTS

Electronic Scholarly Publishing Initiatives
at Industry Canada

David Beattie
David McCallum

SUMMARY. As part of its internationally acclaimed SchoolNet
project, Industry Canada is supporting a series of initiatives in the

David Beattie is Director, Virtual Products Group, Industry Canada/SchoolNet.
David McCallum was Principal Consultant for the Electronic Publishing Promo-
tion Project (EPPP), Industry Canada/SchoolNet, 8th Floor, West Tower, 235
Queen Street, Ottawa, ON K1A 0H5, Canada (email: mccallum.david@ic.gc.ca).
During the course of his work with Industry Canada (1995 to 1997), Mr. McCal-
lum was on leave from the position as Executive Director of the Canadian
Association of Research Libraries/Association des bibliothèques de recherche du
Canada. He also served as a member of the Association of Universities and
Colleges of Canada/CARL Task Force on Academic Libraries and Scholarly
Communication, which issued its final report in November 1996.

[Haworth co-indexing entry note]: "Electronic Scholarly Publishing Initiatives at Industry Canada." Beattie, David, and David McCallum. Co-published simultaneously in *The Serials Librarian* (The
Haworth Press, Inc.) Vol. 33, No. 3/4, 1998, pp. 223-232; and: *E-Serials: Publishers, Libraries, Users,
and Standards* (ed: Wayne Jones) The Haworth Press, Inc., 1998, pp. 223-232.

area of electronic scholarly publishing. This paper provides a brief introduction to Industry Canada and to SchoolNet's activities related to universities, academics and students, describes efforts to promote electronic publishing of scholarly information, and outlines plans for the creation of a Canadian Virtual Centre for Online Scholarly Publishing.

KEYWORDS. Electronic journals, Industry Canada, SchoolNet, online scholarly publishing

INDUSTRY CANADA AND ITS INITIATIVES OF INTEREST TO THE CANADIAN ACADEMIC COMMUNITY

Industry Canada's principal objective is to help make Canada more competitive by fostering the growth of Canadian business; by promoting a fair, efficient marketplace; and by encouraging scientific research and technology diffusion. In 1994, Industry Canada issued a major policy document entitled *Building a More Innovative Economy*.[1] This policy was based on a recognition of the emerging knowledge-based global economy, and emphasized the advancement of education and research as essential means of strengthening Canada's competitive position.

The rapid evolution of the "information highway" was also recognized, as was the need to take full advantage of its potential as an educational tool. This policy thrust was reinforced in *Science and Technology for the New Century*,[2] released in March of 1996, which called for making full use of networking technology to connect Canadian communities, including schools, universities and colleges.

SchoolNet[3] is one of several Industry Canada programs aimed at helping students build skills that will allow them to be more marketable, to transfer from their studies to employment as quickly as possible, and to be well-positioned as entrepreneurs in the new global economy. A multifaceted World Wide Web site, SchoolNet is composed of vetted content for use by the Canadian educational community.

The mandate of SchoolNet is to facilitate the linkage of the 16,000 schools and 3,400 libraries in Canada as well as the 447 native communities that fall under the federal government's jurisdiction. Access to SchoolNet is completely free of charge to students, teachers, and the general public.

Although most SchoolNet applications are oriented to the Kindergarten to Grade 12 levels, some are aimed squarely at the postsecondary sector. One example is the recently launched National Graduate Register (NGR).[4] A companion service to Human Resource Development Canada's Electronic Labour Exchange,[5] the NGR allows students at Canadian universities and colleges to place their resumes online, and to have them accessed by employers within and outside of the country. This will effectively create an electronically searchable national labour pool, thereby allowing firms, even small ones, to do online campus recruiting across Canada.

ELECTRONIC SCHOLARLY PUBLISHING INITIATIVES

Dissemination of new knowledge is an essential aspect of the research process. In a knowledge-driven economy, cost-effective methods for the distribution of scholarly information are vital, particularly in a time of reduced financial support for universities and their libraries.

The academic community in Canada has identified an emerging crisis in scholarly communication. *The Changing World of Scholarly Communication: Challenges and Choices for Canada* (final report of the Association of Universities and Colleges of Canada [AUCC]/Canadian Association of Research Libraries [CARL] Task Force on Academic Libraries and Scholarly Communication, distributed with the December 1996 issue of *University Affairs*)[6] explains how the costs to individuals and libraries of acquiring scholarly information have skyrocketed, due in large part to the pricing policies of commercial publishers. The report argues that the traditional system of scholarly communication is at risk and calls for a transformation of the current model into one that is more dynamic and democratic, "based less on centralized access to print documents, and more on open access via telecommunication to information from various locations in a wide range of electronic formats."[7]

SchoolNet's work to date in the area of electronic scholarly publishing can be grouped under three headings: studies, demonstration projects, and active promotion. SchoolNet is currently exploring the establishment of a virtual centre for online scholarly publishing to allow large-scale conversion of paper-based journals to online publication.

Studies

To explore the viability of electronic publications, in 1995 SchoolNet contracted for two studies concerning the economics of scholarly publishing: *Cost and Revenue Structure of Academic Journals: Paper-Based versus E-journals*,[8] by Dr. Vijay Jog of the Economics Department at Carleton University (Ottawa, Ontario, Canada) and *Funding Electronic Journals on the Internet*[9] by Phoenix Systems Synectics of Ottawa.

Dr. Jog's study identified savings as high as 50% in the costs of online publication, compared to paper-based publication; in theory, these savings could rise even higher if publication were undertaken and managed centrally. The Phoenix study showed the technical feasibility of charging online, and described methods by which publishers could charge for access to their journals.

Demonstration Projects

To develop practical data on the operational aspects of electronic scholarly publishing, SchoolNet assisted the electronic publication of three journals, chosen by means of a formal competition. One was an upgrade of an existing electronic journal, and two were conversions of existing paper-based journals, one of which continues to publish in its original form.

SchoolNet provided support for the multilingual online journal *Surfaces*,[10] Canada's oldest and most respected online journal, now in its fifth year of publication. Activities include the systematization of the production process, standardizing online pagination techniques, and conversion to SGML, all of which have the objective of upgrading the technical platform of the journal to the highest common denominator in electronic scholarly publishing. *Surfaces* will shortly become the first online journal to be published by a Canadian university press, Les Presses de l'Université de Montréal.

Support has also been provided for a parallel (on paper and online) publishing project with the *Canadian Journal of Behavioural Sciences (CJBS)*.[11] This project assessed the impact of parallel publishing on readership of the journal, on subscriptions to it and on issues such as copyright. The reaction from authors and readers has to date been positive; in fact, paid subscriptions to the paper-based journal actually increased following its availability online.

Finally, SchoolNet supported the total conversion of a journal from on paper to online publication. The library reviewing journal, *Canadian Review of Materials (CM)*,[12] ceased paper publication late in 1994 and is now only accessible online, published by the Manitoba Library Association. The journal has been experimenting with various methods of maintaining revenues and has now determined that advertising will be its primary source of revenue.

The demonstration projects with *Surfaces* and *CJBS* have yielded a great deal of information on the management, policy and technical issues concerning the publication of an online scholarly journal. Both journals have written up their experience to date and the studies are accessible from SchoolNet. This information will be an invaluable record of experience for those considering electronic publishing. The record of the *Surfaces*[13] and *CJBS*[14] experiences are available on the Web.

PROMOTIONAL ACTIVITIES

To help break down barriers to the acceptance of electronic publishing of scholarly information, in the spring of 1996 SchoolNet contracted with Mr. David L. McCallum, on professional leave from his position as Executive Director of the Canadian Association of Research Libraries, to head up the Electronic Publishing Promotion Project (EPPP).

The Project has the following objectives:

1. To raise awareness in the Canadian academic community of the soaring costs of traditional scholarly communication methods, and of the potential for electronic publishing to address them.

Key messages being communicated include:

a. The Internet has become a *bona fide* medium for academic information exchange and publishing;
b. Electronic communication of research information allows many advantages over print publishing, including ease of searching, multi-media functionality and global accessibility;
c. It is not difficult for Canadian academics to become Internet users.

2. To seek endorsements from Canadian academic associations and related organizations of peer-reviewed electronic publications as valid outlets for scholarly material; and
3. To encourage the transition of existing Canadian scholarly publications from paper to electronic format, and the creation of entirely new electronic scholarly products.

Objectives 2 and 3 relate directly to Recommendations 21, 22 and 23 under the common heading "Supporting Electronic Publishing: National Action" of the final report of the AUCC/CARL Task Force on Academic Libraries and Scholarly Communication.[15]

Outreach Activities

Initial presentations on the EPPP were made at the Canadian Learned Societies Conference in June of 1996 at Brock University in St. Catharines, Ontario. In the fall of 1996, full information packages were prepared and distributed to Canadian academic organizations. The packages contained a detailed description of the project, excerpts from the project Web site,[16] information on how academics could become computer literate and go online, and a request for the organizations to endorse peer-reviewed electronic scholarly publications.

Feedback on these mail-outs has been most encouraging. The project is being publicized in the newsletters of various associations, and in response to numerous requests, presentations on the project are being made to associations, government organizations, and at universities across the country.

Endorsements of Electronic Scholarly Publishing

Recognizing that Canadian academics will be hesitant to publish electronically unless their publications are officially recognized both by their peers and academic institutions, Canadian scholarly associations and related organizations have been approached to consider formally adopting the following statement:

> This organization recognizes the legitimacy of scholarly material published in electronic form when such information conforms to accepted standards of peer review.

The proposed resolution is based on a similar resolution passed in 1994 by the Higher Education Funding Council for England (HEFCE):[17]

> In the light of the recommendations of the Joint Funding Councils' Libraries Review Group Report[18] (published in December 1993) refereed journal articles published through electronic means will be treated on the same basis as those appearing in printed journals.

The statement of endorsement, or a close variant, has been adopted by the Humanities and Social Sciences Federation of Canada, an umbrella group composed of over fifty scholarly societies, by the Canadian Association of University Teachers, and by CARL. It is expected that other organizations, including the Association of Universities and Colleges of Canada (AUCC), will follow suit in due course.

The Director General of Industry Canada's Science Promotion and Academic Affairs Branch has written to the presidents of the three Canadian Granting Councils (the Medical Research Council, Natural Sciences and Engineering Research Council, and the Social Sciences and Humanities Research Council) requesting that they develop equivalent policy statements. Initial reaction has been positive; in fact, the Medical Research Council has officially adopted this policy.

CESN (Canadian Electronic Scholarly Network)

A Web site on SchoolNet has been developed that groups all EPPP information in one place. CESN[19] identifies and allows access to full-text, peer-reviewed Canadian electronic scholarly publications, contains links to related electronic publishing activities throughout the world, describes Industry Canada's information highway intiatives, and profiles new Canadian full-text, peer-reviewed electronic scholarly journals. The site also provides information on selected Canadian scholarly associations, and on the FESPIC (Forum for Electronic Scholarly Publishing in Canada) discussion group.

Electronic Scholarly Publishing Principles

Electronic publishing is still too new to have established generally recognized standards. Development of and adherence to such standards should accelerate the acceptance of electronic publishing within academia. At the same time, the simple fact that a publication is available electronically does not guarantee that it will not be priced at an unacceptably high level–reasonable pricing policies are also essential.

A draft set of principles[20] intended to describe the characteristics of high-quality electronic scholarly publishing projects was developed by David L. McCallum and will shortly be issued to a variety of electronic publishing and related Internet discussion groups. The principles cover archival, bibliographic, economic, legal and technical aspects, and reflect an academic library perspective. Feedback from Canadian respondents has been positive.

A VIRTUAL CENTRE
FOR ONLINE SCHOLARLY PUBLISHING

A fleeting comment in the study by Dr. Jog (described above) opened the door to an exciting new development. Jog noted that based on work performed at Virginia Tech, significant benefits should be realized by clustering production and proficiency around a common electronic publishing centre. These can be made possible through:

- Greater savings from efficiencies in publication mark-up and preparation;

- A critical mass of expertise in such management issues as copyright, digital integrity, maintenance of subscription revenues and journal operations;
- A coordinated capacity to locate or develop, then to apply, the latest technologies.

Efforts are underway to establish a self-sustaining virtual centre for the online publication of scholarly journals, to be formed through a partnership among university presses and journals, with the goal of creating a national network of online publishing resources for peer-reviewed, non-profit scholarly journals. As of May 1997, four publishing partners have been identified (two university presses, a university library, and a national scholarly society).

Over the initial period of this project, the partners will publish twenty or more journals online, and will promote online publishing within the journals community. The intention is to expand the number of participating organizations as the project develops. New technologies developed will be freely accessible to the partners, and ultimately to the Canadian scholarly community. Progress and results from the project will be published on the Internet.

It is estimated that the overall cost of the project over three years will be about $1 million. The partners will seek financial contributions from other federal programs, provincial governments and educational institutions, and possibly private sector sponsorships.

The results of this project will support several government objectives:

- Employment in new technologies;
- Retention of highly qualified personnel within Canada;
- Lower costs to government and universities (especially libraries), as journal costs decline;
- Construction of research infrastructure; and
- Creation of commercial opportunities for exploitation of new technologies and expertise.

NEXT STEPS

It is hoped that financing for the Virtual Centre will be in place shortly, and that it can begin its activities before the end of 1997.

The founding partners hope to expand the number of non-profit organizations participating in the project over time. The results of their work will be reported on a regular basis through the CESN Website.

The Electronic Publishing Promotion Project has the potential to significantly change the face of scholarly communication in Canada, creating what it is hoped will be an affordable publishing environment that takes full advantage of new technological capabilities, while at the same time respecting the values of the traditional academic publishing system.

NOTES

1. Industry Canada, *Building a More Innovative Economy–Summary.* Available: http://xinfo.ic.gc.ca/ic-data/economy/BAMIE/summary-e.html

2. *Science and Technology for the New Century: A Federal Strategy.* Available: http://canada.gc.ca/depts/science/english/strat-e.html

3. Available: http://www.schoolnet.ca

4. Available: http://ngr.schoolnet.ca

5. Available: http://ele.ingenia.com

6. Available: http://www.aucc.ca/english/sites/aucccarl.htm

7. Ibid., p. 5.

8. Available: http://www.schoolnet.ca/biz/economics/vijayjog.html

9. Available: http://www.schoolnet.ca/biz/economics/phoenix/index.html

10. Available: http://tornade.ere.umontreal.ca/~guedon/Surfaces/

11. Available: http://www.cycor.ca/Psych/ac-main.html

12. Available: http://www.mbnet.mb.ca/cm/

13. Jean-Claude Guédon, "Meta-Surfaces, or Ends and Means to Grow a Viable Electronic Scholarly Journal." Available: http://tornade.ERE.UMontreal.CA/~guedon/Surfaces/meta-surfaces.html

14. Stuart Hickox, "Guidelines for the Conversion of Scholarly Journals to Electronic Form." Available: http://www.cpa.ca/project/guide.html

15. Available: http://www.aucc.ca/english/sites/aucccarl.htm

16. Available: http://www.schoolnet.ca/vp/cesn/

17. Available: http://www.hefce.ac.uk

18. Available: http://ukoln.bath.ac.uk/follett/follett_report.html

19. Available: http://www.schoolnet.ca/vp/cesn/

20. "Principles For Consideration by Canadian Academic Associations in Support of Electronic Publishing." Available: http://www.schoolnet.ca/vp/cesn/princips.htm

Seamless and Integrated Access to the World of Electronic Journals

Jane Beddall
Sue Malin
Kim Hallett

SUMMARY. Blackwell's Electronic Journal Navigator provides a single point of access, reference, control and financial management for electronic journal subscriptions. The service is accessible over the Internet using a World Wide Web browser. Blackwell's have a global network of servers that provide the user with instantaneous access to the full text and abstracts of peer-reviewed scholarly electronic journal articles regardless of their physical format, location, or publisher. Libraries subscribing to electronic journals can benefit from simplified password and access management; standard and customized journal usage analysis and management reports; and assistance with electronic archiving and electronic document delivery. Library users can benefit from a single access and authentication point for all electronic journals; a single search interface and extensive browsing functionality; and alerting services and delivery of full-text electronic articles direct to their PC. *[Article copies available for a fee from The Haworth Document Delivery Service: 1-800-342-9678. E-mail address: getinfo@haworth.com]*

KEYWORDS. Electronic journal, electronic publishing, Blackwell's Electronic Journal Navigator, digital library

Jane Beddall is Electronic Journal Navigator Manager, Sue Malin is Electronic Services Marketing Manager, and Kim Hallett is Marketing and Communications Manager, Blackwell's, Hythe Bridge Street, Oxford OX1 2ET, England (email: kim.hallett@blackwell.co.uk).

[Haworth co-indexing entry note]: "Seamless and Integrated Access to the World of Electronic Journals." Beddall, Jane, Sue Malin, and Kim Hallett. Co-published simultaneously in *The Serials Librarian* (The Haworth Press, Inc.) Vol. 33, No. 3/4, 1998, pp. 233-241; and: *E-Serials: Publishers, Libraries, Users, and Standards* (ed: Wayne Jones) The Haworth Press, Inc., 1998, pp. 233-241. Single or multiple copies of this article are available for a fee from The Haworth Document Delivery Service [1-800-342-9678, 9:00 a.m. - 5:00 p.m. (EST). E-mail address: getinfo@haworth.com].

At Blackwell's the Electronic Journal Navigator is our first step towards integrating a wide body of research literature and ultimately integrating it with multiple user interfaces enabling seamless linking from secondary to primary literature in an electronic environment. Multiple formats, printed books, printed journals, looseleaf, CD-ROM, traditional online, microfiche, portable electronic documents and now Web-based information present significant challenges to researchers and information specialists wishing to access the most *relevant* data regardless of format. Accessing and purchasing smaller units of highly focused relevant information solves a research need. Therefore, an opportunity exists for information intermediaries to provide tools and services which enable integrated searching of diverse research materials.

Engineering Village and BioMedNet are other successful examples of a service integrating research materials and information focused on a virtual community and delivered in a World Wide Web environment.

Blackwell's Electronic Journal Navigator was developed through partnerships with 50 libraries and 12 major publishers worldwide. Added to Blackwell's portfolio of services it provides academics and research libraries with a one-stop shop for research material, regardless of medium.

The development process began with our customers expressing a need for assistance as more electronic journals–free and subscribed– were becoming available from publishers–invariably direct. Complex licensing arrangements, multiplicity of passwords for each publication and end-user resistance to accessing paper-based publications via the World Wide Web were some of the problems encountered by libraries and information centres in 1995.

Blackwell's staff thought through the types of service features that libraries might need as electronic journals became more prevalent and sought out a technology partner collaborator. The most open and expedient technology available at the time was a suite of software developed by ICL/Fujitsu and being used to create Academic Press's IDEAL and APPEAL services, which ICL hosts. Adhering to open standards was an underlying principle of the development while meeting the technological requirements of "the lowest common denominator" customer, making access as wide as possible for *any* customer with *any* web browser, and allowing the publishers to control the content environment with minimal or no interference as well as the pricing/access policies were also requirements.

Blackwell's Electronic Journal Navigator facilitates exchange between all types of publishers–primary, secondary and tertiary/aggregators–hosting content if necessary, validating access through our subscription management system–or in fact *any* subscription management system, even a competitor's. Search results are matched either from a familiar database or through Blackwell's simple article header database then linking to the primary source in electronic form. PDF and RealPage have been the most popular with publishers but TeX, SGML or HTML and later multimedia formats are all possible.

From January to May 1996 Blackwell's recruited North American and European development partners–publishers prepared to give access to some test titles, and libraries willing to provide us with regular feedback on the functioning of the service throughout development. The test service went live July 5, 1996, to our development partners in North America via a server in San Jose, California, and to our European partners via a server in London, England.

There were quite a few ups and downs in the technology partnership. Managing deadlines, testing code and responding to development partner feedback and integrating changes are familiar experiences for any organisation engaged in software development or pioneering new electronic publishing formats.

Simultaneous to the technical development work which stretches from milestone to milestone but never actually ends, is the intense work carried out by our publisher relations team. Many presentations and discussions were held with leading publishers during 1996. By Frankfurt Bookfair 1996 we had an electronic distribution license prepared and many publishers were in a position to sign agreed terms by the end of the year. Basic delivery of electronic journals began to Blackwell's customers in January via Electronic Journal Navigator and the new, enhanced service was launched to the marketplace in April 1997.

Links to secondary databases, document delivery services and monograph-related services such as Collection Manager are all underway both technically and commercially. Profiling and alerting enhancements are fast approaching on the horizon.

We are deploying continuous feedback from customers via a listserv, regular electronic surveys of participants and most recently regular Web-based surveys of end-users in each site in order to gain insight into end-user behaviour with electronic journals. Feeding back input to the development team, marketing team and sales team via our corporate Intranet is becoming a reality and is helping to increase the speed of response to our customers' demands.

BLACKWELL'S ELECTRONIC JOURNAL NAVIGATOR

Blackwell's Electronic Journal Navigator offers a single point of access, reference, control and financial management for all electronic journal subscriptions. The service is accessible over the Internet using a World Wide Web browser. Via a global network of servers the service provides customers with instantaneous access to the full text and abstracts of peer-reviewed scholarly electronic journal articles regardless of their physical format, location or publisher.

Libraries subscribing to electronic journals benefit from:

- Simplified password and access management
- Standard and customised journal usage analysis and management reports
- Assistance with electronic archiving and electronic document delivery.

Library users benefit from:

- A single access and authentication point for all electronic journals
- A single interface that supports searching and browsing
- Alerting services and delivery of full-text electronic articles direct to their PC.

BENEFITS TO LIBRARIES
AND INFORMATION CENTRES

Reduction of the Administrative Load for the Library

Blackwell's Electronic Journal Navigator service handles all electronic journal subscriptions regardless of location, publisher or format. Problems with electronic journals seem to be more about access than acquisition: where it is, how to get it and where it has gone! Blackwell's Navigator service provides a single access route to multiple servers–with a global system coordinating multiple server access for the user. The service also provides a central source for easily downloading (and technically supporting) the different viewer software used by journals produced in formats such as HTML, PDF and RealPage. Other formats will also be supported as they become widely available.

Password Management

Blackwell's Electronic Journal Navigator eliminates the need for the researcher to maintain multiple passwords for different publishers and journals or departments and individuals by supplying a single username and password and linking all journal subscriptions to it. Furthermore, single password access to multiple servers and journals can be allocated at whatever level of access is required within an organisation. So if everyone at a particular institution requires access to all the electronic journals subscriptions then this can be achieved through a single password. If on the other hand access needs to be differentiated by department or site then this can be done as well. Blackwell's Navigator service then handles the validation and access to electronic journals for the user community according to the license provisions indicated by the publisher.

Electronic Subscription Agent

By placing electronic journal subscriptions through Blackwell's, benefits can be gained from the same economies of scale we deliver with paper-based subscriptions such as centralised ordering, consolidated invoicing, and a central point for claims and administration. Blackwell's Electronic Navigator service will also solve problems caused by the multiplicity of pricing and licensing models offered by different publishers of electronic information. The service actually simplifies electronic journal purchasing by removing the need to supply IP addresses or passwords for each subscription. Blackwell's Electronic Journal Navigator service was designed to ensure that it is as easy to create a subscription to an electronic journal as it is to create one for the print equivalent.

Comprehensive Management Reports

The comprehensive range of management reports will enable institutions to track, in detail, the patterns of usage and readership for electronic subscriptions. In addition to regular monthly management reports, Blackwell's Electronic Journal Navigator will allow the customer to interrogate the system interactively and download customised reports, an invaluable aid to local collection management.

An Electronic Archive

Blackwell's are negotiating positively with publishers and other archiving stores to provide customers with a permanent electronic archive for all electronic subscriptions. When Blackwell's serve as the host for publishers, we will maintain at least a 3-year archive or more, subject to publisher negotiation. Blackwell's overall aim is to ensure the preservation of and access to scholarly work, freeing libraries from the costs associated with local data mounting and storage of paper archives.

Electronic Document Delivery

As well as providing access to electronic material on a subscription basis, Blackwell's Electronic Journal Navigator also provides for transactional delivery, i.e., on a "pay per view" basis, for articles from electronic journals to which an organisation does not subscribe (publisher permitting). The exact price for electronic article delivery depends on the copyright fee levied by the publisher, but full pricing details can be viewed on screen prior to placing a request to view the full-text article. Several different payment options are available such as credit card, deposit account or monthly invoice account.

Technical Support

Experienced technical staff can assist customers with all areas of technical support, from loading and maintaining the institution's electronic journal collection, installing and maintaining Internet browsers, and installing and maintaining article-viewing software to offering advice on the support of an institution's network itself.

BENEFITS TO LIBRARY USERS AND RESEARCHERS

Ease of Access

Blackwell's Electronic Journal Navigator service is accessible via the World Wide Web using a common Web browser such as Netscape; special software is not required to access electronic journals. The service provides centralised access to all electronic journals and manages the authentication process. There is no longer any need for the individual user to remember the different locations and passwords for each of the journals to which the organisation subscribes.

Extensive Searching Facilities

The search engine enables the customer to search for articles across a comprehensive collection of electronic journals, regardless of where the journal is actually held. Searches for articles can be activated by keywords, by author and by article title. The search can be limited to the journals to which an institution subscribes, or can be expanded across all journals. The search can also be limited to a particular subject discipline, or expanded across all disciplines. The system also allows the customer to perform keyword and author searches in a particular journal or journal issue. Boolean logic is supported in addition to proximity searching, truncation and wildcards. There is a simple search tool for the first-time user and an advanced search capability that allows the experienced researcher to obtain more finely tuned search results.

Browsing Functionality

Browsing is an important part of research. Blackwell's Electronic Navigator allows the researcher to browse journals in a variety of different ways. The user can have direct access to journals on subscription, browse journals in a particular academic discipline, search through the alphabetical listing of journal titles or browse the journals produced by a particular publisher. Once a journal of interest has been located the researcher can navigate through the issues and tables of contents to the article level.

Instantaneous Electronic Article Delivery

Provided the subscription is valid, once an article has been selected it can be downloaded to the screen and read online or printed out using the appropriate viewer from the viewer store. Alternatively the article can be automatically sent in its original format to an email address to be downloaded and read/printed at a later time. Articles are presented in the exact format in which they were published, including special fonts, tables, graphs and images in colour or black and white. Depending in which format the article is published (typically PDF at present), the system's viewers support full-text searching within the article, thumbnail views of all pages, navigation via bookmarks, magnification and reduction tools and printing at resolutions of up to 600 dpi.

Alerting Services

Blackwell's Electronic Journal Navigator will alert the researcher when new issues of the selected key journals have been published and added to the database, thereby keeping customers up-to-date in their field of research. In most cases the electronic versions are available before their print counterparts (subject to publishers' policies). Also in development is a feature which alerts individuals to new electronic journals which are available in their particular subjects of interest.

Other Features

Some of the other features of the service are:

Context-sensitive help–available on every screen, offering assistance relevant to where the user is in the system.

News feature–Blackwell's will alert users to new developments and enhancements to the service on screen via the "News" button.

Feedback button–the user's questions and feedback can be input directly on screen and sent via automatic email to Blackwell's Electronic Journal Navigator customer service team. This is an effortless way to ask questions or query any aspect of the service.

Index to free electronic journals–Blackwell's are also establishing system links to the contents of a comprehensive and expanding range of free electronic journals.

License store–as electronic versions of journal licenses grow, access can be gained through an integral license store.

Star ratings–highlight key research journals in the library's core collection for all library users.

Technical Knowledge Base–as a user starts to access and use Blackwell's Electronic Journal Navigator, all available data will be collected and made accessible via a searchable database of frequently asked questions. Information is available about the system itself as well as about other issues surrounding electronic journal provision, such as Web browsers, document viewers, networking and software/hardware platforms.

Full Service Package

In addition to the Blackwell's Electronic Journal Navigator System itself, Blackwell's also provides customers with a comprehensive service package including:

- Integrating the customer's site's access to electronic journals via the World Wide Web
- Managing electronic license agreements with publishers
- Providing support and advice on electronic license definitions
- Dedicated customer support
- Dedicated technical support
- Product and software training materials for librarians and end users
- Combined invoicing for print and electronic journals.

Journals in Transition:
From Paper to Electronic Access:
The Decomate Project

Joost Dijkstra, Msc

SUMMARY. The European project Decomate is the first of a series of projects that aims to convert a digital library into a virtual library. By providing more and more services digitally, distributed and across a network, the goal of a virtual library in which end users no longer visit a library building is becoming possible. The aim of the project is to provide end users with electronic access to copyrighted material from their desktop. This paper describes the project's objectives and scope, as well as the design, implementation and integration of generic software which provides access to copyrighted electronic material to the end user's desktop. Furthermore, a first report on the use of the system is presented and the main characteristics of the contents of licenses between publisher and library are addressed. *[Article copies available for a fee from The Haworth Document Delivery Service: 1-800-342-9678. E-mail address: getinfo@haworth.com]*

KEYWORDS. Networked digital library, digitalised journal, copyrighted material, generic system development, user studies, virtual library

Joost Dijkstra is project manager for innovative library projects, and overall project manager for the Decomate project, Tilburg University, Library, P.O. Box 90153, 5000 LE, Tilburg, The Netherlands (email: j.m.m.dijkstra@kub.nl).

The author wishes to thank Nuria Gallart (UAB), Hans Geleijnse (TU), Clare Jenkins (LSE), Ferran Jorba (UAB), Caroline Lloyd (LSE), Teun Nijssen (TU), Thomas Place (TU) and Wietske Sijtsma (TU) for their input.

[Haworth co-indexing entry note]: "Journals in Transition: From Paper to Electronic Access: The Decomate Project." Dijkstra, Joost. Co-published simultaneously in *The Serials Librarian* (The Haworth Press, Inc.) Vol. 33, No. 3/4, 1998, pp. 243-270; and: *E-Serials: Publishers, Libraries, Users, and Standards* (ed: Wayne Jones) The Haworth Press, Inc., 1998, pp. 243-270. Single or multiple copies of this article are available for a fee from The Haworth Document Delivery Service [1-800-342-9678, 9:00 a.m. - 5:00 p.m. (EST). E-mail address: getinfo@haworth.com].

243

1. BACKGROUND

The transition from paper to electronic journals, one of the main themes in the mid-1990s, is a major factor in the development of the digital library. Although databases have been electronically accessible for a long time, the next main development was the introduction of (commercial) electronic document delivery services using scanned journal articles. Almost parallel to that development, institutions and universities started to make their research memoranda and working papers electronically available for everybody free of charge. Then both commercial publishers and universities started new ventures, assisted by new technologies that made it easier to go electronic.[1]

At Tilburg University (TU), the first real project in which end users were able to access journals electronically from their desktop was EASE (Elsevier's Articles Supplied Electronically, 1994-1996). EASE was a local project in cooperation with Elsevier Science— similar to the TULIP project (The University Licensing Project) in the USA but on a much smaller scale. A dedicated software package was implemented which end users could use to access the journal articles.

In many aspects the Decomate project is the follow-up to the EASE project. The dedicated software package had to be replaced by a more open and standardized means of access to databases, more electronic material (not necessarily copyrighted) had to be included, and new document formats were implemented. The advent of the World Wide Web stimulated these developments in that it became easier to integrate systems.

The main goal of the Decomate project has been to provide end users with access to copyrighted materials in electronic form. The project officially started in March 1995 and ended in February 1997. It was carried out by three partners: Tilburg University (TU), the coordinator; Universitat Autònoma de Barcelona (UAB); and the London School of Economics and Political Science (LSE). The European Commission DG XIII C/E (Telematics Applications Programme, Telematics for Libraries) partially funded the Decomate/ LIB-3078 project.

The present article has been organised as follows. Section 2 contains an overview of the project's main objectives and results. An overview of the Decomate system is given in section 3. Sections 4 and 5 describe the implementation and integration of the main parts of the system. The launch of the Decomate system at the sites has been accompanied by fairly extensive user studies. Section 6 contains an overview of the goals, the methodology and the main results of these user studies. For a successful implementation of the Decomate project license agreements with publishers were essential. The main characteristics of these agreements are addressed in section 7. The main conclusions regarding the project are summarised in section 8.

2. PROJECT OBJECTIVES AND APPROACH

Project Objectives

The goal of Decomate was to provide end users access—through the library—to copyrighted materials distributed by commercial publishers in electronic form. In order to achieve this general goal the following subgoals were set:

- The project should integrate a number of existing technologies and ongoing developments in order to create a new and modern type of library service.
- It should demonstrate how electronic distribution of published documents could take place, involving publishers, libraries and end users.
- The technical approach should be based on open, generic solutions which are as independent as possible from the specific technical environment of the Decomate partners in order to ensure a maximum level of transferability to other libraries in the European Community. To demonstrate this transferability, the generic system should be implemented in the technical environment of each partner.
- Attention should be paid to the copyright issue, so as to encourage mutual understanding and future cooperation between libraries and publishers.
- The Decomate software should be based on a pilot system already under development; it should be expanded and gen-

eralised, resulting in a generic system which can handle various types of documents and document formats, and which can be implemented in a variety of technical infrastructures.

- The system should be the subject of intensive user studies in order to study the usefulness and effects of electronic document distribution, especially of mainstream, copyrighted materials.

With these goals in mind, the specific objectives of the project were:

- to create and demonstrate solutions for distribution of scientific publications in electronic form to end users. These solutions are to be based on licensing agreements between publishers and libraries, and on a generic software application that provides the necessary functionality for coping with a variety of document types, formats and technical infrastructures.
- to develop a generic and transferable system for electronic document distribution. The system should include an end user application that would allow access to bibliographic and document databases. This application would provide document browsing, viewing and delivery functions. The system should also include a monitor function for user authorization, usage registration, management information and reporting.
- to develop the system as a set of generic modules, providing the functionality in a way that is as independent as possible of specific document formats, bibliographic databases, document servers and system environments.
- to demonstrate the transferability of the software solution by implementing the Decomate system within the technical infrastructure of the participating libraries.
- to set up a document distribution service to end users in the participating libraries in order to study the usefulness and effects of electronic distribution of mainstream, copyrighted materials.
- to disseminate the results of the project as widely as possible, finishing with an international conference on the Decomate project.

3. OVERVIEW OF THE DECOMATE SYSTEM

Publishers, Journals and User Groups

Decomate covered a wide range of journals mainly in the field of economics (including econometrics), social sciences, arts and (applied) computer science. At the end of the project Tilburg University held approximately 150 journal titles in electronic stock, the London School of Economics about 80 titles and the Universitat Autònoma de Barcelona about 40 titles. Common target groups at all three universities were sought in the faculties of the particular areas that were covered by the journals. The user groups included undergraduate and graduate students and academic staff from the faculties and/or research institutes in the above subject areas.

During the project the partners were successful in getting Elsevier Science, Kluwer Academic Publishers, and Academic Press to deliver copyrighted material. Smaller publishers were also continually being contacted to deliver electronic copyrighted material. Unfortunately they could not manage to set up a production environment before the formal end of the Decomate project.

Decomate's System Environment and Architecture

The Decomate system is running in an environment that can be said to contain three key players: the publisher, the library and the end user. The publisher delivers the copyrighted material in electronic form either by FTP or on CD-ROM. The electronic material consists of both bibliographic data and the corresponding electronic documents. This material is mounted locally. The link (logical pointer) between the bibliographic record and the corresponding document is preserved in the bibliographic record data. The electronic documents are stored in the document base, where the mapping of a logical pointer and the physical address of the document are maintained.

Besides these bibliographic databases and electronic document stores, other systems and/or software interact with the Decomate system as well. These are the management reporting tools (such as spreadsheet software packages) and data from corporate databases that are needed to complement other data in the Decomate database.

The actual processing of the received data until it is mounted in both the bibliographic database and the document store is carried on outside the Decomate system. The reason for this is that there was no generic way in which this process could be implemented within the Decomate system because of differences in the existing systems at all partners' sites. The bibliographic databases were built up in a distinct way at all three places and a common mechanism to store the data could not be identified.

Figure 1 shows a close-up of the core system. The interfaces between the Decomate system and its environment are indicated. The Decomate system itself consists of two parts: the Decomate server and its toolkit. The toolkit collects all kinds of data that are needed to produce a management report. The logfiles, containing data from both the Decomate server and the document store, are the main input to this report. Besides the logfile data, the toolkit needs additional data from corporate databases that contain all kinds of data that cannot be collected from the logfiles, for example, data

FIGURE 1. Internal look at the Decomate system.

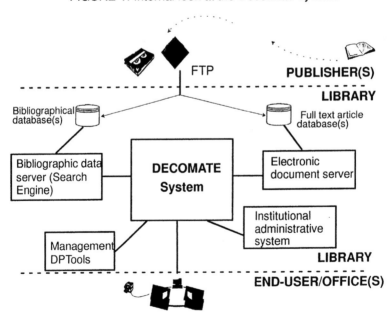

such as the type of user (student, academic, postgraduate), and the faculty/department, but also less typical data items such as location of the equipment of the user (to determine from where–faculty/department, home–users access the system), as well as privileges and authorization data. Finally, an indication of which journal each article is from is added to the system, because the logfiles contain only the article identifier of any article retrieved. These data are usually easy to extract from the bibliographic database.

As one can see, the system uses basically two protocols: Z39.50 to retrieve bibliographic data from the databases and Hypertext Transfer Protocol to retrieve the electronic documents themselves. End users access the Decomate system through a Webclient. The kernel of the Decomate server, the request handler, sends all functional and system requests such as search, browse, present, show and log and authorization to one of the modules: search, browse, log event, user verification, and get document.

For every record returned from the bibliographic server the request handler checks the existence of special tags within the bibliographic record. This check identifies the location of an electronic document. If a certain tag does exist, then the request handler adds the URL to the returned data so that the end user can retrieve the document. This URL contains the location of the document, session identification and security information. These last two are needed in order to prevent unauthorised users from accessing the document store without identification. Time-out data and special security keys are other ways in which the system protects copyrighted material from unauthorised use.

4. IMPLEMENTATION AND INTEGRATION OF THE DECOMATE SERVER

Requirements of a Generic Decomate Server

The main objective of the project was to specify, design and implement a generic piece of software that should be open, as compliant to standards as possible and easily transferable to other distinctive technical environments. But on the other hand the system was also required to adhere to the regulations on the protection of the copyrighted material against abuse as set out in the contract between publisher and library.

The system should consist of a set of generic modules. These should be as independent from each other as possible. The functionality of the system should support the handling of multiple document formats, including derived forms that can be handled by the end user's desktop. Furthermore, neither on the server side nor on the end-user, client side should the software be useable only with specific hardware or desktops, and it should run on a wide variety of platforms. The system should also include a monitoring package for user authorization, usage registration, and reporting management information. To this extent a similar kind of assumption as to what software packages will be used at the front end should be avoided.

The system should support multiple languages (Dutch, Spanish, and English) and should be prepared to provide access to multiple databases and/or CD-ROMs. A final requirement was that the system be able to manage various user authorization schemes because different policies were in place at the three sites.

Implementation and Integration of a Generic Server

Obviously, modularity in itself does not guarantee that a system is generic. But by choosing a particular object-oriented programming language (Object Perl), and by introducing a so-called three-tiered client-server architecture, some main cornerstones were established.

The three-tiered architecture consists of: the end-user level, the data level and the intermediary, server level. The end-user level was actually the one with the lowest impact and the easiest to take care of. A simple Web browser did the trick by making connections to the intermediate level, in our case the Decomate server. Any commonly used desktop on which a Web browser is installed can be used to access the system.

The server level contains the implementation of the functional aspects brought together in the Decomate server. The fact that various classes of differences had to be attributed stimulated the use of a significant number of configuration files to make the software more generic, and to make it a rich customization tool.

The data storage level was taken care of by implementing two types of servers: a document server for the document store with a capacity of multiple Gigabytes and a Z39.50 server for the bibliographic databases. Specially designed programming interfaces preserve the generic character of the server at the boundaries of the Decomate server. One of these interfaces, called the Protocol Layer Interface, connects the Decomate server to a Z39.50 Origin (client side but part of the Decomate server). This interface allows a rather easy substitution of other Z39.50 implementations.

At the so-called Z39.50 target side (server side, where the bibliographic database exists) a similar interface–the Common Database Interface–had been defined and implemented. It maps, again like an API, the Z39.50 layer to the basic functionality that is expected from a full-text search engine that exists on top of a bibliographic database. The Common Database Interface allowed the project partners to have different search engines. LSE and TU implemented their commercially available full-text search engines (respectively BRS/Search and Trip) in the Common Database Interface, while UAB was using the freeware search engine ZEBRA. The fact that UAB could decide not to use the CDI but to connect directly to the Z39.50 layer of the Decomate server was further proof of the generic character of the system.

Decomate did not implement its own Z39.50 protocol. Good source distributions were freely available from specialized sources, such as YAZ and the software from EUROPAGATE, another European project in the Telematics for Libraries framework.

Figure 2 shows the layers and building blocks of a Decomate system. Note that the Decomate system is not a standalone system but can connect to remote Decomate systems. The system is scaleable, as all three types of servers can appear not just once but many times.

The goal of achieving document format independence has been realised by making use of the MIME types that are implemented in a WWW environment. Any currently available document format that is implemented in a WWW browser–be it native, such as a plug-in or a helper application–can be used. Even document for-

FIGURE 2. Layers and building blocks of a Decomate server.

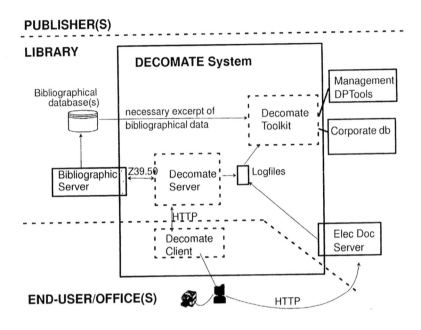

mats that may become available years from now are likely to be manageable in this setup, including real multimedia documents containing audio and video.

The integration of the Decomate generic software in general did not cause too many problems although the implementation of the interface between the commercial/freeware search engines and Decomate's CDI took much more time than expected at LSE and UAB. The reason was that both partners were in the process of selecting a new search engine. They were relatively inexperienced with the newly acquired search engine as well being relatively unaware of the exact implementation details of the Decomate server–and documentation was poor. Evidently, much time was lost by tracing the problem source–search engine or Decomate server– rather than to solving the issue.

There were no other real integration problems, which is a proof of the successful design and implementation of the Decomate software. Successful changes in the user interface through the configuration files were made locally. At present new databases and CD-ROMs have been added to the system without any problem, but little effort is being devoted to plugging in a thesaurus and implementing a document order module.

5. MONITORING AND REPORTING THE USAGE OF THE DECOMATE SYSTEM

Goals and Methodology

Besides the design and implementation of the core system to search and retrieve electronic documents, an equally important part of the project was the design and implementation of a monitoring and reporting package. This package was to provide the means to facilitate the authorization of users, monitor the usage of the system, and provide the capacity to generate management reports.

Prior to the design of the monitoring package, an analysis was carried out to identify:

- what information about the usage of the system was required by management
- what information the contracts prescribed should be reported to the publishers
- what, technically speaking, was feasible to monitor given the limitations set down by law
- what requirements of the qualitative user studies were in place in order to back up and correlate data to be collected from the interviews with end users.

The major goal to design and implement a piece of software as generic as possible applied here as well.

Collected Data

The following data were collected and served as the input for the management report. They are divided into two classes: data on the use of the bibliographic databases, and data on the retrieval of articles from the document server.

Data gathered over specific periods of time from each of the bibliographic databases in the system included:

- number of users per department per type of user searching the database
- number of total sessions
- number of total searches per department per user type
- total number of distinct users per department per user type
- number of times a user moves from a bibliographical database to a document store to retrieve an article, also per department per user type
- search strategy, i.e., use of fields (author, title, free text, boolean operators) per department per user type

The following data from the document server were collected:

- ranking of journals accessed
- ranking of journals per department per user type (student, researcher, academic staff) per publisher per time interval
- location from where articles were accessed (department, library, home)
- number of articles accessed per department per user type per publisher per time interval
- number of times an article was accessed per department per user type per publisher per time interval (ranking of articles)
- number of users accessing articles per department per user type per publisher per time interval
- number of new users accessing articles per department per user type per publisher per time interval

Access, Authorization and Protection of the Material

Decomate is dealing with copyrighted material whose use is restricted by contract to the local university community. To prevent the material from being abused, only authorized users have access to the material. However, within the project access not only to the document material but also to the bibliography was available under restricted access: the same applied for the bibliographic databases that were commercially exploited. Additionally, different access and authorization regimes did apply among the partners.

The Decomate system has been designed in such a way that direct access to the document server is not possible. Users are always forced to access a bibliographic database first. Two access schemes were in place. In the first scheme bibliographic databases could be accessed free of charge, but the user was designated merely as a "guest." As soon as the user made a request for the retrieval of a copyrighted document, identification was required. If the login was successful, the user would not need to identify him/herself again when he/she switched from one database to another. A guest user, however, would have to identify him/herself every time he/she attempted a specific action not permitted to guest users. In the second scheme the bibliographic database was accessible under strict identification at the front door. User identification was required immediately after the selection of a database.

Due to the limitations of real client-server applications, the limitations of the Web and privacy legislation, it was not possible to keep track and to prevent the misuse of the full-text articles once they have been retrieved and displayed at a local desktop. However, the only thing the project partners could do was to make end users aware of the fact that they were going to access copyrighted material by displaying a reference to the license terms at login time. This was one of the clauses in the license agreement.

Collecting Statistical Data and Reporting

The Decomate system logs every significant user or system event in logfiles. The monitoring package processes the logfiles that contain system events. Privacy law must be obeyed and therefore no links between personal names and user events are maintained–neither in the case of access to a bibliographic database nor in the case of access to a document. The usual model that applies, for instance, to statistical analysis in library OPAC logs has been followed: the user's ID is used strictly as an anonymous statistical entry.

Decomate logdata and additional corporate data were stored in a relational database, as it provides a powerful environment for storing, querying and analysing the data, using a standard query language. Although the database presently reflects all the information needs of the project managers, obviously new information needs may arise. Hence the database was built with the standardisation principles as flexible as possible. This facilitates the adding of new modules and indeed allows for making new log and statistical data available.

To comply with the objective of implementing a generic system, it was decided to use commonly available PC reporting tools such as spreadsheets for final analysis and reporting of the results instead of developing a dedicated Decomate reporting system. An additional benefit that is offered is the maximum customisation, flexibility and independence to the local situation.

Standards that are adhered to in this piece of generic software are ANSI C, SQL-92 and X/Open SQL CLI (Call Level Interface, the basis for Microsoft's ODBC interface). Adherence to these standards permitted remote access to any SQL database that complied with them. ANSI C was used to write the loading program in which logdata storage procedures are embedded. The final analysis and reporting of the data were carried out at the PC. Nonetheless, no restrictions were set on the location of the database. In fact it can be installed at a remote server or perhaps on the same PC. When the database was loaded on a remote server, ODBC drivers were used to bridge the client software and the database.

The Decomate partners used Ingres and Oracle as their database management systems, and Microsoft Excel 5.0 for Windows, Microsoft Access 2.0 and Quattro Pro 6.0 as their reporting tools since these packages were the ones in use locally. Two of the three partners had implemented the database on a remote host system while one partner installed both the database and the reporting software on a local PC.

6. THE USAGE AND USERS OF THE DECOMATE SYSTEM: THE USER STUDIES

Objectives of the User Studies

In order to establish the usefulness and effects of electronic distribution, especially of mainstream copyrighted materials, an intensive user study was carried out within the Decomate project. The user study was done at the three sites but was tailored to take local environments into account. End users were involved in testing and using the system in order to foster an understanding of user requirements and changes in behaviour in reaction to the electronic delivery of copyrighted material. The authorisation module in Decomate ensured that a potential user was identified as belonging to the assigned community before allowing access to the copyrighted material. The user study was meant to scrutinise aspects of use both by authorised users in general and by members of a targeted user group. The targeted group was drawn from the academic staff and researchers of the institutions.

The user study sought to collect and analyse data in the following areas:

- *Amount and type of usage.* Investigations were made in order to establish if different types of users exploit the system in different ways and/or to lesser or greater extents.
- *Ergonomic issues.* The user's perception of the efficiency, convenience and ease of use of the system was studied.
- *User acceptance.* Through a qualitative study of the reactions to the system, an understanding was gained of how well expectations have been matched and how effectively the system delivered what the end user required. Shortfalls and benefits of the system were highlighted by end users.

Methodology

In order to collect the data four different approaches were used. These were:

- *An interactive online questionnaire.* Randomly selected end users were asked to complete, when logging in, a short questionnaire displayed on their screen. The questionnaire was concise in order to encourage completion and concentrated mainly on ergonomic issues and information technology facilities already offered.
- *In-depth interviews.* Two sets of in-depth interviews (on a one-to-one basis) were conducted from a representative sample of

users recruited from the academic staff and researchers. One took place before the interviewee had used Decomate, the second towards the end of the project.

• *Focus group meetings.* Complementary to the one-to-one interviews, focus group meetings were organized to explore similar issues, but in an open forum setting. The benefits of such a method are that it allows an investigation of the group culture and that it facilitates the discussion of research methods and the end user's reactions to electronic delivery of copyrighted materials. Due to room capacity and time constraints, this was held only at the LSE.

• *A retrospective analysis of logged-on users.* The data available from the logfiles–logging virtually all system events–was used to ascertain usage according to department or according to status. Other information was also obtained, for example, whether there is any correlation between the subject area of a user and the length of time spent logged into the Decomate system.

Preliminary Results of the Use of the Decomate System

The Decomate system was launched in mid-October 1996. Throughout this section the data relate to the period 1 November 1996 to 28 February 1997.

The number of potential users (including the target group) varied significantly at the three sites. While a slight 170 users at UAB were able to access the system, the user group at LSE was about 2,000 people, and at Tilburg University about 15,000.

Amount of Usage

Detailed information on amount and type of usage was extracted from the logfiles. This was supplemented by the questionnaire, interviews and the focus group.

Table 1 shows the figures for the total number of personalized logins and the number of searches at each site, regardless of target group.

These figures exclude additional guest logins (517 at LSE and

TABLE 1. Total number of personalised logins and the number of searches at each site.

Month	LSE		TU		UAB	
	logins	searches	logins	searches	logins	searches
November	118	945	178	1748	52	151
December	89	810	105	547	48	221
January	126	940	87	721	89	538
February	203	1240	126	911	127	1070
Total	536	3935	496	3927	316	1980

127 at UAB) which occurred during the study. TU's access control was based solely on personalized login and therefore no additional guest logins were occurring.

The information gained from the follow-up interview supports this. At LSE the members of the user group who were interviewed indicated that they had used the system soon after the launch to experiment and test it. After that their use settled down, and in some cases the user did not revisit Decomate. The pattern of use for other users reflected the stage that they were at in their research. Several users commented that the short length of time that Decomate had been available had prevented a regular pattern from developing. The experience of introducing new services has shown that time is needed before usage starts to increase. The increase in usage from January to February, at all sites, demonstrates this. At TU, December and January are months in which exams are scheduled, and this helps explain the lower use.

Amount of Use by User Type

At each site the users were categorised into academic staff, postgraduate students, undergraduate students and guest (at UAB and

LSE only). The logins by user type (excluding guest) are shown in Table 2. The percentage of the total number of logins is given in brackets. The figures in bold indicate the group with the highest level of usage for each site.

Although each site had categories of users called academic staff, postgraduate and undergraduate, the application of the terminology differed among the institutions. This goes some way to explaining the very different usage patterns of the various user types at each site. At the Universitat Autònoma de Barcelona and Tilburg University the majority of postgraduates are registered as staff because they also teach. Therefore users who can be identified as postgraduate from their username represent a small percentage of the entire user population. All Ph.D. students at the LSE were issued a username/password that distinguishes them from academic staff. The higher use by postgraduates at LSE is attributable to the fact that at the time of the user study many academic staff members were not actively engaged in research. The interviews and focus group suggested that postgraduates are more willing to experiment with a service such as Decomate. They have less developed research methods and they possibly also have more time.

The work environment and facilities available to a user affected the use of the service. At LSE, UAB and TU most users had their own computer or had to share one (in public rooms or in private offices) with other people. Those who had to use public rooms felt that the availability of computers had detrimentally affected their use of Decomate, since more effort was required to use the service. Not surprisingly, the computers were generally old and slow, and this discouraged use of the service.

It is remarkable to note that the results of type of use show that

TABLE 2. Logins by user type (excluding guests).

User Type	LSE	TU	UAB
Academic Staff	68 (12.6%)	**218 (44%)**	**201 (63.6%)**
Postgraduate	**402 (75%)**	80 (16%)	16 (5%)
Undergraduate	66 (12.4%)	198 (40%)	99 (31.4%)

undergraduates used the service as much if not more than other user types, although in general undergraduates work from textbooks. Once again, this group seems to be the early adopters of new systems.

Amount of Use by Department

The subject focus of Decomate was mainly on economics and (applied) computer science. At each site there were various departments which were identified as the most likely to benefit from the journals which were made available. However, use was certainly not confined to the target departments and at each site a significant percentage of the use came from beyond the obvious users. This is due to both curiosity and interdisciplinary relevance. The factors that encouraged use by undergraduates, i.e., accessibility via the local network and a familiar interface, contributed to use by a wide number of departments.

At the LSE the highest number of logins was made by a department not in the original target group, Statistics and Mathematics (33%). The next two highest numbers of logins were made by the two most heavily targeted departments. The use of the service by departments such as Geography and Social Administration (21%) demonstrates the interdisciplinary nature of the research undertaken at the LSE, while the Department of Economics accounts for 25% of the total number of logins.

Not surprisingly, the target departments at TU with the highest use of the system from an identifiable group were the Faculty of Economics (15%) and the Faculty of Social Sciences (12%). Unfortunately, the departments of some users (mainly undergraduate students and some staff outside target groups, including librarians) could not be identified but accounted for almost half the total number of logins (respectively, 41% and 26%).

The target departments at Universitat Autònoma de Barcelona were the Department of Applied Economics (36%), the Department of Business Economics (31%) and the Department of Economics and Economic History (22%).

Ergonomic Issues: Reading and Printing

In the preliminary interviews most users stated that they made photocopies of relevant journal articles. The vast majority of interviewees made printouts from Decomate. Only parts of articles (not the whole article) were read from the screen. Most users read the abstract and selected parts of the text before deciding to print: this helped them to avoid printing irrelevant material. Others did not read any of the article but usually this was when the article had been identified as useful by some other means, e.g., a CD-ROM indexing/abstracting service, and so the decision about its validity had already been taken.

Users were asked to comment on the legibility of the full-text articles, both on the screen and when printed. The responses reflected the fact that the full-text files differed depending on the format used by the publisher. Some were true PDF and were clear and easy to read from the screen without needing to enlarge the image. The legibility of the wrapped PDF TIFF files on the screen was considerably less than that of the true PDF and users found it necessary to enlarge the image. The legibility was felt to be sufficient.

Factors Dominating the Usage

The study demonstrated that Decomate is a benefit to the research community. It is a service that is valued by the users and one which, given its various limitations, proved useful in the short period of time allocated to the study. The user study revealed various factors that inhibit use and others that encourage it. Some of these were apparent at all the sites, but others were local characteristics. The factors that inhibited use were the quantity of titles, time span covered, the availability of another place to look for information, legibility of the article on screen and legibility of the article when printed. The factors that encouraged use were: desktop access, 24-hour availability, ability to print, interface ability to navigate around text, and avoidance of the general problems associated with traditional paper journals.

Users recognised that the delivery modes for full-text material are still at an experimental stage and that the legibility should improve with time. The ability to print articles was felt to be essential by most users. The way in which most users work demands that they have a paper copy because it is transportable in a readable format and can be written on. A service such as Decomate that did not permit users to print would not be useful as visits to the library would still be necessary in order to obtain photocopies. Decomate alleviated some of the problems in locating journals. Users could be sure that an article was always available, even if someone else was using it. Material could be printed if necessary.

Several local variations affected the use of Decomate at the three sites. Some factors were: already having a similar service in place, the level of promotion, having older computer equipment on site, having a rather limited number of journals available in electronic form compared to the number of paper journals, and the demography of the user population.

The single most influential factor that affected the user study was the time span over which it was conducted. Users require time to adjust to a new service and to start using it to genuinely support their research rather than just to satisfy curiosity. In order to ascertain the impact on research methods and user behaviour a longer period of time would be required.

7. A BREAKTHROUGH: LIBRARIES AND PUBLISHERS WORKING TOGETHER

Establishing Relationships

The Decomate partners managed to find publishers who were willing to deliver copyrighted material. Some of the talks resulted in signing a license. When licenses were not signed, the reason was either a strategic decision-making process of the publishers, or the fact that they were not (fully) prepared to deliver the copyrighted material for the short period of time required by the project's timetable.

Fruitful talks which resulted in a signing of a contract or the unprecedented delivery of copyrighted material were established with:

- Elsevier Science, Amsterdam, The Netherlands
- Academic Press, London, United Kingdom
- Kluwer Academic Publishers, Dordrecht, The Netherlands
- University Press, Universitat Autònoma de Barcelona, Barcelona, Spain.

A unique project was set up between Swets & Zeitlinger and Tilburg University. Swets & Zeitlinger acted as an intermediary between smaller publishers and the library. The objective of this project was to interest the smaller publisher (mainly British and American) in delivering copyrighted material via the agent. Unfortunately, no real progress could be made during the project, for the reasons mentioned above.

But the second year of the project (1996) may be considered an eye-opener for both the libraries and the publishers. There was a hint of the change in late autumn 1995 when a license agreement with Kluwer Academic Publishers (KAP) was negotiated surprisingly quickly in just two meetings. In the UK a national consortium of both British publishers and British libraries was founded and yielded procedures to access copyrighted material stored at the participating publishers. However, this was not considered to be the best solution since only a hyperlink to the publisher was suggested as the means of access rather than an integrated solution from the library and end user point of view.

License Content

The project partners finally negotiated license agreements. Their contracts, however, were not equal. Nonetheless some general observations can be made on what considerations were taken into account. The following characteristics were identified as part of each contract:

- license type
- rights given to libraries for usage of material
- obligations
- prohibitions
- subscription fee

License Type

During the course of the project two different types of licenses were negotiated: consortium and institution-site-based license. The Decomate project partners engaged in institution-site-based licenses with Elsevier Science (TU, UAB, LSE) and Kluwer Academic Publishers (TU, UAB), while LSE also engaged in a consortium license (Academic Press). A new type of license scheme developed in 1997, by which the cost of the material was based on pay-per-view agreements.

All licenses addressed the definition of authorized users. All users had to be registered at the institution, being either staff, students or fellows who are visiting the university temporarily.

Rights Given to Libraries for Usage of Material

The libraries had the following rights:

- to download images to the desktop computer of the user
- to print one copy of articles resulting from discrete searches for personal use
- to add tables of contents and abstracts onto the University's alerting system
- to reformat files in accordance with technical needs (one publisher)
- to make one back-up copy (one publisher).

Most of the licenses permitted easy cancellations of journals. Each year the library and publishers made a new list of journals that were to be supplied in electronic form. Continuous access to the back issues of cancelled material was also allowed.

Obligations

The partners were obliged:

- to share usage statistics with the publisher
- to control the access to the e-files (authorization, protection) so as to limit user access to the members of the university community and campus
- to include a publisher's copyright notice on the screen and if possible on print-outs
- to allow a publisher to access the system for supervision (one publisher)

- to keep track of suspicious transactions.

The emerging possibilities and growing importance of the World Wide Web necessitated a change in the way in which user access and location were controlled. Now, the focus is on identifying users by username and password. This permits access from home or from any other location.

Prohibitions

The partners were prohibited from:

- altering content and identification of the file
- using files in any form for interlibrary loan purposes or supplying them in any form to third parties.

Providing access to external users and day visitors or providing access through public access points was prohibited. And even though access from project partners to each other's databases was technically possible, this too was prohibited.

Subscription Fee

Of course, a paragraph on the license fee was part of the agreement. The library had to pay a fixed percentage on top of the subscription fee of the printed journals. Discounts were heard of (when the subscription was for the electronic version of the journal only) up to 10% of the subscription fee for paper journals, but this was not applied in the partner's licenses.

Main Observations

The following general observations may be made, based on two years' experience in negotiating contracts with publishers. Some of these observations may be invalid now, as things change quickly:

- The major publishers were taking the lead in electronic subscriptions. They had a strategy and the capability to test and innovate.

- Negotiations with publishers took a lot of time. It also took time to establish all required technical and organizational relations between the publisher and the library.
- In general, most medium-sized and small publishers were reluctant to "go electronic." This is an obstacle for libraries, who want to obtain sufficient critical mass. This continued reluctance may not bode well for the future existence of these publishers.
- Electronic files were not cheaper than printed journals. In most cases libraries had to pay an additional percentage on top of the subscription fee.
- There was/is a clear tendency for publishers to try to make an arrangement on the delivery of electronic files, including non-cancellation agreements with respect to the current subscriptions. Publishers wanted to assure a stability in the sale of their products.
- Experiences with electronic subscriptions provided important information for the publisher. It also provided essential management information for the library. In the long run it can provide a solid basis for decisions on whether to engage in license agreements for certain journals, or whether to use the journals on a pay-per-view basis.
- In the Decomate project all partners stored the electronic files on a local server. Basically the storage location of the full text ought to be a trivial consideration in a networked environment. Performance and the level of use could be the main things to consider when deciding how to store files.

8. MAIN PROJECT CONCLUSIONS

The Decomate project has succeeded in meeting all its objectives and goals. At present a Decomate system is operational as a production system at all partners and delivers copyrighted material from the publisher through the library to the end user. The system has been running as an experimental system since October 1996 at all sites as a testbed for the user studies.

A main characteristic of the system is the WWW application

through which end users have access to both the bibliographical database and the full-text documents. The project succeeded in implementing a system that uses both the standard Z39.50 protocol to access the bibliographical databases and the de facto standard HTTP protocol to retrieve electronic documents in a WWW environment. Both come together in the Decomate server of the system.

The project succeeded in its goal of implementing and integrating a system that is as open, generic, and independent as possible. This is demonstrated by the fact that the same generic software has been successfully implemented in three technically distinct environments. The software was developed without relying on any particular external system, and it adheres to existing standards.

A good technical infrastructure is an important aspect of the system and it helps make it acceptable to end users. Although no particular restrictions were set for any kind of equipment or network–other than that it be fast and robust–it became clear that for printing, high-speed printers are necessary in order to serve end users. And the same requirement for speed seems to be valid for other equipment as well. Waiting for a document to be displayed at the PC or workstation for more than 30 seconds, as an example, is unacceptable. Although the Decomate system runs in virtually any technical environment, this should not be taken too literally. On the other hand, the elements that form the infrastructure (equipment, network, ISDN, for example) seem to improve over time.

The project did lack sufficient validation and demonstration time to allow users to customize, play around with the system and to provide relevant feedback at a deeper level on both the usage of the system and the perception of the system. With the system up and running in October 1996, the end user had time to customize it, yielding so-called playing sessions based on curiosity, but such sessions did not provide useable information about the perception of the system by the user. However, the information gathered on the use of the journals appears to be valuable management information that may provide a basis for decision-making on journal collection development.

The main learning curve during the course of the project was not imposed by technical aspects but by a management aspect. To two of the three partners, negotiating with publishers was a new activity.

This same learning curve applied to the publisher as well. Mutual understanding and a willingness to compromise were normal practice. Nonetheless, after two years, an equilibrium seems to have been established, although it remains to be seen how long it will last. The simple desire to make the project a success influenced economic and political decision-making. On the other hand, all parties are presently in the stage of renewing their original contracts with the publishers, which can be said to be a sign of having reached a certain equilibrium.

Large publishers seem to have prepared themselves better for the digital era than the smaller ones. This explains the observation that not too many more (small) publishers could have been interested in delivering copyrighted material. The Decomate project was carried out during a time of transition for all the key players in the field—end users, facing new technologies at their own doorstep, libraries and publishers–but not all of them responded as we would have expected. End users sometimes surprisingly demanded new developments and wondered why it is taking publishers so long to produce real electronic material instead of simply scanned documents. For smaller publishers there is the more basic concern of making strategic decisions about how to position themselves in the digital era.

One of the main achievements of the Decomate project was the establishment of sound relationships between publishers and libraries, and this is the first step towards the goal of a truly virtual library.

NOTE

1. Throughout this article the term "electronic journal" refers to a printed journal that has been digitized (for instance, by scanning) rather than to a journal that is actually published electronically and may never exist in printed form.

SUGGESTED FURTHER READING

Joost Dijkstra, "Delivery of Copyright Material to End Users: New Unit to the Electronic Document Delivery Chain," in *Proceedings of the International Conference on Library Automation in Central and Eastern Europe* (Budapest, Apr. 1996).

Joost Dijkstra, "From Online Ordering to Document Viewing: Electronic Document Delivery Systems Classified," in *Information Europe*, June 1996.

Joost Dijkstra, "A Generic Approach to the Electronic Access of Scientific Journals: the DECOMATE Project," *Library Acquisitions: Theory and Practice* 21, no. 3 (1997): 393-402.

Hans Geleijnse, "The Digital Library," *Learned Publishing* 9, no. 4 (Oct. 1996): 225-233.

Hans Geleijnse, "Developing an Electronic Library: Strategic and Management Issues," in *Papers from the Third ELVIRA Conference* (London: Aslib, 1996).

Clare Jenkins, "User Studies: Electronic Journals and User Response to New Modes of Information Delivery," *Library Acquisitions: Theory and Practice* 21, no. 3 (1997): 355-364.

Caroline Lloyd, "Evaluating Use of the Decomate System," *Proceedings of the 4th International ELVIRA Conference* (London: Aslib, 1997).

Thomas Place and Joost Dijkstra, "Z39.50 vs WWW: Which Way to Go," in *Proceedings of the Second ELVIRA Conference* (London: Aslib, 1995): 40-53.

A Learning Experience:
The CIC Electronic Journals
Collection Project

Mira Geffner, BA
Bonnie MacEwan, MA

SUMMARY. This paper reviews the history of the CIC Electronic Journals Collection Project. The organizational model used by the consortia for this particular project is described, explored and critiqued. Alternative models of organization are presented and explored. Additionally the staffing and equipment needed to build and maintain such a project are described in detail. A special chal-

Mira Geffner is Project Manager for the CIC Electronic Journals Collection Project and a member of the Task Force on the CIC Electronic Collection, CIC-Net, Inc., 2901 Hubbard Drive, Ann Arbor, MI 48105-2435, USA (email: mrg@cic.net). She has a BA in History from the University of Michigan.

Bonnie MacEwan is Coordinator of Collection Development at the Pennsylvania State University Libraries, E308 Pattee Library, University Park, PA 16802, USA (email: bjm@psulias.psu.edu). She is currently chair of the Task Force on the CIC Electronic Collection, the group charged with oversight of the Electronic Journals Collection Project and similar efforts. She holds an MA in Librarianship from the University of Denver.

The authors wish to thank their colleagues on the Task Force and at the CIC for their continuing support and wisdom. Special thanks go to Barbara Allen, Director of the CIC Center for Library Initiatives, for her intelligence, wise counsel and good humor. Doris Herr deserves special thanks for her patient attention to the preparation of this manuscript as we worked across the miles through computer disasters.

[Haworth co-indexing entry note]: "A Learning Experience: The CIC Electronic Journals Collection Project." Geffner, Mira, and Bonnie MacEwan. Co-published simultaneously in *The Serials Librarian* (The Haworth Press, Inc.) Vol. 33, No. 3/4, 1998, pp. 271-277; and: *E-Serials: Publishers, Libraries, Users, and Standards* (ed: Wayne Jones) The Haworth Press, Inc., 1998, pp. 271-277. Single or multiple copies of this article are available for a fee from The Haworth Document Delivery Service [1-800-342-9678, 9:00 a.m. - 5:00 p.m. (EST). E-mail address: getinfo@haworth.com].

lenge of consortial projects is the need for close coordination and broad communication. Both staffing and organization are discussed in light of these issues. *[Article copies available for a fee from The Haworth Document Delivery Service: 1-800-342-9678. E-mail address: getinfo@haworth.com]*

KEYWORDS. Electronic journals, consortia, coordinated collection development, electronic resources, cooperation

The Committee on Institutional Cooperation's (CIC) Electronic Journals Collection (EJC) was launched in July 1996 as a professionally selected, cataloged and maintained collection of Internet-published scholarly electronic journals. In the preceding years the CICNet staff and CIC librarians had worked to move from an earlier collection to what in the summer of 1995 became the prototype for the current collection. In two years of collaborative acquisition, electronic serials cataloging and technical decision-making we've learned a lot about what has worked for us and what hasn't. In this paper, we use that experience to suggest some ideas for structuring an Internet collection of electronic journals: what type of organization could house such a collection, who could staff it and provide its creative energy, who would lead the project and who would supervise it. For discussion of the current structure and the history of the EJC, please see our article in *PACS-Review*.[1]

We believe that certain organizational elements, described below, are essential to an Internet collection of electronic journals, but that such a collection could work well under many different organizational models, some of which are mentioned in this paper. It is our hope that others will experiment with building scholarly collections of Internet electronic journals within different types of organizations so that the library, research and scholarly publishing communities can learn from a variety of experiences.

ORGANIZATIONAL ISSUES

The CIC, CICNet and the CIC libraries are the principal organizations involved in the CIC EJC. The CIC is a research university consortium encompassing the current and former Big Ten athletic institutions and the University of Chicago. CICNet is the data networking office of the CIC. The CIC libraries' oversight of the EJC has been represented by the Task Force on the CIC Electronic Collection, and ultimately by the CIC Library Directors group which approved joint library funding for the collection in July 1996.

A consortial project of this nature presents many challenges to the group charged with coordination. Not only must the work of the selectors and catalogers at each institution be considered, but the entire project must also be coordinated with CICNet staff. In addition to a group dedicated to oversight and coordination of the consortial aspects of the project, it is essential to have adequate staff to maintain and build the collection. In many cases, an individual is needed to relay input from the Task Force and from other groups such as the CIC Library Automation Directors to the project staff. This person must also be able to respond quickly to questions from staff.

STAFF AND EQUIPMENT NEEDS FOR THE EJC

We have addressed the importance of fully staffing an electronic journals collection elsewhere.[2] Our experience indicates that an electronic collection cannot flourish with fewer staff members than a paper collection. The CIC EJC has operated with an assortment of professional and non-professional staff with representation from the CIC libraries and CICNet, Inc. In conjunction with the Task Force on the CIC Electronic Collection, a project manager at CICNet coordinates project work among CICNet employees and the CIC libraries, and manages the work of the collection assistants.

The initial proposal of the Task Force on the CIC Electronic Collection was to hire masters students in library science at the University of Michigan (the CIC University with which CICNet was affiliated) to do the majority of content management work on the collection. These students, whose work would be supervised by a project manager, would accept title referrals from CIC selectors, correspond with editors and publishers to request permission to include and archive their journals in the EJC, funnel MARC records into the collection database, do some additional database editing to include text descriptions of each journal, and continually check and improve the integrity of the collection database.

CICNet hired three part-time individuals as EJC collection assistants. One was a Sociology B.A. with no library-related experience, the second was an English Literature B.A. with several years of University Press editorial experience, and the third was a recently degreed librarian. Each of these people worked an average of ten hours per week performing the above tasks. Journals in the collection were divided among the three collection assistants according to subject areas, with each individual being responsible for four to seven subject areas. Collection assistants also participated in developing collection procedures and standards.

Beginning with the prototype in the summer of 1995, the E-Journals Collection has used a PC database for data entry and WAIS as the database engine. A CICNet programmer wrote a custom PERL script which converts the data to a Web-readable format. Users have liked the quick and simple title and subject browsing options the collection offers, but manual maintenance of and input to this database make it an unscaleable solution. For future development, we have chosen to stay with the user-friendly Web site design while developing a more robust structure for the collection server.

The EJC runs on an UltraSPARC with Solaris 2.5.1 installed and it will continue on a similar machine when the new database is installed. It is currently connected to the University of Michigan backbone. With 150 titles in the CIC EJC, the collection is using between one and two GB of hard-drive space.

A Web-based collection such as the CIC EJC requires a database which can readily interact with the collection's web server, as well as incorporate MARC records and manual input. A new EJC database is close to completion, written by a PERL programmer in MySQL, an SQL server database engine. The new database, similar to the one currently in use, is based on the format of a MARC serials record. Unlike the current database setup, the MySQL database is a complete package including data entry and search engine. Both databases were designed in consultation with a Web designer who guided both database iterations toward Internet user-friendliness. The new database will conform to the existing simple browsing structure of the collection.

The E-Journals Collection graphic designer and Web administrator worked with the project manager to develop the current interface for the collection. This designer has since worked further with both the project manager and the CIC librarians (including a public services expert) to develop a more attractive page with more of a library look and feel. The new Web page design is in progress but will replace the earlier pages in the near future.

Professional librarians from all of the CIC universities contribute their skills to the Electronic Journals Collection. Titles for the collection have been submitted to the EJC staff by selectors for all 13 libraries. Selectors from each library contribute titles to Electronic Resources Officers (EROs), whose position is analogous to the libraries' Collection Development Officers. Each library's ERO or a designated staff member then uses a Web request form to ask that the title be included in the collection. Six libraries are contributing cataloging records for EJC titles to OCLC, which then makes the records available to CICNet via FTP.

Five years into the popularization of the Web, librarians can easily see that there is great breadth and depth to freely available serials online. And just as there is great potential to their complexity, there is also great impermanence to many of these publications. By doing their jobs (preserving the public record, making that record accessible), libraries implicitly improve the quality of print publications. Publishers understand that their work will be available indefinitely and this offers some incentive for serious publication. This function is vital in the world of Internet publishing as well. Cataloging, together with professional selection, is an important area in which librarians can improve the scholarly value of materials online.

ALTERNATIVE MODELS FOR EJC MANAGEMENT

The EJC project has been a valuable learning experience for the CIC, providing a context in which to wrestle with the challenges of the dynamic environment of networked information and rapidly changing technologies. Additionally it has provided a laboratory for consortial activities, and has brought national and international recognition to the CIC for the content and structure of the project. In light of the changing capabilities of Internet technologies and changes in the CIC brought about by its Virtual Electronic Library project, we are examining new models for managing the EJC.[3]

A key weakness of the CIC EJC has been the lack of direct supervision by the libraries. The collection has relied on technical support to bring project management problems to the attention of the libraries, and on the libraries to bring problems in the collection's appearance and usability to the attention of the project staff. We've identified alternatives for organizing the E-Journals Collection, all of which involve more direct library involvement in project management. Some are based on existing projects, others are variations on our own organizational structure. The following is not intended as a comprehensive review of the electronic resources or electronic journal management options available, but as a quick overview of a few possibilities.

A natural home for a collection of electronic journals is the central office of a national or international library organization. Such a location would give collection staff ready access to library professionals, while giving the collection the secure backing and recognition of an established organization. Many such groups have defined their mission as collecting and archiving materials and making them available to the library community. They are funded through member dues and charges for services. This funding structure could provide a solid financial base for the staff needed to maintain an electronic journals collection project.

A single library or library organization could likewise work through an electronic journals collection to expand its own work in digital documents. Because this collection combines work on selection, cataloging, acquisition and archiving in an Internet environment, it could be a valuable platform for a single library's early experience with this work. If developed by a single library, this project could be made available to other libraries and their users through the Web.

In the consortial environment the greatest challenge and the greatest rewards are in building a collection which takes advantage of existing shared access and retrieval abilities. In our own work, we hope to disperse some of the work currently performed by CICNet and the Task Force on the CIC Electronic Collection.

Building on CICNet's early work on the collection, selectors and catalogers may be able to work directly on the EJC's database–adding and cataloging new serials through a Web interface rather than submitting titles and cataloging records to a central office. This level of direct participation was not possible when the EJC project was first designed.

CONCLUSION

As we write about the CIC Electronic Journals Collection our key concern is that projects like this one continue to flourish in a variety of library settings. We are committed to the EJC as an important type of collection as it represents some of the possibilities for making scholarly material on the Internet both research-accessible and popular. We hope that the descriptive information we have given so far, and the brainstorming we entertain will further open the range of discussions about how librarians work on the Internet and how they continue to build on collections already in place.

NOTES

1. Bonnie MacEwan and Mira Geffner, "The Committee on Institutional Cooperation Electronic Journals Collection (CIC-EJC): A New Model for Library Management of Scholarly Journals Published on the Internet," *The Public-Access Computer Systems Review* 7, no. 4 (1996). Available: http://lib-04.lib.uh.edu/pacsrev/1996/mace7n4.htm
2. Ibid.
3. A brief overview of the Virtual Electronic Library (VEL) is available at http://www.cic.net/cic/velnew.html

Coordination and Collaboration:
A Model
for Electronic Resources Management

Kristin H. Gerhard, MA, MLS

SUMMARY. Library organizations need models for the integration of electronic resources management into library collections and services. The approach taken at Iowa State University was one of coordination and collaboration, with the goal of ensuring that issues arising from the increasing numbers of electronic titles will be handled effectively and efficiently. One part of this approach was the creation of an electronic resources coordinator position within the technical services division. This approach has allowed flexible and responsive management of electronic resources. *[Article copies available for a fee from The Haworth Document Delivery Service: 1-800-342-9678. E-mail address: getinfo@haworth.com]*

KEYWORDS. Electronic resources, library management, technical services, organizational models

INTRODUCTION

In an earlier article, I described the cataloging of electronic resources (including serials) at Iowa State University, and sug-

Kristin H. Gerhard is Electronic Resources Coordinator and Catalog Librarian, Parks Library, Iowa State University, Ames, IA 50011, USA. She holds an MLS from the University of North Carolina at Chapel Hill and an MA in Education from the University of Maine.

[Haworth co-indexing entry note]: "Coordination and Collaboration: A Model for Electronic Resources Management." Gerhard, Kristin H. Co-published simultaneously in *The Serials Librarian* (The Haworth Press, Inc.) Vol. 33, No. 3/4, 1998, pp. 279-286; and: *E-Serials: Publishers, Libraries, Users, and Standards* (ed: Wayne Jones) The Haworth Press, Inc., 1998, pp. 279-286. Single or multiple copies of this article are available for a fee from The Haworth Document Delivery Service [1-800-342-9678, 9:00 a.m. - 5:00 p.m. (EST). E-mail address: getinfo@haworth.com].

gested guidelines for libraries at the beginning of this process.[1] Here, I focus more specifically on our local process, with the goal of providing information to other libraries wrestling with electronic resources (ERs). The model adopted at Iowa State is one of coordinated electronic resources management.

This article looks at the impact of ERs on academic libraries, describes the approach we have taken towards dealing with ER management, and identifies both advantages and disadvantages of this model. While this article is written by a technical services librarian and from the perspective of technical services work, the impact of ERs on libraries is broad enough that the principles have a wider application to the library organization as a whole.

THE IMPACT OF ELECTRONIC RESOURCES

There is no question that libraries must find ways to come to grips with electronic publications. In a recent survey conducted by the American Library Association and Ameritech Library Services, academic libraries were asked a series of questions about electronic services they provided. The result of the study, conducted in the spring of 1996, indicated that 71% of doctorate-granting institutions were providing access to original, free electronic journals. These are journals that have no print counterpart, available to libraries at no cost. Original paid ejournals were provided by 57% of these institutions. A total of 81% of doctorate-granting institutions made full text journals, whether free, paid, or a combination of both, available to their users. "Universally, the most likely method of access is from hard-wired terminals and/or PCs in the library."[2] The report concludes that

> [a]cademic librarians, especially those in the larger and more comprehensive institutions are already offering a wide variety of electronic services and planning to offer more. Also, academic librarians are expanding their traditional role by teaching students and faculty how to use these sources of information.[3]

The boom in electronic resources has brought some important improvements to academic libraries. The number of resources available continues to increase at a rapid rate, with improving, albeit uneven, quality. The phenomenal growth in the Internet, particularly of the World Wide Web, continues. Publishers are increasingly taking steps to make their journals available electronically. Libraries are receiving printed materials in which URLs are noted.

Many electronic reference sources can be searched much more easily than their print counterparts. As Crawford and Gorman have pointed out, this is an ideal format for materials that do not require a linear reading, especially where sophisticated searching would be desirable.[4]

One result of this is that patron expectations have skyrocketed. Information can be delivered to patrons at library workstations, to faculty offices, to dormitories and homes. Not surprisingly, patrons like using electronic resources, sometimes to the point of resisting appropriate referrals to print sources. In order to hold the respect of our users, librarians must negotiate through present circumstances to provide increasing numbers of important electronic titles, which absorb an increasing percentage of library acquisitions budgets. Libraries, and librarians, need to forge a positive, creative way to manage electronic resources.

ORGANIZATIONAL CHALLENGES

Electronic resources are here to stay, and we recognize the importance of what they contribute to our mission. But we have included them in our arsenal of information sources as add-ons more often than we have integrated them into our collections and services. Electronic resources, particularly those available over the Internet, require us to develop new ways of managing. It has been easier to keep these titles in a category labelled "other" and work around them.

An aspect of ER management that poses particular difficulties for technical services is the ethereality of resources available over the Internet. Janet Swan Hill makes this point, among others, in her article, "The Elephant in the Catalog."[5] This lack of a physical piece makes it difficult to fit these titles into existing, standard workflows–acquisitions check-in, cataloging, and provision of access. We don't know how to handle them.

The fact that ER management crosses not only departmental but divisional lines complicates the situation, as adding an ER title necessitates more back and forth communication, rather than a linear pathway through technical services to public services. A title may be selected, but its licensing agreement may turn out to be problematic. It may require additional decisions regarding coverage, number of simultaneous users, or choice of platform. It may have equipment or software requirements that do not mesh with local systems. These issues also serve to draw automated systems staff deeper into an ordering, receipt, and processing system that normally involves systems staff only peripherally.

Further, the unpredictability of ERs also prevents us from writing a simple, one-size-fits-all procedure for handling them. Licensing agreements and technical requirements continue to vary widely from title to title; pricing may include unlimited site access, single user access, or value-added features such as current awareness or full-text options. Access may be by IP number, domain name, or password. Software that works appropriately to provide access through local systems and within local policy constraints may or may not be available for any given title. Rigid, linear processes will not deal adequately with electronic resource management.

Library organizations need models for the integration of electronic resources management into library collections and services. We cannot afford to create solutions ex nihilo in every library. What follows is a description of one possible model, that of collaborative coordination. While we cannot plan with an assumption that the information marketplace will settle down in the future, we can pool our experiences, allowing each library to select the most useful approach for local organizational development.

THE COLLABORATIVE ELECTRONIC RESOURCES COORDINATION APPROACH

Position advertisements for electronic resource or digital resource librarians in academic libraries are increasingly common. In January 1996, Iowa State University Library joined these ranks by creating an electronic resources coordinator position within the technical services division. The underlying goal in creating this position was to ensure that issues arising from the increasing numbers of electronic titles are handled effectively and with some kind of efficiency. Because of cost constraints, this position was created by shuffling existing responsibilities amongst existing staff, de-emphasizing some responsibilities, while adding the tasks necessary to coordinate acquisition and access for electronic resources. It was expected that the position would grow and change over time as needs were assessed and responsibilities assigned.

At the point when this position was created, there was no one person in technical services overseeing the acquisition or cataloging of ERs. Titles were handled largely on a case-by-case basis, with the bulk of the work done by the head of the Acquisitions Department. When cataloging was needed, networked resources (mainly CDs on individual workstations or the Reference Department LAN) were referred to the appropriate staff in the Serials and Monographs Original Cataloging Department. Separate procedures for CD-ROMs had been created by the cataloger responsible for the non-book cataloging workflow, but no provision had been made for cataloging titles available through Internet access.

We were not an unusual academic library. The new environment required adaptation and adjustment. Our initial response was split between assigning responsibilities to those with related existing responsibilities, and establishing task forces to work through policy issues.

In other areas of the library, an ER collection development policy was being drafted. A library-wide task force had made some recommendations about which ERs to catalog; another task force had been working intermittently on the issues of electronic resource management: budget, selection, and so on. The Assistant Director for Collections was responsible for significant license negotiations. The Reference and Informational Services Department was regularly reviewing the electronic reference sources we offer patrons, adjusting the access and products based on budget and usage. Systems staff kept the library's home page up to date, made connections with subject guides to the Internet created by Collection Development and Reference librarians, and kept the Reference resources running. In short, there was a lot to coordinate.

The creation of an electronic resources coordinator position in

Technical Services paralleled the establishment of a series of committees focused on various aspects of electronic resources, with composition based on expertise. The groups included three task forces dealing with various aspects of the library's Web site, a committee on Computer Networking and Architecture, and an Electronic Resources Management Discussion Group, whose charge was to bring issues needing library-wide discussion to the staff and facilitate discussion. Ultimately, virtually every librarian at Iowa State contributed to one or more aspects of the current handling of electronic serials.

ADVANTAGES OF THE COORDINATOR APPROACH

Creating a position in technical services to coordinate work with electronic resources has certain advantages. Having one person coordinating activities related to acquisitions and cataloging means that a critical bulk of information can be unified and maintained by one person. By no means does this diminish the need for others to maintain their own expertise; rather, it provides a mechanism to ensure that there is consistency in library policy and procedures, and consistency in their application. The person in a coordinator role serves as a funnel and gathering point for relevant information from all sources.

A second advantage is that the coordinator role puts a human face on technical services for staff in other parts of the library. Many of the issues involved in managing electronic journals cross departmental lines. Technical services is often the inner temple of the library, where mysterious internal processes eventually yield up the desired materials in organized form. It is important for staff in other areas to have a contact person to whom they can bring questions, issues, and concerns regarding electronic resources. These are complex titles with complex issues. Trying to discern who on an organizational chart or contact list might be responsible for a given aspect of the electronic title with which a reference librarian is dealing is not likely to have a successful outcome. We are in a new world, where we cannot afford linear, isolated processes. We need flexibility and responsiveness.

Thirdly, having a coordinator to keep on top of ERs provides for a series of one-on-one discussions and shared insights. The coordinator is responsible for maintaining a flow of information about electronic resources across and within functions, departments, and divisions. This does not mean being the provider of information so much as trying to facilitate conversations, to listen, and to bring together staff with related information and/or information needs. It also requires periodic checking with library administrators, to ensure that the course being steered is in a desired direction.

POTENTIAL PITFALLS
OF THE COORDINATOR APPROACH

There are two potential pitfalls with the coordinator approach. First, there is no single person to provide backup when the workload is heavy or the coordinator is absent. This can be overcome in a number of ways. It is important to continue to build and support expertise throughout the library, so that various aspects of this work can be covered under varying circumstances. Also, over time, various aspects of the position as initially described will become routinized or established to the point that they can be peeled off to other staff members. Much of the first year at Iowa State was divided between the learning curve and working out procedures for ER cataloging. Since then, maintenance of the divisional Web pages, maintenance of access to cataloged Internet resources, and coordination of cataloging of electronic titles have been moved to others. This has allowed the ER coordinator position to evolve and meet new challenges and needs. The second pitfall is that a coordinating position requires an extraordinary amount of communication: near-constant communication, and within and between a wide variety of individuals and groups. It is all too easy to overlook, unwittingly, an interested party, or a piece of needed information. Vigilance, and the goodwill of one's colleagues, provide the only saving graces.

CONCLUSION

The growth of ERs, in volume and in prominence, requires that library organizations develop a proactive approach to handling these titles. A combination of coordination and collaboration provides one practical model for the management of electronic resources in academic libraries.

In the end, one hopes that this integrated approach to electronic resources management can contribute to a less fragmented vision of what library collections and services might become.

NOTES

1. Kristin H. Gerhard, "Cataloging Internet Resources: Practical Issues and Concerns," *Serials Librarian*, 32, no. 1/2 (1997): 123-137.

2. Mary Jo Lynch, *Electronic Services in Academic Libraries: ALA Survey Report* (Chicago and London: American Library Association, 1996), 6.

3. Ibid., 7.

4. Walt Crawford and Michael Gorman, *Future Libraries: Dreams, Madness, & Reality* (Chicago and London: American Library Association, 1995).

5. Janet Swan Hill, "The Elephant in the Catalog," *Cataloging & Classification Quarterly* 23, no. 1 (1996): 5-25.

ScienceDirect™

Karen Hunter

SUMMARY. ScienceDirect™ has been developed by Elsevier Science to provide a databased, Web host environment for its journals and those of other participating publishers. The target is to create an integrated environment, which will permit efficient and transparent access to the scientific literature by integrating abstracting and indexing searching and by linking to other publishers' sites. *[Article copies available for a fee from The Haworth Document Delivery Service: 1-800-342-9678. E-mail address: getinfo@haworth.com]*

KEYWORDS. ScienceDirect, Elsevier Science, scientific journals

A BRIEF HISTORY

Elsevier Science began to think seriously about using electronic distribution technologies for its journals in the late 1970s. We approached a number of other scientific, technical and medical publishers to form a co-operative venture to scan journals and store them electronically. ADONIS™ was the name given to the consortium. The goal was to encourage article supply services such as the British Library's to use these electronic archives locally as their source for articles, rather than photocopying from the paper origi-

Karen Hunter is Senior Vice President at Elsevier Science, 655 Sixth Avenue, New York, NY 10010, USA (email: k.hunter@elsevier.com).

[Haworth co-indexing entry note]: "ScienceDirect™." Hunter, Karen. Co-published simultaneously in *The Serials Librarian* (The Haworth Press, Inc.) Vol. 33, No. 3/4, 1998, pp. 287-297; and: *E-Serials: Publishers, Libraries, Users, and Standards* (ed: Wayne Jones) The Haworth Press, Inc., 1998, pp. 287-297. Single or multiple copies of this article are available for a fee from The Haworth Document Delivery Service [1-800-342-9678, 9:00 a.m. - 5:00 p.m. (EST). E-mail address: getinfo@haworth.com].

nals. If the electronic system was more efficient than using the paper, then a royalty could be paid to the publishers for the copy made–royalties that were not otherwise being paid.

The notion was a valid one, but it took several years for technology costs to catch up with the theory. The technology of the late 1970s was large optical disks, with $40,000 readers. The technology that ultimately worked was a turnkey CD-ROM system for use with low-cost PCs. ADONIS found its niche in providing weekly CD-ROM delivery of hundreds of biomedical journals to an international group of libraries, which continue to use them for local access and document supply services. What we heard repeatedly, however, was a desire for local networked access, to get the journals to the desktops of the users.

The second major initiative for Elsevier Science was intended to provide that networked access, again consistent with the technology then available. From 1991 to 1995, Elsevier and nine universities participated in an experiment to mount a database of materials science journals for local network access. This experiment was known as TULIP (The University LIcensing Program). As with ADONIS, the electronic journals were delivered to each site. However, in this instance the electronic files for the journals were not accessed through publisher-supplied software (as exists on ADONIS), but rather each university integrated the journals into its own local area network services. The database was large (11 GB per year) and the universities and Elsevier each found unexpected problems, most of which are documented in the experiment's final report.[1] However, from a production and user perspective, this was a viable technology, and there was increased demand for this level of networked access, particularly once the Web took hold and removed the need to customize the access software for different client operating systems on the desktop.

From TULIP came a program called Elsevier Electronic Subscriptions (EES), which is the commercial extension of the TULIP concept. Nearly 1,100 Elsevier journals have been available in electronic form since 1995 through EES. The files are delivered to the subscribing institution, where they are stored and delivered over the local network. An Elsevier-endorsed Web server is available for implementation, if desired. End-user delivery can also be over wide-area networks if the files are licensed for sharing among institutions, as in the case of consortia. This is a service that can be tailored to local needs and integrated with other information relevant to the subscribing institution. At present nearly 2 million users worldwide have desktop access to EES files.

What, then, is ScienceDirect and how does it relate to these other services?

WHAT IS SCIENCEDIRECT™?

ScienceDirect is a logical extension of and complement to the ADONIS, TULIP and EES experiences. It is also a reflection of the potential of the World Wide Web environment to facilitate access to complicated large databases from remote locations. Certainly remote hosting is not a new phenomenon. Dialog, Data Star, Lexis-Nexis and others have been in this business for more than two decades. But the ability to handle color and complex graphics, which are critical to the delivery of scientific material, has been pushed forward by Web developments and, perhaps more significantly, by the enormous increase in computing power and sophistication on the desktop.

ScienceDirect is still in its introductory stages, with the initial "early release" in mid-1997 and general availability scheduled for late 1997 or early 1998. It is a Web-based service that delivers Elsevier Science journals and the journals of other participating publishers via the Internet (or through leased lines). When complete, all 1,100 Elsevier Science journals will be included. The early release collection is focused on the life sciences.

ScienceDirect (http://www.sciencedirect.com) offers a sophisticated service for browsing, searching and printing from the journals database. The service is designed to store both SGML and PDF files for the journals. HTML displays are generated on-the-fly and PDF is available for both viewing and printing. The service can also accommodate journals for which the full text is only available in PDF, but not all features will be implementable in those files.

One such feature which requires SGML is SummaryPlus, a unique feature which provides a capsule of the article for quicker scanning. SummaryPlus includes the full bibliographic information, abstract, index terms, all tables and graphics and all cited references. The references (both in SummaryPlus and in the full text article) are, in turn, linked to abstracts of the referenced articles and, when available, the full text of the referenced article. Users can store searches to rerun on demand and create SDIs (selective dissemination of information profiles) for automatic alerting of new material.

Among the things learned in the TULIP experiment was that the value of the full-text article was greatly increased if one method of access was through the normal method of searching in a more comprehensive abstracting and indexing file. Within ScienceDirect, this is done primarily by providing a five-year abstracting and indexing layer as an integral part of the service. The initial 1,650 journals in this abstracting and indexing component are drawn from the EMBASE database of biomedical journals and include major EMBASE index terms. Over time, this database will grow to include other disciplines, drawn from other abstracting and indexing services or constructed specifically for ScienceDirect. The user will also have access to "power searches" in full EMBASE (which covers 3,500 journals) and, over time, in other specialist databases. In each of these cases–searching within the ScienceDirect layer or searching the full A & I database–there is an option to purchase via a document delivery service any article which is not available in the online collection.

There are also programs under development to permit linking between citations found in a library's locally mounted abstracting and index service and the full text in ScienceDirect, and between ScienceDirect and Web-based services of selected bibliographic services. The goal is to provide access to the service in a wide variety of ways, consistent with library preferences.

In that connection, just as it is important to place the full-text information within a broader context for searching purposes, it is also important to try to provide as much full text in one location as possible. One of the underlying premises of ScienceDirect is that it is more efficient to have a large corpus of information in one location than to have to go to hundreds or thousands of individual Web sites for each title or small cluster of titles.

For that reason, Elsevier Science has invited other publishers to make their material available to ScienceDirect subscribers. There are two ways that can be done: loading the other publishers' materials within ScienceDirect or providing gateways to that material. While there is more functionality possible in the first option, both methods are being pursued. Again, the goal is to provide as comprehensive an environment as possible and to permit users to move from one environment or server to another with a minimum of disruption. That means that whenever possible all publishers should negotiate links between their services, links that recognize common subscribers and remove the need for a separate user verification process.

In this context, Elsevier Science has had discussions on participation in or links to ScienceDirect with a large number of journal publishers. Many scientific societies and small-to-medium sized publishers have indicated an interest in loading their files on ScienceDirect. Most larger publishers, whether society or commercial, prefer a link to their Web sites. This was expected and is consistent with the position that Elsevier itself has taken.

ScienceDirect was built jointly by Elsevier Science and its sister company, Lexis-Nexis. While there will be services for individual subscribers (described below), it was built with the institutional library subscriber in mind. Librarians can customize the terms of access to their users (e.g., enabling or disallowing transactional activities) and track (and charge back) on a departmental level. There are also features which will enable "turning off" of a graduating class, for example, or otherwise putting time restrictions (expiration dates) on user access.

ACCESS TERMS

When ScienceDirect moves from its early release period into broad availability, access will be licensed to institutions based primarily upon subscriptions to the journal titles. ScienceDirect is not intended for a document delivery-type positioning where anyone interested comes into the Web site, browses or searches and then pays for the individual article. The user must be affiliated with a subscribing institution. Access is restricted to a defined Authorized User Community, usually synonymous in an academic institution with the faculty, staff and students whose primary affiliation is with that institution. A subscription entitles the institution's end users to unlimited access to the database and unlimited personal printing or downloading.

One has to say "unlimited" with a caveat, however, as this is still an unknown area for both libraries and publishers and there must be an opportunity to judge from experience whether "unlimited" works. America Online learned at the end of 1996 that "unlimited" access swamped their systems. ScienceDirect and other academic information purveyors have yet to see what the demand will be when a very robust service is offered. ScienceDirect has the benefit of the experience of the Lexis-Nexis operations staff, but as a Web service in science, this is still new territory. Obviously, it is not a question of whether demand can be satisfied, for that is a matter of adding boxes on the floor and telephone lines. But in the happy event that use is very high, the costs associated with providing those services will need to be reviewed in the context of the overall access terms.

Each publisher participating in ScienceDirect establishes its own subscription price for its journals and receives all of the income from that subscription. The libraries decide which journals to subscribe to. In addition, ScienceDirect has a host fee, which is intended to cover some of its costs. ScienceDirect also is paid for certain loading and storage costs by each publisher.

If permitted by the journals' publishers, a library may also purchase articles on a transactional basis for journals to which they do not have a subscription. The cost for these articles has two components: the fee that the publisher of the journal sets for its content (e.g., an equivalent of the Copyright Clearance Center fee) and a ScienceDirect handling charge to cover infrastructure and direct-billing costs. This is consistent with other commercial document delivery services.

Pricing for electronic journals is, in general, a difficult issue for most journal publishers. One of the things Elsevier is doing to learn more is working with the University of Michigan on an experimental project to test six different pricing variations for remotely hosted journals. Called the PEAK (Pricing for Electronic Access to Knowledge) Project, this experiment is being managed at Michigan by a librarian (Wendy Lougee) and an economist associated with the University's School of Information (Jeffrey MacKie-Mason). While PEAK is not directly testing access to ScienceDirect, the results could affect pricing and product options within ScienceDirect. The experiment will run until the end of 1998.

ARCHIVING AND ACCESS AFTER CANCELLATION

One of the regular questions of those who offer electronic access is what is the policy on short- and long-term archival access. Some publishers say that as long as they are also publishing paper, that is the answer: if you want an archive, buy the paper. In the Elsevier Science EES program, the archiving question is moot, as the library takes physical possession of the files. In a remote environment, it is not that simple.

Traditionally, online host services were (and still are) limited to current subscribers and current files. There is no promise of access, for example, to an outdated file that has been removed from Dialog. Similarly, if you had an account in 1996 and dropped it in 1997, you are not given some type of limited access to the 1996 records. But when one moves into the world of online journals, the paper paradigm and notion of what is meant by a subscription seem to continue to prevail. There is an expectation that, having paid "a subscription," one has permanent access. Perhaps one should begin trying to adjust the semantics and talk of an "annual access fee."

Within ScienceDirect it is too early to assert a final policy. There is a need to work with customers over the coming 1-2 years as backfiles build. However, the working assumption is that a current year's subscription will give an institution access to that year plus a fixed number of prior years (probably 3). If the institution cancels that title but continues to subscribe to other titles on ScienceDirect, it can retrieve the backfiles of the subscribed period until the rolling backfile period is over. All backfiles older than the fixed number (3?) of years will be also available, but there will be a charge associated with access for all users (whether or not they are current subscribers).

In this way it should be possible to manage the administrative requirements of maintaining records of cancelled subscriptions for a fixed number of years and cover some of the costs associated with storing and refreshing the archive. As the files age and use lessens, one can actually imagine an increasing rather than decreasing per-use charge. However, right now this is largely speculative and there is considerable work to be done in consultation with libraries to determine the best archival policy. At a minimum, however, Elsevier does guarantee to ensure that there will be a permanent archive of its journals kept by a reliable party.

SCIENCEDIRECT AS A PUBLISHING ENVIRONMENT

In deciding to build this database, Elsevier Science had in mind more than just the services described above. ScienceDirect is also an environment or resource upon which other discipline- or industry-tailored services can be built. Traditional publishing is market-driven, and scholarly publishing is no different. Publishing staff focuses on a specific discipline or subdiscipline in order to understand the scientific and information needs of that community. Historically that has resulted in books and journals for those communities. In the future, one can also expect community-specific electronic services to be common.

The Elsevier Science journals (and the journals of other participating publishers) that are available within ScienceDirect and the software infrastructure offer the opportunity to create niche services for specific disciplines. These community services include a selection of journals and other related publications and services. There may be special services for authors, enhanced multimedia features, access to related Web sites, advertising and moderated forums. These services are targeted in the first instance at individual scientists and their departments and are meant to be complementary, not competitive, to the basic ScienceDirect service. They will not carry the ScienceDirect name, but will have brand names specific to each service.

One example of the synergies that are possible is the links that are planned between ScienceDirect and the ISIS™ service of MDL, the chemical software and information company that joined Elsevier Science in 1997. MDL has specialized software systems, databases, and services in the areas of chemical, biological, and genomic information management, high-throughput synthesis and screening, materials science, chemical sourcing, and environmental health and safety. ISIS (Integrated Scientific Information System) is software that provides, among other things, desktop chemical structure searching and references to the literature about those chemicals. It also includes a database management system for storing and retrieving chemical structures and software to draw and render 2-D and 3-D chemical and biological structures. It would be natural to link through to the full text of the referenced articles, for example, or search the chemical structures in the full text database. The intent is to develop over time sophisticated cross-database access for customers of both services.

FUTURE RELATIONSHIP OF EES AND SCIENCEDIRECT

Elsevier Electronic Subscriptions is a local service limited to the full text and, in theory, limited to Elsevier journals. In fact, we make our standards fully open and accessible and that permits other publishers to link into the same implementations on their own terms and conditions. We encourage other publishers to work with us and we also encourage EES library customers to use the EES standards to make the loading of other journals easier.

ScienceDirect is a sophisticated remote service, with integrated abstracting and indexing services and integrated access to other publishers' journals. As a remotely hosted service, ScienceDirect removes the local need to store and maintain the data. That is traded against the ability to customize an EES implementation. Both services have the option to be linked to locally mounted A & I services.

Some people ask whether EES will continue after all Elsevier journals are available on ScienceDirect. The answer is "yes," as long as customers want the local, customized option (and a significant number of our customers have confirmed that they have this desire). The two services will offer integrated options. The most obvious of these would be to hold some titles locally and integrate into the local search system the bibliographic references to the journals held remotely on ScienceDirect. The local server could then fetch PDFs of those articles, either under a subscription or transactional agreement. The remote files could be titles not used enough to mount locally or could be backfiles of all titles, with the more recent issues held on site. There are other options for integration of the services, including searching within the ScienceDirect environment and serving up high-demand full text from the local server, but the first implementations will be for local searching.

FUTURE TECHNICAL DEVELOPMENT
OF SCIENCEDIRECT

The goal is to work with the library and scientific community to learn how to improve the service in ways that provide better efficiency and effectiveness. Work on enhancements–whether for backoffice and administrative features and user functionality–continues steadily, with essentially the same level of technical staffing as went into the first release (which was designed over a one-year period and brought online over a second one-year period). The level of investment is high, but consistent with providing a distribution system to change a total publishing program from a paper-only to a paper and electronic environment (and anticipating the day when there may be electronic only). It is not intended that the cost of the investment will be recouped solely on added electronic income.

The development has not been without difficulties, as it is a sophisticated undertaking. As most publishers who have tried it have learned, creating database-ready journal files in SGML is a tricky process. However, as more and more material is available in this format, the services that ScienceDirect (and others tuned to using SGML) offer should have a significant impact on the links and access mechanisms that can be provided for the scientific literature.

IN CONCLUSION

ScienceDirect is a major initiative intended to provide a sophisticated set of services and options to our library customers, to our scientist end-users and authors, and to our publishing staff. Its goal is to provide broad access to as many quality scientific journals as possible. In that context, Elsevier Science is pursuing a range of options for linking to other publishers' servers. There is much to learn as online full-text services grow in experience over the next 1-2 years and it is that market experience that will shape the future of ScienceDirect.

NOTE

1. TULIP, *Final Report*. Available: http://www.elsevier.com/inca/homepage/about/resproj/tulip.htm

Evolving
an Integrated Electronic Journals Solution: OCLC FirstSearch Electronic Collections Online

Chip Nilges

SUMMARY. This paper describes the OCLC Online Computer Library Center, Inc.'s electronic publishing program between its introduction in 1992 through the late summer of 1997, focusing on OCLC's ongoing efforts to integrate electronic journals with library acquisition, cataloging, archiving, and online reference systems. The paper begins by describing the OCLC Electronic Journals Online (EJO) service, emphasizing how that service evolved to meet the changing needs of institutional subscribers to electronic journals between 1992 and 1995. It then describes the Electronic Collections Online service, a Web-based service introduced in June of 1997 that provides access to, and archiving for, hundreds of journals from many publishers. *[Article copies available for a fee from The Haworth Document Delivery Service: 1-800-342-9678. E-mail address: getinfo@haworth.com]*

KEYWORDS. OCLC Online Computer Library Center, Inc., electronic journals, serial literature, online reference, World Wide Web

---

Chip Nilges is Manager of Product Management and Marketing, Electronic Journals Division, OCLC Online Computer Library Center, Inc., 6565 Frantz Road, Dublin, OH 43017-3395, USA (email: nilgesc@oclc.org).

[Haworth co-indexing entry note]: "Evolving an Integrated Electronic Journals Solution: OCLC Firstsearch Electronic Collections Online." Nilges, Chip. Co-published simultaneously in *The Serials Librarian* (The Haworth Press, Inc.) Vol. 33, No. 3/4, 1998, pp. 299-318; and: *E-Serials: Publishers, Libraries, Users, and Standards* (ed: Wayne Jones) The Haworth Press, Inc., 1998, pp. 299-318. Single or multiple copies of this article are available for a fee from The Haworth Document Delivery Service [1-800-342-9678, 9:00 a.m. - 5:00 p.m. (EST). E-mail address: getinfo@haworth.com].

The past few years have seen an explosion in the number of academic and professional journals available online. Publishers, subscription agents, and content aggregators have embraced the Web as their primary online distribution channel, with the result that thousands of peer-reviewed academic and professional journals are now available on the Web.

While the rapid growth of Web-accessible journals suggests a revolution in electronic publishing, the online distribution of academic and professional journals has been an evolutionary process. For the OCLC Online Computer Library Center, this process began in the early 1990s with the introduction of a proprietary journal delivery system called Electronic Journals Online (EJO). Through EJO, OCLC helped introduce the world's first electronic peer-reviewed science journal with graphics and completely searchable full text.[1] EJO evolved considerably in its five years of availability, until it was replaced in June of 1997 by an entirely Web-based electronic journals service called Electronic Collections Online. Today, OCLC is working on a "third-generation" system, which will make Electronic Collections Online available through OCLC's online reference system, FirstSearch, in early 1998.

In a number of ways, OCLC's experiences with electronic publishing have mirrored the evolution of the electronic publishing industry as a whole. EJO was one of several early systems that provided online access to electronic journals, and it shared with those systems a number of important characteristics that define systems developed during the early 1990s. Likewise, Electronic Collections Online is one of a number of Web-based services on the market providing access to hundreds of journals from many publishers through a single Web interface. But just as OCLC's electronic journal program reflects the state of the industry, it also reflects OCLC's unique position as a content aggregator and its mission as a library service organization. This mission is evident in Electronic Collections Online's emphasis on preservation, cataloging and the integration of electronic journals with library information systems.

This paper describes OCLC's electronic publishing program between its introduction in 1992 through the late summer of 1997. It begins with a description of the EJO service that emphasizes how that service influenced the development of Electronic Collections Online in 1996-1997. It then describes the Electronic Collections Online service, emphasizing how OCLC's role in the delivery of electronic journals has evolved to meet the changing needs of libraries in managing electronic journals. The paper concludes with a description of OCLC's evolving relationship with journal publishers, its archiving program, and its ongoing efforts to integrate electronic journals into library information systems.

ELECTRONIC JOURNALS ONLINE

Introduced in 1992, the EJO delivery system was based on the use of Standard Generalized Markup Language (SGML) data, with scanned images for graphics and photographs. Publishers participated by providing OCLC with journal data tagged in SGML, accompanied by images for article graphics. OCLC created a single searchable database for each available journal, indexed according to publisher specifications, and made the journal accessible to subscribers over its international telecommunications network, and later, over the Internet and World Wide Web.

The EJO acquisitions model positioned OCLC as a service provider for the publishers participating in the program. Publishers sold journal subscriptions directly to their individual subscribers and institutions. They notified OCLC of each new subscription, and OCLC provided the subscriber with software for logging into EJO and viewing the publication. The viewing software, called Guidon, was a Windows application developed by OCLC that enabled users to search and browse for information in any single journal to which they had subscribed. Guidon provided a high-quality graphical display of full text, including figures, tables and equations. It included a variety of additional functionality, such as links from article references to related records in bibliographic databases, links among related articles in a selected journal, an automatic search capability, and other features.

THE EVOLUTION OF THE EJO MODEL

EJO achieved notable success between 1992 and 1996. The number of available journals grew to almost 50, and the number of participating publishers to 8. During this time the EJO service model evolved considerably, reflecting significant changes in the market for electronic journals–changes that would help shape the development of Electronic Collections Online.

The first of these changes had to do with the type of journal offered through the service. The first two publications mounted on the EJO service were start-up journals available only in electronic form.[2] The success of these experimental titles encouraged several key publishers in science, technology and medicine to make electronic versions of important print journals available through EJO beginning in 1993. This shift signaled the willingness of these "early adopters" to test the waters of electronic publishing by putting online some of their most widely held titles.

A second significant change in the EJO model had to do with the way that journals were presented through the service. Initially, journals were loaded as separately searchable databases. This meant that libraries could subscribe to any or all of the journals available through the service, and access their entire collection through the Guidon interface, but patrons could search and browse only one journal at a time. Beginning in 1993, publishers began making groups of journals available through EJO as searchable clusters, acknowledging the preference of end users to be able to search and browse across a large collection of titles, rather than limiting themselves to a single journal. While these collections represented an important step toward true cross-journal access, they were limited by the fact that they consisted of titles from a single publisher. In addition, they were sold as packages; libraries could not tailor their collection by subscribing to individual titles à la carte.

Probably the most important change in the EJO delivery model was the introduction, in 1995, of a Web interface for the service.[3] The Web dramatically altered OCLC's approach to delivering electronic journals online. EJO was a proprietary system that placed significant financial and technical demands on participating publishers and libraries. For publishers, these demands included the cost and complexity of generating and delivering SGML and scanned images. For libraries, subscribing to EJO meant distributing and providing front-line support for the Guidon interface, a fact that often limited the scope of local implementations to terminals in the library and the offices of select faculty and staff.

The EJO Web interface reduced (and eventually eliminated) the need for the Guidon software, bringing electronic journals to any desktop computer in the library, at the office or at home. It also encouraged publishers to experiment with alternative data formats to SGML, most notably Adobe's Portable Document Format (PDF), which provides for a high-resolution replica of a printed page on the Web. For OCLC, these changes represented a tremendous opportunity to evolve its service by making it easier for libraries to install and distribute electronic journals, and making it easier and less expensive for publishers to make journals available online.

Between 1993 and 1996, the number of electronic journals available to libraries through EJO (and many other services) had grown considerably, and libraries found themselves juggling growing collections of electronic journals from a variety of distributors. In an effort to assess the evolving needs of libraries subscribing to EJO, OCLC gathered information from its library advisory committees and in December of 1995 surveyed three hundred EJO users. Clear priorities emerged from these investigations. These included the desire for a much larger collection of journals (thousands, rather than dozens, of titles); true cross-journal searching and browsing across journals; an archiving solution; usage statistics for tracking activity within individual journals in the collection; support for group purchases; and a number of other features that would make the service work better within an institutional information infrastructure.

OCLC TAKES A NEW APPROACH TO ELECTRONIC JOURNALS

Based on the results of this research and its experience with EJO, OCLC began redesigning its electronic publishing program in early 1996, with the goal of introducing a new, wholly Web-based service in early 1997. OCLC's experience with EJO led the project team to the following parameters for the new service:

- *Reaching a critical mass of journals (hundreds, and eventually thousands, of titles) would require a standardized, scaleable production system*. In practical terms, this meant moving away from the customized indexing associated with the EJO model to standardized indexing and abstracting across journals and publishers. It also meant moving away from the expensive and labor-intensive process of preparing SGML for full-text articles, to a system for delivering articles in data formats that publishers could provide quickly and inexpensively, and that end-users could easily access and display on the Web.

* *Users had to be able to search for information across the entire collection of journals available through the service.* In the EJO user survey mentioned above, OCLC found that 76% of respondents indicated a preference for searching across a collection of journals versus searching a single title. In addition, 93% expressed a strong desire for their search results to show citations for journals to which they subscribe and related journals to which they may not subscribe. As described above, EJO provided only for limited cross-journal searching, and users could access citations only for the journals to which they subscribed.

* *Archiving had to be addressed.* Virtually all of the library groups that provided input into the development of Electronic Collections Online were adamant in their recommendation that the new service include an archiving component to ensure that participating libraries have ongoing access to the journals in their collection. The EJO model had not originally included an archive: the library licensed access to a journal for a specified period, and its rights to the content ended with the license. Within the first few years of its introduction, however, libraries began asking for archival copies of their journals, and some of the publishers participating in the service worked with OCLC to develop CD-ROM archives for interested institutions.

* *In order to adopt electronic journals on a broad scale, institutions would require tools to support local collection management.* These would have to include some of the features mentioned above–à la carte subscriptions and usage statistics, for instance–as well as support for such features as group purchasing and a variety of authentication methods.

- *Integration with online reference services and local systems would be essential to the long-term success of electronic journals.* The tremendous growth in electronic journals between the introduction of the Web and early 1996 made it clear that access would be one of the biggest issues confronting libraries seeking to adopt them on a broad scale. Many of the early electronic journal services were publisher-based and were therefore delivered in isolation from other electronic offerings, such as reference databases, Web-accessible OPACs and other local information systems. Effective implementation of electronic journals, it was clear, would require integrating electronic journals into a variety of existing information resources.

OVERVIEW OF ELECTRONIC COLLECTIONS ONLINE

OCLC began the requirements process for its new service, Electronic Collections Online, in the spring of 1996. Prototyping and usability testing in the summer were followed by rapid development of the service in the fall of 1996 and winter of 1997. In the spring of 1997, OCLC made a preview release of the service available to a group of 18 sites around the world, and released a production version of the service in June.

Electronic Collections Online provides access to a large and growing collection of electronic journals on the World Wide Web. OCLC is building the collection by seeking agreements with publishers to load their journal data and associated indexing at OCLC and then providing access to these data through a single Web interface. Data provided by publishers include indexing and abstracts (in SGML and other tagged formats), as well as full-text articles in standard data formats that are easily viewed on the Web (these include PDF, RealPage, and HTML).

As OCLC receives these data, it normalizes and enhances the indexing and adds it to a single database that links to all articles available through the service. Users can search and browse the database using OCLC's Web interface, which supports cross-journal searching as well as extensive browsing by journal, issue, or topic area. Article citations are available to all users; article abstracts, displayed in HTML, and complete articles, displayed in

PDF, are available to users whose library subscribes to those journals. Libraries participate in the service by purchasing an "access account" from OCLC and then subscribing to individual journals available through the service, either directly with publishers or through subscriptions agents. (Publishers, not OCLC, set the price for the journals available through the service.) An access account enables patrons to log on to the service and search, browse and view article citations for *all* available journals (as opposed to EJO, where users had access to citations only for the journals in their collection). It also entitles the institution to monthly, journal-level usage statistics indicating the number of abstract and article displays by ISSN; archival access to the journals it has subscribed to; and user support and documentation. As libraries subscribe to journals, the publisher or subscription agent that processes the order notifies OCLC of the start and end dates for the subscription. OCLC adds this information to the library's access account profile, which enables patrons to view abstracts and articles for that journal.

OCLC'S EVOLVING ROLE

Under EJO, OCLC was positioned as a publisher service provider, with responsibilities for building, maintaining and supporting the online system. Under Electronic Collections Online, OCLC, on behalf of its members, plays an active role in defining and guiding the development of the service. This role is evident in four areas: (1) OCLC's relationships with publishers, (2) its efforts to ensure archival access to journals, (3) its approach to collection management, and (4) its efforts to integrate electronic journals with library information systems. Each of these areas is discussed below.

Publisher Relations

Reflecting its interests in a large-scale delivery system for institutional subscribers, OCLC's agreements with publishers under Electronic Collections Online differ in four important ways from its publisher agreements under EJO:

1. *OCLC is asking participating publishers to make large numbers (and if possible, all) of the titles from their collections available through the service.* This is in contrast to the EJO model, in which the publishers experimented with the service by making, at most, a handful of titles available. Also, OCLC is initially seeking to make available electronic versions of existing and widely held paper serials, whereas in EJO, the first two journals loaded were electronic only titles. OCLC's goal in taking this approach is to build quickly to a critical mass of titles that are already widely held by libraries. From this base, the collection will expand to include additional electronic-only titles.

2. *OCLC is seeking to lower technical and financial barriers for making journals available online.* Under Electronic Collections Online, OCLC has minimized the cost of mounting data by adopting standard indexing and data formats, both of which are provided by participating publishers in a form that enables OCLC to add them to the database through a more efficient, standardized process than was possible under EJO. OCLC's goal in taking this approach is to reduce subscription costs by minimizing costs for electronic distribution. In addition, by separating the cost of the access account from the cost of journal subscriptions, Electronic Collections Online users share the cost of access, archiving, and other value-added service components with all participating libraries for all available journals. (This is in contrast to a model in which these costs are duplicated by every publisher-distributor, which would tend toward higher costs per journal for these service components.)

3. *Publishers participating in Electronic Collections Online agree to allow OCLC to archive their journal content at OCLC.* OCLC also has the right to provide libraries with perpetual access to the issues of the journals to which they have subscribed, even after the library has canceled a subscription. (Under EJO, publishers sold access only for the online version of the journal, and OCLC's rights to distribute the content ended with the publisher contract.)

4. *In addition to providing archival access, OCLC is seeking to make its online journal collection a print substitute by specifying attributes of the journals made available through the service.* Some of these attributes include delivery dates (on or before print dates); content presented (at minimum, all articles from each issue, and ideally, cover-to-cover content); and data format (to begin with, a replica of the printed page in PDF).

As of late summer 1997, publisher reaction to the Electronic Collections Online model has been very positive. Eighteen publishers have agreed to make more than 650 titles available through the service, and the collection is expected to grow to as many as one thousand titles by the end of the year. The current collection includes titles in science, technology, medicine and the social sciences (a particular area of emphasis for OCLC). Except for two original journals from the EJO service, all of the titles under agreement to date are electronic versions of print journals. The data format of choice for participating publishers is PDF; other formats include CatchWord's RealPage format, which, like PDF, displays an image of the printed page; and, for some of the EJO legacy titles, HTML.

While publishers have taken a number of approaches to subscription pricing for their electronic publications, three basic models predominate. The first is an electronic-only model, in which the publisher sells a subscription to the electronic version of the journal, sometimes at a discount compared to the print subscription price. The second is a bundled model, in which the subscriber pays a premium over and above the print subscription price (usually 10-30%) for both a print subscription and access to the electronic version of the journal. And the third is a version of the bundled model, in which print subscribers are granted a free subscription to the electronic version for a limited period of time. OCLC has also asked participating publishers for the right to sell individual articles from the journals available through the service, and will introduce this document delivery functionality in 1998. Whether subscription or "pay-per-view," it is safe to assume that these pricing models are largely experimental and will likely evolve as publishers and libraries alike accumulate usage statistics for their publications.

Preservation

A significant benefit of electronic journals is their potential to free libraries from the burden of storing archival copies. Unlike paper archiving models, in which materials are stored locally or regionally, the electronic model has made it possible for libraries to share digital archives maintained by external agencies. In a survey of 135 libraries conducted in 1996/97, for instance, Barbara Hall learned that while 91% of respondents offered access to networked electronic journals, 75% were not archiving electronic journals locally.[4]

The trend toward remote archiving of electronic journals has created a need within the library community and among organizations storing these titles for archiving standards and a certification process that will ensure preservation. To date, however, libraries and electronic journal providers have only scratched the surface of archiving standards and their implementation. Hall writes: "Although archiving is a major issue confronting research libraries today, there has been very little comparative information and almost no systematic research available of current practices, policies and solutions."[5]

In spite of the absence of clear standards, a number of required elements for any long-term archiving solution are clear. Essentially, "Libraries will want to know that a subscription to a title gives them permanent access to the contents over time, that the server on which it is found will be consistently available, that the technology will be robust and stable, and that if the supplier . . . ever withdraws the service, then there is a plan for giving them the data they paid for."[6] As these authors point out, the basis for any archiving solution is a purchasing model that ensures the subscribing institution the right to ongoing access to the journal, even after the journal subscription has been canceled–in other words, an access plus ownership model, rather than a simple access model.

In addition, a number of minimum technical standards must be met by the provider. These include standards governing data backup, to ensure the library that redundant copies of journals are available in the event of system failure; availability, to ensure that the data is accessible to patrons when they need it (the ideal being 7 days a week, 24 hours a day); capacity, to ensure that users are not turned away due to system constraints; and interoperability, to ensure that journals are loaded in conformance with standards that support access from local systems as well as through the provider's interface.

Archiving standards must also anticipate technical change and provide for migration of data and the systems that house it to emerging formats and systems. In its final report, the Task Force on the Archiving of Digital Information describes a "migration" strategy for preserving digital information. This strategy involves

> the periodic transfer of digital materials from one hardware/ software configuration to another, or from one generation of computer technology to a subsequent generation. The purpose of migration is to preserve the integrity of digital objects and to retain the ability for clients to retrieve, display, and otherwise use them in the face of constantly changing technology.[7]

Migration as defined above has two facets: (1) preserving the integrity of the objects (journal articles, abstracts and indexing) themselves and (2) migrating the system to provide *convenient* ongoing access to those objects. The first component requires that the intellectual integrity of information stored in the archive is preserved over time–that it is not tampered with and does not decay as it is backed up or archived, or the format is migrated. The second component requires that the provider migrate the data formats and the system as technology evolves to ensure that the content in the archive, as well as the system used to access it, remain accessible.

OCLC's Archiving Policy

OCLC's approach to archiving is based on a centralized model, in which copies of all journals available through the service are stored at OCLC. OCLC has adopted this approach to ensure that technical standards like those described above will be consistently applied across all of the journals available through the service. The core of this approach is OCLC's agreement with publishers, which grants OCLC the right to mount a copy of all journal content distributed through the service at OCLC. The agreement also grants OCLC the right to store, in perpetuity, all of the journal content delivered to OCLC during the period of the contract and provide ongoing access to libraries that have subscribed to this content, even if the publisher terminates its agreement with OCLC.

OCLC tracks library journal subscriptions on a title-by-title basis through the Electronic Collections access account. The access account serves as an "electronic shelf" that enables libraries to start and stop journal subscriptions at any time. For each subscription, OCLC maintains the start date and end date and associates it with that institution's account. Because the access account is not tied to particular journal subscriptions, as long as the library maintains it, patrons will be able to view abstracts and articles for all journals in the library's collection. (This includes current journal subscriptions and, where the library has discontinued a subscription, the volumes and issues to which it subscribed.) Should the library discontinue its access account, OCLC will maintain its subscription profile for five years. If the library renews its account during this time, this profile will be associated with the account, assuring the library of access to its archive.

Technical standards for the Electronic Collections Online archive include daily on-site backups; off-site storage of all content and system software; accessibility approaching 7 days a week, 24 hours a day; and reliability consistent with other OCLC online services. OCLC's approach to data migration is to provide as much current content in as few formats as possible. As data formats become outmoded, OCLC will encourage participating publishers to provide their current data in a single, widely used format. At its discretion, and based on available technology and usage information, OCLC will also migrate journal backfiles to new data formats if current formats (such as PDF) become outmoded. In cases where OCLC does not migrate backfiles to emerging data formats, it intends to provide libraries with access through an adequate and available mechanism.

OCLC also intends to migrate the Electronic Collections Online service to new technology as needed to match the ubiquity and convenience of the original, Web-based system. As a fail-safe mechanism, OCLC has requested participating publishers to allow

OCLC to distribute copies of journal content on a digital medium (such as CD-ROM) to libraries that have subscribed to these journals, in the event the service is discontinued.

Supporting Local Collection Management

The growth of electronic resources has in many cases substantially increased the work of libraries to select, acquire, and circulate resources. This increased labor has ranged from identifying and researching options, to licensing content and providing access. These tasks absorb library resources, and can slow collection growth.

OCLC is following a three-pronged strategy to reduce this burden and support local electronic collection management for electronic journals. For common collection management tasks–such as archiving–OCLC seeks to achieve economies of scale by centralizing the activity. For aspects of collection management where local control is preferable–selection, for instance–OCLC has developed tools to support local collection control. And where technology offers opportunities to dramatically improve collection management activity, OCLC will follow one of two approaches: (1) build new tools to support this activity; or (2) leverage existing tools and systems to ease the library's workload.

OCLC is also working with a number of subscription agents to provide libraries with centralized purchasing of available titles. In this partnership, OCLC aggregates, stores and provides online access to journal content, while subscription agents provide centralized purchasing, support for licensing efforts, and integration with paper-purchasing procedures. OCLC believes that many of the subscription agents' traditional roles in supporting serials selection and acquisition will also apply to the electronic environment. These roles will include centralized purchasing, arranging common subscription start dates, managing the renewal process, and notifying subscribers of available journals. To date, OCLC has signed agreements with almost one dozen subscription agents to provide subscription support for journals available through Electronic Collections Online.

Providing Integrated Access to Electronic Journals

As Richard E. Quandt notes, since "the ultimate purpose of research libraries has to be the provision of scholarly information, the quality of a library must be measured not so much by the physical objects within its walls, but by the ease with which it permits access to relevant scholarly materials."[8] Providing easy access to electronic journals will require integration of these resources with the library's complete digital and physical collections. These will include the materials in the library's stacks, as well as materials available through interlibrary loan, online reference information (including abstracting and indexing databases and online full text), document delivery resources, and online library catalogs and other finding aids. The library community has also increased its demand for standards-based, open systems that will allow libraries to link directly from a local system into one or more repositories of electronic journal data and retrieve the desired material on the fly.

In developing Electronic Collections Online, OCLC has adopted an access strategy that supports these emerging access trends for electronic journals. This strategy encompasses *vertical integration* of electronic journals with OCLC's online reference service, First-Search; *horizontal integration* with other electronic journals and library catalogs; and standards-based *systems integration* to support the efforts of libraries to integrate electronic journals with local systems.

Vertical Integration of Electronic Collections Online with FirstSearch

One of EJO's most popular features consisted of links from endnotes in articles available through the service to bibliographic records in databases such as Medline and INSPEC. In order for the circle of electronic journals and abstracting and indexing databases to be complete, however, users must be given the freedom to move seamlessly between journals and finding aids. They must be able to link directly from abstracting and indexing databases to journal articles, and also initiate searches of abstracting and indexing databases from within journal articles.

Electronic Collections Online has rapidly moved in this direction. The first release of the service supported links between article end notes and records in bibliographic databases. Electronic Collections Online is also being integrated with FirstSearch, which provides access to a collection of almost 70 citation, abstract and full-text databases, bibliographic and holdings information for OCLC members, document ordering and interlibrary loan functionality. This integration, which will be complete in early 1998, will operate on two levels:

- Libraries that subscribe to FirstSearch will be able to subscribe to journals available through Electronic Collections Online and search and browse their Electronic Collections Online journal collection from within the FirstSearch interface. This level of integration will provide libraries with a single point of access for electronic journals, other full-text resources and online reference.
- Journal articles available through Electronic Collections Online will be linked to FirstSearch third-party databases that index those journals. This feature will enable users to search their preferred pointer file (Medline, for instance), and link directly from records in that file to the journal article described. Articles will be available to users in cases where the library subscribes to the journal through Electronic Collections Online. OCLC will also support online document ordering to enable libraries to purchase articles from journals to which they do not subscribe.

*Horizontal Integration with Other Electronic Serials
and Library Holdings*

As appealing as the one-stop shopping approach to electronic journals may be, in practice libraries juggle access to electronic journals from many sources. To date, library strategies for integrating access to electronic journals across providers have centered on easily implemented HTML links between the library homepage and/or links from the library's Web-accessible online catalog to the journal in question on the distributor's server.

While linking from the library catalog is used less frequently than simply listing available titles, it will undoubtedly grow in popularity because it adds so much value as an access point to information. The catalog allows the library to display availability of (and provide access to) electronic resources in the context of the library's entire collection. Used as a gateway to electronic resources, library catalogs can provide "a coherent view of the holdings of multiple libraries or library collections" and consistent indexing across holdings.[9] In addition, as "a high-quality, *managed* information access system," a catalog is reliable, available, and provides users with behavior that is "highly repeatable from session to session."[10]

To facilitate "catalog access" to the journals available through its collection, OCLC ensures that WorldCat (the OCLC Online Union Catalog) contains complete and authoritative cataloging for each journal that is accessible through Electronic Collections Online. As new journals are loaded on the service, corresponding records are made available through WorldCat. When a record exists, it is reviewed and enhanced by cataloging experts in OCLC's TechPro service; where a record is needed, these same catalogers create one. Two hot links are included in each record: one to the Electronic Collections Online logon screen, for users with authorization numbers and passwords, and a second to the URL for users whose IP address has been authorized to access the title in question. These links take the user directly to the title page of the journal in question. From here, the user can navigate to a search screen, display a list of issues, table of contents for a current issue, or scan an author/title page. For institutions that do not catalog through OCLC, OCLC also provides the means to build hypertext links that will authenticate the user (either through IP address or authorization/ password), log them on to the service, and present them with the electronic title page of the specified journal from which the user can navigate through the entire contents of the publication.

OCLC's cataloging efforts for Electronic Collections Online journals have created a foundation for more closely integrating these resources with abstracting and indexing databases. Today, records for Electronic Collections Online journals are accessible on WorldCat through FirstSearch. Libraries subscribing to journals available through Electronic Collections Online can attach their holdings symbol to the WorldCat record describing those journals. When they do, their holdings symbol will be displayed within First-Search databases, alongside the library's paper holdings (and holdings for other electronic serials). WorldCat records will also be available to OCLC member libraries for use in their local catalogs.

CONCLUSION

At its peak in December of 1996, EJO provided access to 48 journals. At this writing, OCLC had signed agreements to make well over 650 journals available through Electronic Collections Online, with a number of contracts in process. This kind of growth is not unique to OCLC; a number of providers are making hundreds of titles available on the Web, with expectations of delivery collections numbering in the thousands by the turn of the century. The implications of this growth for libraries are clear: academic and professional journals are moving online at an accelerated rate, and it appears that libraries will have the opportunity in the next few years to migrate large portions of their paper collections online.

If the evolution of OCLC's electronic journals program is an indicator of the direction the industry is taking, libraries can expect significant changes in the way that electronic journals are delivered in the next few years. Leading these changes will be increasing integration of electronic journals into library information systems and improvements in standards-based, open systems that will allow libraries to link directly from a local system into one or more repositories of electronic journal data. In many ways, it appears that this integration will follow the trend of the late 1980s and early 1990s that saw the consolidation of bibliographic, and then abstracting and indexing, and finally full-text databases, into a group of services designed specifically for libraries.

Even if this scenario is played out, electronic journals will differ substantially from their predecessors in a number of ways, starting with the content that is distributed. As they evolve, for instance, these publications will increasingly diverge from their paper counterparts, as authors and publishers increasingly seek to incorporate a variety of digital supplements into their journal "articles." At the same time, as publishers and libraries gain experience with electronic journals, pricing issues are likely to be addressed, and new models–more than likely, hybrids of current subscription and pay-per-view models–will emerge and gain acceptance. Finally–and this is already happening–we can expect that new technical models for connecting end users to journals will continue to evolve.

For its part, OCLC will focus on the rapid development of its electronic journals program to meet the needs of the library commu-nity it serves. This will involve supporting the library's efforts to make the transition from print to large-scale electronic journal collections that support the acquisition, circulation, and preserva-tion of these publications. Electronic Collections Online represents only the current phase in this ongoing process.

NOTES

1. Andrea Keyhani, "The Online Journal of Current Clinical Trails: an Innovation in Electronic Journal Publishing," *Database* 16, no. 1 (Feb. 1993): 14-23. EJO was a joint venture between the American Association for the Advancement of Science (AAAS), which developed the editorial content and focus, and OCLC, which developed the interface and online system, and distrib-uted the journal over its telecommunications network.

2. These publications included the *Online Journal of Current Clinical Trials*, published by the American Association for the Advancement of Science (pub-lished today by Chapman & Hall, North America); and the *Online Journal of Knowledge Synthesis for Nursing*, published by Sigma Theta Tau. Both journals are available through Electronic Collections Online.

3. *Applied Physics Letters Online*, published by the American Institute of Physics, was the first journal mounted under this interface; other journals quickly followed.

4. Barbara Hall, "Archiving Electronic Journals: Current Practices and Poli-cies in Academic Research Libraries" (summary of presentation on Archiving the Internet by Barbara Hall at the ALCTS Computer Files Discussion Group, June 28, 1997, American Library Association Annual Conference). Available: http://www-lib.usc.edu/Info/Acqui/research.html

5. Ibid.

6. Charles B. Lowry and Denise A. Troll. "Carnegie Mellon University and University Microfilms International 'Virtual Library Project'," *The Serials Librarian* 28, no. 1/2 (1996): 143-169.

7. Commission on Preservation and Access and Research Libraries Group, *Preserving Digital Information: Report of the Task Force on Archiving Digital Information*, May 1, 1996.

8. Richard E. Quandt. "Electronic Publishing and Virtual Libraries: Issues and an Agenda for the Andrew W. Mellon Foundation," *Serials Review* 22 (summer 1996): 9-24.

9. Clifford A. Lynch, "Building the Infrastructure of Resource Sharing: Union Catalogs, Distributed Search, and Cross-Database Linkage," *Library Trends* 45 (winter 1997): 449.

10. Ibid., 450.

INDEXING

Indexing Electronic Journals

Cathy Rentschler, MLS

SUMMARY. The staff of *Library Literature* has been indexing three electronic journals since 1995. This article provides an overview of the process, including selection of titles, subscriptions, procedures and problems. *[Article copies available for a fee from The Haworth Document Delivery Service: 1-800-342-9678. E-mail address: getinfo@haworth. com]*

KEYWORDS. Electronic journals, indexing, library literature

In 1995, *Library Literature* became the first H. W. Wilson index to include electronic journals. The company has recognized that

Cathy Rentschler has been the editor of *Library Literature* since 1975 (email: crentschler@hwwilson.com). She is the current chair of the Library Science Librarians Discussion Group of the Association of College and Research Libraries.

[Haworth co-indexing entry note]: "Indexing Electronic Journals." Rentschler, Cathy. Co-published simultaneously in *The Serials Librarian* (The Haworth Press, Inc.) Vol. 33, No. 3/4, 1998, pp. 319-324; and: *E-Serials: Publishers, Libraries, Users, and Standards* (ed: Wayne Jones) The Haworth Press, Inc., 1998, pp. 319-324. Single or multiple copies of this article are available for a fee from The Haworth Document Delivery Service [1-800-342-9678, 9:00 a.m. - 5:00 p.m. (EST). E-mail address: getinfo@haworth.com].

electronic journals are an important new source of information for *Library Literature* subscribers. Each step in the process has meant changes to our procedures, and the staff and I have acquired some new skills. Others who work with electronic journals may be interested in our experiences.

THE SELECTION PROCESS

A proposal to index electronic journals was presented to the in-house committee that studies *Library Literature* every two years. Barbara Chen, Associate Director of Indexing Services, and I were given the assignment to examine titles and make recommendations.

The first change came during the selection process. Studying journals to be indexed in *Library Literature* usually means sitting around a large table piled with stacks of sample issues. The journals are passed around, examined and evaluated against the criteria for inclusion. In contrast, the examination process for electronic journals meant that Barbara and I sat in front of her computer looking at titles on the screen. The *Directory of Electronic Journals, Newsletters and Academic Discussion Lists*, published by the Association of Research Libraries, was a valuable resource for identifying titles to examine.[1] *Library Literature* itself was another resource, and we noted titles that had been mentioned in the literature of the field. I had done some preliminary work by identifying sites where back issues of journals were archived. Archives had to be located for two reasons. We didn't want to index ephemeral material that wasn't being archived, and we needed to look at issues that had been "published," rather than subscribe and wait for issues to appear. The first criterion for electronic journals was thereby established: archiving of published issues.

In examining several titles, we excluded those which, despite being categorized as journals, consisted of nothing more than announcements or short news items. This became our second criterion (one used for print titles as well): articles of reference and research value. We also excluded titles with invalid addresses, and titles with only one archived issue. Print publications must have published several issues, ideally at least one volume, before they are considered for *Library Literature*.

Barbara and I recommended three titles for inclusion: *LIBRES,* *MC Journal* and *Public-Access Computer Systems Review.* The committee agreed to our recommendations.

SUBSCRIPTIONS

The next step was to subscribe to each of the titles. For print titles, we would have entered subscriptions through our serials vendor. However, anyone who has joined a listserv or subscribed to an electronic journal knows that "subscribing" is handled via electronic mail. Subscribers receive an e-mail message notifying them whenever an issue has been published. Subscribers then request the contents, also via e-mail. The staff learned how to set up the subscriptions and to save the confirmation message explaining listserv commands. A separate folder for each title was created in our mail system. As we received messages about a new issue, they were moved to that folder.

PROCEDURES AND SYSTEM SPECIFICATIONS

As we eagerly awaited the first issue, we began to consider the details of the indexing process and any necessary changes to our system specifications. We had considered doing all of the indexing and keyboarding on a personal computer that would be connected to our data entry system. At that time, there was only one personal computer in the department. (Our work is normally done on dumb terminals connected to a mainframe.) The indexer and the data entry clerk would have to leave their desks to use the PC, and no one else could use it during that time. We decided that we would print a hard copy of each issue. Once the hard copy is printed, an indexer indexes it just like any print publication. I check the indexing and the hard copy is given to a data entry clerk for keyboarding.

We realized that citations to electronic journals wouldn't look like those for a print publication. We also knew that the bibliographic records in the *Library Literature* database had to be MARC-compatible. We began to look at style manuals for electronic citations to determine what elements are usually included. A print publication normally has a volume and/or issue number, an issue date and paging. This information, along with the author's name and article title, allows a user to locate that article. Electronic journals, in turn, have retrieval methods, server addresses, file sizes, article addresses and archive sites. They may in fact have multiple retrieval methods and addresses. At the time we decided to include electronic journals, the MARC fields and the citation styles were still in development. Fortunately there are staff members at the Wilson Company who monitor these developments and could advise me. We had to consider fields for the Wilson Journal File[2] as well as the *Library Literature* database.

Since electronic journals are in fact computer files, we would need to include the general material designation (GMD) in each bibliographic record. We would keyboard paging as given by the journal. If no paging was noted, we would use the number of lines or bytes, as cited by the journal. Electronic addresses for a particular article also would be keyboarded in each bibliographic record, including e-mail instructions, where necessary. Articles might have an e-mail, ftp, gopher, telnet or Internet address as their retrieval method; some articles had multiple methods. Later, we began to see separate addresses for ASCII and HTML versions of an article. We included all the retrieval methods at first, but eventually omitted gopher addresses as journals began to establish Web sites. We decided to use only HTML addresses, and to ignore archival site addresses.

In the Wilson Journal File, print publications have publisher name and address fields. No change would be needed for the publisher name field, but we substituted retrieval methods (electronic addresses) for the usual street address, city, etc. All retrieval methods, including gopher, would be included in the Journal File record. Subscription instructions, such as "send the message SUBSCRIBE PACS-P to the listserv address" would be included in a note field.

PROBLEMS AND DEVELOPMENTS

Excluding questions about subject headings and matters of style, problems with indexing print publications usually involve typographical errors or missing issues. Our problems with electronic journals have followed the same pattern, but the methods of solving them were different, and were handled more quickly.

One of our first problems was a minor one, an apparent typographical error. For a print journal we would have waited to see if a correction appeared in a subsequent issue. If it were a serious error we might try to alert our users, perhaps by adding "[sic]" in a title, for example. In this case, I e-mailed the editor. She replied immediately, was grateful for my alerting her to the problem and made an online correction to the article.

A subsequent problem was more serious. We received one issue by e-mail when we hadn't received the previous issue. The problem was caused by the journal's server being changed. This explained why no subscriber activity was being recorded on the server. The editor gave me the new address and sent the missing issue by e-mail.

As time went on, we began to realize that our electronic journals were establishing Web sites. This meant we didn't have to "subscribe" or to wait for e-mail messages, but could periodically check the Web for new issues. It's still easier for us to wait for notification via e-mail rather than spend time searching the Web, which can be very time-consuming. Although the H. W. Wilson Company has its own node on the Internet (and its own Web site, http://www.hwwilson.com) even we find searching slow going at times.

We have bookmarked the Web sites of our three electronic journals. When an additional PC was installed in our department, another problem was identified. In transferring the bookmarks to the new PC we discovered that one of the addresses was no longer valid. We instituted a new procedure of testing the URL for each site on a regular basis. When a change occurs, the Journal File record is updated, just as we update addresses for print publications. We also update the bookmarks on our personal computers. A staff member also regularly checks the "What's New" section of journal Web sites for possible changes.

We still find it more convenient to print a hard copy of the journals for indexing and data entry. We have experienced an occasional problem with missing lines of text or lines running off the screen or the page. Modifying printer commands and an e-mail query to the journal editor didn't resolve the problem. We have found that printing the Web version has worked better. We also learned that other subscribers hadn't reported any problems, leading the journal editor and myself to believe that most users are migrating from e-mail to the Web site.

It was exciting to be editor of the first and only H. W. Wilson index to include electronic journals, but that is no longer the case. *Education Index* now includes an electronic journal, and I expect other Wilson indexes will follow suit. Our staff served as a resource for the staff of *Education Index* and will do the same for other departments. And as Wilson indexes become available through WilsonWeb, there will be the opportunity for users to link directly to an article by clicking on the address included in the *Library Literature* citation. We also expect that more electronic journals will be included in the future. Whenever we study *Library Literature* we will be looking for new titles which meet our criteria. We have three additional electronic titles on our list for consideration during the next study.

In the early 1980s, the H. W. Wilson Company began offering its indexes in electronic formats through Wilsonline. Later, CD-ROM versions and magnetic tape formats were added. Original abstracts are being created for many products and full-text options are under way. Wilson products have certainly entered the digital age. As the company approaches its centennial, "Celebrating the Future, Commemorating the Past," its mission remains the same: to give its users the information they want in the way that they want it.

NOTES

1. Michael Strangelove and Diane Kovacs, *Directory of Electronic Journals, Newsletters and Academic Discussion Lists*, 3rd. ed. (Washington, D.C.: Association of Research Libraries, 1993).

2. The Wilson Journal File is the company-wide database of all journals indexed by H. W. Wilson Company indexes. The database includes such information as journal title, publisher, frequency, price, etc. It also includes who indexes what (e.g., *Journal of Academic Librarianship* is indexed in *Library Literature* and in *Education Index*), along with start and end dates. Title changes, cessations, etc., are also available. Currently there are nearly 6000 records in the file, of which 4700 are active titles. The full file is available only in electronic format.

Uniform Resource Identifiers and Online Serials

Leslie Daigle
Ron Daniel Jr.
Cecilia Preston

SUMMARY. The widespread acceptance of the World Wide Web makes it the method of choice for publishing online serials. However, concerns ranging from rights management to the long-term integrity of citations are just two of the issues which continue to impede the widespread adoption of such a mode of publication. This paper discusses the history and purposes of Uniform Resource Iden-

Leslie Daigle is Vice President, Research, Bunyip Information Systems Inc. (email: leslie@bunyip.com).
Ron Daniel Jr. is a Technical Staff Member, Los Alamos National Laboratory (email: rdaniel@lanl.gov).
Cecilia Preston is a partner, Preston & Lynch (email: cecilia@well.com).

The authors would like to thank Patrik Fältström, Michael Mealling, and Renato Ianella for their cooperation on an earlier paper, parts of which provided the basis for this paper's discussion of URN abstract architecture.

[Haworth co-indexing entry note]: "Uniform Resource Identifiers and Online Serials." Daigle, Leslie, Ron Daniel Jr., and Cecilia Preston. Co-published simultaneously in *The Serials Librarian* (The Haworth Press, Inc.) Vol. 33, No. 3/4, 1998, pp. 325-341; and: *E-Serials: Publishers, Libraries, Users, and Standards* (ed: Wayne Jones) The Haworth Press, Inc., 1998, pp. 325-341. Single or multiple copies of this article are available for a fee from The Haworth Document Delivery Service [1-800-342-9678, 9:00 a.m. - 5:00 p.m. (EST). E-mail address: getinfo@haworth.com].

325

tifiers (URIs) as well as the role identifiers will play in the deployment of online serials. Particular attention is paid to development of Uniform Resource Names (URNs), one of the goals of which is to use existing identifier systems, such as ISBNs, ISSNs, and SICIs. The paper describes URN syntax and resolution, then presents some illustrations of how WWW-based publication of online serials might use different forms of URIs. *[Article copies available for a fee from The Haworth Document Delivery Service: 1-800-342-9678. E-mail address: getinfo@haworth.com]*

KEYWORDS. URN, URI, resource naming, identifier

INTRODUCTION

The publication of serials online is of considerable current interest. Numerous small-scale experiments are being conducted, but widespread use of such publication systems still seems a few years away. The ultimate shape of the world of online serials will be the result of compromises between many communities. By virtue of its (near) ubiquity and popularity, the Internet is the de facto standard network for use by online publications with an eye to global accessibility. To date, the application software infrastructure of the Internet and the World Wide Web (WWW) has not been sufficient to meet the needs of serious online serial publications. This paper outlines the work that is being done to address some of those issues, in particular in the area of providing infrastructure for robust Internet identifiers for online resources.

Publishers form one of the most obvious of the communities involved in the shaping of online publication systems. They are particularly concerned about the ease of copying digital works, and are loath to provide much of their content until rights management systems can offer solid protection. Rights management systems such as IBM's Cryptolopes [IBM] and InterTrust's DigiBox [InterTrust] are actively being developed and marketed to publishers to address their concerns. But publishers do not operate in a vacuum. They rely on customers–readers and librarians. While publishers might wish to impose extremely strong licensing and/or copyright management systems which charge for even trivial access to a document, readers and librarians will reject solutions that are too expensive or cumbersome. This is not a problem that will be solved by Internet technology, but the appropriate infrastructure must be available to support solutions that are adopted by the publishing community.

Scholars and archivists are another community with legitimate concerns about online publication of serials and its impact on the long-term integrity of the literature. Procedures for storing paper over long periods of time are well understood; storing digital data over such timescales is an area of current work. The desires of this community for very strong guarantees on the longevity and integrity of the literature have a downside–cost. The cold fact of the matter is that century-old articles are rarely accessed, making it difficult to justify a massive infrastructure for their preservation. Instead, an approach to preservation that is less expensive than the current model for physical works is needed. This may imply that fewer sites will store copies of a work, and other sites that access the work will pay to do so. These, too, are important issues that must be resolved in order for online publications to gain the stature and respect of their physically published counterparts. Again, the solution must come from the interested communities, and the technical advancement of the WWW infrastructure must be such that it can support the practices that these communities promulgate.

The rest of this paper focuses on the specific issues of Internet infrastructure for one component of the technological solution–resource identifiers.

ONLINE PUBLISHING AND THE WWW–TODAY

One strength of the serial literature is the integrity of citations between articles. The hyperlink mechanism of the WWW is the natural way for referencing one article from another. That linking mechanism will also be used for including figures in articles (including animation, video, audio and links to the underlying data sets, for example), obtaining articles from a table of contents, and returning articles that meet search criteria. In fact, these links are the heart of the WWW. Currently these links are implemented using Uniform Resource Locators (URLs), the "addresses" of resources on the WWW. URLs provide a "compact representation of the location and access method for a resource available on the Internet" [Fielding]. This compact representation for protocol-specific information made it very easy to build the WWW from the bottom up, and to bring in a great deal of information that already existed in FTP and Gopher sites. The WWW simply could not have been created any other way.

This low barrier to entry has downsides as well. Since it is so easy to start providing resources on the WWW, very little advance planning is needed. Longevity of links has not been a major consideration of most providers of WWW resources. As a consequence, all users of the WWW are familiar with the problem of broken links. The brief history of the WWW already provides numerous examples of such problems. The best known example concerns the seminal documents on the origin of the WWW itself. Initially these documents were all provided from the CERN WWW server, and consequently were identified using URLs of the form http://info.cern.ch/ These documents were widely cited. When the World Wide Web Consortium (W3C) was formed, the documents were moved off CERN's machines. For about a year CERN provided a forwarding service, but now, old links to those documents are broken. If you happen to know that almost all those documents are available at http://www.w3.org/ then it is easy to find them again. However, no software currently exists that will perform that mapping, or mappings for other document repositories that have similarly moved.

The WWW has been in general use for only four years. We are concerned about the availability of WWW resources over much longer timescales–on the order of a century. As Tim Berners-Lee notes [TimBL], much of the fragility of WWW links arises due to poor choice of the identifiers. But we are confronted with a tradeoff. Embedding particular access technology information, such as protocol, host, port, and path, in an identifier makes it easy to resolve but limits its lifetime. Identifiers without such information can have long lifetimes, but require extra steps to resolve. The simple fact of the matter is that using identifiers based on technologies of the late 20th century, such as HTTP, DNS, and HTML, is a high-risk strategy to achieve long-lived identifiers. Using the WWW to publish online serials requires the development of an identification system and resolution mechanism that avoids the use of such potentially transient information. Of course, half of that requirement already exists. Numerous bibliographic identification systems, such as ISBNs, ISSNs, SICIs (Serial Issue and Contribution Identifiers), Library of Congress Control Numbers, and SUDOC numbers are currently in use. These identifiers do not display the dependence on specific technology that current URLs do. The remainder of this paper discusses how such identifiers might be resolved, and the issues that arise.

DEVELOPMENTS IN INTERNET IDENTIFIERS

Broken links are not the only problem that can be attributed to the use of retrieval information as an identifier. Since URLs incorporate domain names, common practice is to contact the first machine that is associated with that name. This results in overloaded servers and duplicated intercontinental traffic. All these problems became apparent very early in the development of the WWW. The Internet Engineering Task Force (IETF) is the de facto standards body for defining the necessary technology infrastructure for the Internet. In 1992, it established a working group on Uniform Resource Identifiers (URIs) that was to standardize various URL schemes which were emerging at the time, as well as to consider what could be done about other related problems. That working group developed a model that allows resources to be identified by a Uniform Resource Name (URN), which would be a persistent identifier for a resource, independent of information such as protocol, host, port, etc. One of the requirements placed on URNs by the working group was that URNs be able to utilize older forms of identifiers such as ISBNs, ISSNs, LC control numbers, etc. URLs and URNs were defined to be the two classes of URI.

To obtain a copy of a resource, a URN would be mapped to a set of URLs that are the current locations of the resource. The browser or other client software would then pick one URL from the set and use it to fetch the resource. This would add a measure of fault-tolerance to obtaining resources. If the first server was down, the client could use one of the other URLs in the list. Replicating a resource could be achieved by copying the resource to a new location, then adding the URL for that new location to the list. Moving a resource to a new location would be like replicating it, followed by deleting the old URL and resource instance.

The data structure for mapping URNs to URLs was called the Uniform Resource Characteristics (URC). This name was given because, in addition to the URN and URL information, the URC was to be a carrier for information about the format of a resource at a particular URL, bibliographic information on the resource, and perhaps a digital signature to ensure that the resource had not been tampered with. The URC ultimately became a generalized metadata structure for a resource.

This model is described in the IETF documents RFC 1630, RFC 1737 and RFC 1738 ([TimBL2], [Sollins], and [TimBL3]).

Following on the work of the URI group, an IETF URN working group was formed with the consensus viewpoint that no single naming scheme would suit all needs. What was needed was a technical infrastructure, or framework, that would support many different schemes. This paper describes the outcome of the work of that group.

A URC-WG has not formed, although there are several projects that are now tackling related problems. The IETF has a working group on Web Distributed Authoring and Versioning (WEB-DAV) that is working in coordination with the W3C. The W3C also has the follow-on to the PICS (Platform for Internet Content Selection) effort [PICS], now known as the Resource Description Framework. Some of the people involved in the URC effort are now participating in those related projects.

URNs AND THE INTERNET INFORMATION INFRASTRUCTURE

The initial experience of circular discussions and no development progress that plagued the URN work within the IETF was caused by the fact that many efforts were attempting to solve both the Internet technical infrastructure issues and the problems of different end-user communities (publishers, network-level software developers, etc.). Indeed, many of the original proposals for URN systems featured resource naming structures that were tightly coupled to a resolution mechanism that was geared to solve one community's needs. From the IETF's perspective, the critical step was to focus strictly on finding the technical infrastructure for Internet identifiers that would provide persistent identifiers and support the solutions such communities developed within their own frameworks of discussion. To achieve this, two important things were needed: a separation of the structure of the name (identifier) from the resolution mechanics, and a resolution infrastructure that is multitiered and permits distributed information management at all levels.

There are three primary reasons why the separation of the name from the particulars of the resolution process is necessary. The first is only underscored by the success of the WWW–there is a real need for Internet identifiers that are not dependent on resource location, and that have some capacity for persistence. This alone would reduce the frequency with which resources "disappear" because the filename is changed, or the machine on which a resource resides is changed, and so forth. Beyond that, resource access robustness would be improved considerably by providing access to a particular resource from one of several suggested locations. URNs are meant to address all of these issues. Therefore, the temptation is to start by proposing specific techniques to solve these Web-general problems. Extensions can be made to servers, registration services can be added to already-popular services, and no doubt there is some organization willing to accept money in return for the privilege of storing copies of documents on their disk farms.

However, the second reason for which the separation between identifier and resolution process is necessary stems from the very fact that different communities have very different resolution needs. Thus, the technical infrastructure for URNs must be capable of supporting the resolution mechanisms developed by those individual communities, and not just for specific application software. Two key needs for which the solutions are often in opposition are: speed of access and strongly authenticated security mechanisms. Taking a minute to locate a deeply archived document anywhere in the world can be considered fast. Then, having located that document, it would probably be important to authenticate that it is indeed the expected resource (through a signing or certification of the resource itself, the URC referencing it, or even the URN referring to it). That part of the process takes time. On the other hand, various networked systems rely on the ability to consistently refer to configuration data or other resources that are stored and maintained at remote locations. These resources may be created, used, and destroyed in a period of less than an hour, which is a lifetime for machine accesses. While it might be reasonable to take a day to assign an appropriate identifier to a book, and 30 seconds to verify access rights and account information to view it, speed (of assignment as well as of resolution of identifiers) may take precedence over ability to charge for access to one of these network resources. No one end-to-end resolution mechanism can solve all such communities' needs.

The third reason for which the separation between name and resolution process is necessary is simply to allow resolution systems to evolve and be changed over time.

As part of the effort to recognize the naming needs of different communities, and to allow the re-use of existing names, URN identifiers are divided into "namespaces." In rough terms, a namespace is a collection of identifiers that are related through some (externally defined) relationship. ISBNs form a namespace in that they are assigned through a known process and the initiated eye can extract information from the string of digits. The collection of HTTP URLs could be considered a namespace, in that they refer to the set of WWW-accessible resources available at an instant in time. A "URN namespace" is now defined to be an existing or new namespace that has a well-defined mapping to the URN syntax and that also has support systems for resolution using the URN infrastructure. Those support systems may change over time. It is presumed that different URN namespaces will be proposed for identifying different types of resources and different assignment policies. Individual communities will establish resolution systems that are tailored to their needs, but there is nothing inherent in the identifier that precludes the use of other resolution systems.

Dividing URNs into different namespaces is the first step in supporting the second important infrastructural goal of the URN work: a multitiered resolution infrastructure with distributed information management. This is important because centralizing information away from its caretaker tends to lead to lags in updating and other errors. The resolution services for a URN must be provided by parties responsible for maintenance of the information about that URN (directly or through arrangement with another party). Since the resources named by a URN may change ownership over time, the resolution services for a URN must be able to change without modifications to the URN itself. The URN system abstract description outlines a method of handling URN identifiers with these necessary modular layers of information management. In addition to accommodating differences across namespaces, this approach is also designed to distribute authority in such a way as to keep all information maintenance close to the responsible entity. For example, if a resource location changes, only the final level of resolution needs to be made aware of the change.

While the namespace itself can also be used to distribute the load of resolution work to servers nearest the resource, some namespaces will not want to publish details of the structure of their names. Such namespaces can either opt to include other indications of subauthorities in translating their names into URN representations, or these will fall into the category of URNs which are handled by a single external resolution system for the entire namespace.

Rules for individual namespaces are determined by the owners of the namespace before they are registered as URN namespaces. Authority of assignment of individual names within the namespace is also dependent on the individual namespace, and is not part of the URN resolution framework.

From the standpoint of client software, this distributed authority also means that sites may have local procedures to follow. As an example, consider a user working for a corporation whose library has licensed *Books in Print* on CD-ROM. If that user were to click on a link that used an ISBN-based URN, it would be feasible to send the resolution request to software at the library that could search the CD-ROM and return bibliographic information on the book, instead of requiring access to the global Internet to interact with a remote resolver service.

OUTPUT–WHAT THE URN WORKING GROUP HAS DELIVERED TO DATE

The previous section explained the basic principles that formed the foundation of the IETF's URN working group efforts. A year later, URNs are more a reality than a theory, as important steps have been taken in capturing the proposed structure and mechanics in IETF documents ("Requests for Comments"–RFCs) and some basic implementations.

Syntax

The first standards-track document from the URN-WG defines the syntax for URNs (RFC 2141 [Moats]). An example URN would be–urn:isbn:0670856053. This example illustrates two important points. First, URNs are structured into three components which are delimited by the colon character: a literal string "urn," the namespace identifier (NID), "isbn" in this case, and the namespace specific string (NSS). The NSS is a legal identifier from the namespace identified by the NID. In this example, the string "0670856053" is a valid ISBN; the hyphenated form, "0-670-85605-3," would have also been valid. The URN shown above uses identifiers from existing namespaces such as ISBNs, with only minor recoding to get them into a unified syntax.

The URN-WG is not defining the one true method for resolving URNs. Instead, there is a proposal for a method that can be used as a "fallback" if local methods fail, or if there is no local method defined for a particular URN namespace. This solution is based on a two-step resolution procedure. The first step is to locate a resolver, which can map from URIs to information about the resources the URIs identify (e.g., through a database, or some other mechanism). The second step is to communicate with the resolver to find out about a particular URI. Those two steps are discussed in the next two sections.

Resolver Discovery

The URN-WG has recommended one particular approach to resolver discovery for experimental status. This approach, documented in RFC 2168 [Daniel1], is called the NAPTR (Naming Authority PoinTeR) method. It uses a new DNS resource record, called the NAPTR record, which carries the rule stating how to extract parts of a URI and rewrite those parts into a domain name. Although there are questions as to whether this approach can support the needs of a fully operational system, it was selected as an experimental system because it will make use of the already globally deployed DNS infrastructure. The nature of the approach to URNs is such that this system can be replaced with a more suitable one when the operational requirements are understood through experience, without perturbing the then-existing URNs. Here, we will illustrate the NAPTR process with a simple example of how ISBNs might be handled. Recall that our example of an ISBN-based URN looked like: urn:isbn:0670856053.

The first step in the NAPTR method is to discover the rewrite rule(s) for the namespace. To do this, the NAPTR method specifies that there be an apparently centralized site, urn.net, which registers the rewrite rules for all namespaces. The process of finding a resolver begins by extracting the NID, "isbn" in this example, and asking the Domain Name System for any NAPTR records associated with the name isbn.urn.net. ISBNs are an ISO standard. For the purposes of this example, let us assume that ISO has licensed Bowker to run the resolution service for ISBN URNs. (Bowker is a national registration agency for ISBNs, so this is not a wholly implausible assumption.) With those assumptions, the DNS might return a NAPTR record that told clients the next domain name to query was bip.bowker.com, that they could expect to find a resolver at that name, and that they could use either the Z39.50 or the HTTP protocol to talk with that resolver. Finally, the NAPTR record might tell the clients that the URN resolver could provide information about the resource identified by the URN, but that the resource itself was not available from that site.

The details of the NAPTR record, and how it encodes all the information above, are not germane to this article. We refer any interested readers to the NAPTR specification for those details as well as additional examples. Of import here is the fact that the owner of a namespace does not have to be the entity that manages operation of the resolution system.

The information at the namespace_identifier.urn.net level can be quite small. Also, it only appears to be centralized. The design of the DNS is such that the administrators of urn.net do not have to be the administrators of namespace_identifier.urn.net.

Use of one and only one protocol to communicate with the resolver is not necessary. The example mentioned that either Z39.50 or HTTP could be used to query the resolver. Any other protocol can also be used. This is one way that NAPTR accommodates future developments.

Resolvers will have different information available, and will be prepared to answer different sorts of requests. Some resolvers will have the resources themselves, and could answer requests for the resources with their data. Other resolvers might have only bibliographic information, or a single URL for the resource. These different forms of requests types, known as resolution services, are described further in the NAPTR specification. The URN-WG is preparing a more extensive document on resolution services and how they should be handled in different protocols.

Communicating with a Resolver

The previous section discussed how a client could use the NAPTR procedure to find a resolver and determine the protocol to use and the queries to ask when speaking with the resolver. The URN-WG has approved one proposal for such a resolution protocol for experimental use. That proposal is a simple convention for encoding resolution service requests and responses as HTTP requests and responses. Known as THTTP (Trivial HTTP), it was developed with the intention of being easy to retrofit onto existing HTTP servers and is documented in RFC 2169 [Daniel2].

Resolution services, such as mapping an Identifier to a Resource (I2R), an Identifier to a URL (I2L), or an Identifier to a description of the resource (I2C), are encoded as HTTP GET requests. All of HTTP's features for format negotiation are available. The THTTP specification has also been developed to use some of the special capabilities of HTTP in order to make life easier for users. For example, the I2L request returns the URL in a Location: header. This makes the browser automatically try to fetch the resource for the common case of a simple citation to a resource using a URN.

Other protocols can be used for communicating with a resolver. Encodings in Z39.50, LDAP, and CORBA IIOP are all possibilities. Our experimental system already utilizes the Handle resolution protocol from the Corporation for National Research Initiatives (CNRI). Protocols such as these are expected to be an area of rapid development.

Additional Documents

Additional supporting documentation is being developed to describe the architecture of the approach to URNs, as well as guidelines for developing and registering new namespaces.

Although the work on standardizing URNs and the support infrastructure is not complete, some first steps in making the use of URNs a reality for publishers have been taken. As a proof-of-concept that the URN proposal is capable of supporting names from existing name schemes, URN-WG put together a paper describing a possible carrier mechanism of ISBNs, ISSNs, and SICIs. To become "the" representation of these identifiers in URNs will require coordination with the organizations responsible for the relevant standards.

URN IMPLEMENTATION STATUS

Currently the two most popular WWW browsers, Netscape Corporation's Navigator and Microsoft's Internet Explorer, do not offer native support for URNs. It is logical to ask how URNs can be deployed. The Netscape browsers have offered special treatment of URIs that begin with "urn:" for quite some time. These are sent to the HTTP proxy. This means that organizations with firewalls can modify their proxy server to understand URNs, and all the Netscape browsers behind the firewall will instantly gain URN support. This forms the basis of current URN demonstrations. Starting with version 4.0, Internet Explorer offers the ability for custom "protocol handlers" to be downloaded and installed. This feature can be used to add URN support in situations where there is no proxy, or modifying it is infeasible.

Beyond the client issues, URN deployment software is in good shape. The NAPTR resource record has been part of the two most recent releases of BIND (Berkeley Internet Name Demon), the de facto standard DNS server distribution. Support for the THTTP protocol is easy to develop using CGI scripts.

ISSUES IN URNs

While the previous sections of the paper have presented URNs as a possible technology to use in the publication of online serials, there are still open issues about how URNs should evolve. At this time the thorniest issues arise about namespaces. In addition there are operational concerns about the migration of resources and the consequent maintenance of information in the resolution system(s).

The major issue currently facing the URN-WG concerns namespaces and namespace identifiers. As discussed previously, a namespace is a system for assigning identifiers according to a particular scheme. The scheme may imply delegation of authority when binding an identifier to a work, such as in ISBNs. There may be even more freedom in the choice of identifiers, such as the Domain Name System.

One of the problems the URN-WG is dealing with is the result of the IETF's bitter experience with the top-levels of the Domain Name System. Currently the .com, .edu, .org, and .net domain registries are being run by Network Solutions Inc. Because that company has the sole right to assign names in those domains, they are the target of an anti-trust suit. This same sort of battle occurs at the root of the domain tree. Currently, it is not possible for anyone to create new top-level domains (such as .web, .biz, or .realestate). Coming up with a scheme that will allow new top-level domains to be created in a controlled manner has occupied much of the efforts of the Internet Architecture Board. These same sorts of problems will arise in registries of URN namespaces.

From a technical standpoint, there is also a certain tension between easily conceived hierarchies and stable systems. For example, a hierarchy of names based strictly on geographic boundaries is subject to the very real external events of countries that split and/or change boundaries.

Like the deployment of the WWW and URLs initially, some of these issues will best be exposed through the adoption and use of URNs. The basic architecture for URNs is now set; operational experience will guide future refinements.

ILLUSTRATIONS OF URIs IN ONLINE PUBLISHING

There are 3 important steps to consider in the use of URNs for online serials publishing–the creation of a URN namespace (and the maintenance of it), the publishing of a resource with a URN, and the resolution of the URN into the desired resource, once it has been published. The URN becomes the focal URI in this process, with URLs and URCs supporting the operations.

As mentioned previously, a URN namespace may be constructed from an already-existing namespace, such as ISSNs. In that case, the only necessary step is the formalized registration of the namespace and any necessary mappings into URN syntax and structure. Alternatively, an organization may choose to develop its own namespace. In either situation, creation of a URN namespace implies a certain commitment, undertaken directly or delegated to another party, to provide the ability to resolve published URNs to resources. Consideration of the necessary resources to provide this service must be given before the serious undertaking of creating a new URN namespace where an existing one might suffice.

The envisioned publishing process using URNs is not so different from the standard "WWW publishing" as it stands today. However, it is expected that publishers will provide (or delegate) resolution services to access the resources they publish with URNs. Thus, a published resource must have a name assigned to it (through the namespace's particular name assignment process–e.g., the standard ISSN assignment process), and the resource and its information must be made available to the service that will provide resolution to the resource.

Finally, the consumer of the URN–the reader of the online serial– will encounter URNs in citations and references from other online material. Resolution, carried out by a browser or intermediary software, will entail the iterative lookup described in previous sections. The user (or the user's agent) may select a particular copy of a resource based on availability, proximity, quality of reproduction, etc. It is this step that is most heavily supported by the proposed URC construct–standardized metadata describing the various locations, costs, and characteristics of the desired resource. The final resolution step, of course, is still achieved through a URL which indicates current locations of the resource, and the protocol(s) needed to access it.

CONCLUSIONS

Online serials publication, in the context of today's Internet, relies heavily on the use of the Internet's identifier infrastructure. Although it has not previously been robust enough to adequately support the real-life needs and requirements of commercial publishers, steps are being made through the definition and nascent deployment of URN systems. Clearly, issues remain, and operational shortcomings will only be illustrated through usage. The URN infrastructure is timely, and support for more exploration of operational issues will lead to more robust, flexible systems for the future.

NOTES

[IBM] International Business Machines, Cryptolope home page, http://www.cryptolope.ibm.com

[InterTrust] InterTrust home page, http://www.intertrust.com

[Fielding] Roy Fielding, "Relative Uniform Resource Identifiers," RFC 1808, Internet Engineering Task Force, http://ds.internic.com/rfc/rfc1808.txt, June 1995.

[TimBL] Tim Berners-Lee, "The Myth of Names and Addresses," http://www.w3.org/DesignIssues/NameMyth.html

[TimBL2] Tim Berners-Lee, "Universal Resource Identifiers in WWW," RFC 1630, Internet Engineering Task Force, June 1994.

[Sollins] Karen Sollins and Larry Masinter, "Functional Requirements for Uniform Resource Names," RFC 1737, Internet Engineering Task Force, December 1994.

[TimBL3] Tim Berners-Lee, Larry Masinter, and Mark McCahill, "Uniform Resource Locators (URL)," RFC 1738, Internet Engineering Task Force, December 1994.

[PICS] Paul Resnick and Jim Miller, "PICS: Internet Access Controls without

Censorship," *Communications of the ACM*, 1996, vol. 39 (10), pp. 87-93, http://www.w3.org/PICS/iacwcv2.htm

[Moats] Ryan Moats, "URN Syntax," RFC 2141, Internet Engineering Task Force, http://ds.internic.com/rfc/rfc2141.txt, May 1997.

[Daniel1] Ron Daniel Jr. and Michael Mealling, "Resolution of Uniform Resource Identifiers using the Domain Name System," RFC 2168, Internet Engineering Task Force, http://ds.internic.com/rfc/rfc2168.txt, June 1997.

[Daniel2] Ron Daniel Jr., "A Trivial Convention for Using HTTP in URN Resolution," RFC 2169, Internet Engineering Task Force, http://ds.internic.com/rfc/rfc2169.txt, June 1997.

CITATION

Citing Serials:
Online Serial Publications
and Citation Systems

Janice R. Walker

SUMMARY. This article examines in detail the major citation styles as they apply to electronic sources and to online serial publications. The examination reveals difficulties with all of the major styles. The author, therefore, briefly explains an approach that translates the elements of online sources into those needed for citation of these sources in print or electronic formats. This element approach allows authors to translate the necessary information to cite electronic sources in any style. *[Article copies available for a fee from The Haworth Document Delivery Service: 1-800-342-9678. E-mail address: getinfo@ haworth.com]*

Janice R. Walker is Coordinator, Computers and Writing Program, Department of English, University of South Florida, 4202 East Fowler Avenue, CPR 358, Tampa, FL 33620, USA (email: jwalker@chuma.cas.usf.edu).

[Haworth co-indexing entry note]: "Citing Serials: Online Serial Publications and Citation Systems." Walker, Janice R. Co-published simultaneously in *The Serials Librarian* (The Haworth Press, Inc.) Vol. 33, No. 3/4, 1998, pp. 343-356; and: *E-Serials: Publishers, Libraries, Users, and Standards* (ed: Wayne Jones) The Haworth Press, Inc., 1998, pp. 343-356. Single or multiple copies of this article are available for a fee from The Haworth Document Delivery Service [1-800-342-9678, 9:00 a.m. - 5:00 p.m. (EST). E-mail address: getinfo@haworth.com].

343

KEYWORDS. Citations, bibliographies, style guides, documentation, Internet

Electronic versions of serial publications pose unique citation problems. Many of the existing formats for scholarly citations fail to take into account the unique structure of electronic publications, or fail to adequately address some of the specific issues prompted by online serial publications. Thus, as Phyllis Franklin notes in the Foreword to the *MLA Handbook*, "the rules for citing electronic material that the MLA committee established are not presented as definitive, and they will surely change as the technology and practices governing electronic communication evolve."[1] An examination of some of the major proposals for citing electronic sources reveals that these formats all fail to adequately address important differences between Internet publications and print publications.

This article examines the problems inherent in these proposed formats as they pertain to electronic publications and outline the tenets of the Columbia Style, an expansion of the Walker Style for citation of electronic sources. Further, it examines the specific structures of some common online serial publications and shows how these elements can be translated using the Columbia Style to fit the purpose of scholarly citations for both print and online publications.

THE MODERN LANGUAGE ASSOCIATION

For almost fifty years the Modern Language Association has been the authority for writing in English and literature subject areas. In the fourth edition of the *MLA Handbook*, the MLA committee recognized the need to include formats for citing publications accessed by computers and attempted to address two important considerations of electronic sources: (1) how to locate the text again, and (2) how to ensure that the text consulted will still be available for verification. Franklin sees the problem of locating Internet sources as primarily one of infrastructure:

A reader who wishes to locate a book can take a few pieces of information–such as the author's name and the title–to a library or bookstore in this country and many others and readily determine whether the volume is available. Publication practices, copyright laws, and the organization of libraries provide an infrastructure that makes locating print publications a relatively simple matter. Consequently, references to print sources can be brief. Because no comparable infrastructure yet exists for electronic publications, citations of them must provide more information than references to print sources normally contain.[2]

However, MLA's answer to this problem was to include the word "Online" as the publication medium, followed by the "name of the computer network," i.e., "Internet." The *Handbook* further suggests that the writer may want to include the electronic address used to access the document, preceded by the word *"Available,"* as supplementary information only.[3] By allowing the omission of electronic addresses, however, MLA defeated its own goal of providing sufficient information to re-locate the source. The Internet, contrary to what Franklin has said, does have an infrastructure, albeit one that may not be readily apparent to those not familiar with the cyber-terrain. Internet protocols and addresses–URLs, FTP, Gopher, Telnet, etc.–can usually provide the knowledgeable reader with sufficient information to re-locate a source. Without the address, however, the sheer volume of information online makes locating a specific file sort of like looking for the proverbial needle in the haystack–only much more difficult.

The second consideration which the MLA committee attempted to address is the ability to ensure the availability of a text:

> After considerable discussion, committee members agreed that electronic texts will and probably should change but that readers must be able to get back to the original texts (or "archival copies") a writer consulted and cited. Ways must be found to archive electronic texts reliably at specific times in their history. A minimal standard is for electronic documents to be dated. In electronic research as in print research, only the ability of readers to verify an author's use of a source can discourage the circulation of error. How this important goal will be achieved remains to be seen.[4]

The MLA committee recognizes the fluidity of electronic publications, but they see this fluidity as problematic. However, attempting to ensure the verifiability of a writer's sources, while a worthwhile goal, entails additional problems, including limited computer resources and sometimes lack of sufficient knowledge of protocols, which may preclude the ability of many authors to provide a reliable means of archiving or accessing texts. The Working Group on Intellectual Property Rights also addressed the need to archive information; however, the exemption for libraries pertaining to archival copies under copyright law "does not allow for preservation in electronic or digital form."[5] They suggest that hard (paper) copies of electronic documents be filed with the Copyright office. However, a hard copy of an electronically published work may not ultimately be the same work–one cannot point a mouse and click on a hard (paper) copy of electronic links and visit other sites–and it is features such as this hypertextuality that make electronically published works unique.

These suggestions and the MLA formats for citing electronic sources reflect a vision of electronic documents as print-based, available through technological means, rather than as work published electronically that may or may not translate into print. Even the inclusion of the word "available" before the electronic address furthers this perception of online publishing as somehow not "real" publishing but only a virtual space where "real" (i.e., print) publications may be stored for future access. This conception of electronic publications has precipitated much of the confusion over citation formats. Thus the formats devised by the MLA for citing electronic sources fail to follow the same logic as that used for citation of print sources, thereby adding to both the marginalization of electronic publications and to the confusion of scholars.

The American Psychological Association Style

Xia Li's and Nancy Crane's groundbreaking work was the first widely disseminated attempt to codify a system of documentation specifically for electronic sources. Although they omit some important Internet sources, they add that "we believe . . . the basic forms can be adapted to other sources." Their book, *Electronic Style: A Guide to Citing Electronic Information*, follows the documentation guidelines of the American Psychological Association (APA) most used in the social sciences and, for the most part, presents a clear and concise system that includes electronic addresses as a required element.[6]

However, Li and Crane continue to dichotomize print and electronic sources unnecessarily by inclusion of the "available" wording, making it appear as though an electronic work is somehow not really published (we don't say "available in print"). Additionally, there is no guarantee that a work *will* still be available. It would actually be more accurate, then, to say "originally located at" or "accessed by the author at." Again, however, this is unnecessary information and unwieldy to work with. Li and Crane justify this addition of elements and the exclusion of other elements usually found in citation formats, such as page numbers and publication information, by saying,

> Although this guide adheres closely to the APA style of citation, it also introduces new elements, for example: "Type of medium," and "Available" which help to better describe the newer formats. In preparing this guide it was necessary to discard some elements which are usually found in descriptions of printed sources, such as "paging," "place of publication," and even "publisher." The primary objective in making reference to an item, whether in print or electronic format, is to give enough information so that it can be located.[7]

However, the inclusion of these extraneous elements is unnecessary to fulfill the stated purpose of providing sufficient information to locate the source.

The end punctuation in the URL (Uniform Resource Locator) or Internet address in Li and Crane's format can be misleading as well, since punctuation is an integral part of Internet addresses. As Li and Crane themselves state: "Punctuation, in the context of availability statements, can present real problems. Every effort has been made to use punctuation sparingly because a stray period, comma, or slash can be mistaken for part of an address."[8] Li and Crane's examples avoid this problem by simply omitting end punctuation altogether in their cites. And, although they recognize that the date "is often of paramount importance in electronic sources,"[9] they do not make it clear which date is to be included in the parentheses–the date of the work itself, which may or may not be available, or the date of access, which, as we will see, is an essential element in electronic documentation.

In their new book, *Electronic Styles: A Handbook for Citing Electronic Information*, parts of which have been published on the World Wide Web, Li and Crane expand their format to include MLA as well as APA formats and to correct some of the problems in their original work. For example, they now include the date accessed as a separate element in both APA and MLA formats, using square brackets ("[" and "]") to separate the date in APA style, as well as to delineate the publication medium (e.g., "CD-ROM"). In the MLA-style format, they now include a full-stop after the document address. As noted in their previous work, however, this punctuation can be confusing, since punctuation is a crucial part of Internet addresses.[10]

There are inconsistencies in the presentation and examples of protocols as well. For instance, whereas the model shows "Available Protocol (e.g., HTTP):" as the basic structure of the format for citing Internet documents, their examples for APA style omit the protocol for "commercial supplier[s]." And their citation formats for Internet sites include unnecessary repetition of key elements, such as "http" (hypertext transfer protocol) in the citation as both the protocol and as part of the address. Further, Li and Crane's format does not clearly delineate between "online" sources and those available from "commercial suppliers" and could be confusing. For example, if I access the *MLA Bibliography* online using telnet protocols through the World Wide Web, following links from my university library home page, do I cite the information retrieved as the database (a "commercial supplier"), or as the Internet protocol I used to access it? What if I log on to America Online to access the site?

In both the MLA and APA styles, Li and Crane's formats for citing e-mail include the full e-mail addresses for both the sender and the recipient of personal e-mail messages. This is analogous to including the home addresses or phone numbers for senders and recipients of "snail mail" cited in publications–not only is it unnecessary, it could also be dangerous. And Li and Crane continue, as does the MLA committee, to include the nebulous term "online" in their citation of Internet sources. I am not certain exactly what the word "online" refers to–one can be "online" when one is connected to a Local Area Network (LAN) or to a Wide Area Network (WAN), to a local bulletin board service, or to the Internet. And the same publication or software application may be published on CD-ROM, diskette, or installed on a hard drive, so citing the publication medium may also be unnecessary or confusing.

One interesting idea Li and Crane propose is the use of paragraph numbers in a work to designate location or length. However, counting the number of paragraphs in lengthy works can be extremely troublesome, and, sometimes, impossible. Further, with search features found in most word processing and browser programs, it is unnecessary. Li and Crane also add to the confusion about the nature of listservs on the Internet, citing a listserv posting by including the statement "Available E-mail: listname@address" in their citation. This format can be confusing, making it appear that one can simply send an e-mail to the address cited and receive a copy of the referenced work. Of course, this is not how online discussion lists work. Most discussion lists require sending a subscription request to a separate address to join the list, and messages may or may not be archived, depending on the software and the decision of the list owner. Further, even when messages are archived, they are generally available only by sending certain specific commands to a listserv, listproc, or majordomo address, or they may be available at a separate WWW, FTP, or gopher site. Messages sent to the listserv address will be distributed to all members of the list and will not provide the sender with the archival copy, even if there is one.

Turabian Style

Melvin H. Page has also addressed the citation of electronic sources. Like the MLA committee, he does not intend for this work to be definitive but, instead, presents it as "suggestions for citations of Internet sources . . . derived from the essential principles of academic citation" in Turabian style. His work, too, uses additional punctuation, in this case, square brackets ("[" and "]"), in addition to inclusion of the word "available," but he omits mention of protocols and includes the author's Internet, or e-mail, address in his citation format, which, as we saw in the discussion of Li and Crane's format for citation of e-mail and listserv messages, is problematic. By enclosing the Internet address in square brackets he adds punctuation that may tend to be confusing as well as extraneous, further categorizing electronic publications as "different," or somehow "not real." Further, his use of the word "in" to indicate a work included in a larger body of material is confusing and, perhaps, erroneous in electronic documents since documents in cyberspace are not enclosed within a binding as in traditional print formats. Page also does not specify which date is to be included–the date of publication or the date the material is accessed. Lastly, Page's examples for citing listserv messages include unnecessary duplication, repeating the name of the listserv which is already included as part of the listserv address, e.g., "H-AFRICA [h-africa@msu.edu]."[11]

Probably the most troublesome aspect of Page's formats for citation of Gopher and FTP sites is that they omit the protocols necessary to access the work. For example, he gives the following format for citing a file found at a Gopher site:

"Democratic Party Platform, 1860." [wiretap.spies.com Wiretap Online Library/Civic and Historical/Political Platforms of the U.S.] 18 June 1860.

Without knowing this is a Gopher site, the reader trying to access it could easily confuse the address "wiretap.spies.com" as either an FTP, Gopher, e-mail, newsgroup, or other type of Internet site, making it impossible, or at least difficult, to locate the source. Page also does not explain his placement of the directories, or path, followed from a site to access a document (the path is separated in his example from the Internet address by a space, and then each level directory is separated by a forward slash). In the foregoing example, too, apparently the date Page uses ("18 June 1860") is the date of the document itself. However, his placement is where traditional print citation formats include the date of publication. Obviously this document was not published on a Gopher site in 1860. So if the date is referring to the date the document is originally published elsewhere, then this date would more correctly be placed directly after the document title.

Harnack and Kleppinger's Style

Andrew Harnack and Gene Kleppinger also attempted to address the problem of academic citation of Internet sources in their article, "Beyond the *MLA Handbook*: Documenting Electronic Sources on the Internet" published in the online journal *Kairos: A Journal for Teachers in Webbed Writing Environments*. However, their conclusions, like so many others, reflect a print-based model. For instance, they recommend that teachers require students to "print copies of cited material."[12] One needs to be careful about making recommendations that not only can be construed as copyright violation but that seem to assume that student writing itself is print-based and needs some kind of print-based support. Why not, for example, recommend that teachers, instead, require students to obtain permission to "copy" referenced documents to a diskette? Online documents are not (or perhaps should not be) intended for print, and conventions of style and documentation, therefore, need to keep this in mind as well.

Harnack and Kleppinger point out four major areas of concern:

1. distinguishing between Internet addresses and command sequences,
2. distinguishing between dates of publication and dates of user access,
3. distinguishing between addresses of publication and addresses for retrieval, and
4. providing for the "openness" of many Internet pathways to the same (authentic) source.

In order to distinguish between the Internet address and the command sequence necessary to access a given electronic document, Harnack and Kleppinger suggest adding angle brackets ("<" and ">") around the Internet address. This addition of angle brackets, however, is unnecessary, confusing, and does not solve the problem it purports to address. Most directory pathways are encountered, not in WWW documents, which have a distinct URL, but in gopher and FTP sites. But Harnack and Kleppinger's models do not include angle brackets around the Internet addresses for Gopher and FTP sites. Additionally, many Gopher and FTP addresses may also be

352 E-SERIALS: PUBLISHERS, LIBRARIES, USERS, AND STANDARDS

accessed through Web browsers. Thus, "ftp ftp.media.mit.edu" becomes "ftp://ftp.media.mit.edu." The same Internet address, then, could be cited either with or without the angle brackets, depending upon the software the author uses to access the work. Angle brackets, too, cannot easily be incorporated into documents written for the World Wide Web, since Web browsers recognize these brackets as part of the HyperText Markup Language (HTML) tag. The text enclosed within the angle brackets will not show up at all, then, since the browser will search for an HTML command sequence when it encounters the angle brackets. In order to circumvent this problem in WWW documents, Harnack and Kleppinger, in their own source code, added additional HTML commands, which entails that the author, then, be familiar not only with the format for citing sources, but also with relatively uncommon HTML commands (i.e., ">" and "<").

Harnack and Kleppinger recommend that the date of the document or message, or the date of the last revision, if available, be placed following the title of a work. I agree with this placement, which treats the actual document date as an edition or revision in a print publication. However, the access date may sometimes be the only date available on an electronic work, and may be the only acknowledgment that the document may have changed without any apparent notice to the reader. According to *A Manual for Writers of Term Papers, Theses, and Dissertations*, online sources "may be continually revised, making the precise date of access especially important."[13] The Turabian manual places the access date after the publication information, preceded by the word "accessed" in their note format (the manual does not provide examples of bibliographic or reference listings including this information). The APA manual recommends that, if a document or publication date is not available, then it should be replaced by the date the information is accessed by the writer.[14] Both the document date and the access date are important in referencing electronic works, however, and the placement of the dates within the citation should be sufficient to delineate the information without adding unnecessary explanations, such as the word "accessed." Thus, too, when the date of publication and the access date are the same, repetition of dates should be unnecessary.

The third ambiguity that Harnack and Kleppinger point out is the use of the address of the publication rather than the archival address, if any, for Internet sources. Most Internet sources are not archived; however, Harnack and Kleppinger are right in pointing out that, if an archival file is available, the address should be included in the citation. They recommend adding the word "via" followed by the archive address after the address of the listserv where the information was originally published. For example,

Carbone, Nick. "NN960126: Followup to Don's comments about citing URLs." 26 Jan. 1996. <acw-l@unicorn.acs.ttu.edu> via <http://www.ttu.edu/lists/acw-l>. (17 Feb. 1996).

I believe this is adding an unnecessary layer of complexity. If the archive address is known, then it would be preferable to cite that address rather than the listserv address, which could be omitted in favor of the archive name. This would fulfill the requirement of providing the reader with access to the referenced source without including unnecessary information.

Lastly, Harnack and Kleppinger point out that many WWW files are available as links from, or incorporated in, other works. Thus, they point out, these "relative addresses," may often be used in citations rather than the original, or "authentic," address of an electronically published work. To denote these files, Harnack and Kleppinger recommend using the abbreviation "lkd." equivalent to the "qtd." abbreviation used in the *MLA Handbook* for "treatment of indirect references." Links are an important component of most World Wide Web pages, and I agree they should be acknowledged. Often, however, especially with graphic files, it may not be readily apparent that a file is not actually part of a given work. Where the link is apparent and where it is important to cite the source from which the work is linked in addition to the file itself, then both addresses should be acknowledged, and the "lkd." analog suggested by Harnack and Kleppinger is an excellent way to make the connection between the documents apparent.

Proposal for Citation of Electronic Sources

The "Walker/ACW Style for Citation of Electronic Sources"[15] published on the Web has been expanded to address author-date as well as humanities styles of citations, and will be available within the coming year (hopefully) from Columbia University Press, to be titled *The Columbia Guide to Online Style* by Janice R. Walker and Todd Taylor.[16] This *Guide* offers specific formats for citing electronically available publications of all types–from WWW publications to CD-ROM serials and software publications–and uses an element approach that allows users to translate information for any style. Elements of citation include author's name, title of article, title of complete work, version, edition, or volume numbers, publication information and date published, and, for electronic works, date accessed. Additionally, electronic serial publications pose unique problems for citation purposes, including how to cite page references and whether or not an electronic version of a print publication can be cited as a primary source.

The basic format for citing electronic sources in humanities style is as follows:

Author's Lastname, Author's Firstname. "Title of Document." *Title of Complete Work* (if applicable). Version or File Number, if applicable. Document date or date of last revision (if different from access date). Protocol or electronic medium and address or access path (date of access).

For example:

Walker, Janice R. "MLA-Style Citations of Electronic Sources." Ver. 1.1. Rev. Aug. 1996. http://www.cas.usf.edu/english/walker/mla. html (23 Jul. 1997).

To cite sources in author-date style:

Author's Lastname, Author's Initials. (Date of document, if available and different from date of access). Title of document. *Title of complete work* (if applicable) (Version, Edition, or other identifying information). Protocol or electronic medium and address or access path (date of access).

The example in author-date format, then, would be:

Walker, J. R. (1996). MLA-style citations of electronic sources (Ver. 1.1). http://www.cas.usf.edu/english/walker/mla.html (23 Jul. 1997).

I believe these formats present the information necessary to accomplish the purpose of bibliographic citations–to recognize authorship and to allow the reader to access the original material–in a way that is clear and concise. The formats as given are readable both in print and electronic publications, and, thus, too, may help to make our transition from a print culture to an electronic one a little easier.

The general format for citing an article in an online journal in humanities style would include the author's name, last name first, the title of the article enclosed in quotation marks, the title of the journal in italics, the volume number, a colon, and the issue number, the date of publication in parentheses, followed by a period, the URL for the document, and the date of access enclosed in parentheses. For example,

Blais, Ellen. "O Brave New Net!" *Computer Mediated Communication Magazine* 3:8 (1996). http://www.december.com/cmc/mag/1996/aug/last.html (5 Aug. 1996).

For author-date styles, include the author's last name and first initial, followed by the publication date in parentheses and a period, the title of the article, the title of the journal and volume number, in italics, separated by a comma, followed by the issue number in parentheses, the URL for the document, and the date of access enclosed in parentheses. For example,

Blais, E. (1996). O brave new Net! *Computer Mediated Communication Magazine*, 3(8). http://www.december.com/cmc/mag/1996/aug/last.html (5 Aug. 1996).

There is, of course, no single format for online serial publications. Print-based journals may offer online counterparts; however, electronic versions of journals may be substantially different from their print counterparts. Even the electronic address may be different depending on the route taken to access a given work. And searchable full-text databases may create document addresses based on a search path rather than a distinct document location. Thus, this type of element approach makes sense as we move into this new era of publishing.

NOTES

1. Phyllis Franklin, foreword to *MLA Handbook for Writers of Research Papers*, 4th ed. (New York: MLA, 1995), xvi.

2. Ibid., xv.

3. Joseph Gibaldi, *MLA Handbook for Writers of Research Papers*, 4th ed. (New York: MLA, 1995), 165.

4. See note 1 above.

5. United States Patent and Trademarks Office, "Intellectual Property and the National Information Infrastructure: The Report of the Working Group on Intellectual Property Rights," Sep. 1995. http://www.uspto.gov/web/ipnii/ipnii.txt (4 Jan. 1996).

6. Xia Li and Nancy Crane, *Electronic Style: A Guide to Citing Electronic Information* (Westport: Meckler, 1993), 1.

7. Ibid.

8. Li and Crane, *Electronic Style*, 3.

9. Ibid., x.

10. Xia Li and Nancy Crane, "Bibliographic Formats for Citing Electronic Information," revised 20 May 1996. http://ac.grin.edu/~hunter/achon/lecture.html (17 Jul. 1996).

11. Melvin H. Page, "A Brief Citation Guide for Internet Sources in History and the Humanities," Ver. 1.1, 30 Oct. 1995. http://www.hivolda.no/asf/kkf/citation.html (2 Jan. 1996).

12. Andrew Harnack and Gene Kleppinger, "Beyond the *MLA Handbook*: Documenting Electronic Sources on the Internet," *Kairos: A Journal for Teachers of Writing in Webbed Environments* 1, no. 3 (1996). http://www.csc.eku.edu/honors/beyond-mla (14 June 1996).

13. Kate L. Turabian, *A Manual for Writers of Term Papers, Theses, and Dissertations*, 6th ed. Revised by John Grossman and Alice Bennett (Chicago: U of Chicago P, 1996), 158.

14. *Publication Manual of the American Psychological Association*, 4th ed. (Washington, DC: APA, 1994), 219.

15. Janice R. Walker, "Walker/ACW Style Sheet for Citation of Electronic Sources," Ver. 1.1, revised August 1996. http://www.cas.usf.edu/english/walker/mla.html (28 Jul. 1997).

16. Janice R. Walker and Todd Taylor, *The Columbia Guide to Online Style* (New York: Columbia UP, in press).

Index

AACR, 147-166
  definition of a serial, 149-152
Academic Press, 247,263,265
  see also APPEAL; IDEAL
acquisitions, 83-106,109-110,114
  check-in, 95-96
  claiming, 95-96
  renewals, 99-101
  staffing, 92-95
  workflow, 86-92,95-96
Adobe Acrobat
  see PDF
ADONIS, 31-32,206,207,287-288
aggregators, 60-62
America Online, 37,292
American Association for the
    Advancement of Science,
    317n1,n2
American Chemical Society, 56,
    63-64,206,208
American Institute of Physics, 56,
    63,317n3
American Mathematical Society, 63
American Psychological
    Association, 346-349,352
American Society for Biochemistry
    and Molecular Biology,
    63-64
American University, 94
Anglo-American Cataloguing Rules
  see AACR
ANSI C, 256
APPEAL, 65,234
Applied Physics Letters Online, 317n3
archives, 212,215
archiving
  see preservation
ASCII, 130,207,208,211,322
  see also formats

Association for Computing
    Machinery, 62-63
Association of American Publishers,
    76,77,208
Association of Universities and
    Colleges of Canada, 225
association periodicals, 62-65
The Astrophysical Journal, 67
attention, 45-54
Australian Academy of Science, 63

Berkeley Internet Name Demon, 338
BIG5 (format), 131
  see also formats
Big Ten, 273
biomedical journals, 24-26
  see also STM serials
BioMedNet, 234
Birmingham and Loughborough
    Electronic Network
    Development, 203
Blackwell's, 37,65,206
  see also Electronic Journal
    Navigator
Bowker, 77,335
Brigham Young University, 93
British Library, 215,287
browsing, 34,38,239-240
BRS/Search, 251

Canada. Human Resource
    Development Canada, 225
Canada. Industry Canada, 224,230
Canadian Association of Research
    Libraries, 225,229
Canadian Association of University
    Teachers, 229
Canadian Electronic Scholarly
    Network, 229-230

MDL, 294-295
Medical Research Council (Canada),
    229
MEDLINE, 33,313,314
metadata, 167-178,179-198,210,211,
    220n55,330,340
  conversion, 186-194
  definition, 168-169,180
  formats, 181-183
  repository, 183-187
Microsoft Access, 256
Microsoft Excel, 256
Microsoft Internet Explorer, 39,337
MIT Libraries, 85-105
MIT Press, 56
*Modeling and Simulation in Materials
    Science and Engineering*,
    208
Modern Language Association,
    344-346,348,353
Mosaic, 39
multimedia, 33

naming, 4-15,326-340
Naming Authority Pointer
  see NAPTR
NAPTR, 335-338
NASA, 3,20n1
National Endowment for the
    Humanities, 2
National Engineering Education
    Delivery System
  see NEEDS
National Graduate Register, 225
National Library of Canada, 215
National Preservation Office (UK),
    215
National Research Council
    (Norway), 29
National Science Foundation, 3,20n1
National Serials Data Program, 124
Natural Sciences and Engineering
    Research Council, 229
NEEDS, 173
Netscape, 39,207-208,337
Network Solutions Inc., 338

Neuroscience-Net, 66
*The Nordic Journal of Philosophical
    Logic*, 24,27,28,29-30
North Carolina State University, 94
North-Holland Publishing, 206
Norwegian Health Network, 30
Norwegian National Library, 27

OCLC, 39,102
  cataloging, 133-145,163-165,275
  Electronic Collections Online,
    57-58,61,299-318
  Electronic Journals Online,
    300-305,317n1
  see also FirstSearch; Intercat;
    SiteSearch
  TechPro, 315
  WorldCat, 315-316
ODBC, 256
offprints, 34
Olive Tree, 150
*Online Journal of Current Clinical
    Trials*, 317n2
*Online Journal of Knowledge
    Synthesis for Nursing*, 317n2
OPAC, 184-187,190-193,314-315
Oracle, 256
Oregon Flora Project, 156-160
Ovid, 59
Oxford University Press, 32

Page, Melvin H., 349-350
Panorama, 182,186
PDF, 28,29,31-32,130,207-208,211,
    235,240,262,289,303,
    305-306,308,311
  see also formats
PEAK Project, 292-293
peer review, 2,4,25,27,30,33,36,45-54,
    205,216
Pergamon, 206
Perl, 250,274
PICS, 183,330
PII, 38
Platform for Internet Content Selection
  see PICS

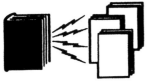

Haworth
DOCUMENT DELIVERY
SERVICE

This valuable service provides a single-article order form for any article from a Haworth journal.

- *Time Saving:* No running around from library to library to find a specific article.
- *Cost Effective:* All costs are kept down to a minimum.
- *Fast Delivery:* Choose from several options, including same-day FAX.
- *No Copyright Hassles:* You will be supplied by the original publisher.
- *Easy Payment:* Choose from several easy payment methods.

Open Accounts Welcome for ...
- Library Interlibrary Loan Departments
- Library Network/Consortia Wishing to Provide Single-Article Services
- Indexing/Abstracting Services with Single Article Provision Services
- Document Provision Brokers and Freelance Information Service Providers

---

MAIL or *FAX* THIS ENTIRE ORDER FORM TO:

Haworth Document Delivery Service
The Haworth Press, Inc.
10 Alice Street
Binghamton, NY 13904-1580

or FAX: 1-800-895-0582
or CALL: 1-800-342-9678
9am-5pm EST

PLEASE SEND ME PHOTOCOPIES OF THE FOLLOWING SINGLE ARTICLES:

1) Journal Title: _____
   Vol/Issue/Year:_____Starting & Ending Pages:_____
   Article Title:_____
   _____

2) Journal Title: _____
   Vol/Issue/Year:_____Starting & Ending Pages:_____
   Article Title:_____
   _____

3) Journal Title: _____
   Vol/Issue/Year:_____Starting & Ending Pages:_____
   Article Title:_____
   _____

4) Journal Title: _____
   Vol/Issue/Year:_____Starting & Ending Pages:_____
   Article Title:_____
   _____

(See other side for Costs and Payment Information)

COSTS: Please figure your cost to order quality copies of an article.

1. Set-up charge per article: $8.00
   ($8.00 × number of separate articles) _____

2. Photocopying charge for each article:
   1-10 pages: $1.00 _____

   11-19 pages: $3.00 _____

   20-29 pages: $5.00 _____

   30+ pages: $2.00/10 pages _____

3. Flexicover (optional): $2.00/article _____

4. Postage & Handling: US: $1.00 for the first article/
   $.50 each additional article _____

   Federal Express: $25.00 _____

   Outside US: $2.00 for first article/
   $.50 each additional article _____

5. Same-day FAX service: $.35 per page _____

GRAND TOTAL: _____

METHOD OF PAYMENT: (please check one)

❏ Check enclosed ❏ Please ship and bill. PO # _____
(sorry we can ship and bill to bookstores only! All others must pre-pay)

❏ Charge to my credit card: ❏ Visa; ❏ MasterCard; ❏ Discover;
❏ American Express;

Account Number: _____ Expiration date: _____

Signature: ✗ _____

Name: _____ Institution: _____

Address: _____

_____

City: _____ State: _____ Zip: _____

Phone Number: _____ FAX Number: _____

MAIL or *FAX* THIS ENTIRE ORDER FORM TO:

Haworth Document Delivery Service	**or FAX:** 1-800-895-0582
The Haworth Press, Inc.	**or CALL:** 1-800-342-9678
10 Alice Street	9am-5pm EST)
Binghamton, NY 13904-1580	

OTHER NEW BOOKS FROM HAWORTH LIBRARY SCIENCE

THE HOLOCAUST

Memories, Research, Reference
Edited by Robert Hauptman, PhD
Helps you guide others in Holocaust research
and shows you how you can avoid contributing to the
popularization and trivialization of the Holocaust.
(A monograph published simultaneously as
The Reference Librarian, Vol. 29, Nos. 61/62.)
$49.95 hard. ISBN: 0-7890-0379-1.
Text price (5+ copies): $29.95.
Available Spring 1998. Approx. 336 pp. with Index.

Over 300 Pages!

PUBLISHING GLAD TIDINGS

Essays on Christmas Music
William E. Studwell, MSLS, and
co-author and editor, Dorothy E. Jones, MLS, MRE
Helps you see how major, but nearly forgotten,
Christmas carols have stayed with us throughout
the years.
(A monograph published simultaneously as
Music Reference Services Quarterly, Vol. 6, No. 4.)
$29.95 hard. ISBN: 0-7890-0398-8.
Text price (5+ copies): $19.95.
1998. Available now. 157 pp. with Index.

FICTION ACQUISITION/FICTION MANAGEMENT

Education and Training
Edited by Georgine N. Olson, MLS
Discusses the need for education and training of librarians for
skills necessary to successful fiction acquisition and fiction
collection management.
(A monograph published simultaneously as
The Acquisitions Librarian, Volume 10, No. 19.)
$29.95 hard. ISBN: 0-7890-0391-0.
Text price (5+ copies): $14.95.
1998. Available now. 120 pp. with Index.

COLLECTION DEVELOPMENT

Access in the Virtual Library
Edited by Maureen Pastine, MLS
A guide to balancing traditional collection issues
with electronic access and document delivery demands.
(A monograph published simultaneously as
Collection Development, Vol. 22, Nos. 1/2.)
$49.95 hard. ISBN: 0-7890-0385-6.
1997. 225 pp. with Index and an extensive bibliography.

Over 200 Pages!

CHEMICAL LIBRARIANSHIP

Challenges and Opportunities
Edited by Arleen N. Somerville
Shows you how you can adapt your methods to
the rapidly evolving demands of twentieth-century
chemical researchers without sacrificing your high standards
of service.
(A monograph published simultaneously as
Science & Technology Libraries, Vol. 16, Nos. 3/4.)
$49.95 hard. ISBN: 0-7890-0388-0.
Text price (5+ copies): $24.95. 1997. 240 pp. with Index.

Over 225 Pages!

STATE SONGS OF THE UNITED STATES

An Annotated Anthology
William E. Studwell, MSLS,
and Bruce R. Schueneman, MLS, MS
This anthology offers a unique look at music,
America's past, and the pride of our 50 states.
(A monograph published simultaneously as
Music Reference Services Quarterly, Vol. 6, Nos. 1/2.)
$39.95 hard. ISBN: 0-7890-0397-X. 1997. 225 pp. with Index.

Over 200 Pages!

ACQUISITIONS AND COLLECTION DEVELOPMENT IN THE HUMANITIES

Edited by Irene Owens, PhD
Helps you keep up with changes in the information environment
and shows you how the tools you've developed for selecting
traditional library materials will be useful as you grapple with
electronic texts, "spider" search mechanisms on the Web,
becoming a webliographer, and budget shortfalls.
(A monograph published simultaneously as
The Acquisitions Librarian, Vol. 9, Nos. 17 & 19.)
$34.95 hard. ISBN: 0-7890-0368-6.
Text price (5+ copies): $24.95.
1997. 194 pp. with Index.

SERIALS CATALOGING AT THE TURN OF THE CENTURY

Edited by Jeanne M.K. Boydston, MSLIS,
James W. Williams, MSLS, and Jim Cole, MLS
Gives you the plain facts on the specific challenges
serials catalogers have been facing and how they're meeting
adversity head-on, ready to gain the advantage in the rumble
with proliferating information and formats.
(A monograph published simultaneously as
The Serials Librarian, Vol, 32, Nos. 1/2.)
$39.95 hard. ISBN: 0-7890-0373-2.
Text price (5+ copies): $24.95. 1997. 209 pp. with Index.

Over 200 Pages!

ECONOMICS OF DIGITAL INFORMATION

Collection, Storage, and Delivery
Edited by Sul H. Lee
Highlights key concepts and issues vital to a library's successful
venture into the digital environment and helps you understand
why the transition from the printed page to the digital packet has
been problematic for both creators of proprietary materials and
users of those materials.
(A monograph published simultaneously as the
Journal of Library Administration, Vol. 24, No. 4.)
$29.95 hard. ISBN: 0-7890-0369-4.
Text price (5+ copies): $19.95. 1997. 117 pp. with Index.

PHILOSOPHIES OF REFERENCE SERVICE

Edited by Celia Hales Mabry
Discusses the origins of reference service, its
founding principles, the pleasures and pitfalls of the
reference encounter, delivering high-quality service,
and much more!
(A monograph published simultaneously as
The Reference Librarian, Vol. 28, No. 59.)
$49.95 hard. ISBN: 0-7890-0371-6.
Text price (5+ copies): $29.95. 1997. 224 pp. with Index.

Over 200 Pages!

CALL OUR TOLL-FREE NUMBER: 1-800-HAWORTH
US & Canada only / 8am-5pm ET; Monday-Friday
Outside US/Canada: + 607-722-5857
FAX YOUR ORDER TO US: 1-800-895-0582
Outside US/Canada: + 607-771-0012

E-MAIL YOUR ORDER TO US: getinfo@haworth.com

VISIT OUR WEB SITE AT: http://www.haworth.com